Challenges to
Chinese Foreign Policy

Asia in the New Millennium

SERIES EDITOR: Shiping Hua, Center for Asian Democracy, University of Louisville

This series publishes manuscripts that examine the challenges and opportunities of Asia in the new millennium, from the perspectives of politics, economics, cultural tradition, and history. Priority will be given to manuscripts dealing with the democratization process in Asia. Projects studying the impact of Asia on the world also are welcome, as are theoretical, empirical, and policy-oriented work suitable for educational use at either the undergraduate or graduate level.

Challenges to Chinese Foreign Policy

DIPLOMACY, GLOBALIZATION, AND THE NEXT WORLD POWER

Edited by
Yufan Hao, C. X. George Wei,
and Lowell Dittmer

The University Press of Kentucky

Copyright © 2009 by The University Press of Kentucky

Scholarly publisher for the Commonwealth, serving Bellarmine University,
Berea College, Centre College of Kentucky, Eastern Kentucky University, The
Filson Historical Society, Georgetown College, Kentucky Historical Society,
Kentucky State University, Morehead State University, Murray State University,
Northern Kentucky University, Transylvania University, University of
Kentucky, University of Louisville, and Western Kentucky University.
All rights reserved.

Editorial and Sales Offices: The University Press of Kentucky
663 South Limestone Street, Lexington, Kentucky 40508-4008
www.kentuckypress.com

13 12 11 10 09   5 4 3 2 1

Library of Congress Cataloging-in-Publication Data

Challenges to Chinese foreign policy : diplomacy, globalization, and the next
world power / edited by Yufan Hao, C. X. George Wei.
        p. cm. — (Asia in the new millennium)
    Includes bibliographical references and index.
    ISBN 978-0-8131-2529-9 (hardcover : alk. paper)
    ISBN 978-0-8131-9202-4 (pbk. : alk. paper)
    1. China—Foreign relations—1976– I. Hao, Yufan. II. Wei, C. X. George.
    JZ1734.C47 2009
    327.51—dc22   2008041541

This book is printed on acid-free recycled paper meeting the requirements of the
American National Standard for Permanence in Paper for Printed Library
Materials.

Manufactured in the United States of America.

Member of the Association of
American University Presses

Contents

Introduction, *Yufan Hao*   1

1. Overview: The Evolution of China's Diplomacy and Foreign Relations in the Era of Reform, 1976–2005, *Zhang Baijia*   15

Part I. China's Relations with the United States

2. Building a New Conceptual Framework for U.S.-China Relations, *Jianwei Wang*   37

3. China's New Leadership and Strategic Relations with the United States, *Jia Qingguo*   57

4. American Nuclear Primacy or Mutually Assured Destruction: The Future of the U.S.-China Strategic Balance of Power, *Baohui Zhang*   71

Part II. China's Relations with Other Major Powers

5. The Sino-Russian Strategic Relationship: Ghost of the "Strategic Triangle"? *Lowell Dittmer*   87

6. The European Union and China: Partnership with Competition, *Xinning Song*   115

7. China's Japan Policy: Beijing's View of the U.S.-Japan Alliance, *Quansheng Zhao*   133

Part III. China's Regional Relations

8. The Korean Peninsula: A Chinese View on the North Korean Nuclear Issue, *Yufan Hao*   155

9. China's Dilemma over the North Korean Nuclear Problem, *Shi Yinhong*   173

10. Changes in South Asia since 9/11 and China's Policy Options, *Du Youkang*   183

11. After the Anti-Secession Law: Cross-Strait and U.S.-China Relations, *Zhidong Hao*   197

12. Hong Kong and Macao: In between China and the West, *Ting Wai*   217

Part IV. Chinese Diplomacy with Chinese Characteristics

13. Between Rhetoric and Pragmatism: Nationalism as a Driving Force of Chinese Foreign Policy, *Suisheng Zhao*   239

14. Engagement or Sanction? U.S. Economic Diplomacy toward China since the Cold War, *C. X. George Wei*   253

15. The Rupture of the Sino-Soviet Alliance: An Assessment of the National Intelligence Evaluation, *Shen Zhihua*   275

16. A Misty Cold War in the Himalayas: China's Historical Temperament in International Relations, *Xiaoyuan Liu*   295

17. An Intercultural Communication Model of International Relations: The Case of China, *Wenshan Jia*   319

Conclusion, *Lowell Dittmer*   335

English-Chinese Terms   349

About the Contributors   361

Index   365

Introduction

Yufan Hao

China's increasing economic and military capabilities have attracted much attention in recent years. Within the span of a single generation, China has moved from an almost isolated state to a hub of a globalized economy, from an obsolete and bloated army to a professional force possessing high-tech excellence, and from hostility toward global institutions to active participation in multilateral organizations. China has the fastest growing economy in the world, and its diplomacy has also become increasingly sophisticated, expanding its influence both in Asia and elsewhere. Chinese foreign policy has become less personal, less radical, less ideological, and more pragmatic and professional. China's national interests are more specifically defined, and the pursuit of these interests has become more realistic and flexible.

The rise of China has led many to wonder how an increasingly powerful China will behave in the foreseeable future. Will this power eventually lead the Chinese leadership to challenge the existing international norms, rules, and institutions? Or will China's integration into the international economy, its growing middle class, and its increasing participation in international institutions lead to China's becoming a "status quo" power? How should the world respond to this newly emerged great power?

Currently, two views dominate the debate over this issue. Conservatives with a realist's understanding of international relations believe that China will become assertive and expansive and may eventually dominate the region. These power theorists express the need to contain a rising China because they believe that China's desire to alter the rules of the game will grow as its capabilities increase. Others believe that China's reform and growing economic integration with the world will make it a more open and pluralistic nation, which may lead to more predictable behavior. This

1

view recognizes the importance of China's growing interdependence with the rest of the world and argues in favor of engaging China further. In fact, there is an increasingly popular belief among China observers that economic interdependence may gradually create a context, on both the international and the domestic level, within which China's foreign behavior will be constrained, thus making it more cooperative and more stable. Both views reveal a deep concern about the future role of Chinese foreign policy in world affairs.

A rising China and the direction of China's foreign policy have dominated policy discourse worldwide. Several basic questions are at the forefront of the discussion: What is the nature of the change in Chinese foreign behavior in the past three decades? Will this behavior remain the same, or is it subject to rapid change? What factors will affect Chinese foreign policy in the coming decade? What are the sources of change in Chinese foreign policy?

For years, China specialists and an attentive public around the world have been puzzled by the unpredictability of Chinese foreign policy. The major changes in Chinese foreign policy, especially toward the two superpowers, were often unanticipated. For instance, in 1978, when the United States and the People's Republic of China (PRC) agreed to establish formal diplomatic relations, one of the Chinese leaders' major objectives was Sino–American strategic cooperation against the Soviet Union. But a few years later, the Chinese government publicly disavowed its interest in cooperating with Washington against Moscow and began to pursue a policy designed to reduce tensions with the Soviet Union, even though political consultation on various regional security issues in Asia and military exchange programs between China and the United States continued to expand.

Studies on Chinese foreign policy have become abundant in the last two decades, as voluminous new materials have become available. Generally speaking, there are three major schools of thought in explaining the source of change in Chinese foreign policy. The first school focuses on China's domestic change and development. It believes that, unlike the other major powers' foreign policies, China's foreign policy is "domestically driven"—determined by Chinese culture, tradition, leadership, ideology, politics, and economic development. No matter how the international environment changes, Chinese leaders form and pursue foreign policy only according to their own preferences and perceptions of the world. Chinese foreign policy, this school believes, is a simple extension of the country's domestic development.

The second school believes that China's foreign policy is theoretically no different from that of any other major power. That is, China's international behavior is determined by its position in the international system. Like any other nation, China has to protect its national interests, defined in terms of survival, security, power, and economic well-being. Unlike the domestic-centered approach, in which the ideological preferences and objectives of key decision makers are paramount, this school argues that no matter what is going on in China's domestic politics and economy, it has to act according to the dynamics of the international environment. Chinese foreign policy, this school believes, is the country's reaction to its international environment.

The third school lies somewhere between the first two. Chinese foreign policy, it argues, is determined by both its internal development and its international environment. While carefully analyzing Chinese culture, tradition, politics, social development, economy, and leadership, this school also looks at the dynamics of the international system that China must deal with, emphasizing the interaction and mutual reinforcement between China's domestic concerns and its international concerns. As a nation-state, China cannot ignore the nature of the contemporary international system. To survive and pursue economic interests, China must act according to its position in the international system. Meanwhile, due to its specific internal structure, tradition, and emerging social challenges, Chinese leaders have to balance their foreign policy with China's domestic development.

One of the major weaknesses in the field of Chinese foreign policy studies is that some academics are interested in explaining and analyzing Chinese foreign policy with Western theoretical methodologies, while others analyze only what is going on in Chinese foreign policy, with less emphasis placed on how a specific policy was made. Since the Chinese foreign policy–making process appears as a "black box" to outsiders, its study is more or less reduced to an analysis of the policy and a speculative examination of the factors affecting the decisions. Yet some scholars have developed a more sophisticated methodology to make their analyses more professional and scientific by examining various factors such as system determinants, domestic determinants, cognitive factors, and so forth.

Although Western studies on China's foreign policy are abundant, it is more important for people outside China to know how the Chinese themselves understand their country's foreign policy and how they predict changes in it. This volume is a collective effort of Chinese scholars who share an interest in understanding and explaining Chinese foreign policy. We take the third approach to Chinese foreign policy, seeing it as a response to both domestic and foreign challenges, and exploring the interaction of the two.

We believe that Chinese foreign policy is determined by cultural heritage; domestic, political, and economic concerns; personal characteristics of leaders; and reform politics. Yet China has increasingly become a part of the world system, which provides opportunities as well as places constraints on its policy options. Chinese leaders have to be sensitive to the changing international environment, which China has only limited power to shape. As a result, the Beijing leadership has developed a pragmatic strategy to deal with the existing system and the major powers. This pragmatism has little to do with communist ideology; it requires Beijing to be responsive to the outside world, even though ideological rhetoric may occasionally be used to further domestic stability and regime survival. It is a firmly goal-fulfilling and national interest–driven strategy conditioned substantially by China's historical experiences and geostrategic environment.[1]

Obviously, the need to understand the trends in Chinese foreign policy and the factors shaping it is more urgent than ever. This volume provides an assessment of China's increasingly active foreign policy from the Chinese perspective, with a focus on China's foreign relations challenges and the strategies it has adopted and will adopt to pursue its interests in the twenty-first century. This volume is not intended to be a comprehensive study of Chinese foreign policy. Instead, it analyzes aspects of change in Chinese foreign policy as well as challenges deemed important in influencing China's policy options.

A sophisticated analysis of Chinese foreign relations in recent years indicates that the following factors have played a vital role in shaping the PRC's foreign relations: its historical, cultural, and political heritage; its newly gained confidence owing to rapid economic growth in the last three decades; its domestic, social, and developmental concerns; its perceived role and position in world affairs; its perceived security threats inside and outside China; and its perceived external environment. We believe that both external and internal stimuli and restraints have been and will continue to be major sources of Chinese foreign policy options. Therefore, the contributors to this book examine the changes in China's external environment in the last two decades, China's efforts to foster favorable conditions for its continued modernization, and the internal changes and constraints that may limit and influence Chinese foreign policy options. Only by exploring the sources of Chinese behavior can we develop a better framework for understanding how and why Chinese foreign policy is the way it is, how it might change, and what factors might shape these changes in the foreseeable future.

The specific questions this book addresses include the following: What are the changes in China's external environment as perceived by the Beijing leadership? Does Beijing have a grand strategy to cope with these perceived changes? What is the concept of "peaceful rise" that Beijing has been advocating? What alternatives are available to China? What does China's current strategy imply for international peace and security in the coming years? Is China's current approach yielding the results it anticipated? How can China reduce its risks if others decide that a rising China is a threat and must be countered? How is the United States perceived in Chinese foreign relations? What is Beijing's strategy in dealing with the United States? What are the prospects for an increasingly prominent China and a dominant United States to manage their inevitable disagreements? How are Europe, Japan, and Russia viewed in the Chinese global strategy? What challenges are inherent in Beijing's relations with the European Union (EU), Russia, and Japan? What has changed and what remains constant in China's relations with its Asian neighbors? What basic policy challenges will China have to deal with in the coming decade? What basic policy options or policy guidelines will China use in dealing with various international issues? And, most critically, what has China learned from its past diplomatic experience that will shape future Chinese foreign policy?

This volume, developed from two international conferences held at Nanchang University in 2005 and the University of Macao in 2006,[2] is divided into four parts. To better understand the possible changes and trends in Chinese foreign policy, one has to understand the basic forces and factors that shape the continuity of policy and the context of change. Thus, chapter 1 is an overview in which Zhang Baijia reviews the historical changes and developments in Chinese foreign policy. He outlines both external and internal stimuli that made the post–Mao leadership fundamentally shift Chinese foreign policy from the "Three Worlds" strategy to a pragmatic one that allowed China to substantially improve its relations with the United States, Japan, and other major Western powers. Zhang provides a concise yet comprehensive overview of the origin and development of fundamental changes in Chinese foreign policy after the death of Mao and the adjustment in foreign policy since the early 1980s. He identifies the features of China's full-dimensional and multilateral foreign policy in response to the new structure of relations among the major powers, as well as the challenges of Chinese foreign relations in the twenty-first century. In examining the Chinese government's response to international challenges in the past thirty years, Zhang identifies three features of Chinese foreign policy: the involvement of economics and political issues such as human rights and environmental protection; the increasing role of personal diplomacy by top leaders; and the implementation of diplomacy in all directions, trying to improve relations with almost all countries.

There is no doubt that dealing with the United States has been the most challenging task for the Chinese leadership when formulating foreign policy. The United States, as the sole superpower in the world, is the only country that can substantially undermine or assist China's modernization program, and to a large extent, it may determine China's future and the pace of its development. An analysis of this major external element in Chinese foreign relations can illustrate the alternatives available to China in the formation of reactive foreign policies and behaviors. Therefore, the first part of the book focuses on Sino–American relations. In chapters 2 and 3, Jianwei Wang and Jia Qingguo trace and analyze the development and conceptualization of China's foreign policy toward the United States. Wang expounds the diplomatic discourse and conceptualizes the terms used to describe U.S.-China relations since the 1970s, including the evolution from "strategic partners" to "strategic adversaries" to "strategic competitors" to "3C" (i.e., candid, constructive, and cooperative). Although both the United States and China have attempted to find a new conceptual framework to broaden and stabilize their relationship since the end of the Cold War, Wang believes that the U.S.-China diplomatic discourse did not dramatically change until the 9/11 terrorist attacks. Changes in the American diplomatic discourse on China and hence Sino–American relations began with a behavioral adaptation to a new geopolitical reality and advanced to a profound perceptual adjustment that recognized China as an international actor and put U.S. relations with China in a more realistic and positive light. This reconceptualization process is still in a preliminary stage, however, with many unanswered and unsettled issues and with both countries still harboring a deep-rooted skepticism and wariness about the other.

Jia examines the switch in Chinese foreign policy from an ideological to a more conventional orientation and argues that the mentality of the new Chinese leaders has contributed to China's reconceptualization of its relations with the outside world. Likewise, the objectives of China's security policy have been redefined to reassure the international community, espe-

cially the United States, that a peaceful and constructive China is now focusing on cultivating good foreign relations, multilateral cooperation, and
reciprocity. For instance, China's eight-part nuclear policy reflects its intention to address the concerns of the other major powers. Yet the voices of
power politics and pessimists within China are urging an increased nuclear
deterrence power and the elimination of China's no-first-use policy.

Baohui Zhang takes a different view of the China-U.S. nuclear balance
in chapter 4. He argues that the illusion of U.S. nuclear primacy could lure
Washington into aggressive behavior, lead to an American propensity to
disregard the Chinese nuclear threat, and use war to pursue its interests in
a conflict with China. China's nuclear power, according to Zhang, is on the
verge of achieving breakthroughs. In the next two decades, U.S. nuclear
primacy will be challenged as China dramatically improves the overall balance of power with the United States by changing the strategic nuclear
force ratio from the current 200:1 to 4:1 or even 3:1.

Aside from the United States, the most important countries to Chinese
foreign policy makers are Russia, Japan, and the EU, which are the focus of
the second part. As the international influence of the United States has suffered in the wake of the war in Iraq, China's relations with the other major
powers have improved accordingly, except for its relations with Japan. In
chapter 5, Lowell Dittmer examines Sino-Russian interactions in relation to
the triangular power structure before and after the Cold War. After a brief
review of the development of the bilateral relationship from the era of the
Mongol Golden Horde, he argues that although China and Russia have never
been able to agree on ideology, they have now formed a far more meaningful
relationship than is generally credited. They have achieved this "strategic cooperative partnership" under straitened international circumstances and in
the absence of shared ideological assumptions by dovetailing their strategic
and material interests and institutionalizing this convergence at the elite level.
Dittmer believes that Russia's disappointing embrace of capitalism and the
fact that Russia is still the most plausible strategic counterweight to U.S. hegemony have sweetened the relationship between Moscow and Beijing. Domestic political developments in both countries after the end of the Cold War
removed the obstacles to their convergence, and the rise of terrorism has
helped strengthen their partnership. As a result, China and Russia have made
great progress in terms of border disputes, foreign trade, emigration, arms,
and energy trade. The remaining problems in this new strategic partnership
derive from the power vacuum left in Central Asia by Moscow's withdrawal

and the weakness of the new independent republics, as well as the divergence of the Russian and Chinese grand designs for Asia. Although Russia has repudiated communism and lost the wherewithal to sustain a bipolar confrontation, and although the communist ideology has been deradicalized in both Russia and China, the ghost of the strategic triangle lingers, and the three powers can still "tilt" the international balance of power.

In chapter 6, Xinning Song examines the recent development of China-EU relations. Song argues that in the wake of 9/11, China-EU relations not only substantially improved but also became institutionalized. Bilateral trade between China and the EU has reached unprecedented levels, and although there are still differences in the area of human rights, China-EU relations seem to be maturing.

Whereas Sino-Russian and Sino-EU relations have improved, the Sino-Japanese relationship seems to be sliding into trouble. In chapter 7, Quansheng Zhao traces the evolution of China's Japan policy and Beijing's view of the U.S.-Japan alliance. He argues that three approaches have guided Chinese foreign policy toward Japan in the past half century: the history-embedded approach, the national interest–driven approach, and the more recent comanagement approach. Beijing recently adopted the third approach in dealing with the Korean peninsula and the Taiwan Strait crises, as Chinese leaders began to recognize that the United States and Japan have major stakes and interests in these regions and that antagonistic political relations might promote hostile security policies. Although the two issues are different in nature, they both require China to adopt a more cooperative attitude toward the major powers. The United States is the primary partner for comanagement in both cases, with Japan playing a minor but significant role.

Most analysts agree that China has neither the intention nor the capability to directly challenge the United States on a global scale, but there is no consensus regarding China's policy toward the rest of Asia. China's position as the center of a growing web of trade and a "locomotive" of Asian economic growth, along with its political arrangements with other Asian countries, has raised concerns about China's intention toward the region. How is Asia perceived in Beijing's foreign policy design? What kind of policy is China promoting among its neighbors? What are the pressing issues in China's regional policy? What can China do to reduce concerns in the region and ameliorate relations with its neighbors? Part III addresses these questions. Because the North Korean nuclear issue is one of the most challenging in terms of regional security, there are two chapters dealing with it. In chapter 8, I examine the pact signed on February 13, 2007, by the United States and North Korea in which Pyongyang agreed to freeze its nuclear program in exchange for economic assistance and the improvement of Pyongyang-Washington relations. What are the prospects for the denuclearization of the peninsula? What can China do to push for the nonproliferation of North Korean nuclear technology? I take an optimistic perspective, arguing that the successful denuclearization of the Korean peninsula in a peaceful manner is possible and that China will continue to play an active role in facilitating it. Beijing's handling of the North Korean nuclear issue demonstrates how pragmatic and flexible Chinese foreign policy has become.

In chapter 9, Shi Yinhong explores why China abandoned its neutral position and became an active participant in the North Korean nuclear crisis. He identifies three major Chinese interests: (1) peace and stability on the peninsula, (2) denuclearization of North Korea to prevent a dangerous chain reaction and an arms race, and (3) maintenance of its special strategic relationship with North Korea. Shi believes that it has been difficult for China to prioritize these three objectives, which is why Beijing remained passive until the recent crisis emerged.

South Asia is becoming a concern for Chinese foreign policy makers. In chapter 10, Du Youkang reviews the changes in South Asia since the 9/11 terrorist attacks and their impact on China's policy toward the region. The significance of South Asia in the international geostrategic setting has markedly risen, and Indo-Pakistani relations have improved from confrontation to relaxation. However, nontraditional security issues such as attacks by al Qaeda, the peasant movement (Naxalite) in India, Nepal's antigovernment forces, the Liberation Tigers of Tamil Eelam, Jamaat ul Mujahedin Bangladesh, and Afghanistan's opium production have become the main threats to the stability and economic development of the region. Du believes that the new situation in South Asia will improve China-U.S., China-India, and China-Pakistan relations. Thus, he believes that China needs to maximize its geographic advantage and restrain negative factors by taking positive steps in advance, rather than passively reacting to events that may endanger the region.

Any analysis of Chinese foreign relations would be incomplete without examining the issue of Taiwan. Indeed, the Taiwan problem has been the most serious challenge in Chinese foreign relations. With a focus on the percussion caused by passage of an anti-secession law on the mainland, Zhidong Hao's chapter 11 addresses what can and cannot be changed in the future.

Hao argues that the interests of the United States and China have emerged in terms of regional stability and status quo. What each side *can* change—but not without difficulty—is the definition of *China* for both the mainland and Taiwan. Also, the United States can accept the association between the two. Although the anti-secession law brought forth a crisis, it seems to have provided an opportunity as well.

With the return of Hong Kong and Macao to China at the end of twentieth century, Chinese foreign policy took on some new elements that deserve our attention. In chapter 12, Ting Wai examines the roles of Hong Kong and Macao in the history and development of China and the impact of Chinese foreign policy toward these two entities. He concludes that the distance between China and the world has been "shortened" because of Hong Kong's role as a bridgehead, gateway, and middleman. The historical and current connections and interests of Europe, Japan, and the United States in Hong Kong and Macao; Hong Kong's role as Asia's "world city" and a regional hub; and China's "one country, two systems" policy mean that the two cities continue to be important to the development of the mainland. Meanwhile, Hong Kong and Macao have benefited enormously as China has opened its market and developed multiple linkages at all levels with the outside world. China's increasing interests in its neighbors have empowered the two special administrative regions.

Since Chinese foreign policy has been a function of domestic and external changes, most of the contributors to this volume touch on how other countries' policies toward China have changed and how these changes may affect Chinese foreign policy. In part IV, written mostly by historians, we examine the dynamic changes in external relations as well as the new and lasting internal elements that have influenced Chinese policy making. In chapter 13, Suisheng Zhao examines the development of Chinese nationalism and its impact on Chinese foreign policy. He argues that at least three strands of nationalism have occurred in modern China that deserve attention: ethnic nationalism, state nationalism, and liberal nationalism. Zhao also defines a fourth type—pragmatic nationalism—that does not have a fixed, objectified, or defined content, nor is it driven by any ideological or religious beliefs. He argues that pragmatic nationalism is an instrument used by a political entity to hold a nation together and bolster the faith of its people during times of rapid and turbulent transformation. This type of nationalism is currently influential and has an indirect effect on Chinese foreign policy.

With an emphasis on the conflicting approaches of engagement and sanction practiced by the Economic Cooperation Administration (ECA) and the Department of State, George Wei evaluates U.S. economic diplomacy toward China since the Cold War era and its impact on China's policy options. Throughout the Cold War, U.S. foreign policy makers applied economic "soft power" in a negative way to achieve the diplomatic goals that military "hard power" could not. This policy orientation was largely attributable to the mind-set of American policy makers that developed during the Cold War and politicized U.S. economic diplomacy; it was clearly demonstrated by the evolution of U.S. economic policy toward China since the end of World War II. Yet twenty years of sanctions against China achieved nothing but a more defiant, isolated, consolidated, and dangerous communist regime in China and the loss of huge profits for the United States from U.S.-China trade. In contrast, the early ECA's engagement approach, as well as the U.S. policy of engagement with China since the late 1980s, has worked.

In chapter 15, Shen Zhihua argues that during the Cold War era, ideology played a less important role in the Sino-Russian relationship than the Americans thought. The most serious mistake made by the CIA was its failure to foresee the breakup of the Sino-Russian alliance in the late 1950s. Contrary to CIA predictions, China bombed Jinmen Island even though this military action might have led to a military confrontation with the United States. Mao Zedong thought he had the Sino-Russian alliance to back him up; however, the Soviet Union would not use nuclear weapons for the sake of China. Shen believes that the bombing of Jinmen was the first step that led to the split with the Soviet Union, accelerated by the Soviets' opposition to Mao's Great Leap Forward. Thus, two factors led to the final breakdown of the Sino-Russian alliance. First, the communist international bloc lacked a system for compromise, so that conflicts between communist countries could not be easily mitigated and thus could get out of hand. Second, the communists placed party above nation and ideological goals above national interests. As a result, the line between the party-to-party relationship and the state-to-state relationship was blurred, and party goals and power superseded national interests and authority. When national conflicts could not be addressed and solved in a timely manner, alliances could rupture.

The paramount task when studying Chinese foreign policy and foreign relations is to identify the fundamental ways of Chinese thinking and the Chinese characteristics that play a role, which is the intent of the authors of the last two chapters. To detect changes in Chinese foreign policy, it is necessary to sort out the lasting elements to identify continuities and discontinuities in Chinese diplomacy. After carefully examining the Tibet issue and the policies of the Qing, the Kuomintang (KMT), and the Chinese Communist Party (CCP) toward Tibet, Xiaoyuan Liu in chapter 16 points out the historical characteristics of Chinese foreign relations. He argues that the CCP policy toward Tibet was in continuity with that of the Qing court and the Nationalist Party. China consolidated its modern sovereignty in Tibet at a special juncture in history—an era of continuous revolution in China and bipolarization of the world. The communist movement for power, the rise of India, Tibet's unique culture and medieval system, and the United States' destabilizing influence all converged in the Tibet issue. Although the CCP planned the reform of Tibet differently from the Qing and the KMT—waiting for the maturation of the mass movement in Tibet to implement reform from the bottom—it shared with its predecessors a historical consensus about breaking the status quo of the Tibetan theocratic system, involving Tibet in China's process of building a modern nation-state, and thus completing China's territorial sovereignty. Ideology played a role in Beijing's foreign policy, and the CCP's tolerance of the Tibetan Lamaist leadership was temporary and expedient, just as the KMT seized Buddhism and used it to maintain its tenuous ties with Tibetan society. Also at work was a more profound historical logic—a nation-state temperament that had taken shape since the nineteenth century but was overshadowed by the communist dogma that became prevalent in China after 1949. Chinese nationalism was a fundamental character forged during China's process of nation-state building, and the communist ideology was more instrumental than characteristic in Beijing's coping with the Cold War.

Chapter 17 by Wenshan Jia interprets China's diplomatic behavior from a cultural perspective. Social constructionism conceptualizes communication as a contextual force that shapes and reshapes culture, rather than culture dictating the form of communication. After surveying the existing literature on the subject, Jia argues that contemporary Chinese diplomatic behavior can be seen as largely governed by the deep Chinese culture, which is an extension of the Chinese relational-hierarchical model of interpersonal relationships. In contrast, Western countries use the rational model, which is self-interest centered, and Japan's model is rationalist in substance and relational in form or appearance. Thus, although Chinese officials have been remarkably successful in using their rhetorical skills to identify China with the West since 1978, certain events reveal the failure of China's intercultural understanding. For example, when Japanese prime

minister Koizumi announced his decision to make a personal (versus official) visit to the Yasukuni Shrine, Chinese leaders were outraged because
they mistook Japanese culture as entirely relational rather than partly rational. Likewise, yielding to the American request to inflate the Chinese
currency without tenacious bargaining revealed the Chinese misjudgment
of American culture, which values self-interest and would expect China to
be tough during negotiations. Thus, the Chinese international relations
model has to be intercultural rather than Sinocentric.

In the conclusion, Lowell Dittmer offers a historical perspective and overview of Chinese foreign relations and an assessment of possible future trends.
In brief, the overall objective of this volume is to provide a better understanding of the various factors affecting current Chinese leaders' perceptions of
foreign relations and the potential factors that may affect Chinese foreign policy. The main point of this book is that although China's security environment seems to have improved, the challenges remain significant, and some of
them come from within. China is still in an early stage of developing a grand
global strategy, with the hope of achieving a peaceful rise and international
harmony. China has been a status quo power since the mid-1990s and will remain so in the foreseeable future.

Notes

1. Zhao Shuisheng, ed., *Chinese Foreign Policy: Pragmatism and Strategic Behavior* (Armonk, N.Y.: M. E. Sharpe, 2004), 4–5.
2. We are grateful to the University of Macao and Nanchang University, especially Dr. Mo Yaping, dean of the College of Foreign Languages and deputy dean
of the College of Sciences and Technology of Nanchang University, for their generous support in hosting and convening the two conferences.

1. Overview

The Evolution of China's Diplomacy and Foreign Relations in the Era of Reform, 1976–2005

Zhang Baijia

This chapter traces the development of China's diplomacy since that nation undertook economic reform and opened itself up to the outside world. There have been two major stages: the initial, unfolding stage of reform from 1978 to 1991, and the stage of constructing an economic system and socialist market from 1992 to 2000. Since then, China' reform has been guided by the goal of achieving comprehensive, harmonious, and sustainable development, and its need for political and social reform has become increasingly urgent. Therefore, this can be considered the third stage in the development of China's diplomacy. In each stage, the problems facing China have been different, and its diplomacy has been constantly adjusted along with its reform agenda.

Formation of Foreign Policy in the Spirit of Reform

After the end of the Cultural Revolution in 1976, China's diplomatic activities quickly became vitalized. From 1977 to 1978, Chinese leaders and various kinds of delegations made numerous visits overseas. The mission of most of these trips was to investigate foreign economies, technologies, and educational institutions, as preparation for reform and opening up. Before the Third Plenary Session of the Eleventh Central Committee of the Chinese Communist Party (CCP) at the end of 1978, which marked the beginning of reform, Deng Xiaoping made two important diplomatic decisions: to sign the Sino-Japanese Peace and Friendship Treaty, and to normalize China-U.S. diplomatic relations. These two decisions were based not only on realistic, long-term diplomatic considerations but also on domestic political considerations. He wanted to ensure the smooth transformation of the CCP's political line and to provide China with a more stable and favorable international environment. During this period, Mao Zedong's "Three Worlds" concept and "One Battle Line" strategy, which emphasized China's alliance with the United States against the Soviet Union, were still the underlying principles of Chinese diplomacy. Although Deng Xiaoping had inherited this strategy, his main purpose was to open China up to the United States and other Western countries and to promote China's economic development rather than to merely safeguard its national security. After the normalization of China-U.S. diplomatic relations in 1979, China hoped to reinforce that relationship, but when the U.S. Congress passed the Taiwan Relations Act, the development of bilateral relations suffered a setback.

Although, on the surface, Chinese foreign policy underwent no great changes until 1982, the thinking on diplomacy and the content of diplomatic activities were already quite different from those of the past. In December 1981, China and the United States began to negotiate on the issue of U.S. weapons sales to Taiwan. In the spring of 1982, an opportunity to ameliorate Sino-Soviet relations appeared. When Soviet leader Leonid Brezhnev made a long speech in Tashkent on March 24 and expressed his willingness to improve relations with China, Deng Xiaoping instructed the Foreign Ministry to respond immediately. On March 26, the Chinese Foreign Ministry hosted its first press conference since its founding more than thirty years earlier and released a brief statement on Sino-Soviet relations, attracting international attention. Although Deng Xiaoping considered Sino-Soviet relations important, he believed that it would be to China's advantage to reach an agreement with the United States on the sale of weapons to Taiwan and to stabilize Sino-American relations before turning to the Soviet Union.[1]

The late summer and early autumn of 1982 was a key period for the transformation of Chinese foreign policy. In July and August, Deng met with several leaders of the Central Committee and the Foreign Ministry and suggested that China make a big move by sending a message to the Soviet Union aimed at bettering relations between the two countries. According to Deng, improved Sino-Soviet ties would rely on the Soviet Union making the first move to resolve the "three barriers" issue.[2] On August 17, China and the United States signed a new joint communiqué that set out the principles for a gradual reduction of U.S. arms sales to Taiwan. Although the United States eventually failed to keep its commitment, this communiqué marked a general stabilization in Sino–American relations. At the same time, the Foreign Ministry began work to improve Sino–Soviet relations. In the middle of August, Yu Hongliang, director general in charge of Eastern Europe and the Soviet Union, visited Moscow to conduct a regular inspection of the work at the embassy and to communicate to the Soviets the Chinese government's willingness to improve the relationship between the two countries.[3]

China's new foreign policy first became public on August 21, when Deng Xiaoping met Javier Pérez de Cuéllar, the secretary-general of the United Nations. Deng emphasized that opposing hegemony, safeguarding world peace, and reinforcing cooperation with third-world countries were the main focus of Chinese foreign policy.[4] In September, the CCP held its Twelfth National Congress, which marked the outspread of reform and the opening of China to the outside world. In his report to the congress, party chairman Hu Yaobang stated that the CCP would maintain its independent foreign policy and that the "Five Principles of Peaceful Coexistence" would continue to guide China in constructing and developing relations with other countries. He also noted that as long as the Soviet Union took practical measures to remove the threat to China's security, Sino–Soviet relations would likely proceed toward normalization. In October, China and the Soviet Union hosted the first round of negotiations at the deputy-ministerial level, indicating a formal resumption of the long-interrupted political dialogue. After the Twelfth National Congress, Chinese leaders stopped mentioning in public Mao's "Three Worlds" and "One Battle Line" concepts. Under its new policies, China started to establish more balanced foreign relations by consciously keeping its distance from the United States.

In March 1986, Zhao Ziyang, premier of the State Council, delivered the "Report on the Seventh Five-Year Plan" in the Fourth Session of the Sixth National People's Congress. The fourth part of his report elaborated on China's "Independent Foreign Policy for Peace" and listed its ten basic principles: (1) the fundamental goal of China's foreign activities is to oppose hegemony, maintain world peace, develop friendly relations and cooperation with all countries, and promote common prosperity; (2) China believes that all countries, big or small, strong or weak, rich or poor, are equal members of the international community; (3) China adheres to the principle of independence, and with regard to international affairs, China's stance and policy will be based on the merits or demerits of a matter; (4) China will not be dependent on any superpower, nor will China form an alliance with any superpower; (5) China adheres to the Five Principles of Peaceful Coexistence and strives to establish, restore, and develop normalized relations with all countries of the world; (6) China belongs to the third world, and a fundamental element of China's foreign policy is to strengthen its solidarity and cooperation with other third-world countries; (7) China opposes arms races; (8) China intends to pursue a long-term policy of opening itself up to the world; (9) China follows the goals and principles of the Charter of the United Nations, participates in all kinds of international organizations, and takes an active part in multilateral diplomatic activities; and (10) China values communication with people in all countries.[5] With this report, the reform of China's foreign policy was finalized.

From 1982 to 1988, China ameliorated relations with surrounding countries through a series of diplomatic activities and reinforced its political and economic cooperation with third-world countries. Although China purposely kept its distance from the United States, the development of relations between the two countries went smoothly during these years. Meanwhile, China also improved and eventually normalized relations with the USSR in 1989. China continued to develop political and economic ties with Western countries as well as Eastern European countries. In addition, China strengthened its cooperation with the United Nations, participating in multilateral economic activities and contributing to the resolution of regional disputes.

From the end of the 1970s to the mid-1980s, more notable than this policy shift was the profound change in the principles of Chinese diplomacy. In the 1960s, China's diplomatic relations were deeply affected by ideology. Then, China was squeezed by the confrontation between the two superpowers— the United States and the Soviet Union. The CCP considered itself the standard-bearer of the international communist movement, and support of revolutionary movements worldwide was the main goal of China's diplomacy. As a result, the Chinese government based its relations with other countries on ideological principles and evaluated the political nature of each country with an ideological gauge. Moreover, the CCP overestimated the seriousness of the international situation and believed that a third world war was imminent, which would lead to a global revolution. Or, alternatively, revolution would stop the imminent war. By the 1970s, the fanaticism caused by the Cultural Revolution in China began to fade, but there had been no significant change in the Chinese view of the international situation.

In contrast with China's diplomacy in the 1960s and 1970s, there were significant changes in Chinese diplomatic thought in the era of reform. For instance, the task of diplomatic work was clarified; that is, to continue to safeguard national independence, sovereignty, and the socialist system, but also to create a peaceful international environment and especially an environment favorable to national economic construction and national reunification. New concepts that emphasized the practical preservation of national interests, the opposition of hegemony, the application of nonalignment, and the disavowal of leadership among third-world countries or in the international communist movement were added to the Independent Foreign Policy for Peace. In carrying out exchanges with other countries, China would follow the trend of world development and its own national interests rather than defining friend and foe by ideology or adopting the strategy of uniting with certain countries to oppose others.

In the meantime, Chinese leaders came to see major international problems and relations between China and the world in a new light. They reevaluated the international situation and gradually discarded the previous view that a large-scale world war was inevitable. By the end of the 1970s, Deng Xiaoping began to believe that a third world war could be postponed. By the middle of the 1980s, he had concluded that world war could be avoided and saw the world's main problems as involving peace and development. Chinese leaders recognized the diversity of the existing world and how its various components struggled with the opposing forces of incompatibility and mutual dependence. It was both possible and necessary for states, especially the great powers, to cooperate, since they shared a common interest in dealing with a number of international issues. The Chinese recognized that a closed-door policy was not the basis of independence and that self-reliance was not blind xenophobia. China needed to strengthen its economic cooperation and trade with other countries and absorb advanced science, technology, and management experience from foreign nations.

During this period, the impetus for change in Chinese foreign policy came not only from recognition of the need for political and economic reform but also from reflection on past experiences and lessons. China's new diplomatic guidelines, recognition of major international problems, and determination to change the relationship between it and the world showed that China had bid farewell to its "revolutionary diplomacy," with its strong ideological colors. China was on the way toward integrating itself into the existing international system and taking a consciously active stance. At the same time, China realized that to play a greater role in international affairs and to finally resolve the issue of national reunification, its most important task was to do its own job well.[6]

Those who are familiar with the diplomatic history of China know the saying that "China's diplomacy changes every ten years."[7] Thus, the period of the late 1980s and early 1990s was just another window of time during which a series of major events occurred: the Tiananmen incident, the sanctions imposed by the United States and other Western nations, the dramatic transformation of Eastern Europe, the Persian Gulf War, and the collapse of the Soviet Union. Yet, in terms of diplomacy, China maintained its stability and continuity and did not make any major changes during this period.

There are four main reasons that China's foreign policy remained stable. First, facing a complicated international situation, Deng Xiaoping put forward this strategic principle: "Observe cool-headedly, hold position firmly, cope with affairs calmly, conceal our capacities and bide our time, be good at maintaining a low profile, never claim leadership, and make some contributions."[8] Insisting on separating ideological struggles from state-to-state relations, he thus saved China from returning to its old path. Second, the third generation of Chinese leadership, with Jiang Zemin at its core, inherited the foreign policy determined by Deng Xiaoping. Third, China adopted a series of measures on the diplomatic front: actively engaging in diplomatic activities in Asia, the Middle East, and Africa and establishing diplomatic ties with twenty-three countries, including Singapore, South Korea, Saudi Arabia, Israel, and South Africa; seizing the opportunity of the Gulf crisis to quickly break the West's sanctions while resuming and stabilizing relations with Western countries; consistently fighting against activities infringing on China's sovereignty with regard to Taiwan, Hong Kong, Tibet, and Macao; and emphasizing self-determination in implementing development and reform based on China's domestic situation. Finally, a deeper-rooted reason for China's diplomatic stability was that continuity was guaranteed by the domestic political line and the popular support for it. Moreover, once China had opened itself and established connections to the rest of the world, it was impossible to return to its introverted state. In addition, Western countries were worried that excessive pressure on China would be detrimental to their own interests.

Domestic and diplomatic problems caused by the Tiananmen incident were generally resolved by 1992, and the progress on the diplomatic front exceeded Chinese leaders' expectations. After the experience of this serious crisis, China's new foreign policy was further consolidated.

Globalization and Establishment of the Socialist Market Economy

Unlike in the 1980s, both international and domestic factors exerted great influence on the development of China's foreign policy in the 1990s. The two main international factors were the end of the Cold War and the acceleration of economic globalization; the two main domestic factors were the establishment of a socialist market economy and China's resumption of administrative power over Hong Kong and Macao.

The international situation underwent a series of major changes in the early 1990s. The one that most concerned Chinese leaders was the political change in the Soviet Union. The disintegration of the Soviet Union sent shock waves through the CCP, and the party discussed what lessons could be learned from this event. The viewpoint of "preventing peaceful evolution" was advanced, and some even advocated an ideological debate with the Soviet Union. However, Deng Xiaoping's determined policy was that no matter what changes took place within the Soviet Union, China must stabilize relations with the Soviets rather than engage in ideological debate.[9] When summing up the discussion, Jiang Zemin pointed out that the best way to prevent peaceful evolution was for China to manage its domestic affairs well; China had to continue both reform and openness, and economic construction should be the central task.[10] The result of this discussion was significant to the stabilization of China's domestic and foreign policies, which enabled China to establish a new relationship with Russia on the basis of mutual respect and good-neighborliness after the breakup of the Soviet Union. Thus, China took a key step in adapting to the post–Cold War world.

During a period of observation and reflection in the summer of 1991, Jiang Zemin and other Chinese leaders considered the international situation—specifically, the termination of the bipolar system and the move toward multipolarization. Despite the unstable and volatile international situation, the theme of peace and development in Chinese foreign policy had not changed.[11] Chinese leaders decided to continue to promote domestic reform and opening up, yet they were determined to adjust the structure of China's foreign relations in accordance with the new situation. Initially, China's leaders were rather optimistic about the prospects of multipolar development, but in the mid-1990s, they came to the realization that this would be a long and arduous process. This understanding led China's diplomacy to take a more pragmatic direction.

At the beginning of the 1990s, along with major changes in the international situation, China's reform entered a crucial phase. Although China's reform policies had been in effect for more than ten years, no clear goals had been set for reform of the economic system. Some economists believed that the only goal of reform was to improve the existing economic system; others held that the ultimate goal of reform was to establish a market economy. Without a clear objective in mind, China's approach had been one of "groping around in the pebbles to find a way to cross the river," which meant that the Chinese government dealt only with emerging problems that could be solved and shelved those that could not. As a result, many of the reform measures of the 1980s were tinged by an aura of transition and compromise. One typical example was the double-track price system implemented at that time. At the end of 1980s, faced with unprecedented inflation, the Chinese were increasingly aware that the goals of economic reform must be clarified as soon as possible.

In 1992, with Deng Xiaoping's well-known "talk during the tour of South China" and the Fourteenth CCP National Congress as symbols, China accelerated the pace of reform and opening up. The National Congress decided to establish a socialist market system, which became the most important domestic event of the decade in China. From then on, China's reform moved away from the "groping around" phase and entered a phase of comprehensive and systematic development. The confirmation of economic reform goals eliminated the political instability caused by differing opinions and greatly reduced the influence of the conservative force. Beginning in 1993, the Chinese government systematically implemented a series of reforms focused on the central task of establishing the socialist market system, including changing the operating mechanism of state-owned enterprises, converting the mandatory plan to an instructional plan, and carrying out coordinated reforms in prices, financial and trade management systems, the social security system, housing, the land-use system, and so forth. China's political reform took on a new impetus, and the main thrust was to transform and adapt the government's function to the needs of a market economy. In the last few years of the twentieth century, China overcame internal inflationary pressure and the external impact of the Asian financial crisis, and its economy enjoyed a sustained and rapid growth. By the end of twentieth century, China had established a market economy with national macroguidance and control. This development quickly turned China into a major player in the world economy. When dealing with foreign affairs, Chinese leaders paid more attention to economic issues, and other countries began to take seriously China's position in the global economy.

From a retrospective point of view, there were several reasons for the relatively smooth transition of China's economic system. First, the delay in defining its economic reform goals was probably a good thing. After more than ten years of experimentation and practice, China was able to avoid the type of trauma suffered by Russia, which had always seemed to have a clear goal. Second, from the very beginning, China's reform was characterized by extroversion, and Chinese scholars and officials always paid great attention to the importance of "converting" China's economy to align with the global economy. Thus, from the 1980s to the 1990s, China's economy continued to strengthen its ties with the world market. Third, the timing of China's decision to build a market economy was slightly ahead of the trend of accelerated development and economic globalization; this enabled China to hold the initiative and benefit from the trend of economic globalization, instead of being its passive victim, as some other developing countries were. Fourth, the Chinese government set the procedures and pace of opening up to accord with China's actual situation; this prevented Chinese interests from being damaged by giving outsiders too rapid access to the homeland. In the 1990s, these concerns were important factors in economic and diplomatic negotiations between China and Western countries.

Throughout the 1990s, the resumption of sovereignty over Hong Kong and Macao occupied an important place on the agenda of the Chinese government. Although, as a diplomatic issue, the taking back of Hong Kong and Macao was a relatively independent event, it had far-reaching implications. In fact, Chinese leaders were somewhat preoccupied with the return of these territories, to the extent that they did not feel free to deal with other diplomatic issues until the turnover was accomplished. On July 1, 1997, the Chinese government resumed the exercise of sovereignty over Hong Kong, and on December 20, 1999, it resumed the exercise of sovereignty over Macao. On the whole, the process went smoothly; there were neither major disruptions nor confusion. The return of Hong Kong and Macao put an end to the history of foreigners seeking colonies in China. For the Chinese people, this was a major event that wiped out a century of humiliation and disgrace, and it greatly enhanced their national self-confidence.

In the second half of the 1990s, China was increasingly challenged by the effects of globalization. China's economy was now closely linked with the world economy. The intense competition among various types of foreign and native enterprises affected not only China's domestic market but also the international market. For the first time, the Asian financial crisis of 1997 exposed China's economy to the influences of external events. Although China's losses were relatively small, the crisis taught the Chinese people a great lesson. In 1998, Jiang Zemin warned that the trend of economic globalization and the rapid development of information technology would make the competition among national powers increasingly intense.

Aware of the tremendous impact of globalization, Chinese leaders increasingly and consciously combined political, economic, and diplomatic factors in their policy-making considerations. The most typical case was the negotiation over China's entry into the World Trade Organization (WTO). These negotiations started in 1986 and lasted for fifteen years. Although WTO members repeatedly raised the bar for entry, the Chinese government was determined to join the organization and finally managed to prevail over all dissenting views. Chinese leaders' objective was very clear: to create a more favorable external environment for reform and economic development by acquiring WTO membership. This was considered key to China's active participation in the process of economic globalization and to its promotion of domestic industrial restructuring by making use of external pressure. By the end of 2001, China had become a formal member of the WTO.

Construction of a Multilevel Foreign Relations Pattern

Generally speaking, Chinese diplomacy involves four groups: major powers, neighboring countries, third-world countries, and international organizations. In different periods, China's focus has been on different groups. On the whole, China's diplomacy did not become balanced until the 1980s.

After 1982, China began to move toward building a more balanced foreign policy. In the second half of the1980s, the trend was relatively clear— toward an all-around, multilevel diplomacy—and this direction was strongly reinforced by both international and domestic factors in the 1990s. By the turn of the twenty-first century, China's diplomatic pattern took into account not only its relations with the major powers and developed countries but also its relations with its neighbors and developing countries. China went to great lengths to establish bilateral relations with other countries and was actively involved in multilateral diplomatic activities.

The establishment of an all-around, multilevel diplomatic pattern was related to three major tasks faced by China. The first was to deal with the many changes in international relations after the end of the Cold War in general and the overall adjustment between the great powers in particular, as well as the situation caused by the flourishing of various regional and intercontinental cooperative organizations. The second was to safeguard world peace and oppose hegemony, power politics, and terrorism and to promote the establishment of a fair and reasonable new international political and economic order. The third was to deal with the impacts of economic globalization and the rapid development of science and technology in China.

China's twenty-first-century diplomacy exhibits three new features in terms of form and content. First, the content of foreign affairs has expanded significantly to include the areas of economy, security, human rights, environmental protection, and other regional and global issues. Second, the diplomatic activities of top leaders play an increasingly vital role. Dialogue and communication between the heads of nations directly promote the development of bilateral and multilateral relations, and some problems that are difficult to solve by low-level coordination and negotiation are resolved at this highest level. Third, China seeks to establish partnerships on a global scale. In these partnerships and other cooperative relationships between China and other countries or regional organizations, regular meetings, negotiations, and dialogues on different levels are established. This new mode of operation not only improves the effectiveness of bilateral and multilateral cooperation but also contributes to the stability of ongoing relations between the parties.

In the 1990s, China's efforts to establish a pattern of omnidirectional external relations began with good-neighbor diplomacy. At the beginning of the decade, China finally normalized relations with all neighboring countries. Since then, China has continued to develop its relations with its neighbors, and the pact between China and the Association of Southeast Asian Nations (ASEAN) is the most conspicuous example. At the end of 1997, the two sides issued the "Joint Statement of the China-ASEAN Summit Meeting," in which the two sides confirmed the goal of establishing a partnership based on neighborliness and mutual trust. During the Asian financial crisis, China provided aid to the countries involved through both bilateral and multilateral channels, and the government ensured that the fixed rate of the renminbi (RMB) would not be changed. These measures were widely praised by the international community. After the normalization of Sino-Vietnamese relations in 1991, the two countries established a framework for their relationship in 1999 with a focus on long-term stability, friendship, and comprehensive cooperation. China's relations with Pakistan and India also steadily improved. In 1996, China and India established a cooperative partnership based on the Five Principles of Peaceful Coexistence, and China and Pakistan announced their intention to build a comprehensive, cooperative partnership for the twenty-first century. In Northeast Asia, China paid close attention to safeguarding the peace and stability of the Korean peninsula. While maintaining its traditional friendly and cooperative relations with the Democratic People's Republic of Korea, China's political and economic relations with South Korea developed rapidly. Likewise, China has good relations with other neighboring countries.

It is apparent that China has made significant progress in resolving historical border disputes with its neighbors. China and Russia reached five border agreements and protocols, and except for several specific regions, their border disputes have essentially been resolved. China and Vietnam signed a land border treaty and an agreement on the mare clausum issue. Although the Sino-Indian border issue remains unresolved, the situation has greatly improved. The governments of the two countries have signed a number of agreements aimed at maintaining the status quo and creating conditions for the development of bilateral relations. On the South China Sea issue, China clearly stated in the joint declaration with ASEAN its willingness to work with the involved countries to properly settle the dispute through peaceful negotiations and in accordance with the universally accepted norms of international law and the basic principles established by the modern law of the sea. China has taken the same position toward other similar disputes.

China's relations with the major powers have long been an important factor in its foreign policy. Traditionally, China's relations with the major powers were in a sense limited to the realm of neighboring countries, and safety issues were of paramount concern. After reform and opening up, the situation changed dramatically. First, economic matters have assumed an important place in China's relations with the major powers. Second, there are many more regional and global issues that require mutual concern and cooperation. Developing and stabilizing relations with the major powers and the developed countries have played an important role in China's modernization and continue to have great significance in terms of maintaining world peace.

In the mid-1990s, Chinese leaders pointed out that China had to actively work to develop a new relationship with the major powers. In this spirit, China took the lead in 1996 in establishing a relationship with Russia based on equality, mutual trust, and a strategic, cooperative partnership. The two countries signed the Sino-Russian Good-Neighborhood Treaty of Friendship and Cooperation in 2001. Despite some concerns by both parties, Sino-Russian relations have generally proceeded smoothly.

China-U.S. relations have gone through some ups and downs since normalization. In November 1993, President Jiang Zemin and President Bill Clinton met in Seattle, Washington—the first sign of real progress since the establishment of diplomatic relations. In 1997, China and the United States announced a joint effort to establish a constructive, strategic partnership for the twenty-first century. Over the next several years, China-U.S. relations experienced two crises: the U.S. bombing of the Chinese embassy in Belgrade in 1999, and the collision between a U.S. Navy surveillance plane and a Chinese fighter jet in April 2001. After the terrorist attacks of September 11, 2001, China-U.S. relations finally stabilized. President George W. Bush visited China in October 2001 and again in February 2002, and the leaders of the two countries reached an important consensus on promoting China-U.S. relations. The facts show that although there are many conflicts between the two countries, they share vital interests. After nearly twenty years, the depth and breadth of relations between the two countries mean that neither party can treat the relationship carelessly.

In the last few years of the twentieth century, China also established partnerships with France, Britain, Canada, Japan, and the European Union. China has maintained relatively good relations and cooperation with all the major powers and the developed countries, which is unprecedented.

At the turn of the century, relations between China and the countries of Africa, West Asia, and Latin America also advanced. In 1999, China and Egypt signed a joint communiqué to establish strategic and cooperative relations in the twenty-first century. In October 2000, the Forum on China-Africa Cooperation Ministerial Conference was held in Beijing. Participants adopted the "Beijing Declaration of the Forum on China-Africa Cooperation" and the "Program for China-Africa Cooperation in Economic and Social Development." The Chinese government announced that it would deduct the debt of 10 billion RMB owed by Africa's most heavily indebted and least developed countries over the next two years to assist in solving the African debt problem. China established diplomatic relations with most Latin American countries and developed economic and trade relations and people-to-people exchanges with some countries that lack diplomatic relations with China.

Being actively engaged in multilateral diplomacy is now a prominent feature of China's foreign policy. After resuming its legitimate seat in the United Nations in 1971, China gradually began to participate in UN activities involving multilateral diplomacy. In the mid-1980s, China clearly adopted multilateral diplomacy as an important part of its Independent Foreign Policy for Peace. In the 1990s, China became increasingly active in the field of multilateral diplomacy, actively advocating for the establishment of a new international political and economic order based on the Five Principles of Peaceful Coexistence, opposing hegemony and power politics, and defending the interests of developing countries.

The United Nations is an important stage for China to exhibit its multilateral diplomacy. As a permanent member of the UN Security Council, China has fulfilled its responsibilities and made its own contribution toward maintaining international peace and security, as well as promoting just and fair solutions to major regional conflicts. On China's initiative, the five permanent members of the UN Security Council held a summit meeting in 2000—the first of its kind in history. China has also participated extensively in the work of the various UN agencies and in multilateral economic and social activities in various fields, as well as promoting international cooperation.

In the 1990s, China took part in a number of regional and multilateral organizations. It clearly showed its support for regional dialogue and cooperation in a variety of forms, based on equal participation, negotiation for consensus, the seeking of common ground, and the following of a progressive order. China actively promoted the formation of multilateral confidence-building measures with neighboring countries, maintained regional security and stability, and promoted regional economic development. China also actively participated in Asia Pacific Economic Cooperation (APEC) activities and hosted the APEC informal leadership meeting in Shanghai in October 2001. In the second half of the 1990s, China, Russia, Kazakhstan, Kyrgyzstan, and Tajikistan jointly established the "Shanghai Five" working mechanism. They originated a new security concept based on mutual trust, disarmament, and cooperative security and provided a new model of regional cooperation among both large and small countries. On this basis, in June 2001, the Shanghai Cooperation Organization was set up. China, Russia, Kazakhstan, Kyrgyzstan, Tajikistan, and Uzbekistan reached a broad consensus on cooperating in the future to fight the "three evil forces" of terrorism, extremism, and separatism. Subsequent developments proved that this was an excellent example of foresight.

China's Diplomacy in the Twenty-first Century

At the beginning of the twenty-first century, the world was still at a transitional stage after the disintegration of the bipolar structure. No matter how the outside world had changed, however, China's most important objective was domestic—to build an all-around "well-off" society in the first twenty-five years of the century. China's diplomacy would be carried out with this objective in mind. At the end of 2002, a smooth transition in Chinese leadership was realized at the Sixteenth National Congress of the CCP. Judging by developments in the first few years of the new century, China's diplomacy has undergone certain adjustments owing to the evolution of the international situation and China's increased strength.

At the dawn of the new century, there were four main factors promoting the continuity and stability of China's foreign policy. First, the framework for China's foreign policy and foreign relations was quite clear and comprehensive, and China's main diplomatic task was to perfect that framework. Meanwhile, a stable and consistent foreign policy not only promoted China's image as a responsible power but also increased other countries' trust in China. This was especially important because China's policy-making process was not yet transparent.

Second, from the 1990s to the first decade of the twenty-first century, China's foreign relations predictably experienced a period of increased sensitivity. On the one hand, with the deepening of reform, China faced many new problems and a buildup of internal pressures. On the other hand, the international pattern was still undergoing changes, and with the growth of China's comprehensive national power, other countries were reexamining China and thus adding external pressures. The crucial stage of China's own development happened to coincide with changes in the external environment, which made dealing with diplomatic and security issues more complicated. Under such circumstances, any change in the existing foreign policy without serious consideration could result in an uncontrollable and unpredictable chain reaction.

Third, since the beginning of reform and opening up, China has been the beneficiary of the existing international order. As the world has moved in the direction of multipolarity and democratization, China has advocated for the establishment of a just and fair international political and economic order through cooperation rather than confrontation. In dealing with issues between itself and the outside world, China recognizes that its own ability to shape the international order and structure is limited. China knows that such a transformation will be a long and tortuous process and that the final outcome will depend on all kinds of changes in the relative strengths of various forces.

Finally, China still has much to learn about international affairs. In fact, China as a great power lacks diplomatic experience. The world is full of uncertainties, and all sorts of unexpected emergencies may come to pass. Because of China's limited strength and inexperience, it is important and practical for it to maintain policy flexibility.

After the Sixteenth National Congress of the CCP, there were some adjustments in China's foreign policy, three of which are noteworthy. First, this congress more accurately pointed out that peace, development, and cooperation are the main tenets of international relations and emphasized the handling of international affairs with mutual respect and the seeking of common ground. It also stressed that the main task of China's diplomatic work is to safeguard strategic opportunities for the building of China's well-off society.

Second, the thinking behind China's diplomacy is more explicit. Based on historical experience and present needs, the overall framework has been clarified: the major powers are pivotal, neighboring countries are a priority, developing countries are the foundation, and multilateral relations are vital. In recent years, China has made progress in all these areas, but especially noteworthy are two major changes in China's multilateral diplomacy: the issues discussed between China and other countries are essentially global rather than regional, and China's multilateral diplomatic activities are now being conducted at a higher level, with the United Nations as a main arena. A typical example is China's attendance at the G-8 meeting with leaders of developing countries after 2003.

Third, China's diplomacy has become more transparent, more practical, and more active. This has been demonstrated by China's handling of some hot international issues, including the prevention and treatment of serious infectious diseases, the war in Iraq, and reform of the United Nations. The most salient example is China's active effort to end the North Korean nuclear crisis. China promoted the six-party talks among China, the United States, North Korea, South Korea, Japan, and Russia, held five times between 2003 and 2005. These talks prevented the crisis from escalating out of control and opened the way for a peaceful solution. As a matter of fact, all the parties have accepted the goal of a nonnuclear Korean peninsula. China's transition from its initial noninvolvement in the North Korean nuclear crisis to its limited involvement in the three-party talks among China, the United States, and North Korea to its active promotion of the six-party talks demonstrates that China is a responsible power ready to play a bigger role in maintaining regional security.

Generally speaking, China's foreign policy in recent years has been to pursue development through stability. However, some new issues have arisen that need to be resolved. First, a rapidly rising China needs to express its domestic and diplomatic goals to the external world, strengthen its bilateral and multilateral cooperation with other countries through a more active approach, and further establish its image as a reliable, trustworthy power. Thus, China has to assume greater responsibility in dealing with major global issues such as world and regional peace, economic prosperity, antiterrorism, arms control, and environmental protection, and it must play a more active and constructive role in resolving hot regional issues.

Second, China needs to establish a more effective system to coordinate its foreign policies. Along with the implementation of reform and the establishment of a market system, the dimensions of China's foreign affairs have greatly broadened. The number of governmental departments and offices that participate in policy making has increased, and the interaction between domestic and international factors is increasing. Under these circumstances, the need to conciliate various domestic interests has become a salient issue in making and implementing foreign policy. If there is no conciliation in policy making, this will not only adversely affect the efficiency of dealing with foreign affairs but also cause some unexpected negative consequences.

Third, with China's economic development and the enhancement of its national power, it is faced with the issue of readjusting its own position. How China defines its position will have a broad impact on other countries. For the time being, it may be best for China to play the role of a bridge—

facilitating contact between developed and developing countries. Although China is becoming an economic power, in many ways it is still a developing country and will continue to be so for quite a while.

Conclusion

In retrospect, the most critical and profound period of China's diplomatic development was from the end of the 1970s to the mid-1980s. These years can be regarded as a transitional period in the diplomatic history of the People's Republic of China during which its basic foreign policy was revised to match reform and its opening up to the world. The adjustment in China's foreign policy in the 1990s was necessary to accommodate further domestic reform and adapt to a post–Cold War world. It is premature to comment on China's diplomatic development in the twenty-first century, but so far, China has clearly demonstrated its desire to revitalize the nation through peaceful development and cooperation.

Notes

1. Wang Taiping, ed., *Fifty Years of PRC's Diplomacy* (Beijing: Beijing Press, 1999), 1388.

2. Party Literature Research Center of the CCP Central Committee, ed., *Annals of Deng Xiaoping, 1975–1997* (Beijing: Central Literature Press, 2004), 835. The "three barriers" mentioned by Deng Xiaoping referred to the USSR's stationing of large forces on the China-Soviet border and in Mongolia, its support of Vietnam's invasion and occupation of Cambodia, and its armed intrusion into Afghanistan.

3. Qian Qichen, *Ten Episodes in China's Diplomacy* (Hong Kong: Sanlian Shudian, 2002), 9–10.

4. Party Literature Research Center, *Annals of Deng Xiaoping,* 841.

5. *Selections of Important Literature since the 12th National Congress of CCP (II)* (Beijing: Renmin Press, 1982), 960–64.

6. *Selections of Deng Xiaoping II* (Beijing: Renmin Press, 1994), 240.

7. In the 1950s, China adopted the policy of "leaning to one side," aligning with the Soviet Union against the United States; in the 1960s, it adopted the policy of "opposing two hegemonies"—the Soviet Union and the United States; in the 1970s, it adopted a "one line" policy, uniting with the United States, Japan, and Western Europe against the Soviet Union; and in the 1980s, it gradually developed an omni-directional foreign policy.

8. Party History Research Center of the CCP Central Committee, ed., *Brief History of the Chinese Communist Party* (Beijing: Chinese Communist Party History Press, 2001), 201.

9. *Selections of Deng Xiaoping III* (Beijing: Renmin Press, 1993), 353.

10. Jiang Zemin's comments during internal meetings of the CCP on June 10, July 24, July 31, and December 7, 1991.

11. Jiang Zemin's and Li Peng's speeches during an internal meeting of the CCP on July 24, 1991.

Part I

CHINA'S RELATIONS WITH THE UNITED STATES

2. Building a New Conceptual Framework
for U.S.-China Relations
Jianwei Wang

One constant challenge for the policy makers in China and the United States since the end of the Cold War has been to find a new, mutually agreeable conceptual framework for the relationship between the two giants. During the Cold War period, the nature of the relationship was more utility oriented than anything else. The two countries sought not a convergence of their ideologies or values but rather a convergence of their interests. Those interests were narrowly defined within a framework of anti–Soviet expansionism. For the purpose of thwarting the perceived Soviet threat, China and United States formed a quasi-strategic alliance against their common adversary. That kind of overarching framework, though very limited, served to control the conflict of interests and values in secondary domains such as trade, the Taiwan issue, and human rights. Both sides were careful not to let friction in one issue area "spill over" to damage the perceived predominant common strategic interest.

With the disintegration of the Soviet empire and the collapse of world communism, this anti–Soviet framework had clearly run its course. One consequence of the disappearance of this conceptual framework has been a drifting in the relationship between China and the United States, and nobody knows where this relationship is headed. Moreover, without this framework to provide a cushion, disputes between the two countries could get out of hand at any time. As a result, uncertainty has increased and predictability has decreased, leading to frequent vacillations in recent U.S.-China relations.

Needless to say, the political leaders and elite in both countries fully understand the importance of their relationship because of their countries' respective critical mass and growing interdependence. Both sides have attempted to find a new conceptual framework to stabilize the relationship, but this process has not been easy. Whereas China's description and definition of the relationship have remained relatively constant, the United States' definition of its China policy and hence Sino-American relations have experienced sea changes from one administration to another, keeping the Chinese busy reacting and responding to these changes. This situation has been most dramatic during the presidency of George W. Bush, highlighting the flexuous and complex nature of the relationship. Nevertheless, after a lot of twists and turns, it seems that both countries are gradually moving toward a new conceptual framework to guide the relationship, although the final configuration of this reconceptualization is still far from clear and its durability is uncertain.

From "Strategic Partners" to "Strategic Adversaries"

Looking at the history of U.S.-China relations since the 1970s, it seems that until recently, China was often in a position to define that relationship. The decades of the 1970s and 1980s were basically guided by the "anti-hegemony" clause in the Shanghai Communiqué, which the Chinese insisted on. This pattern continued even during the Clinton administration. China was actively pursuing a common conceptual framework to define its relationship with the United States, and the main thrust of its endeavor was to retain as many strategic elements of the relationship established during the Cold War as possible. "Strategic partnership" became the mantra of China's major-power diplomacy. Beijing had never clearly defined this term, but for the Chinese, it implied something important, cooperative, and long term in nature. It was value free and based purely on the comprehension of common interests. It should be noted that this concept did not apply only to U.S.-China relations. Establishing a strategic partnership became China's foreign policy objective with any country or group of countries possessing significant clout in world and regional affairs. To some extent, this also reflected Beijing's desire to standardize its dealings with major powers and to lock up cooperative relations with other potential power centers in the post–Cold War era.

Initially, the Clinton administration was not interested in this kind of conceptualization. During his first term, Bill Clinton tried to use human rights as the organizing principle to define U.S. relations with China. To do so, he was prepared to challenge the domestic legitimacy of the Chinese government, even to the extent of sacrificing practical American interests such as trade. This was a major departure from the policy of his predecessor, George H. W. Bush, whose mind-set had been largely similar to that of his Chinese counterpart Deng Xiaoping. Bush and Deng did their best, under the circumstances, to rescue the relationship from the storm of the Tiananmen incident. Bush strongly believed that no matter what happened within China, for better or worse, U.S.-China relations were too important to be compromised for value purposes.

But Clinton's attempt to handle the relationship within a conceptual framework of human rights soon proved unworkable. The stake in U.S.-China trade relations and the pressure from the U.S. business community were simply too great for him to implement the most-favored nation–human rights linkage. Then in 1996, the Taiwan Strait crisis further convinced him and his foreign policy advisers that the most serious issue in Sino-American relations was not the fate of some Chinese dissidents but rather war and peace, which could involve the lives of thousands of Americans. With the exchange of state visits during Clinton's second term, China got what it wanted from the United States: a "constructive strategic partnership" that was supposed to protect China's so-called core national interest—Taiwan.

The Chinese thought that this was the end of story and that the relationship between the two countries would once again be stable under a new conceptual framework. This complacence, however, proved to be short-lived. When Republican George W. Bush launched his bid for the presidency, his first assault against Clinton's China policy targeted this conceptual framework of "strategic partner." He declared that China was actually a "strategic competitor" of the United States, and Bush's chief foreign policy adviser Condoleezza Rice developed a rationale for this reconceptualization. She argued that because China had "unresolved vital interests" concerning Taiwan and the South China Sea, it resented the role of the United States. This suggested that China was not satisfied with the status quo and would like to alter the balance of power in Asia in its own favor. That alone made China a strategic competitor rather than a strategic partner. Rice stated that although cooperation should be pursued whenever possible, the United States "should never be afraid to confront Beijing when interests collide."[1]

The Bush foreign policy team's drastic reconceptualization of Sino-American relations from "strategic partner" to "strategic competitor" was closely related to a grand global strategy long advocated by some of its main players, such as Dick Cheney and Paul Wolfowitz. That strategy's goal was U.S. primacy in world affairs. It envisioned a world structure in which the United States would prevent any other nation or alliance from becoming a great power and preclude the rise of another global rival for an indefinite time.[2] Since China was the only country in a position to possibly challenge U.S. hegemony, it had to be considered a strategic competitor.

Scholars endorsing this redefinition of Sino-American relations further elaborated this concept. David Shambaugh, for example, argued that strategic competition might be a more apt description of the current U.S.-China relationship because the two countries did not share much in terms of worldviews, strategic interests, political systems, intelligence, or military relations. The key assumption underlying his analysis was that "the two nations [were] vying for strategic pre-eminence in East Asia."[3] Along the same lines, strategy reviews from early in the Bush administration exhibited a China-centered feature. The various classified and unclassified reviews and studies, particularly the reports by Andrew Marshall and Zalmay Khalizad, indicated that China policy left a deep imprint on the overall U.S. strategy, and they reflected an obsession with China as a potential military threat. For the first time since the end of the Cold War—or, for that matter, since World War II—the United States was forming a China-centered grand strategy.

Caught off guard, the Chinese initially seemed unable to counter with their own cognitive framework. Apparently, Washington had taken away Beijing's initiative to conceptually define the relationship. This was consistent with the mentality of some Bush administration officials that the relationship should be defined according to American rather than Chinese terms. To avoid a direct confrontation with a more assertive America, China largely took an approach of "crouching tiger and hidden dragon" in both conceptual and policy terms (with the exception of the unfortunate incident involving the collision of a U.S. Navy EP-3 surveillance plane and a Chinese fighter jet in April 2001). Chinese leaders just repeated President Jiang Zemin's formula for dealing with the United States: enhancing mutual trust, minimizing trouble, developing cooperation, and avoiding confrontation. Contrary to its normal practice, China took pains to send three missions—all "self-invited"—to Washington to court the new president. To highlight Beijing's eagerness to get off to a good start with the new administration, Jiang Zemin even sent premature congratulations to President-elect Bush. Facing a series of challenges and provocations from the American side, ranging from human rights to Taiwan, China's response was unusually muted, designed to avoid the escalation of conflict whenever possible. In the words of some Chinese scholars, while the Bush administration was taking a position of full offense, China should "avoid its fruits" and wait for later opportunities.

From "Strategic Competitor" to "3C" Conceptualization

Interestingly, the concept of "strategic competitor" was almost as short-lived as that of "strategic partner." At the beginning of the Bush administration, China was largely ignored, and top Republican foreign policy advisers were talking about downgrading U.S.-China relations and upgrading U.S.-Japan relations. However, the midair collision of the U.S. surveillance plane and the Chinese fighter jet near Hainan Island in April 2001 forced the China issue back in the spotlight of American foreign policy and acted as a catalyst for both sides to change course. Just as Clinton had realized the necessity of managing Sino-American relations more carefully after the 1996 Taiwan Strait crisis, some of the more pragmatic heads in the Bush administration, such as Secretary of State Colin Powell, began to sense the possibly dire consequences of neglecting China. Depicting China as a strategic competitor might indeed turn Beijing into one, so that term quietly disappeared from the Bush administration's vocabulary. By the time of Powell's trip to Beijing in July 2001, the crisis mood was pretty much over, and preparations for President Bush's first visit to China were well under way.

It goes without saying that the September 11, 2001, terrorist attacks on the United States and the American reaction dramatically changed the geopolitical environment in which Sino-American relations functioned. The Bush administration was suddenly faced with a real enemy that presented a more immediate danger to U.S. security than the potential threat posed by China. Consequently, the formation of a China-centered global strategy was put on hold, at least for the time being. China's swift strategic decision to support the U.S. war on terror put Beijing and Washington on the same side once again, at least on the surface.[4] Bush was obviously impressed by China's lack of hesitation in supporting the United States.[5] As an acknowledgment of Beijing's goodwill, Bush decided to attend the Asia Pacific Economic Cooperation meeting in Shanghai, irrespective of the ongoing war in Afghanistan. In his first encounter with the Chinese president, Bush formally dropped the usage of "strategic competitor" and called China "a great country and not an enemy of the United States." In fact, he asserted that he regarded "China as a friend of the United States."[6] In defining the nature of the relationship, he now moved closer to what the Chinese preferred and declared that the United States sought a relationship that was "candid, constructive, and cooperative."[7] The adjectives "constructive" and "cooperative" were what the Chinese wanted to hear; "candid" was added by the United States to cover any possible fallout in the relationship in the future. Interestingly, Bush put "candid" before "constructive" and "cooperative," indicating his awareness that the two countries still did not see eye to eye on many issues. This "3C" definition was the first clear departure from the original "1C" concept: competitor. During his first meeting with Bush, Jiang Zemin also began to push for a high-level strategic dialogue mechanism between the two countries, which did not materialize until 2005. In his testimony before Congress in April 2002, Secretary of State Powell reiterated the 3C formula to describe U.S.-China relations: "A candid, constructive and cooperative relationship is what we are building with China: candid where we disagree; constructive where we can see some daylight; and cooperative where we have common regional, global or economic interests."[8] At a dinner to honor visiting Chinese premier Wen Jiabao in December 2003, Powell further emphasized this 3C relationship when he told Wen: "You have been candid, constructive, and you have sought cooperative relationships, and that is precisely what we seek with China." He added, "We need such a relationship in future generations to deepen and expand the peace."[9]

After 9/11, new opportunities for strategic cooperation between China and the United States, as exemplified by the war on terror and the North Korean nuclear crisis, moved the U.S. conceptualization further away from one of competition. Bush's decision to launch a war against Iraq significantly diverted U.S. attention from East Asia to the Middle East. Washington certainly did not need a strategic competitor in East Asia when it was engaged in nasty urban guerrilla warfare in Iraq. On the contrary, it needed China's cooperation more than ever to maintain stability in the Asian Pacific. In other words, for the immediate future, the main security threat to the United States did not come from major powers but from "shadowy networks" of international terrorists. In a speech at West Point in June 2002, President Bush pointed out that the cooperation provided by major powers in the war against terrorism had convinced him that "we have our best chance since the rise of the nation-state in the seventeenth century to build a world where the great powers compete in peace instead of prepare for war."[10] The National Security Strategy, released by the White House the following September, reconfirmed this idea. It asserted, "Today, the world's great powers find themselves on the same side—united by common dangers of terrorist violence and chaos."[11] Based on these new cognitions, Secretary of State Powell developed a "strategy of partnership" before he stepped down. He argued that the war on terror and the nurturing of constructive relationships among the major powers were not mutually exclusive. The United States was conducting the war on terror "with an eye toward great-power cooperation." With regard to Sino-American relations, Powell declared that the most significant cognitive breakthrough was that neither side believed "there is anything inevitable about our relationship any longer." In other words, China and the United States did not have to be strategic competitors. With that kind of conceptual modification, the U.S.-China relationship warmed up significantly. By the end of Bush's first term, some people on both sides were calling the relationship the best since Nixon's historic visit to China in 1972.[12]

From "Peaceful Rise" to "Stakeholder"

Although use of the term "strategic competitor" to describe China had been suspended, this did not mean suspension of the mutual suspicion between the two countries. This was particularly true for the United States. As a matter of fact, strategic planners in the Department of Defense never took their wary eyes away from China. China's rapid economic growth and the subsequent enhancement of its military power constantly haunted the American policy makers. In other words, the ghost of the China threat never totally disappeared from the psyche of the American public. After its relegation to the sidelines for three years, the China issue suddenly reemerged in the forefront during the first year of Bush's second term. China made headlines in the media almost on a daily basis. Prominent think tanks engaged in major projects related to China. Various Defense Department and congressional reports carried ominous tones about China's military buildup. Some saw this as another wave of "China fever" among the American public; others called this a return of the "China threat xenophobia." But whatever it was called, the underlying reason for this new wave of China bashing was China's rise as a formidable economic and military power. Apparently, some U.S. political and military leaders and elite had been caught off guard by the speed of China's rise, particularly in the military domain. The Iraq quagmire further increased their anxiety. These perceptions—whether accurate or not—were dictated not only by ideology and values but also by historical experience and precedent.

The Chinese foreign policy establishment was fully aware of this perception of a "China threat." They understood that without effectively addressing this issue among the American public, even if Washington agreed to define the relationship as one of "strategic partnership," there could be no real stability. Therefore, beginning in 2002, the Chinese elite, represented by Zheng Bijian, a former aide to current Chinese leader Hu Jintao, began to develop and disseminate the theory of "peaceful rise" in an attempt to address the deep-rooted suspicion of China in the West in general and the United States in particular. In his speeches delivered during various trips to the United States, Zheng tried hard to drive his point home: Americans needed a new conceptual framework to view China's rise as a world power. He declared that China would take a brand-new route of peaceful rise that was totally different from that of Germany, Japan, or the former Soviet Union.[13] This new path was characterized by China's connection with rather than detachment from the process of economic globalization. Its success relied on China's own development, its market openness, its institutional self-improvement, and its mutually beneficial relations with other countries. China had been on this path of peaceful development for two decades and had benefited greatly from it; there was no reason to change.[14] Zheng defined China's peaceful rise as equivalent to its modernization. He argued that the experience of the past twenty-five years had proved that unlike other rising powers in history that had used aggression and war to accomplish their ascendance, China could secure the necessary capital, technology, and resources through peaceful means because it had opened itself to the world market. Economic globalization made China's peaceful rise feasible. China's development required a peaceful international environment, and in turn, its development would strengthen world peace. In sum, China's peaceful rise would bring opportunities rather than threats to the international community.[15] The promotion of this "peaceful rise" theory in the United States reached a climax when Zheng Bijian's article was published in the most influential foreign policy journal—*Foreign Affairs*.[16]

China's bombardment of the "peaceful rise" theory obviously had an impact on American officials. Deputy Secretary of State Robert Zoellick's seminal speech on U.S.-China relations in September 2005 was apparently triggered by his discussions with Zheng on the theme of "peaceful rise." In that speech, Zoellick broke new ground in defining China and U.S.-China relations. He pointed out that China was not like the Soviet Union of the 1940s because China did not have an anti-American or radical ideology and was not seeking to overthrow the existing international system. This statement by a U.S. official basically put an end to the debate whether China should be considered the next Soviet Union in the post–Cold War era. Zoellick also declared that China was no longer an outsider; after two decades of reform and openness, China had become a full-fledged member of the international community. Although China was not a democracy, he noted, it did not engage in a struggle against democracy. Therefore, the United States should not preclude long-term cooperation with China. The most interesting concept put forward in his speech was an appeal for China to become a "responsible stakeholder" in the international system, although Zoellick did not explain what he meant by this.[17]

The new discourse of "stakeholder" trigged a heated discussion among China's America watchers. Owing to the term's vagueness and the difficulty of translating it into a Chinese equivalent, a variety of different meanings emerged from the Chinese media. Some Chinese analysts took it as an indication that the United States was forming a new China strategy and was ready to accept a rising China. Others were more skeptical about the real intention behind the concept. They pointed out that although it indicated Washington's official recognition of China as a legitimate member of the international system, it could also mean that Washington would now set a higher standard for China's domestic and international conduct. Whereas in the past the United States had given China—still considered an outsider—special treatment in terms of trade, human rights, and weapons proliferation, that kind of special treatment would not be warranted for an inside stakeholder.

A more formal response from the Chinese side came when the official *People's Daily* published an article by Zheng Bijian on its front page. Zheng called Zoellick's speech "the most definitive political comment by the United Sates on Sino-U.S. relations" and argued that a permanent improvement in U.S.-China relations would require a fundamental understanding of the Communist Party of China and its basic direction for the twenty-first century. He pointed out that beginning in the late 1970s, China had embarked on a very different path from the former Soviet Union. In 1979, while the

Soviet Union was invading Afghanistan, the Communist Party of China was making its historic decision to reform and open up to the outside world. He made it crystal clear that China was not disposed to challenge the existing international order and would never advocate the use of force to destroy or sabotage it. He said that China embraced economic globalization because globalization made it possible for China to remain peaceful and still obtain the necessary international resources to support its modernization drive. In other words, because of economic globalization, there was no need for China to seize other countries' resources by way of territorial expansion and contesting for colonies. He then articulated the key concept of China's internal and external policies, which in Chinese, stands for three peaces: international peace, internal harmony, and reconciliation across the Taiwan Strait.[18]

This type of conceptual dialogue in the public domain was unprecedented in the history of U.S.-China relations. It indicated that both countries realized the necessity and importance of finding a new conceptual framework to define and stabilize the relationship. Washington needed to find a new conceptual rationale to accept and even accommodate the arrival of China as a major power. Gradually, the "stakeholder" concept has taken hold in the American discourse about China, and the term has been incorporated in official documents emanating from various governmental agencies from the State Department to the White House to the Pentagon. When Chinese president Hu Jintao visited the United States in April 2006, the leaders of both countries apparently endorsed this discourse. In his welcome address on the South Lawn of the White House, President Bush used this phrase for the first time.[19] In response, President Hu's remarks at the White House luncheon also mentioned "stakeholder," although he quickly added that China and the United States should also become "constructive partners."[20]

In later speeches and interviews, Zoellick elaborated on the meaning and purpose of "stakeholder." He pointed out that in the seven U.S. administrations in the last thirty years, the primary goal of U.S. policy toward China had been to integrate it into the international system. By all measures, that objective had now been accomplished. The question then became, integrate China for what purpose? That purpose, according to Zoellick, was to make China a "responsible stakeholder" in the international system. The argument went like this: For the last twenty years, China had benefited enormously from this system, which had been created and maintained largely by the United States after World War II. Now it was time for China to give something in return. In other words, China and the United States had a common interest in the system, and China had a responsibility to join the United States in making it work. This required that interaction between the two countries go "beyond pure national interest" to recognize "how one develops a national interest in the strength of the international system."[21] On another occasion, Zoellick stated that it was difficult to summarize the meaning of "stakeholder" in one simple line and to understand its pros and cons. The concept, he said, was meant to set an agenda for long-term dialogue with the Chinese.[22] The term "stakeholder" seems to have survived Zoellick's departure from the State Department in June 2006, and government officials continue to use it in their diplomatic discourse on China.

Senior policy makers in the Bush administration have tried hard to come up with a new vocabulary to define China and U.S. policy toward it. So far, the United States is not ready to go back to the Clinton-era discourse and call China a "strategic partner" in clear-cut fashion. It seems that the Bush White House still has a lot of trouble using the word "strategic" to describe U.S. relations with China, and some ideologues insist that the term "strategic partner" be reserved for U.S. allies and democracies. Nevertheless, under the influence of the "stakeholder" conceptualization, the United States is now more willing to discuss strategic issues in the relationship and to admit that the United States and China share some strategic interests.

Another effect of this "stakeholder" business is that it has made it easier for policy makers to differentiate China not just from the former Soviet Union but also from other authoritarian countries characterized by the United States as "rogue states." In March 2006, President Bush was asked at a press conference which country—Iran, North Korea, or China—posed the greatest threat to the United States. Interestingly, Bush pointed out that the U.S. relationship with China was certainly different from its relationships with Iran and North Korea. Although China is not a democracy, he said, "it is a country [that] has chosen the path, by and large, of markets and enterprise." So in terms of trade relations, China was already a strategic partner.[23] This was a more nuanced and sophisticated view of China compared with Bush's mind-set when he first took office. However, the differentiation between a political strategic partner and an economic strategic partner reflected Bush's continued ambivalence about China and indicated that he was still constrained by his declared global strategy of "eliminating tyranny in the world." Bush's changing perception of China was further demonstrated by his endorsement of the U.S.-China Strategic Economic Dialogue, announced by Treasury Secretary Henry Paulson during his visit to China in September 2006.[24] Before he went to Beijing, Paulson delivered a speech in which he continued the perceptual evolution started by Zoellick. He pointed out that "China is already a global economic leader and deserves to be recognized as a leader." However, with leadership comes with responsibility, and he noted that China should "accept its responsibility as a steward of the international system of open trade and investment." Compared with other U.S. officials, Paulson more forcefully rejected the myth of the "China threat" by saying that the United States actually had a huge stake in a prosperous and stable China and that it should welcome Chinese competition. In the meantime, he also advised Beijing that the most effective way to counter the growing anti-Chinese sentiment was to move forward with further economic reform and liberalization.[25]

Since China was not the second Soviet Union, as Zoellick declared, the United States was no longer justified in trying to "contain" China's rise. During her visit to Australia in March 2006, Secretary of State Condoleezza Rice took pains to avoid the word "containment" to describe the U.S. policy toward China. Although she declined to state clearly that the U.S. policy toward China was *not* containment, she did point out that containment was a product of the Cold War and specifically described U.S. relations with the Soviet Union. She did not think it was appropriate to use the word to describe Sino-American relations and tried to use a softer vocabulary to explain the U.S. strategy. She asserted that the U.S. policy was to create environments or conditions in which China would emerge as a "positive force."[26] She indicated that the United States' policy objective was to ensure that China's "energies" and "growth" were "channeled in a way that is stabilizing for the international system."[27]

Conclusion

In recent years, both the United States and China have made an effort to find a new conceptual framework to broaden and stabilize their relationship. At the beginning of the Bush administration, Washington was developing a China-centered global strategy that sought to redefine China from a "strategic partner" to a "strategic competitor" that posed a threat to long-term American interests. The September 11 terrorist attacks, however, proved the invalidity of that conceptualization—at least in the short term. The Bush administration began to adjust its China policy immediately after 9/11, but this was more a behavioral adaptation to a new geopolitical reality rather than a profound perceptual change regarding the nature and character of China as a nation and as an international actor. Late in his first term and particularly during his second, Bush and his administration displayed some "new thinking" about China. The post-9/11 behavioral adaptation led to some perceptual changes that put U.S. relations with China in a more realistic and positive light. In some respects, the United States now regards China as a partner rather than an adversary. To some extent, the concept of "stakeholder" has put China and the United States on the same side. This reconceptualization has also differentiated China from the former Soviet Union and modern-day "rogue states." As a result, the nondemocratic nature of the Chinese regime has not prevented the United States from cooperating with China when their common interests converge. In short, the Bush administration has come a long way in modifying its perception of China.

Overall, China has been reactive in this reconceptualization process. Beijing was able to define the relationship in terms favorable to itself during the Clinton administration, but to its dismay, the conceptual framework of "strategic partner" failed to survive the neoconservative assault of the new Bush administration. For a while, Beijing had no new thinking to offer in the relationship, and its attention was focused on practical crisis management. When Hu Jintao took office in 2002, China's American establishment, represented by Zheng Bijian, became more proactive in conceptualizing U.S.-China relations by coining the theory of "peaceful rise." The purpose of this theory was to undermine the deep-rooted fear of the "China threat" in the United States, and it succeeded in triggering conceptual and strategic dialogues between the two countries and facilitated the rethinking process on the American side that led to the invention of the "stakeholder" concept.

These reconceptualization efforts are still in a preliminary stage. Both sides still have a lot of unanswered questions about each other. We will have to wait and see whether these cognitive changes from both sides will constitute a sufficient foundation for more stable Sino–American relations. Take the concept of "stakeholder," for example. Clearly, it was a positive step for the United States to emphasize the two countries' common stakes in maintaining the existing international order. But the concept does not necessarily constitute a sufficient operational condition for a more robust relationship because each side might have a very different understanding and definition of the essence of this concept, as well as the means of realizing a stakeholder relationship.

First of all, it must be recognized that this concept was initially put forward as a demand on China by the United States. As discussed earlier, once China was fully integrated into the international system, the United States expected it to become a "responsible stakeholder"—the implication being that China did not yet have that status. In his "stakeholder" speech Zoellick also listed a number of areas in which China's behavior was perceived as problematic. In recent years, a pattern has emerged: every time American leaders meet with Chinese leaders, they deliver a long laundry list of complaints and demands, and the Chinese scramble to address U.S. concerns. If the stakeholder concept is used only to facilitate constant American demands on China, it can hardly serve as a solid basis for a stable relationship. The United States must be willing to deal with China in more of a give-and-take fashion. In other words, acting as responsible stakeholders should be the common objective of both sides rather than a demand of one side on the other. Neither side has the right to make a unilateral judgment about whether the other side is a responsible stakeholder. Instead, there should be a mechanism of mutual supervision through consultation rather than unilateral accusation.

Some policy makers on the American side are aware of the problem. In an interview in April 2006, Zoellick correctly pointed out that the United States and other countries "also need to be responsible stakeholders in the system."[28] In his welcoming speech to Hu, President Bush referred to both the United States and China as "stakeholders" in the international system.[29] In his speech on China in September 2006, Paulson also emphasized that the United States has responsibilities as a stakeholder in the global system.[30] In short, "stakeholder" needs to become a common device for self-discipline and mutual examination, not a unilateral stick wielded by one side against the other.

The key questions are: Who will define the "stake"? And how will it be defined? If each side uses only its own narrow national interests as criteria to judge the behavior of the other side, the concept of stakeholder is meaningless; it turns out to be nothing more than asking one side to subordinate its interests to the other side. In this respect, Washington has to avoid the tendency to equate its own interests with the interests of the international system; it cannot use Chinese behavior that is at odds with the interests of U.S. foreign policy as a yardstick to judge whether China is a responsible stakeholder.

It goes without saying that today we are living in a U.S.-centered international system. It is only natural that the interests of the United States and the interests of the existing international system would overlap to a significant extent. Therefore, it is not unreasonable for the United States to have a greater say in defining the "stake" in the international system. Beijing has to accept this reality. However, this does not mean that the United States can automatically claim its own interests as the interests of the entire international system. As a matter of fact, some American foreign policy practices during the Bush administration have weakened rather than strengthened the effectiveness of the international system the United States helped create. For its part, China must resist the temptation to maximize its parochial interests at the expense of the global system; it needs to accommodate more to the system stakes defined by the United States. Conversely, the United States should be careful not to neglect and jeopardize the core national interests cherished by the Chinese. Simply put, for Sino-American relations to have truly global significance, in Zoellick's words, both countries have to go "beyond their pure national interest" and recognize "how one develops a national interest in the strength of the international system."[31]

As a result of globalization and integration, the common stakes for China and the United States have been increasing. Today, the two countries can claim common interests in almost all important international issues, including antiterrorism, nonproliferation, trade liberalization, environmental protection, energy, transnational crime, and various epidemics. Even with regard to the most historically divisive issue—Taiwan— the maintenance of peace and stability in the Taiwan Strait has become the common goal of both sides. From this perspective, the concept of "stakeholder" reflects the reality. The existence of numerous common interests makes it easier to set up common objectives in dealing with urgent international issues, thus reducing the possibility of conflict. However, having a common objective is no guarantee of effective and fruitful cooperation. For example, although the United States and China have a common goal in preventing Iran from acquiring nuclear weapons, they may have different views about the means of achieving that goal. Indeed, the same is true of many other international issues, such as the war on terror, the North Korean nuclear issue, and the Darfur humanitarian crisis. In the final analysis, such differences are caused by different priorities in American and Chinese foreign policy resulting from their different status in the international system and their different value orientations. Put another way, behind the unity of common objectives, there are still disparate relative gains, which often manifest as different preferences in terms of the means and tactics used to resolve an issue. This divergence in tactics is no small matter because it often leads to skepticism about the other side's commitment to the common objective. The American reaction to China's performance in the six-party talks is a typical example. With no consensus on means and tactics, the common objective often seems hollow. However, China's extraordinary diplomatic adjustments with regard to the North Korean and Iranian nuclear issue indicates Beijing's willingness to close the gap with Washington in dealing with high-stakes international issues.

Finally, the concept of "stakeholder" has not significantly reduced either side's suspicions about the other's long-term strategic intentions. According to Zoellick, China is not another Soviet Union; it does not have a radical anti-American ideology, does not seek to overthrow the existing international system, and does not see itself in conflict with capitalism and democracy. But if that is the case, why does China's domestic political system and its military modernization cause such alarm in the United States? Indeed, such suspicions seem to be deepening among the American elite. The recently published *Quadrennial Defense Review Report* and the National Security Strategy further highlight the United States' strategic anxiety about a militarily strong China. How China will use its power and influence is still a big question in the minds of many Americans. As Americans like to say, "The jury is still out." From time to time, American leaders publicly express their concern that Beijing's military buildup "outsizes" its regional role.[32] That kind of wariness is used to justify an increasingly visible hedging strategy against China. Related to this, the new concept of China's peaceful rise has not found an enthusiastic audience in the United States, and so far, it has changed few minds in Washington. Even Zoellick was not persuaded by it. As he put it, "Many countries hope China will pursue a 'Peaceful Rise,' but none will bet their future on it."[33] Likewise, Zoellick's stakeholder concept was met with skepticism, as some in Congress asked whether it was more accurate to depict China as a "robust rival" rather than a stakeholder.

The Chinese also have a deep-rooted skepticism about whether the United States can genuinely accept a rising China as an equal partner. American leaders first began to express the idea that the United States would welcome a strong and prosperous China as early as the 1940s. Of course, it did not take a lot of courage to say that when China was still a weak nation. The real test is yet to come. Will this rhetoric prove to be "Lord Ye's love of dragon"—professed love of what one really fears—now that China is evolving into a new superpower? Beijing has tried hard to assure Washington that China has no intention of challenging the U.S. leadership position in world affairs. But even so, China's rise would inevitably offset some of the American global influence. To what extent the United States will embrace this prospect is a big question in the minds of many Chinese. Washington still shies away from placing the relationship squarely on a strategic basis, and after Hu Jintao's 2006 visit to the White House, many Chinese still believe that the United States does not take China seriously.

In conclusion, more than a decade after the end of the Cold War, the United States and China are still struggling to find a lasting conceptual framework for their relationship—a relationship that is critical to peace in the twenty-first century. Recent efforts by both governments are positive first steps, but at this point, the new framework is largely a skeleton that needs much more flesh. The two nations have a long way to go before they can declare that they have found a viable way to coexist peacefully and cooperatively in the twenty-first century.

Notes

An earlier version of this chapter appeared in *Journal of Comparative Asian Development* 1 (2006).

1. Condoleezza Rice, "Promoting the National Interest," *Foreign Affairs* (January–February 2000): 57.

2. Nicolas Lemann, "The Next World Order, the Bush Administration May Have a Brand-New Doctrine of Power," *New Yorker*, April 1, 2002, 43–44.

3. David Shambaugh, "Sino-American Strategic Relations: From Partners to Competitors," *Survival* 42, no. 1 (2000): 99.

4. Chinese leader Jiang Zemin called President Bush five hours after the attack to express his sympathy and support, which was extraordinary, given China's traditional slowness in reacting to international events. "Wu Jianmin Reveals Inside Stories of Handling the U.S.-China Airplane Collision Incident and 9/11," *China News Service*, January 17, 2008, http://www.chinanews.com.cn/gn/news/2008/01–17/1137807.shtml.

5. George W. Bush and Jiang Zemin, "U.S., China Stand against Terrorism," White House press release, October 19, 2001, http://www.whitehouse.gov/news/releases/2001/10/20011019–4.html.

6. "Jiang Zemin and Bush Holds Talks," *People's Daily*, October 20, 2001.

7. Bush and Jiang Zemin, "U.S., China Stand against Terrorism."

8. Colin Powell, testimony before the Senate Appropriations Subcommittee on Foreign Operations, Export Financing, April 24, 2002, http://www.state.gov/secretary/former/powell/remarks/2002/9685.htm.

9. Colin Powell, remarks at dinner honoring Chinese premier Wen Jiabao, December 8, 2003, http://www.state.gov/secretary/former/powell/remarks/2003/26973.htm.

10. George W. Bush, "Remarks by the President at 2002 Graduation Exercise of the United States Military Academy," June 1, 2002, http://www.whitehouse.gov/news/releases/2002/06/20020601–3.html.

11. White House, "The National Security Strategy of the United States of America," September 2002, http://www.whitehouse.gov/nsc/nss.pdf.

12. Colin Powell, "A Strategy of Partnerships," *Foreign Affairs* (January–February 2004): 4, 6, http://www.foreignaffairs.org/20040101faessay83104-p60/colin-l-powell/a-strategy-of-partnerships.htmlp.

13. Zheng Bijian, "The 16th Party Congress of CPC and China's New Path of Peaceful Rise," in *Collection of Zheng Bijian's Essays*, vol. 3 (Shanghai: Shanghai People's Press, 2005), 1122.

14. Zheng Bijian, "The Suggestion to Carry out Research about China's Development Path of Peaceful Rise," in *Collection of Zheng Bijian's Essays*, 3:1130–31.

15. Zheng Bijian, "Ten Points about China's Development Path of Peaceful Rise," in *Collection of Zheng Bijian's Essays*, 3:1281–83.

16. Zheng Bijian, "China's 'Peaceful Rise' to Great Power Status," *Foreign Affairs* 5 (September–October 2005): 18–24.

17. Robert Zoellick, "Whither China: From Membership to Responsibility," remarks to the National Committee on U.S.-China Relations, September 21, 2005, http://www.ncuscr.org/articlesandspeeches/Zoellick.htm.

18. Zheng Bijian, "Way that Communist Party of China Takes in 21st Century," *People's Daily*, November 22, 2005.

19. George W. Bush and Hu Jingtao, "President Bush and President Hu of People's Republic of China Participate in Arrival Ceremony," April 20, 2006, http://www.whitehouse.gov/news/releases/2006/04/images/20060420_v042006db-0046jpg-515h.html.

20. George W. Bush and Hu Jingtao, "President Bush and People's Republic of China President Hu Exchange Luncheon Toasts," April 20, 2006, http://www.whitehouse.gov/news/releases/2006/04/20060420–2.html.

21. Robert Zoellick, "Remarks and Q & A at the Institute of Economic Economics," April 17, 2006, http://www.state.gov/s/d/former/zoellick/rem/2006/64700.htm.

22. Robert Zoellick, "Interview with Phoenix TV," April 18, 2006, http://www.state.gov/s/d/former/zoellick/rem/2006/64796.htm.

23. George W. Bush, "President Addresses National Newspaper Association Conference," March 10, 2006, http://www.whitehouse.gov/news/releases/2006/03/20060310–2.html.

24. U.S. Department of Treasury press release, "The Joint Statement between the United States of America and the People's Republic of China on the Inaugura-

tion of the U.S.-China Strategic Economic Dialogue," September 20, 2006, http://www.treas.gov/press/releases/hp105.htm.

25. Henry Paulson, "Remarks by Treasury Secretary Henry M. Paulson on the International Economy," September 13, 2006, http://www.treas.gov/press/releases/hp95.htm.

26. Condoleezza Rice, "Interview with Greg Sheridan of the Australia Broadcasting Company," March 15, 2006, http://www.state.gov/secretary/rm/2006/63347.htm; "Interview with Kerry O'Brien of the Australian Broadcasting Company," March 16, 2006, http://www.state.gov/secretary/rm/2006/63167.htm.

27. Condoleezza Rice, "Interview with Maura Fogarty of CNBC Asia," November 17, 2006, http://www.state.gov/secretary/rm/2006/76221.htm.

28. Robert Zoellick, "Interview with Phoenix TV."

29. Bush and Hu Jingtao, "Arrival Ceremony."

30. Paulson, "Remarks."

31. Zoellick, "Interview with Phoenix TV."

32. Rice, "Interview with Maura Fogarty."

33. Zoellick, "Whither China."

3. China's New Leadership and Strategic Relations with the United States
Jia Qingguo

China's current government has been in office for more than five years. During this time, China's relations with the United States have received unprecedented international attention. Although most people agree that the relationship is of unparalleled importance to the world as well as to the two countries, people disagree about how this relationship is going to evolve. Optimists point at the growing interdependence and expanding base of the relationship and argue that China and the United States will be able to manage their relationship in a rational and mutually beneficial manner. Pessimists call attention to the so-called logic of great-power politics and assert that the two countries are destined to experience confrontation and conflict.[1] Many factors will shape the eventual outcome of the relationship.

This chapter discusses how China's new leadership has approached strategic relations with the United States. It argues that, like their predecessors, China's current leaders attach great importance to the relationship, and they believe that it is in China's best interests to develop a constructive strategic partnership with the United States. Accordingly, the Chinese government has carefully avoided actions that would jeopardize the relationship and has sought every opportunity to improve it. In the meantime, however, it has also taken measures to hedge against the potential threat posed by the United States. China's nuclear policy can only be understood within this context. This discussion first outlines the broad strategic orientation of China's new leadership. It then analyzes China's nuclear policy and finally examines opportunities and challenges relevant to China-U.S. strategic cooperation.

China's Strategic Orientation

China's attitude toward its strategic relationship with the United States is part and parcel of its overall strategic orientation. In short, this orientation is peaceful development. Like their predecessors, China's current leaders believe that China's future lies in sustained economic growth and social and political improvements. In a carefully prepared speech at the Bo'ao Forum in April 2004, President Hu Jintao stated that China's goal for the first two decades of the twenty-first century was to "quadruple the 2000 GDP [gross domestic product] to US$4 trillion with a per capita GDP of US$3,000" and to "further develop the economy, improve democracy, advance science and education, enrich culture, foster greater social harmony and upgrade the texture of life for the people."[2]

By any standards, these goals are extremely ambitious. To begin with, quadrupling China's GDP in twenty years would require at least 7.2 percent annual growth.[3] This is a very difficult task. After more than two decades of rapid growth, China's economic base is already quite large. It has become increasingly difficult to sustain such growth, especially when China is already facing economic problems such as sharp price hikes for energy and raw materials and saturation of the international market with made-in-China products. Moreover, China's scientific, educational, and social goals demand a drastic increase in investment in scientific research, education, and cultural development, as well as improvements in the social welfare and public health systems and enhanced income redistribution through a more rigorously implemented, progressive tax system. Finally, it is equally difficult, if not more so, to undertake political reforms to make decision making and the selection of leaders more transparent and the government more accountable. To attain these ambitious objectives, the Chinese government needs time and all the resources it can muster. Iit needs to strive for a peaceful international environment so that it can focus on attaining these goals.

After more than two decades of integration with the outside world, China has acquired a higher stake in international political and economic arrangements. Greater political and economic linkages with the outside world have given China normal channels to express its views, defend its legitimate interests, and promote reform of the existing international order, if necessary. Meanwhile, economic relations between China and the outside world have given China an even larger stake in international stability and prosperity. In 2004, China became the world's third largest trading partner, with a foreign trade volume of US$1,154.74 billion.[4] The same year, it also attracted US$64.072 billion in foreign investment.[5] In March 2005, its foreign reserve stood at US$659.1 billion, second only to that of Japan.[6] As a result, China has little need to resort to nonpeaceful means to defend and promote its vital interests.

Finally, China's view of international relations has undergone three broad changes: (1) from an ideological view to a more conventional one,[7] (2) from a zero-sum to a positive-sum game, and (3) from suspicion and hostility to identification with the international system. These attitudinal changes in turn have contributed to China's conceptualization of its relations with the outside world and the goals and objectives of its security policy in terms of peace and cooperation. This also helps explain the Chinese government's advocacy of peaceful development in recent years.

For peaceful development to occur, China must take several steps in its external relations. First, China needs to cultivate good relations with the outside world. According to President Hu Jintao, "China will promote the steady growth of relations with major countries, stick to the principles of building friendship and partnerships as well as security and prosperity with neighbors while combining bilateral friendship with regional co-operation. . . . China will also strengthen unity and co-operation with developing countries and support their just and rational appeals in international affairs."[8]

Second, China needs to resolve international problems through multilateral cooperation. The Chinese government believes that multilateral cooperation is required for the maintenance of peace. Accordingly, former vice premier Qian Qichen said in 2004, "We should opt for multilateralism and give full play to the important role of the UN. Our world is one big family. Naturally, family affairs should be handled by all its members through consultations." The United Nations, Qian said, is "the core of the collective security mechanism and the best venue for multilateral interchanges." It should therefore "continue to play its important role in international affairs. Facts have proved that no major international issues can be tackled by just one or two countries or a group of countries laying down the law."[9]

Third, multilateral cooperation is also required for the promotion of development. The Chinese government believes that the international community should work together to ensure that all countries—not just a few countries—benefit from world economic development. As Chinese foreign minister Tang Jiaxuan put it in 2002, "It would not be in the interest of a sound world economy if the laws of the marketplace were given a free rein to dominate globalization. The international community needs to reform the current rules in the world economy, strengthen guidance and management of the globalization process, take account of fairness and reduce risks while seeking efficiency, and steer globalization in an 'all-win' direction of coexistence."[10]

Finally, the Chinese government realizes that its good intentions may not be reciprocated. Therefore, while it strives for a peaceful international environment and subscribes to multilateralism in dealing with international issues, it also needs to protect against potential security threats by building up its national defense capabilities. The Chinese government believes that this is especially necessary in the age of high-tech warfare. The 1991 Gulf War demonstrated to the world that technology has fundamentally changed the way war is fought. As Chinese military analysts put it, "The forms of war are undergoing changes from mechanization to informationalization. Informationalization has become the key factor in enhancing the war fighting capability of the armed forces. Confrontation between systems has become the principal feature of confrontation on the battlefield. Asymmetrical, non-contiguous and non-linear operations have become important patterns of operations."[11] Accordingly, the Chinese government has decided that it must do more to modernize its military. The significant increase in defense spending in 1989 and 1990 represented a reward to the People's Liberation Army (PLA) for standing firm on the side of the Chinese government during the political crisis in 1989; the continued hefty growth in defense spending since 1991 reflects its keen awareness of China's vulnerability in the face of the revolution in military affairs. As China's 2004 defense white paper put it, "The world's major countries are making readjustments in their security and military strategies and stepping up transformation of their armed forces by way of developing high-tech weaponry and military equipment and putting forth new military doctrines." Consequently, "the generation gap in military technology between informationalization on the one hand and mechanization and semi-mechanization on the other is still widening, and military imbalance worldwide has further increased. The role played by military power in safeguarding national security is assuming greater prominence."[12] Under the circumstances, China has no alternative but to keep up with this trend if it wants to assure its security.

As the only superpower in the world, the United States has great influence on China's external environment. Fully appreciating this fact, China has sought every opportunity to develop a cooperative relationship with the United States. During his visit to the United States in May 2002, then–Vice President Hu Jintao said: "History and the reality tell us that cooperation between China and the U.S. will benefit both while confrontation will leave neither unharmed. A steady, sound and growing China-U.S. relationship serves the fundamental interests of the two peoples and the people of the world and is also in line with the historical trend of human progress."[13]

On the whole, China's leadership is quite satisfied with the current state of China-U.S. relations. In his meeting with President Bush during the informal gathering of the Asia Pacific Economic Cooperation on November 20, 2004, President Hu noted that relations between the two countries had made headway during the previous four years. High-level dialogue and exchanges at various levels were increasing; coordination and cooperation in such areas as economy and trade, antiterrorism, reconstruction of Iraq, and law enforcement were advancing steadily; and military exchanges between the two countries had basically resumed. He was positive that China and the United States shared extensive common interests and had good reason to engage in mutually beneficial cooperation in a wide range of areas.[14]

At the same time, China's leadership is concerned about problems between the two countries—in particular, the Taiwan problem. In his meetings with U.S. leaders, President Hu has repeatedly pointed out that proper handling of the Taiwan issue is the key to sound China-U.S. relations. He is hopeful that the United States recognizes the danger of Taiwan separatist forces and will honor the commitments reiterated by President Bush on many occasions to adhere to the one-China policy, observe the three Sino-American joint communiqués, and oppose Taiwan's independence. Hu has also asked the United States to support the Chinese government's efforts to safeguard national sovereignty and territorial integrity and to achieve peaceful reunification between the Chinese mainland and Taiwan. He has asked the United States not to send the wrong signals to Taiwan separatist forces.[15]

China's leadership hopes that the two countries can enhance their cooperation and develop a strategic partnership. Toward this end, President Hu has made the following proposals to President Bush: (1) maintain the momentum of high-level exchanges between the two countries; (2) strengthen the strategic dialogue between them; (3) promote bilateral cooperation through the China-U.S. Joint Commission on Commerce and Trade, the Joint Economic Committee, and the Joint Committee on Science and Technology; and (4) continue to follow the principles of reciprocity and mutual benefit to strengthen cooperation in antiterrorism, law enforcement, health, and environmental protection. In addition, Hu believes that both sides should continue to consult and coordinate on the North Korean nuclear issue, the reconstruction of Iraq, and other regional and international issues.[16]

China's Nuclear Policy

China's nuclear policy is an integral part of its strategic orientation. China has maintained a nuclear force essentially for two purposes: to free China from nuclear blackmail, and to enhance China's security at minimal cost. In retrospect, one can identify eight basic components in China's nuclear policy: minimal deterrence, no first use, no proliferation, security assurance to non–nuclear weapon states, security assurance to nuclear weapon states, nuclear disarmament, opposition to ballistic missile defense systems, and peaceful resolution of nuclear crisis.

Minimal Deterrence

For many years, China has pursued a policy of minimal deterrence. Although, over time, its technological sophistication and growing resources have made it possible to drastically expand its nuclear arsenal, China has chosen not to do so. Instead, it has maintained the "barest of abilities to retaliate with nuclear force should they come under nuclear attack."[17] In the words of Chinese ambassador Sha Zukang, "China's nuclear arsenal is the smallest and least advanced among the five nuclear powers."[18] As Lieutenant General Li Jijun, vice president of the PLA's Academy of Military Science, put it in a speech to the U.S. Army War College on July 15, 1997, "A small arsenal is retained only for the purpose of self-defense. . . . China's strategy is completely defensive, focused only on deterring the possibility of nuclear blackmail being used against China by other nuclear powers."[19]

No First Use

China announced its no–first–use policy when it tested its first nuclear bomb in 1964, and it has adhered to that policy ever since. According to its 1998 white paper on national defense, "From the first day it possessed nuclear weapons, China has solemnly declared its determination not to be the first to use such weapons at any time and in any circumstances, and later undertook unconditionally not to use or threaten to use nuclear weapons against non-nuclear-weapon states or nuclear-weapon-free zones."[20] According to Chinese ambassador Hu Xiaodi, "China initiated that nuclear-weapon states should conclude a treaty on no–first–use of nuclear weapons and undertake unconditionally not to use nuclear weapons against non–nuclear-weapon states. China actively supports the Conference of Disarmament in Geneva to re-establish an ad hoc committee on negative security assurances and start without delay substantive work and negotiations. China also supports the negotiation of a protocol on security assurances for non–nuclear-weapon states within the NPT [Non-Proliferation Treaty] framework."[21]

No Proliferation

For quite some time after China acquired nuclear weapons, it was critical of the nonproliferation regime. China argued that this was nothing but an instrument of the nuclear powers to maintain their nuclear monopoly and was therefore unfair and unjust. Despite the criticism, however, China publicly stated that it would not engage in nuclear proliferation. Eventually, China formally subscribed to the nonproliferation regime in 1992. Subsequently, the Chinese government has taken many steps to comply with the nonproliferation rules.[22] For example, in December 2001, the Chinese legislature adopted the Amendments to the Criminal Law of the People's Republic of China, designating the illegal manufacturing, trafficking, and transporting of radioactive substances as criminal offenses. Also, in February 2002, the Chinese government promulgated the Provisions on the Administration of Safeguard and Supervision of Nuclear Import and Export and Foreign Nuclear Cooperation.

Assurance to Non–Nuclear Weapon States

China provides non–nuclear weapon states with unconditional security assurances. It participates in several nuclear weapon–free zone treaties in Latin America, the South Pacific, Southeast Asia, and Africa, under which China is prohibited from deploying, using, or threatening to use nuclear weapons in these regions. On April 11, 1995, in UN Security Council Resolution 984, China joined the other four declared nuclear weapon states (United States, Russia, United Kingdom, and France) in providing legally binding positive security assurances to come to the aid of non–nuclear weapon states in the event of a nuclear attack against them.[23]

Assurance to Other Nuclear Weapon States

China has also provided assurances to some of the other declared nuclear weapon states as their relations have improved. For example, China promised not to target its nuclear weapons against Russia in 1994 and made the same promise to the United States in 1998. In addition, it has agreed to keep its nuclear weapons at a very low level of alert.

Nuclear Disarmament

China has been a champion of nuclear disarmament. China's 1998 defense white paper stated that "all states should negotiate and conclude an international convention on the complete prohibition and thorough destruction of nuclear weapons." China believes that the countries with the largest nuclear arsenals (meaning the United States and Russia) should take the lead in nuclear disarmament.[24] It has repeatedly urged these two countries to make deep cuts in their nuclear forces.

Opposition to Ballistic Missile Defense Systems

China is opposed to ballistic missile defense systems. It believes that the development of such systems would be destabilizing and encourage a nuclear arms race. As far as China is concerned, it would be compelled to build more nuclear weapons against its will. According to Ambassador Sha Zukang, China is opposed to the U.S. national missile defense (NMD) because it would weaken or neutralize China's already limited deterrence capability. "China will not allow its legitimate means of self-defense to be weakened or even taken away by anyone in any way. This is one of the most important aspects of China's national security."[25]

Peaceful Resolution of Nuclear Crisis

Although China is firmly supportive of nonproliferation, it does not favor the use of force to deal with proliferation; rather, it believes that such problems should be dealt with through negotiation and dialogue. Force should be used only as a last resort, consistent with international law and with explicit authorization from the UN Security Council. Prior to the U.S. invasion of Iraq, China took the position that force should not be used until all peaceful options had been exhausted. Since the outbreak of the ongoing North Korean nuclear crisis, China has repeatedly expressed its opposition to the use of force to deal with that crisis.

Changes in the Making?

Most people in the Chinese foreign policy circle support China's nuclear weapons policy. They agree that, given the current domestic and international circumstances, China's policy is the most sensible approach. Some people, however, have argued for changes to the policy to reflect what they believe are new international and domestic realities.

Some Chinese analysts point out that the real motive behind the United

States' development of NMD is to neutralize China's limited nuclear deterrence capabilities. They argue that China should respond by increasing the number of its nuclear weapons or improving its existing stocks so that China can penetrate NMD and maintain its minimal deterrence capabilities. On March 14, 2000, Sha Zukang, then director general of the Arms Control Department, said that China was opposed to NMD and would not tolerate a weakening or deprivation of its limited means of self-defense.[26]

In addition, in light of the fact that none of the other four nuclear weapon states maintains a no-first-use policy, some argue that China's adherence to this policy puts it in an unfavorable position. The widely reported remarks by Major General Zhu Chenghu in 2005 on the possible use of nuclear weapons against the United States in the event of a Taiwan Strait military confrontation, for example, reflect such a view.[27]

Finally, as Taiwan separatists have pushed for independence more aggressively in recent years, some Chinese analysts have taken a pessimistic view about the future of cross-strait relations. Under the circumstances, they argue that China should sharply increase its nuclear arsenal to deter the United States from intervening should military action become necessary to eliminate the separatist problem in Taiwan. They point out that the United States did not intervene in Russia's military operations to deal with the Chechen problem primarily because of Russia's large nuclear arsenal.

Despite these and other views, the Chinese government has not changed its nuclear policy in any significant way. It still believes that its current time-honored approach best serves China's national interests. However, new international developments are making the Chinese rethink some components of this policy. Whether this will eventually lead to significant changes depends on how China and the outside world interact and how such interactions affect the Chinese perception of how China's nuclear policy can best promote its national security interests.

Opportunities for and Challenges to Sino-American Strategic Cooperation

With the rise of China, the relationship between China and the United States has become one of the most important bilateral relationships in the twenty-first century. How these two countries manage this relationship will influence not only their respective vital interests but also the peace, stability, and prosperity of the world. First, China and the United States need to enhance their existing cooperation against the proliferation of weapons of mass destruction. They should step up their efforts to consult with each other, share intelligence, enforce existing international agreements to prevent proliferation, and develop effective measures to close loopholes in those agreements. They should also promote and support multilateral cooperation to combat the proliferation of weapons of mass destruction.

Second, the two countries need to enhance and expand confidence-building measures between them. The recent agreement to hold high-level strategic dialogues to discuss a wide range of issues is a step in the right direction. They should also expand and deepen their existing military-to-military contacts, continue and enhance talks on military maritime safety, and support each other's constructive role in security cooperation in Asia.

Third, the two countries need to promote and support existing regional and global mechanisms of multilateral security cooperation. It is time for the United States to shift its efforts from enhancing exclusive bilateral security arrangements to developing inclusive multilateral mechanisms. At the regional level, the two countries should work more closely to attain a peaceful resolution of the North Korean nuclear problem through the six-party talks. They should also consider the possibility of developing the six-party-talk framework into an East Asian security organization. At the global level, they should work together to enhance the UN Security Council's effectiveness and develop a new set of international norms to enable the international community to tackle security problems such as weapons of mass destruction, terrorism, and transnational criminal activities. It is time to drop ideological pretensions in doing so. The United States should welcome China's participation in the G-8 summit meetings, and China should be prepared to play a constructive role in those meetings.

Finally, for effective cooperation, the two countries need to develop better understanding and strategic trust between them. The Taiwan problem has been an obstacle for too long; it is still limiting and eroding strategic cooperation between the two countries and even carries the threat of military confrontation. As long as the United States withholds support for China's unification, China will find it impossible to take a benign view of U.S. intentions. Accordingly, it may be time for the two countries to consider a new communiqué in which the United States clearly and unambiguously states its support for China's peaceful unification (if it wishes, it could add the term "democratic"). Only by doing so can the United States convince the Chinese that it has no "evil" intention of splitting the island province from China. For its part, China should state clearly and unambiguously that it will not use force to deal with the Taiwan problem as long as Taiwanese authorities refrain from taking drastic steps to separate Taiwan from China. These actions may encounter domestic political opposition in both countries. However, unless they are taken, China and the United States will find it impossible to overcome strategic distrust, let alone attain an adequate level of strategic cooperation.

Conclusion

Strategic cooperation between China and the United States is not just desirable but also indispensable. Given the nature of their relationship, achieving such cooperation will be difficult, especially in the context of domestic politics. However, they must recognize that their interests and fate are bound together; there is no better alternative to cooperation. It is time for the leaders of both countries to actually assume leadership rather than catering to ever-shifting popular political sentiments. They must educate their people about the importance of the relationship and the need to make concessions to attain understanding, trust, and cooperation between the two countries. They should also take the lead in the fight against ideological fundamentalism, explicit and disguised racism, and offensive realism and ensure that people with these agendas do not take center stage and trash the relationship. It is time for these leaders to show that they have the necessary political courage, wisdom, and vision.

Notes

1. John J. Mearsheimer, *The Tragedy of Great Power Politics* (New York: W. W. Norton, 2001); Richard Bernstein and Ross H. Munro, "The Coming Conflict with America," *Foreign Affairs* (March–April 1997): 20–32.

2. "Full Text of Hu Jintao's Speech at BFA Annual Conference 2004," Bo'ao, April 24, 2004, http://www.china.org.cn/english/features/93897.htm.

3. See *Zhongguo jingji zhoukan* [China Economic Weekly] at http://finance.sina.com.cn/g/20050512/14491582048.shtml.

4. *Liang'an Jingmao Tongxun* [Bulletin of Economic and Trade Relations across the Taiwan Strait] 6 (1998): 47.

5. See Foreign Investment Administration of the Ministry of Commerce at http://www.fdi.gov.cn/common/info.jsp?id=ABC00000000000019228.

6. "Zhu: Zhongguo shi Yazhou zuijia touzidi" [Zhu: China is the best investment place in Asia], *Wenhuibao* [Wenhui Daily], Hong Kong ed., April 7, 1998, A3.

7. Here, the concept "ideology" is defined narrowly to refer to Marxist or communist ideology.

8. "President Outlines Foreign Policy," *Xinhua*, August 8, 2004, http://www2.chinadaily.com.cn/english/doc/2004–08/31/content_370199.htm.

9. "Multilateralism, the Way to Respond to Threats and Challenges: Statement by H. E. Mr. Qian Qichen, Former Vice Premier of China at the New Delhi Conference," July 2, 2004, http://www.fmprc.gov.cn/eng/wjdt/zyjh/t142393.htm.

10. "Statement by H. E. Tang Jiaxuan, Minister of Foreign Affairs of the People's Republic of China, and Head of the Chinese Delegation, at the General Debate of the 57th Session of the United Nations General Assembly," September 13, 2002, http://www.fmprc.gov.cn/eng/wjdt/zyjh/t25092.htm.

11. See Federation of American Scientists at http://www.fas.org/nuke/guide/china/doctrine/natdef2004.html#5.

12. Ibid.

13. "Vice President Hu Jintao: Enhanced Mutual Understanding and Trust towards a Constructive and Cooperative Relationship between China and the United States," May 1, 2002, http://www.china-embassy.org/eng/zt/hjtfm/t36335.htm.

14. "President Hu Jintao Meets with U.S. President Bush," http://www.fmprc.gov.cn/eng/wjb/zzjg/bmdyzs/xwlb/t171299.htm.

15. Ibid.; "President Hu Jintao Meets with U.S. Secretary of State Condoleeza Rice," http://www.fmprc.gov.cn/eng/zxxx/t188470.htm.

16. "President Hu Jintao Meets with U.S. President Bush."

17. Bates Gill, "China's Nuclear Agenda," *New York Times*, September 7, 2001.

18. "Speech at the NMD Briefing by Ambassador Sha Zukang," March 14, 2001, Permanent Mission of the PRC to the UN Mission at Geneva.

19. "Traditional Military Thinking and the Defensive Strategy of China: An Address at the U.S. Army War College," Letort Paper No. 1, August 29, 1997, 7. See "China's Nuclear Doctrine," http://cns.miis.edu/research/china/coxrep/doctrine.htm.

20. Information Office of the State Council of the People's Republic of China, "China's National Defense," July 1998, http://russia.shaps.hawaii.edu/security/china-defense-july1998.html#5a.

21. "Statement by Ambassador Hu Xiaodi, Head of the Chinese Delegation, on Security Assurances for Non-Nuclear-Weapon States at the 3rd Session of the PrepCom for the 2005 NPT Review Conference," April 30, 2004, http://www.china-un.org/eng/xw/t94693.htm.

22. Ministry of Foreign Affairs of the People's Republic of China, "Fact Sheet:

China: Nuclear-Weapon Proliferation Prevention," April 27, 2004, http://www
.globalsecurity.org/wmd/library/report/2004/prcnuclear-proli-prevention-
factsheet_27apr2004.htm.

23. "Statement by Ambassador Hu Xiaodi."

24. Information Office, "China's National Defense."

25. "Speech at the NMD Briefing by Ambassador Sha Zukang."

26. "Sha Zukang qiangdiao Zhongguo fandui Meiguo gao NMD" [Sha Zukang stresses that China is opposed to U.S. development of NMD], http://www .chinamil.com.cn/item/nmd/content/news1987666-nmd.htm. In December 2001, Professor Wu Xinbo also said that U.S. development of NMD would encourage China to increase its nuclear weapons and its penetration capability; see http://www .zaobao.com/special/us/pages1/nmd151201b.html.

27. "If the Americans draw their missiles and position-guided ammunition on to the target zone on China's territory, I think we will have to respond with nuclear weapons," said General Zhu Chenghu, *Financial Times*, July 15, 2005, http://news .ft.com/cms/s/28cfe55a-f4a7–11d9–9dd1–00000e2511c8.html.

4. American Nuclear Primacy
or Mutually Assured Destruction
The Future of the U.S.-China Strategic Balance of Power
Baohui Zhang

The nuclear balance of power between the United States and China will be a major security issue in the twenty-first century. On the one hand, China is rapidly expanding its offensive nuclear forces. According to the Pentagon, the Chinese are deploying a new generation of land- and sea-based strategic weapon systems.[1] On the other hand, the United States has begun the deployment of a multitiered ballistic missile defense system. As Stephen J. Cimbala has observed, "Absent an unknown and unforeseeable technology breakthrough in offense or defense, we are in for a period of competition between the two kinds of technologies."[2] Indeed, the dynamics of the nuclear relationship between China and the United States will be driven mostly by the expanding offensive capabilities of the former and the current and future defensive capabilities of the latter.

It is important to examine whether China and the United States will be able to achieve stable mutual deterrence in the coming decades. To do this, an accurate assessment of China's emerging nuclear capability is vital, along with an analysis of the future trends in the nuclear relationship between the two countries. With the emerging global rivalries between them, not to mention the flash point of the Taiwan Strait, China and the United States need to establish a framework of mutual deterrence that can stabilize any potential crisis situation between them. And stable mutual deterrence will be possible only if China can develop and deploy an offensive capacity that at least keeps pace with the U.S. defensive capability.

First, this chapter criticizes the idea of American nuclear primacy promoted by some U.S. scholars. I suggest that the idea is based on unrealistic assumptions that cannot be applied to nuclear deterrence in the context of Sino-American relations. The chapter then analyzes the current and forthcoming modernization efforts that will lead to a secure second-strike nuclear capability for China. In the next section, I examine whether the U.S. defensive system will be able to seriously degrade China's nuclear deterrence and I argue that even under the best assumptions, the United States will not be able to remove the nuclear shadow in the Sino-American strategic relationship. Finally, I suggest that the logic of mutually assured destruction gives the advantage to the offensive side, especially when it chooses to target the enemy's population for maximal effect. Therefore, China will be able to exercise a robust strategic deterrence if it can penetrate the U.S. defensive system with just several dozen nuclear warheads. My conclusion is that, in the medium future, mutual deterrence will continue to be the foundation of the strategic relationship between China and the United States.

The Myth of American Nuclear Primacy

The idea of American nuclear primacy is largely the result of research by Keir A. Lieber and Daryl G. Press, two scholars who have published a number of articles in important foreign policy journals.[3] They argue that the nuclear balance of power has shifted tremendously in favor of the United States in recent decades. While the U.S. nuclear arsenal has significantly improved, deploying more accurate missiles with stealth bombers such as the B-2, Russia's strategic nuclear force has steadily declined. Russia's major weapons systems, such as submarine-launched ballistic missiles (SLBMs) and nuclear submarines, are dated and poorly maintained. At the same time, China still adheres to a minimal deterrence strategy by maintaining only a tiny nuclear capability. In particular, China's no-first-use doctrine makes its bare-bones strategic force an easy target for a surprise attack. Lieber and Press thus claim that due to the United States' lopsided nuclear primacy, mutually assured destruction (MAD) is no longer the foundation of the strategic relationship with these countries.

Lieber and Press not only exaggerate the significance of the current U.S. nuclear advantage but also demonstrate a persistent American tendency to underestimate China's strategic capability. As observed by a report from the Council on Foreign Relations in 2000, "The tendency in Washington to dismiss China as an inconsequential nuclear actor must be set aside in favor of a clearer appreciation of China's significance, both current and potential. Over the coming decade, China could very substantially increase the size, sophistication, and overall capability of its strategic force."[4]

Recent U.S. intelligence recognizes the rapidity and significance of Chinese nuclear modernization. For example, a 2007 report by the Pentagon notes that the Chinese military has already started to deploy a new generation of land-based strategic nuclear missiles called DF-31s. The missile is solid fueled and road mobile, making it less vulnerable than older Chinese missiles that were silo deployed.[5] Further, the possibility that China will soon deploy the longer-range DF-31A seemed to be confirmed by a public display of new Chinese intercontinental ballistic missiles (ICBMs) in the summer of 2007. The Chinese military organized a large-scale exhibition of its latest weapons to celebrate the eightieth anniversary of the founding of the People's Liberation Army (PLA). At the exhibition, a scale model of a new road-mobile ICBM was displayed. *Kanwa Defense Review*, an overseas-based Chinese military magazine, speculates that this is the long-awaited DF-31A, with improved range over the standard DF-31.[6] The Pentagon report also predicts that China will soon deploy the long-awaited Type 094 class SSBN (the U.S. Navy designation for a nuclear-powered, ballistic missile–carrying submarine) with its JL-2 SLBM, which is based on the DF-31. There is evidence that the new submarine may already be in service. Pictures of the submarine are available on the Internet, and *Kanwa Defense Review* recently published a photograph that showed two Type 094s moored at the Huludao submarine factory.[7]

These new and forthcoming capabilities debunk the suggestion by Lieber and Press that the United States will be able to destroy all Chinese nuclear weapons in a preemptive strike. Neither Lieber nor Press is a China expert, and they are misreading the real Chinese nuclear capability both now and in the near future. They are largely unaware of China's latest progress toward nuclear modernization. In fact, in the next ten to fifteen years, China will achieve a secure second-strike capability through the deployment of new-generation nuclear submarines armed with multiple warhead missiles capable of striking anywhere in the United States. They will be complemented by a new generation of mobile land-based intercontinental missiles that can carry multiple, independently guided warheads. These new capabilities will significantly change the nuclear balance of power between China and the United States.

There are other problems with Lieber and Press's analysis of the Chinese strategic nuclear forces and their vulnerability to a preemptive strike. As pointed out by Li Bin, a Chinese nuclear expert, several assumptions by

Lieber and Press are unreasonable at best. For example, the primacy argument is based on the belief that the United States now possesses the capability to destroy almost all of China's strategic missiles in a preemptive strike. However, Li Bin notes that this assumption "misses the central point of whether the entirety of Chinese long-range nuclear weapons have been identified and located by U.S. intelligence or whether all the objects that are identified in China are real nuclear weapons."[8]

As various studies have shown, China has made a tremendous effort to ensure that its small, bare-bones nuclear forces can survive a preemptive strike. To do so, China has employed a variety of countermeasures, such as camouflage and mobility, to make sure that the enemy cannot identify all its strategic weapons.[9] Further, there are reports that China has deployed some of its mobile missiles in hardened facilities buried deep in the mountains, mostly in the northern part of the country. Therefore, Li Bin observes that given the large size of the Chinese territory, it is possible that U.S. intelligence failures will undermine any preemptive strike against China's nuclear forces.[10]

Another problem with the idea of American nuclear primacy, as pointed out by Bruce G. Blair and Chen Yali, is the assumption that Russia or China would be completely unaware of a forthcoming preemptive strike by the United States. The primacy model assumes that the United States could prepare for a sneak attack without being detected. However, in the real world, that assumption is unrealistic. As Blair and Chen conclude, such a "complete intelligence failure is not plausible."[11] In any crisis situation that threatened to escalate toward war, China would take precautions against a U.S. preemptive strike on its nuclear forces. As a result, it would be very difficult for the United States to destroy the entirety of an alerted Chinese nuclear force.

Finally, an equally serious problem is that the idea of American nuclear primacy could create a dangerous illusion of superiority, leading American decision makers to pursue unwise policies. If China's or Russia's nuclear deterrence capabilities are perceived to be lacking in credibility, this might encourage an American president to ignore their warnings and take aggressive action. This would be particularly dangerous in the event of a major crisis in the Taiwan Strait. As Lieber and Press argue, "As U.S. nuclear primacy grows, China's leaders may act more cautiously on issues such as Taiwan, realizing that their vulnerable nuclear forces will not deter U.S. intervention, and that Chinese nuclear threats could invite a U.S. strike on Beijing's arsenal."[12] Thus, U.S. leaders might ignore Chinese nuclear warnings, such as the one suggested in 2005 by General Zhu Chenghu of the PLA, who argued that China should threaten to use nuclear weapons to deter American military intervention in the Taiwan Strait.[13] American nuclear primacy simply makes this kind of threat unbelievable, since it would invite a devastating U.S. preemptive strike. In their article, even Lieber and Press agree that it is reasonable to worry that nuclear primacy "might lure Washington into more aggressive behavior."[14]

The Rise of Chinese Nuclear Deterrence

It is important to understand China's real nuclear capability so that no American president underestimates the effectiveness of Chinese nuclear deterrence in a crisis situation. Unfortunately, Lieber and Press are not China specialists, and they have committed the critical error of not tracing the dynamic development of Chinese nuclear forces in recent years. Indeed, a dynamic analysis of the Chinese strategic nuclear force predicts the emergence of stable mutual deterrence between China and the United States in the next decade. In fact, China will acquire a force capability *at least* as potent as that of Britain and France.

Since the first explosion of a Chinese nuclear bomb in 1964, China has expended enormous efforts to acquire a nuclear force that incorporates intermediate-range and intercontinental ballistic missiles.[15] Consistent with its minimal deterrence strategy, China's intercontinental capability is the smallest among the major nuclear powers. China believes that a small retaliatory force is sufficient to deter a much larger nuclear power, since no country is willing to see its largest cities destroyed by a few large Chinese nuclear bombs. Until very recently, this capability was represented by an estimated twenty to thirty deployed DF-5 ICBMs, which have a range of 13,000 kilometers (8,060 miles) and are armed with single multimegaton warheads. This is the basis of Lieber and Press's claim that China's strategic nuclear force remains minimal and vulnerable.

The problem is that Lieber and Press are unaware of several ongoing Chinese nuclear modernization programs that have achieved major breakthroughs in recent years. One important program involves a new generation of land-based ICBMs—the aforementioned DF-31 and DF-31A. Both are land mobile and solid fueled, making them less vulnerable to a preemptive strike by the United States. The strike ranges of the DF-31 and DF-31A are 8,000 and 12,000 kilometers (4,960 and 7,440 miles), respectively.

Although Lieber and Press claim that the new missiles will be equipped with single warheads, all Chinese sources indicate that the new missiles can be armed with at least three multiple and independently guided warheads. In fact, the U.S. National Intelligence Council concluded in 1999 that China has had the technical capability to produce multiple reentry vehicles for two decades.[16] Perhaps the most important confirmation of this capability came from two PLA officers who revealed that the DF-31 had its first successful test on August 2, 1999. The missile's maiden flight included experiments with dummy warheads, indicating that the DF-31 is capable of carrying multiple warheads in its payload.[17]

A far more important modernization program concerns the next generation of submarine-based strike capability. Ironically, this sea-based capability is not even mentioned in Lieber and Press's analysis. The program centers around the previously mentioned Type 094 submarine and its JL-2 SLBM, which is based on the DF-31 ICBM and has a similar range. Photographs available on the Internet indicate that the submarine carries twelve missiles instead of the previously rumored sixteen. However, Chinese sources suggest that each JL-2 is capable of carrying at least three independently guided warheads.[18]

One way to predict the future size of the Chinese offensive nuclear capability is to look at the improvements in U.S. defensive capability. As argued by Brad Roberts, although China has chosen to adopt the smallest nuclear force among the major countries, this policy may change in the face of American ballistic missile defense, which is now a multitiered system deployed on land and sea. Roberts argues that China may need to pace its offense to keep up with the United States' defense.[19] Indeed, Chinese strategists believe that China could defeat the American missile defense system by expanding its offensive capability. As argued by Wu Chunsi, a leading Chinese expert on ballistic missile defense, "The most direct response to missile defense is to increase the number of offensive missiles. Within a significant period of time in the future, the U.S. ballistic missile system will only be able to handle an attack by several dozen missiles. Thus, China can maintain its deterrence against the U.S. by modestly increasing its offensive capability."[20]

Research by the Rand Corporation suggests that China may be able to field a strategic force of seventy-five to 100 warheads in the next decade.[21] However, this estimate is obviously too conservative, since it is based on the assumption that the Chinese strategic nuclear force will rely overwhelmingly on land-based missiles, such as a mixture of the DF-5 and the newer DF-31 and DF-31A. It also assumes that these land-based missiles will continue to be armed with single warheads. This analysis commits the same basic factual error made by Lieber and Press—namely, their disregard of China's new sea-based capability. The Rand study, which was completed before the launching of the Type 094 SSBN and the successful test of the JL-2 SLBM, did not foresee these new strategic nuclear systems. Indeed, with regard to the Type 094 submarine, the Rand study concluded that "political and technological constraints may delay or even suspend the deployment of this boat."[22] This prediction has turned out to be a major mistake.

Given China's rapid progress in the last two years, it will be able to increase its strategic nuclear capability to approach that of Britain and France. For example, if China deploys six Type 094s, and if each of its twelve JL-2 missiles carries three warheads, it will acquire a sea-based nuclear deterrence of 216 warheads. Aided by several dozen new-generation land-based missiles such as the DF-31 and DF-31A, some of which could also carry multiple warheads, the total number of Chinese strategic warheads could easily exceed 300 and approach the deployment level of France and Britain. Therefore, a recent U.S. Naval War College study claims that "China's nuclear forces appear to be on the threshold of a new qualitative level."[23] A Chinese analysis echoes the same view by arguing that recent developments "mean that China's sea-based nuclear strike force is no longer just a theoretical deterrence. Now it is marching toward the direction of real war-fighting capability."[24]

This emerging Chinese strategic nuclear capability will certainly look very different from the one described by Lieber and Press. Rather than basing its nuclear deterrence on twenty or so land-based strategic missiles that are very vulnerable to a preemptive strike by the United States, China will possess a robust nuclear deterrence that is capable of retaliating against a first strike by another country. Indeed, for the first time, China will have a truly secure second-strike capability.

U.S. Ballistic Missile Defense

An analysis of the future strategic balance of power between China and the United States also needs to consider the emerging American defensive capability, which could potentially undermine China's offensive nuclear forces and weaken the effectiveness of mutual deterrence. The Bush administration's deployment plan for the national missile defense (NMD) system is limited to 100 to 200 ground-based interceptors. The immediate intention is to deploy only forty interceptors in five years.[25] However, as many have pointed out, this system would allow the United States to defend against only a limited attack by a rouge state such as North Korea, not an overwhelming attack by a major nuclear power such as Russia or China.

As two PLA strategists have argued, given the current technology, it would be very difficult, if not impossible, to achieve a foolproof defensive system.[26] An attacker could deploy a wide range of countermeasures to defeat a ballistic missile defense system. These include the use of radar decoys, radar-absorbing materials, deceptive jamming, trajectory changing, and submunitions. According to a study by the U.S. Army War College, China is actively developing all these countermeasures.[27]

Stephen J. Cimbala recently conducted research on the role of missile defense in nuclear deterrence between Russia and the United States. According to his model, if Russia merely maintained a strategic force of 500 warheads, it could still deliver twenty warheads against the United States after a preemptive strike by the latter and if American missile defense managed an interception rate of 60 percent.[28] Given the massive destructive power of a single nuclear warhead, a counterstrike by twenty warheads would constitute sufficient deterrence against any country. Indeed, Cimbala argues that an interception rate of 60 percent is not realistic at present, given the various technological constraints.

A similar analysis can be applied to a future nuclear scenario between China and the United States. If China deployed six Type 094 submarines and each of its missiles carried three warheads, two surviving Chinese submarines could launch a total of seventy-two warheads. Again assuming a success rate of 60 percent by American missile defense, about twenty-eight Chinese warheads would strike the United States. Thus, without a major technological breakthrough, U.S. missile defense will not be able to deter the emerging Chinese nuclear capability. This means that in the coming decades, China will be able to maintain an effective mutual deterrence with a medium-sized strategic nuclear force.

According to PLA strategists, nuclear deterrence gives the advantage to the offensive side. Due to the extraordinary destructive power of nuclear weapons, any missile defense system would need to achieve a success rate of 95 percent to be effective. Therefore, they argue that in the foreseeable future, no country, including the United States, will possess the necessary technology to mount an effective defense.[29]

Mutually Assured Destruction and
Sino-American Relations

The ongoing modernization of China's nuclear forces will dramatically improve its strategic balance of power against the United States, since mutually assured destruction (MAD) levels the playing field between a superpower and a medium-sized nuclear power such as China. As Henry Rowen notes in a recent study by the U.S. Army, MAD is "city-busting" in nature. He states that the succinct strategy of MAD is: "Don't attack weapons, aim at people."[30] MAD enables a small nuclear force to achieve maximal deterrence against a major nuclear power. This is best represented by France, which is a classic medium-sized nuclear power. Its nuclear doctrine is to hold a stronger country's population hostage to prevent it from endangering France's vital national interests. According to a French official's elaboration of the rationale behind its nuclear strategy, "The neutralization of the adversary (state's) administrative, economic, and social structures, the destruction of the framework of life and activity of millions of persons constitutes damage that would be difficult to accept, even if a part of the population concerned by these destructions escapes immediate death."[31] France thus deems a medium-sized force sufficient to deter a larger nuclear power. The current French nuclear deterrence is based on only four strategic submarines carrying about 300 warheads.

As stated earlier, China is likely to acquire a nuclear force with at least 300 strategic nuclear warheads, most of which will be securely deployed on submarines. Therefore, China's strategic nuclear capability will be *at least* as potent as that of France. In fact, there is good reason to believe that the future Chinese capability could significantly exceed that of the French. A recent Chinese analysis suggests that the reason the Type 094 submarine carries only twelve missiles instead of sixteen is related to cost-effectiveness; it lowers the displacement of the submarine and thus its construction cost. The net benefit is that China can build and deploy a greater number of Type 094s and thus increase the probability that a few would survive a first strike by the United States. If this is indeed the Chinese strategy, China's sea-based strike capability will certainly exceed that of France and Britain.

As recently observed by Blair and Chen, Chinese nuclear doctrine "places no value on achieving nuclear parity with anyone."[32] The logic behind Chinese nuclear deterrence is fundamentally the same as that of the French: a smaller nuclear force will be able to deter a larger one if it targets the latter's population centers. This logic is best elaborated by Major General Peng Guangqian, an influential strategist at the PLA National Defense University. During an interview with Hong Kong–based Phoenix TV, General Peng commented that although the United States possesses the capability to destroy China multiple times, China need only destroy the United States once. As he put it, "the cost for both sides in this context is the same: what is the difference between a person dying one hundred times and him dying just once." General Peng thus emphasizes that China does not seek nuclear parity because it is pointless in the real world. Although the Chinese nuclear capability represents only a tiny fraction of the U.S. capability, "its effect is the same. In China's view, the United States cannot even stand the attack by just one nuclear bomb."[33]

Therefore, China's emerging nuclear capability will profoundly impact the overall balance of power between it and the United States. As Stephen W. Walt observes in a study on U.S. primacy, the spread of nuclear weapons represents the greatest threat to American hegemony because it will undermine U.S. dominance in conventional military power.[34] A potent Chinese nuclear force will be able to neutralize a significant portion of U.S. conventional military power by rendering it unusable in specific contexts such as the Taiwan Strait. This is essentially the French logic of nuclear deterrence, and it is the logic espoused by General Zhu Chenghu in 2005 when he indicated that China should threaten to use nuclear weapons to deter American intervention in the Taiwan Strait. As first analyzed by Alastair Iain Johnston, some Chinese nuclear experts had already started to discuss the need to modify the no–first-use doctrine in the 1990s to compensate for China's disadvantage in conventional military power.[35] The emerging Chinese nuclear capability would certainly give more credibility to such threats. Although the Chinese government has repeatedly denied that it is modifying its no–first-use doctrine, a crisis situation in the Taiwan Strait might compel China's leaders to rely on nuclear deterrence to prevent an inevitable and humiliating conventional military defeat by the United States.

Conclusion

It is simply a myth that the United States will soon enjoy a lopsided nuclear advantage over China. The Chinese strategic nuclear forces are on the verge of achieving real breakthroughs. New land- and sea-based strategic weapons systems will provide China, for the first time, with a secure second-strike capability.

In fact, MAD will continue to be the foundation of the strategic relationship between the United States and China. This will be the case because MAD, by nature, targets the population centers of the enemy state. China's long-standing practice of targeting the largest American cities will continue, and any new defensive capabilities of the United States will not be sufficient to deter future Chinese nuclear forces. Even after a preemptive strike by the United States, China will still be able to retaliate with sufficient warheads to overwhelm American defensive systems. Therefore, MAD will continue to be a vital factor in the Sino-American strategic relationship. This prospect was recently analyzed by Aaron Friedberg in a survey of the future of U.S.-China relations. According to him, mutual deterrence may turn out to be a critical stabilizing factor for U.S.-China relations.[36]

China and the United States should recognize that maintaining stable mutual deterrence is in the best interests of both countries. Therefore, they need to establish a cooperative framework to avoid an arms race between China's offensive capabilities and the United States' defensive capabilities. Such as arms race would only serve to deepen the mistrust between the two countries and worsen their security dilemma. The recent Chinese antisatellite test may indicate the direction of a future strategic arms race. According to Chinese war doctrine, the effectiveness of its nuclear deterrence is critically linked to its ability to destroy American space-based assets, which perform the role of early warning for missile defense.[37] Further, some Chinese experts argue that it is merely a matter of time before the United States starts to establish a space-based missile defense. To ensure the effectiveness of its nuclear deterrence, the Chinese military believes it must develop its own space war capability. For example, as pointed out by General Ge Dongsheng, deputy commandant of the Academy of Military Sciences of the PLA, space war should be integrated into China's nuclear strategy. As he observes, "It is critical to develop space capabilities and construct an integrated space–nuclear strategic force. The space capability is vital in clearing a pass way for nuclear missiles. It will enable our nuclear force to survive, penetrate and hit their targets."[38]

It is thus vital for China and the United States to establish a stable deterrence framework to avoid an arms race that will inevitably expand into outer space. This will require the leaders from both countries to engage in open and frank discussions of all the issues related to strategic nuclear deterrence.

Notes

1. Department of Defense, *Military Power of the People's Republic of China 2007* (Washington, D.C.: Department of Defense, 2007).

2. Stephen J. Cimbala, "Parity in Peril? The Continuing Vitality of Russian-U.S. Strategic Nuclear Deterrence," *Contemporary Security Policy* 27, no. 3 (December 2006): 431.

3. Keir A. Lieber and Daryl G. Press, "The Rise of U.S. Nuclear Primacy," *Foreign Affairs* 85, no. 2 (March–April 2006): 42–54. The two authors provide more details of their argument in a longer article, "The End of MAD? The Nuclear Dimension of U.S. Primacy," *International Security* 30, no. 4 (spring 2006).

4. Robert A. Manning, Ronald Montaperto, and Brad Roberts, *China, Nuclear Weapons, and Arms Control: A Preliminary Assessment* (New York: Council on Foreign Relations, 2000), vi.

5. Department of Defense, *Military Power of the People's Republic of China 2007*, 19.

6. See "Zhongguo jinyibu xianshi dandao daodan weishe liliang" [China further displays deterrence through its ballistic missiles], *Kanwa Defense Review* (September 2007): 25.

7. For photos of the Type 094 submarine, see "Zhongguo guoli zengqiang bupa junli dui shijie touming hua" [China is increasing its national power and thus no longer concerned about revealing its military capability to the world], http://mil.news.sina.com.cn/p/2007–11–07/0733470765.html; "Huludao he qian gongchang zhuangkuang" [The situation at the Huludao nuclear submarine factory], *Kanwa Defense Review* (December 2007): 22.

8. Li Bin, "Paper Tiger with Whitened Teeth," *China Security* (autumn 2006): 81.

9. Paul H. B. Godwin, "China's Nuclear Forces: An Assessment," *Current History* 98, no. 629 (September 1999): 260–65.

10. Li Bin, "Paper Tiger," 81.

11. Bruce G. Blair and Chen Yali, "The Fallacy of Nuclear Primacy," *China Security* (autumn 2006): 63.

12. Lieber and Press, "The Rise of U.S. Nuclear Primacy," 43.

13. For more details about this comment by General Zhu Chenghu, see "Zhonguo Zhu chenghu shaojiang: jiang yong hewu kang Mei" [Chinese Major General Zhu Chenghu will use nuclear weapons against the U.S.], *Xingtao Daily*, July 16, 2005.

14. Lieber and Press, "The Rise of U.S. Nuclear Primacy," 43.

15. For more on the development of Chinese nuclear forces, see Shirley Kan and Robert Shuey, *China: Ballistic and Cruise Missiles* (Washington, D.C.: Congressional Research Service, 2000); Bates Gill, James Mulvenon, and Mark Stokes, "The Chinese Second Artillery Corps: Transition to Credible Deterrence," in *The People's Liberation Army as Organization*, ed. James Mulverson and Andrew N. D. Yang (Santa Monica, Calif.: Rand Corporation, 2002); John Wilson Lewis and Xue Litai,

China's Strategic Seapower: The Politics of Force Modernization in the Nuclear Age (Stanford, Calif.: Stanford University Press, 1994).

16. National Intelligence Council, *Foreign Missile Development and the Ballistic Missile Threat to the United States through 2015* (Washington, D.C.: National Intelligence Council, 2001), 11.

17. Hou Xiaohe and Zhang Hui, *Meiguo dandao daodan fangyu jihua toushi* [A look at the U.S. ballistic missile defense system] (Beijing: Zhongguo minhang chubanshe, 2001), 256. Both authors are PLA officers teaching at the National Defense University.

18. The JL-2 missile was successfully tested on June 16, 2005. Most Chinese sources indicate that the missile can carry at least three independent guided warheads. See Zhao Dexi, "Zoujin jinri Zhongguo wuqiku" [Walking into China's arsenal], *Zhongguo guoqing guoli*, March 2002; Yi Ming, "Zhuanjia kan Zhongguo he qianting zonghe zhanli" [Experts' views on the combat capabilities of Chinese nuclear submarines], *Zhanlue yianjiu* [Strategic Studies], October 2006.

19. Brad Roberts, "Alternative Futures," in *China's Nuclear Future*, ed. Paul J. Bolt and Albert S. Willner (Boulder, Colo.: Lynne Rienner, 2006), 167–92.

20. Wu Chunsi, "Zhong-Mei he guanxi de zouxiang" [Future direction for China-U.S. nuclear relationship], in *Weishe yu wending, Zhong-Mei he guanxi* [Deterrence and stability: China-U.S. nuclear relationship], ed. Zhu Mingquan, Wu Chunsi, and Su Changhe (Beijing: Shishi zhubanshe, 2005), 306.

21. *Chinese Response to U.S. Military Transformation and Implications for the Department of Defense* (Santa Monica, Calif.: Rand Corporation, 2006), 103.

22. Gill, Mulvenon, and Stokes, "The Chinese Second Artillery Corps," 551.

23. Lyle Goldstein, "Introduction," in *China's Nuclear Force Modernization*, ed. Lyle Goldstein (Newport, R.I.: Naval War College, 2006), 2.

24. See "Situation at the Huludao Nuclear Submarine Factory," 22.

25. Carl Hulse, "The Great-Grandson of Star Wars, Now Ground Based, Is Back on the Agenda," *New York Times*, June 8, 2003.

26. Hou Xiaohe and Zhang Hui, *A Look at the U.S. Ballistic Missile Defense System*, 248–52.

27. Mark A. Stoke, *China's Strategic Modernization: Implications for the United States* (Carlisle, Pa.: Strategic Studies Institute, U.S. Army War College, 1999), 89–91.

28. Cimbala, "Parity in Peril?" 430.

29. This argument was made by Hou Xiaohe and Zhang Hui in *A Look at the U.S. Ballistic Missile Defense System*, 251.

30. Henry S. Rowen, "Introduction," in *Getting MAD: Nuclear Mutual Assured Destruction, Its Origins and Practice*, ed. Henry D. Sokolski (Carlisle, Pa.: Strategic Studies Institute, U.S. Army War College, 2004), 3.

31. David S. Yost, "France's Nuclear Deterrence Strategy: Concepts and Operational Implementation," in Sokolski, *Getting MAD*, 203.

32. Blair and Chen, "The Fallacy of Nuclear Primacy," 68.

33. Peng Guangqian, *Zhongguo junshi wenti yanjiu* [Research on Chinese military issues] (Beijing: PLA Press, 2006), 351, 354.

34. Stephen W. Walt, *Taming American Power: The Global Response to U.S. Primacy* (New York: W. W. Norton, 2005), 138–39.

35. Alastair Iain Johnston, "China's New 'Old Thinking': The Concept of Limited Deterrence," *International Security* 20, no. 3 (winter 1995–1996): 5–42.

36. Aaron Friedberg, "The Future of U.S.-China Relations: Is Conflict Inevitable?" *International Security* 30, no. 2 (fall 2005): 28.

37. For the Chinese military's view on space war, see Major General Cai Fengxia, "Kongjian zhanchang yu guojia kongjian anquan tixi chutan" [Space war and national space security: an initial exploration], *Zhongguo junshi kexue* [Chinese Military Sciences] 19, no. 2 (February 2006): 44–51.

38. General Ge Dongsheng, "Yi fazhan hangtian liliang wei tupokou, tuijin wuojun xinxihua jianshe, wei weihu guojia fazhan zhongyao jiyu ji tigong anquan baozhang" [Developing a space capability to promote military digitization and to provide security protection for national development], in *Zhanlue jiyuqi de bawo he liyong* [Mastering the strategic opportunity], ed. Ba Zhongyan (Beijing: Shishi chubanshe, 2006), 22.

Part II

CHINA'S RELATIONS WITH OTHER MAJOR POWERS

5. The Sino-Russian Strategic Relationship
Ghost of the "Strategic Triangle"?
Lowell Dittmer

The relationship between the two vast empires astride the Eurasian heart-land has been troubled for centuries, despite certain superficial similarities in size and in political and economic structure. The Mongol Golden Horde in-vaded Russia in the thirteenth century, burning Moscow and taking Kiev, and continued to rule southern Russia and extort tribute from the north for the next 200 years, leaving a historical legacy of dread. Russia would lag China developmentally for the next several centuries. Its population did not reach 13 million until 1725 (compared with China's brilliant civilization and, by that time, about 150 million people), and the first Russian visitors to Bei-jing in the modern era (beginning in the mid-seventeenth century) were obliged to prostrate themselves (kowtow) before the Qing emperor. Yet the decline of the Manchu dynasty coincided with Russian industrialization fol-lowing the defeat of Napoleon, and subsequent Russian appetites for trade and territorial expansion led to increasing infringement on imperial China. The Russian imperialist strategy was that of a "free rider": Russian forces typically pressed their claims when China was already preoccupied with other threats. Thus in 1854–1859, while China was engulfed by the Taiping Rebellion (1851–1864), General N. N. Murawjew and 20,000 troops occupied the delta and north shore of the Amur (or Heilong) River and the maritime provinces without firing a shot. During the second Opium War, Russian forces made additional opportunistic territorial grabs, formalized in the 1860 Sino-Russian Treaty of Beijing. During the Yakub Beg Rebellion in Xinjiang, Russian troops occupied part of the Yili region, formalized in the Treaty of Livadia (later modified slightly in China's favor by the Treaty of St. Peters-burg). Completion of the trans-Siberian railway and the decline of the Qing offered further opportunities for cheap gains, and in 1898 Russia made Port

Arthur and Dalian imperial treaty ports, occupied Manchuria in the wake of the Boxer Rebellion, and extended its sphere of influence over China's northeast in 1905. After encouraging the Mongols to rebel in 1910, Russia established a protectorate over Outer Mongolia in the midst of the 1911 Xinhai revolution.

Moscow and the Chinese Civil War

After the Bolshevik Revolution the new Soviet regime renounced its share of the Boxer reparations as well as most imperialist privileges in China, and it quickly established diplomatic relations with the short-lived Peking Republic (1924). It also helped organize and advised the Chinese Communist Party (CCP) and assisted importantly in the 1924–1925 reorganization of the Nationalist Party (Kuomintang, or KMT). Thus the Soviet Union commenced its long two-level game with China. The rise of Chiang Kai-shek following Sun Yat-sen's death in 1925 put the relationship in temporary jeopardy, as the Nationalists violently split with the CCP and entered into an agreement with Japan to intervene militarily in the Russian Far East; this threat was withdrawn, however, when Nationalist China normalized relations with the USSR in 1932.[1] Although the Bolshevik regime's relationship with the rival CCP was, for ideological reasons, far more intimate, Joseph Stalin also cultivated cordial relations with the Nationalists for geostrategic reasons. Thus, in 1937, threatened on his flank by the Japanese takeover of Manchuria in the Mukden incident, he persuaded CCP leaders to cooperate with the KMT in a second United Front rather than executing Chiang in the December 1936 Xian incident. Stalin even signed a nonaggression pact with the Nationalist regime in 1937, including the provision of war materiel. When the CCP ultimately drove the KMT from the mainland and turned to the Communist Party of the Soviet Union for help in consolidating its revolution, the USSR immediately recognized the new regime and invited its new leader to Moscow. After prolonged and wary negotiations, Mao Zedong and Stalin signed a thirty-year Sino-Soviet Treaty of Friendship, Alliance, and Mutual Assistance (February 14, 1950) to establish a Eurasian partnership in pursuit of worldwide revolution.[2] Moscow agreed to provide a loan of US$300 million over five years (at a concessionary interest rate of 1 percent) plus construction aid in building fifty (eventually thrice that) massive heavy industrial projects.

In addition, it ceded most of the concessions it had recently gained in negotiations with the Nationalist regime (e.g., returning Port Arthur). But not until Beijing sent "volunteers" into the Korean War, and soon after contributed generous aid and advisers to the first Indochina War (particularly at Dien Bien Phu), was Stalin fully satisfied with the Chinese commitment to world revolution. By 1959, bilateral trade amounted to 2 billion yuan, five times that in 1950, accounting for 48 percent of China's foreign trade; the composition of this was colonial, however, with China exporting mostly agricultural products and raw materials while importing machinery, technology, and turnkey plants.[3] Although this massive exercise in transplanting modern (socialist) industrial culture from one country to another was to end badly, for amply documented reasons, the period of cooperation made an enduring contribution to Chinese political and economic development, while also establishing "old school" ties of lasting value to coming generations of Chinese and Russian leaders.[4]

Mao and Stalin's Successors

The alliance fell apart in the 1960s in the wake of a snarl of perceived betrayals, China's ill-conceived and ideologically presumptuous Great Leap Forward, a long-simmering Chinese impatience with an oft-deferred Soviet promise to provide nuclear weapons (which Mao sought to underscore by boldly challenging Nationalist occupation of the offshore islands in 1958, without warning Moscow he was doing so), diverging priorities over whether to win the third world through people's war or parliamentary coalition building, and disagreement over the future direction of political and economic development in established socialist regimes. The period of friendship thus ended in the late 1950s and devolved into three decades of fratricidal polemics, geopolitical encirclement and counterencirclement schemes, an intense arms race and border fortification, and occasional border violence. This conflict obsessed both sides at the time and has puzzled them since. As we now know, the most sensitive phase of this rivalry was touched off by the Soviet invasion of Czechoslovakia in August 1968, exciting Chinese apprehensions of an analogous application of the incipient Brezhnev Doctrine to the People's Republic of China (PRC) and leading to a series of border clashes preemptively initiated by Beijing in March 1969.

Post-Mao Reconciliation

After Mao's death in August 1976 the ideological animus against "socialist hegemony" began to dissipate, while the rise of Ronald Reagan's crusade against the "evil empire" led to a new cold war and bipolar arms race. Beijing interpreted this exclusively in "superpower" terms, a status to which China did not yet aspire. This new cold war hence relieved Beijing of some of its security concerns: PRC arms spending was reduced by some 7 percent per annum as a proportion of gross domestic product (GDP) from 1979 to 1989, and these funds were plowed into domestic industrial investment. Whereas the Chinese quietly allowed the thirty-year Sino-Soviet treaty to lapse upon its expiry in 1981, they agreed to continuing dialogue over mutual problems. Beginning in 1982, after normalization and the Third Communiqué had placed the Sino-American relationship on a stable footing, a new series of Sino-Soviet normalization talks were held, alternating semiannually between the two capitals in the spring and fall of each year and usually involving the same team of officials on either side. Progress was initially glacial due to Soviet intransigence over what Beijing called the "three fundamental obstacles": heavy fortification of the Sino-Soviet border and Outer Mongolia, Soviet troops in Afghanistan, and support of the Vietnamese threat to China's southeastern flank (and to China's ally Cambodia). Talks nevertheless continued on schedule, accompanied by gradually increasing trade and cultural exchanges, and this helped to contain and stabilize the dispute during the post-Mao and post-Brezhnev succession crises.

Mikhail Gorbachev decided to rationalize Soviet foreign policy in the late 1980s. While retrenching high-risk ventures in the third world, he tried to revive the Sino-Soviet friendship in the hope of creating a Eurasian socialist redoubt. In speeches at Vladivostok (July 1986) and Krasnoyarsk (September 1988) he proposed a freeze on the deployment of nuclear weapons in the Asian Pacific region, Soviet withdrawal from the Cam Ranh Bay naval facility in Vietnam, and unilateral reduction of the Soviet military by 500,000 troops within two years, nearly half (200,000) of which would come from the region east of the Urals. This Soviet "new thinking" (*novo myshlenie*), according to which Brezhnev's vaunted achievement of "strategic parity" had redounded in few substantial gains at immense cost, eventually included the removal of all three obstacles to further progress with China. Meanwhile, both countries' economies were running aground on the limits of "extensive development" under command planning—the Soviet Union after years of stagnation under Brezhnev, and China after radical Maoism had exhausted itself in the Cultural Revolution. Fresh leadership teams in both capitals thus turned to "socialist reform" in an attempt at revitalization referred to as *perestroika* and *gaige kaifang,* respectively. There was again a sense that both countries, with symmetrically structured and ideologically oriented economies, might learn from each other. Because China had been the first to experiment with reform, much of the initial learning was by the Soviet Union. But China also paid close attention to Soviet experiments, and in fact, the liberalization that culminated in the 1986 protest movement that would lead to the fall of Hu Yaobang was inspired by Gorbachev's call for Soviet political reform (and Deng Xiaoping's vague echoing encouragement of the same). Whereas such mutual learning was selective and ultimately led in divergent directions—with the Russians embracing ever more radical political reform due to bureaucratic resistance to economic reform, and the Chinese continuing to implement economic reform without very much political reform—the fact that both countries were engaged in broadly analogous socioeconomic experiments and were interested in each other's experiences helped orchestrate their détente.[5]

Based on both foreign policy and domestic policy convergence, by the end of the 1980s it was possible to convene a summit meeting sealing the normalization of party-to-party relations. This summit, held in the second week of May 1989, quite unexpectedly marked both the climax and the terminus of this process of convergence around socialist reform. Student demonstrations at Tiananmen Square had necessitated moving all the summit ceremonies indoors. The sanguinary Chinese solution to the spontaneous protests, implemented within a fortnight of Gorbachev's departure, led to international sanctions and to a Soviet decision to preclude any analogous crackdown either domestically or among fellow Warsaw Pact signatories.[6] But without resort to outside force, the European socialist regimes could not stand, and by the end of 1990, all but China, North Korea, Laos, Vietnam, Cuba, and the Soviet Union had fallen like dominoes to a wave of protest movements.

After the Cold War

Throughout this period, the Chinese leadership, still defending both Marxism-Leninism and their own violent "solution" to mass protest, deplored this turn of events, criticizing Gorbachev's leadership for "deviating from the path of socialism" and thereby contributing to the collapse of the bloc. In early 1990 Deng Liqun and the more ideologically orthodox (leftist) wing of the CCP even advocated a public critique of Soviet errors, which Deng Xiaoping vetoed. After the Gulf War (January–February 1991), some joint socialist response to the triumphalist American "new world order" seemed advisable, but no sooner had Beijing become reconciled to cooperating with Gorbachev than the Soviet leader's survival was threatened by the August 1991 coup attempt by his own left wing. Though Beijing came perilously close to supporting the coup publicly before its consolidation, it recovered in time to reaffirm its commitment to noninterference, only to witness (with mounting dismay) the ensuing dissolution of the Soviet Union into fifteen republics, twelve of which agreed to join the Commonwealth of Independent States (CIS).

Part of the reason for the PRC's quick recognition of this new political reality was that, had it not, many alternative options would have been available to the former USSR. After letting the empire break away, there seemed every likelihood of reconciling the old Russo-Japanese territorial dispute (involving three small islands and a tiny archipelago north of Hokkaido) and signing a peace treaty with Japan. South Korea had just granted Moscow a US$3 billion concessionary loan in appreciation of its recognition of Seoul, and Taiwan had briefly established consular relations with Latvia and nearly exchanged ambassadors with Ukraine and Outer Mongolia before being deterred from further diplomatic inroads by PRC warnings. The new line in the Kremlin under China's least favored candidates for succession—Boris Yeltsin and Andrei Kozyrev—was anticommunist and pro-American. The Russians, in turn, plausibly suspected the CCP of siding with the August 1991 coup conspirators. Thus, the first post–Cold War "strategic partnership" to be proclaimed (in 1992) was between the United States and the fledgling Russian Federation. Chinese strategic analysts fretted lest successful Russian economic reform lure foreign direct investment (FDI) from China, undermining an increasingly performance-based CCP legitimacy.

Yet Moscow's new international prospects in the world of bourgeois democracy proved to be greatly exaggerated. The decisive domestic factor was that the Russian "double bang" of marketization and privatization utterly failed to revive the economy, which went into free fall: real GDP declined 13 percent in 1991, 19 percent in 1992, 12 percent in 1993, and 15 percent in 1994. Privatization via management buyouts ushered in a two-tiered market consisting of "oligarchs" at the top—former managers of state-owned enterprises who simply grabbed the country's major industrial assets—and a geographically balkanized patchwork below. In addition, the country's distribution network collapsed. Meanwhile, the leading Western industrial powers, still overburdened with debt in the wake of the arms race and a worldwide recession following a second price hike by the Organization of Petroleum Exporting Countries (OPEC), were far less munificent with financial support than had been expected; only Germany, now reunified thanks to Gorbachev's refusal to invoke the Brezhnev Doctrine, made substantial subventions to Russian economic development (more than US$20 billion in 1993 alone). In the West, Russian arms were discredited (and a former ally was defeated) in the 1991 Gulf War in which Moscow, after voting to support the enabling UN Security Council resolution, played no visible role. Russia was, in effect, demoted from bipolar nemesis to diplomatic nonentity; it was excluded from any role in resolving the Balkan imbroglio and, though finally invited into the Group of Seven, was initially only an observer. Yeltsin's emergent political rivals, both on the Left (Zyuganov and the revived Communist Party) and on the Right (Lebed), challenged his nationalist bona fides and urged a shift from West to East, arguing on geostrategic grounds in favor of a more "balanced" international posture between East and West. In the East, however, hopes of new breakthroughs were quickly dispelled. Negotiations with Japan premised on a territorial compromise realizing Khrushchev's (never implemented) 1958 agreement (provisionally splitting the four islands, then phasing in a more comprehensive settlement, including complete retrocession) aroused unexpectedly passionate military and local opposition, as well as hesitation in Tokyo. This prompted Yeltsin to postpone his visit twice, and when he finally arrived in Tokyo in October 1993, he did not even bring a proposal to the table. With regard to Korea, the initial euphoria elicited by Gorbachev's 1988 Krasnoyarsk speech and by the September 1990 establishment of diplomatic relations (to Pyongyang's outrage) did not survive the disarray of the new post-Soviet regime, and although bilateral trade has since revived, it has not lured much South Korean investment. The last in a series of diplomatic setbacks involved the 1993 admission of six former satellites to the Council of Europe[7] and the 1994 proposal to enlarge the North Atlantic Treaty Organization (NATO) to include three former Eastern European satellites; the latter was finalized in 1997 in apparent appreciation of U.S. election-year constituency concerns rather than any realistically perceived security threat. Having dissolved the Warsaw

Pact upon the collapse of the Iron Curtain, Moscow could see no further point to NATO but to push Russia out of Europe, piling Ossa on Pelion.

Strategic Partnership

Ironically, two nations that had never been able to agree on the same Marxist ideology now found it possible, in the absence of shared ideological assumptions but under straitened international circumstances (post-Tiananmen Chinese ostracism and the Russian economic meltdown), to converge on a "strategic cooperative partnership" (*zhanlue xiezuo huoban guanxi*), a coinage the Chinese attribute to the Soviets.[8] This was first proposed in the form of a "constructive partnership" by Yeltsin in September 1994 (at the inaugural presidential summit in Moscow); it was then elevated to a "strategic partnership for the twenty-first century" during Yeltsin's April 1996 summit in Beijing (a month after China's confrontation with the United States over Taiwan, and in the context of President Clinton's reaffirmation of a strengthened Japanese-American security alliance). *Partnership* has since become a fungible term of endearment in the diplomatic lexicon of both powers, as China has formed partnerships with Pakistan, France, Germany, the European Union, Japan, Korea, and the United States, and Russia claims partnerships with Japan, Iran, India, and the United States. The implication is to vaguely privilege a relationship without making (or demanding) any specific commitments to (or of) one's "partner"—and one can have any number of partners at once. Yet for both countries, the Sino-Russian partnership has remained pivotal, an admission ticket back to what Jiang Zemin called "great-power strategy" (*da guo zhanlue*), precisely because this is the only relationship with sufficient leverage to pose a credible alternative to the lone superpower. The partnership disavows any threat to a third party (i.e., the United States), from whom each in fact has more to gain in economic terms than from its partner. The United States has long been China's most important trade partner, for example, accounting for ten times as much trade as with Russia; nor is China Russia's most important trade partner. With limited economic stakes, and without mutually agreed strategic objectives or common foes, just how meaningful can this partnership be?

The argument here is that the Sino-Russian partnership is far more meaningful than is generally credited, held together by dovetailing strategic and material interests and a painstakingly institutionalized convergence.

There is perhaps a degree of analytical vested interest among Western observers of the relationship, leading first to a tendency to discount the possibility of schism after the thirty-year alliance was signed (see chapter 15), then to an equally stubborn tendency to discount the prospect of reconciliation in the wake of a thirty-year dispute. Yet since its christening in 1998, the strategic partnership has only deepened, leading the director of the East European, Russian, and Central Asian Studies Institute at the Chinese Academy of Social Sciences to call the ensuing decade "the best in the history of bilateral relations."[9] To be sure, the relationship is not based on overwhelming popular support. Although a December 2000 poll showed that the majority of Russian politicians, journalists, and business leaders considered China to be Russia's most important strategic partner (by far outweighing the United States, which was fifth on the list), in the parts of Russia most directly affected by the opening to China, there was strong antipathy. For instance, in the south of Primorski Krai, residents preferred cooperation with the United States, Japan, South Korea, or even Germany —not China. Nor is there much popular enthusiasm (despite a legacy of Soviet assistance in the early years) for Sino-Russian cooperation in China, where Russian bids for large contracts or commercial sales are routinely rejected. It is at the elite level that an institutionalized momentum has been established, with seven presidential summits between 1992 and 1999 and six exchanges of premiers plus countless other official delegations. Despite pessimistic predictions, momentum has not been derailed by leadership successions. Dmitry Medvedev made China his first foreign destination within weeks after his presidential inauguration in May 2008, and Hu Jintao has kept summit diplomacy running on schedule.

Domestic constituencies of the relationship have shifted over time, from the committed socialist reformers of the 1980s to a "red-brown" coalition of communists and nationalists in the aftermath of Tiananmen to Putin's power pragmatists of the early 2000s. The collapse of the communist bloc threw both opponents and proponents of the relationship into temporary disarray. Before that time, the relationship had been endorsed by reformers on both sides of the Ussuri and opposed by the old guard; since then, there has been an ironic reversal of roles. In China, despite the Yeltsin regime's repudiation of the ideological legacy they once shared, two factors now sweeten the relationship: First, the fact that Russia's embrace of capitalism failed to correct the Soviet malaise has made it an effective object lesson, allowing the CCP to vindicate its own post-Tiananmen hard line. Second, despite its supposed ideological transformation (and subsequent military drawdown), Russia remains the world's most plausible strategic counterweight to U.S. hegemony. Global unipolarity and American unilateralism have been feared and resented by both powers since the end of the Cold War. China's radical reformers were more wary of the partnership because, by raising the specter of a Sino-Soviet alliance within a "strategic triangle," it threatened to alienate China from the West—but then, most of those reformers did not survive Tiananmen. In the former Soviet Union, while Tiananmen momentarily disabused Gorbachev and his supporters of their illusions about Chinese reform, their lease on political life proved almost as brief. Meanwhile, in Russia, the fact that the CCP was able to crush liberal opposition and prevail while communism was self-destructing elsewhere inspired the forces of orthodoxy that had once been among China's most vociferous critics.[10] The pro-China stance of the Communist Party of the Russian Federation—still one of the most powerful parties in the Duma—reflects this group's ideological assumptions. At the same time, the former pro-China liberals, including scholars such as Lev Delyusin and former diplomats such as Yevgeniy Bazhanov, though on guard against any nostalgia for fraternal solidarity, remain basically sympathetic with the PRC. The now marginalized anti-China bloc consists of two quite disparate currents: (1) the radical pro-Western bloc, intellectually led by the Moscow Institute of Foreign Relations (affiliated with the Russian Foreign Ministry) and linked politically to such figures as Yegor Gaydar and the Yabloko movement, and (2) radical nationalists such as Vladimir Zhirinovsky (whose Liberal Democratic Party had an unexpected electoral success in 1993), who regard China as an alien security threat. The local political leaders (now appointed) of contiguous regions of the Russian Far East, particularly Primorski and Khabarovski Krais, share some of this radical nationalism in their obsession with the border threat and inflated estimates of the problems of smuggling and illegal migration. At the same time, the economic prosperity of their domains has become so closely linked to that of the PRC that they must reluctantly accede to growing economic integration. At the top, a pragmatic majority under Yeltsin, Putin, and Medvedev has, since the mid-1990s, favored a "balanced" pro-China tilt.

Certainly one important dimension of the partnership is internal or bilateral, turning their 2,700-mile land border—still the world's longest—from a concentration of troops, tanks, and land mines into an economic thoroughfare and generally improving relations between two of the largest countries in the world.[11] Since 1992 there have been dozens of high-level diplomatic exchanges, and summit meetings have been regularized on an annual basis. These meetings have resulted in hundreds of agreements, including the 1991 agreement to delimit the eastern borders and initiate border demarcation; the 1993 Five-Year Military Cooperation Pact; the September 1994 agreement on mutual nonaggression, mutual detargeting of strategic weapons, and no first use of nuclear force; and the 1997 agreements on trade, oil and gas development, and cultural cooperation. Substantial progress on mutual force reduction had already been achieved under Gorbachev, and at the 1992 summit Yeltsin followed suit with a proposal for mutual but gradual demilitarization (thus avoiding the dislocation occasioned by rapid Soviet withdrawal from Eastern Europe) to the minimal number of troops required for peaceful border patrolling (now numbering some 200,000). This permitted both countries to shift priorities, with China moving troops from the border to face Taiwan and the South China Sea and Russia redeploying troops to face the security threat created by Chechnya and the expansion of NATO.

The most significant development since 1992 has been the set of five-power agreements among China, Russia, and the three bordering Central Asian republics of Kazakhstan, Kyrgyzstan, and Tajikistan signed in Beijing in April 1996 and in Moscow in April 1997. In the former, both sides agreed on mutual force reductions and military confidence-building measures on their respective borders; the latter established a "zone of stability" restricting military activity to a depth of 100 kilometers (62 miles) along the frontier and making border security exercises more transparent. Although Moscow jealously guards its strategic interest in these loyal members of the CIS, it has seen fit to chaperone this somewhat unusual negotiating teamwork, thereby facilitating Chinese border agreements with all three Central Asian republics (subsequent border demarcation has lagged, however, in the case of war-ravaged Tajikistan). China has since become neighboring Kazakhstan's largest trade partner, agreeing in 1997 to invest US$9.7 billion (the equivalent of half Kazakhstan's gross national product and China's largest FDI project on record) to build oil and gas pipelines from the Caspian oil fields to the Xinjiang region and ultimately on to Shanghai. Kazakhstan in turn has promised to control Uighur acolytes of an independent "Eastern Turkistan" (whose borders would coincide with those of ethnically riven Xinjiang province). This negotiating exercise between China and the four former Soviet republics was regularized in annual meetings, and in the summer of 2001 it was expanded to include Uzbekistan and formalized as the Shanghai Cooperative Organization (SCO), thereby forming the largest security-related international organization in the world in which the United States is not a member. In view of the salience of militant Islamic nationalism to these still secular dictatorships, the SCO's mandate was expanded to include drug trafficking and terrorism, and an antiterrorist center was subsequently established at Bishkek, Kyrgyzstan (later shifted to new member Uzbekistan). Although at least temporarily eclipsed by the incursion of U.S. forces in the Central Asian republics during the attack on the Taliban regime in 2001, the SCO in 2005 requested the United States to vacate its bases as soon as possible. In April 2006 the SCO expanded again, adding Mongolia, Iran, India, and Pakistan as observers. There is a certain amount of subsurface tension over resources, as the Russian Federation continues to regard Central Asia as being in its own sphere of interest, while China views the SCO as a vehicle to cultivate ties with Central Asia and build oil and gas pipelines eastward; however, several successful mutual military exercises have been conducted.

Jiang Zemin and Gorbachev, during their April–May 1991 Moscow summit, had already agreed in principle on how to "delimit" the borders; for instance, Moscow accepted the Thalweg, or the deepest part of the main channel, as the "line" dividing the Ussuri (Wussuli) and Amur (Heilong) rivers. Demarcation was then conducted during the next seven years, over the vociferous objections of local Russian politicians. This resulted, among other things, in giving China access to the Sea of Japan via the Tumen River, whose development was foreseen in a cooperative project supported by the United Nations Development Program and also involving North Korea. China also regained sovereignty of one-square-mile Damansky (Chenbao) Island, where the 1969 border clash had started. At the November 1997 Beijing summit, the two sides signed a demarcation treaty for the eastern sector, including an agreement suspending the sovereignty issue for joint development of three still disputed small islands on the Amur River (including Heixia or Black Bear Island) in sensitive proximity to the cities of Khabarovsk and Blagoveschensk. At the November 1998 "hospital summit" in Moscow, both sides expressed satisfaction that the eastern and western sections of the border had finally been accurately demarcated, with the exception of those three small islands (which were also decided upon completion of demarcation in July 2008).

One possibly advantageous aspect of the bilateral relationship, virtually frozen since the 1950s, involves trade. There is substantial complementarity between China's need for raw materials for its booming economy and Russia's substantial natural resource deposits, and between China's surplus but relatively neglected border population and Russia's sparse and declining regional population. Bilateral trade made a great leap forward in the early 1990s to fill the vacuum left by the Tiananmen sanctions (the value of all Western investment in China dropped 22 percent during the first half of 1990) and by the collapse of the centralized Russian distribution system upon dissolution of the Soviet Union. While total Soviet foreign trade dropped 6.4 percent for 1990, the Sino-Soviet trade volume increased to US$5.3 billion, a quarter of which was border trade. Several Sino-Russian special economic regions were established in emulation of the thriving special economic zones in the southeast. More than 200 cooperative projects were initiated between localities in the two countries, and China dispatched some 15,000 citizens to the Soviet Far East for temporary labor service. But these steep early rates of commercial growth could not be sustained; the 1991–1992 economic crisis left Russians unable to repay Chinese exporters, and the Russians complained of shabby product quality and disruption of their (hitherto state-monopolized) retail networks. Moscow's subsequent imposition of steep border duties, cuts in transport subsidies, and restrictions on organizations entitled to engage in foreign trade caused Sino-Russian trade to plunge by nearly 40 percent (largely at the expense of border trade) in the first half of 1994. It began to recover in 1995, reaching US$5.1 billion that year and US$6.85 billion in 1996; however, it sank to US$6.12 billion in 1997 and dropped even further to US$5.48 million in 1998, particularly after Yeltsin's mid-August devaluation of the ruble and debt restructuring. This obviously foreclosed Yeltsin's goal to raise bilateral trade to US$20 billion by 2000. However, as Russian GDP revived after the turn of the millennium, Sino-Russian trade picked up as well, doubling from 1996 to 2002 and continuing to grow at a double-digit rate: US$12 billion in 2002, US$15.8 billion in 2003, US$20 billion in 2004, US$29.1 billion in 2005, and US$40 billion in 2007. By 2007, China was Russia's fourth biggest trade partner, and Russia was China's eighth biggest. Russia has incurred a rapidly increasing account surplus: for 2000–2002, this surplus was 50 percent of trade volume.[12] Since 2006, the imbalance has abruptly shifted in China's favor by dint of a large influx of value-added Chinese exports.

Whereas bilateral trade has been growing, this must be put in the context of an overall increase in foreign trade. Thus for China, Russia has declined in relative importance, particularly as an export market. China's 2002 trade volume with Russia was only around one-tenth its volume with either the United States or Japan, China's top trading partners. Conversely, China's importance to Russia as a market has increased, accounting for 6 percent of Russian exports in 2002. In terms of commodity composition, the two partners have to some extent reversed positions since the 1950s, with China importing a growing proportion of fuel, timber, and raw materials and exporting manufactured products. Yet this is an incomplete and misleading picture: the Chinese still import heavy machinery and nuclear reactors, and a large proportion of Chinese imports (often more than 20 percent) consists of sophisticated arms and military technology. Since the early 1990s, there has also been a mutual increase in FDI. In a recent assessment of FDI between China and Russia for the first half of 2003, Li Jianmin reports that US$329 million was contributed by Russian investors for 1,471 projects in China, and US$350 million was contributed by Chinese investors for 503 projects in Russia.[13] Because the two economies are so disparate in their ability to attract FDI (China drew US$140 billion in 2000–2002), Russian FDI is insignificant for China; however, the two countries are just beginning to engage in foreign investment, and their reciprocal investments are a substantial form of economic integration for both (the Russian share of all Chinese outward FDI is 25 percent, and the Chinese share of all Russian outward FDI is 20 percent).[14]

A relatively controversial aspect of this increasing economic interdependence is emigration, in view of the large disparity in populations. According to data from Chinese and Russian statistical yearbooks, the population in the Chinese border provinces in 2002 exceeded 130 million, whereas the Russian population stood at less than 7 million and had been declining due to out-migration and an overall decline in Russian population growth. Exact figures are hard to find, but a rough estimate of 300,000 Chinese citizens currently residing in the Russian Far East appears reasonable. Fears that Chinese immigrants could eventually outnumber Russian citizens, forcing a reconsideration of the border settlement, seem exaggerated, however. In addition to the bureaucratic obstacles erected to regulate immigration (such as contract labor quotas), the distribution of economic opportunity is likely to equilibrate. At present, per capita income is still higher in the Russian border region than in China's northeast, but unemployment is also higher; given China's faster growth rate, income and employment can be expected to rise there.

Arms exports may be the most important facet of the trade relationship, although their significance transcends economics. Some 95 percent of China's arms imports since 1985 have come from Russia or Ukraine, often constituting more than one-fifth of total Chinese imports from Russia.[15] One of the few Western sanctions to be sustained by both Europe and the

United States since Tiananmen has been arms sales, so the Chinese turned to Russia, which had experienced a drastic drop in worldwide arms sales after the Gulf War (which saw Soviet arms bested by high-tech Western weaponry). From 1992 to 1995, China bought seventy-two Su-27 fighters, four Kilo-class submarines, ten Ilyushin transport planes, and 100 S-100 air-defense missile systems. The first contingent of Chinese pilots was sent to Moscow in June 1992 to undergo a one-and-a-half-year training course, and by the turn of the millennium, some 4,000 Russian experts had gone to China by "private" contractual arrangement to modernize Chinese nuclear and missile capabilities.[16] The 1995–1996 confrontation over the Taiwan Strait whetted Chinese appetites for further acquisitions, and in November 1996 the two sides renewed their military cooperation pact, allowing China to purchase thirty to fifty Su-30MKK multipurpose fighters, four diesel-powered (Kilo-class) submarines, four Sovremenniy-class destroyers with accompanying Sunburn antiship missiles designed to counter U.S. carrier fleets, and a fifteen-year licensing agreement to produce up to 200 additional Su-27s (as Chinese F-11s) at a production line in Shenyang (with a restriction against exporting them). By early 1997, China was the leading purchaser of Russian arms, machinery, and equipment (surpassing India). More than half of Russia's military production is financed by proceeds from arms sales, much of which comes from China (in 2000, 74 percent of Russia's arms exports went to Asia, of which 52.6 percent went to China and 18.2 percent to India).[17] Reportedly annoyed by the private contract to license Chinese production of Su-27s, the Russian Foreign Ministry vetoed sales of Tu-22 Backfire long-range bombers and Su-35 fighters, but the Chinese were able to purchase Russian in-flight refueling technology to extend the range of Chinese bombers to more than 1,000 miles, as well as Russian space technology. In early 2000 the Russian and Israeli media divulged an arrangement (denied by the Chinese) whereby China would purchase sophisticated radar surveillance aircraft (similar to American AWACS) produced in Russia and electronically equipped in Israel. When Washington forced the Israelis to renege, the Russians agreed to sell China their own Il-76 electronic surveillance aircraft. Since 2006, however, there has been a virtual freeze on new Chinese arms purchases, perhaps due to such complaints. The Russians have also endeavored, with some success, to interest the Chinese in civilian technology—some 25 percent of the Chinese commercial aircraft pool is now Russian.[18] In interviews, the Russians dismiss Western concerns that these weapon sales might upset the military balance, pointing out that if they do not sell arms to the PRC some other country will, with the worst conceivable consequences for Russian security.

Although the relationship has been deprecated as "hot" on top and "cool" on the bottom, the following set of symbiotic constituencies has emerged to provide institutionalized support for the partnership. First, Russia's military-industrial complex finds it simpler to continue production runs rather than undergo defense conversion, at least in the short run, and China is its largest customer. Heavy industry (e.g., the machine tool industry, oil and gas companies, nuclear and hydropower industries) is oriented toward market-opening initiatives for similar reasons, although here the Russians may be overly optimistic; whereas the Chinese have been ready purchasers of Russian weaponry, they have by and large not sought to upgrade aging Soviet plant technology, preferring to leapfrog to the most advanced (Western) levels, even if that means starting from scratch in many enterprises.[19] Still, the Russians may be competitive (certainly in terms of price) in hydroelectric power and nuclear energy development projects, provided they are able to swing attractive financing deals. Second, the state trading companies, which, since the 1994 Russian tariff and immigration legislation, have regained control over bilateral trade, are now staunch supporters of expanded economic relations. At the same time, both Chinese and Russian shuttle traders continue to evade bureaucratic control, and border trade has revived, constituting some 30 percent of the total (with illegal barter trade adding an unknown percentage) by the late 1990s, serving a broad market on both sides of the border. Third, regional governors, now appointed from Moscow with local legislative approval, have reluctantly come to appreciate their regions' growing dependence on the Chinese economy as a locomotive for their own.

Although less avidly discussed by the principals, the relationship does have a strategic as well as a bilateral utility—after all, it is a "strategic partnership." While jointly criticizing hegemony or unilateralism, both sides deny that the partnership is aimed at any third party. But both share certain strategic interests and concerns, including a resentment at being left on the periphery of the "new world order" being constructed by the United States. The Russian Federation survived its experiment with communism in a rather ravaged condition—though it inherited four-fifths of the former USSR's territory, it was left with half its GDP (equivalent to half of China's current GDP) and less than half its population (about 148 million, which has since declined). The Soviet military of 6 million men has shrunk to a demoralized force of 2.3

million, overburdened for years by a rebellion in tiny Chechnya. Within Asia, India and China emerge as the twin pillars of Russian foreign policy. In 1998, Yevgeny Primakov suggested a strategic triangle to concert policy among the three; India expressed interest, but China has been unenthusiastic.

Clearly there are limits to mutually supportive activities, including residual suspicion on the Russian side at the Chinese accumulation of advanced weaponry (although border demilitarization has proceeded apace, and most of this weaponry is deployed in the south). Yet there is abundant indication of mutually supportive diplomatic demarches: Russia has unqualifiedly supported China's claim to Taiwan and Tibet and defended China's human rights record against UN sanctions. China endorsed Russia's right to take whatever measures it deemed necessary to deal with the Chechen uprising. Both countries opposed NATO expansion, U.S. withdrawal from the Anti-Ballistic Missile (ABM) Treaty and introduction of missile defense, humanitarian interventions, sanctions on North Korea for its nuclear program, expanded 1997 guidelines of the Japanese-American security alliance, and involvement of the Central Asian republics in NATO's Partnership for Peace and joint military exercises. In some cases, such cooperation has been reasonably effective. Thus, the joint Russian-Chinese opposition to (i.e., their implicit threat to veto) UN intervention in Kosovo in 1999 obliged the United States to turn to NATO. And joint Russian-Chinese opposition to escalating pressure on North Korea seems to have thwarted any American notion of invoking sanctions or resorting to a preemptive strike. But more often than not, Sino-Russian collaboration has been insufficient. Joint opposition to U.S. missile defense failed, and President Bush withdrew from the ABM Treaty anyway; joint opposition to the U.S. invasion of Iraq (not to mention Western European opposition) was equally unavailing. Perhaps part of the reason is that mutual support has been solely declaratory. Unlike during the Korean War, there has been no call for military support—no Chinese troops were sent to Chechnya, and there has been no discussion of using the Russian navy in a Chinese invasion of Taiwan. When Russia bids for a Chinese construction project, its partnership status is not a trump card; similarly, Chinese interest in an oil pipeline to Angarsk could not trump a more lucrative Japanese offer (in compensation, Putin promised to increase oil shipments via railroad to China and to increase Sino-Russian cooperation in developing natural gas, but bargaining continues). Maintenance of the partnership seems to have relatively little premium over bids for the best price in the global marketplace.

One of the emerging challenges to the strategic partnership has been the power vacuum left in Central Asia by the withdrawal of the Soviet Union and the advent of relatively weak independent republics in its place—some with attractive oil and mineral deposits, and all with large and increasingly self-conscious Islamic populations. What seemed to have been a Sino-Russian condominium for mutual mentorship under the auspices of the SCO was interrupted by the September 11, 2001, terrorist attacks and the subsequent U.S. intervention in Afghanistan and then Iraq, leading to the establishment of large U.S. bases in Uzbekistan and Kyrgyzstan. This made the region a relatively open field for triangular competition. From the perspective of the Central Asian republics, the American involvement was initially welcome, introducing a new, well-endowed bidder in their natural resources auction. Although Putin agreed to Bush's request for basing rights (perhaps in response to the prior agreement by the republics involved), he later came under criticism from Russian military officials for doing so without a quid pro quo or an agreed-on departure date. The Iraq venture, having lost its original rationale when no WMDs could be found, was redefined in 2004 in terms of the promotion of freedom, and the Central Asian republics lost their interest in the American connection. A consensus emerged to terminate basing rights, and the Americans accordingly abandoned all bases in Uzbekistan, retaining only the Kyrgyzstan facility. Meanwhile, Putin had shored up Russian defense fortifications along the CIS frontier and resolved in 2002 to reinforce the Kant air force base outside Bishkek with Su-27 fighters, Su-25 attack jets, and various transports and helicopters. The implication was that the American base at Manas had failed to provide sufficient support to the Akayev administration in its efforts to clear the region of terrorism. The Chinese, unlike the Americans, have recognized Russia's leading strategic role in the CIS and have limited their interest to oil, which they have continued to pursue in pipeline deals with Kazakhstan and more recently with Iran. This has resulted in a certain cleavage over the future role of the SCO: Russia thinks the organization should focus on fighting terrorism qua fundamentalist religious separatism, while China's main hope is to extend the SCO's role to the field of economic cooperation. During Wen Jiabao's September 2002 visit to Moscow, he repeatedly suggested a free-trade zone within the region, but Russia has been reluctant, apparently fearing that the Central Asian economies would fall under the sway of the Chinese dynamo and Russia would be crowded out.

The rise of terrorism has actually helped strengthen the partnership to some extent. Although the American pursuit of al Qaeda and the (allegedly) related invasion of Iraq are quite distinct from the obsession with separatism that drives the Russian and Chinese campaigns in Chechnya and Xinjiang, respectively, all three now share a concern with fighting Islamic extremism, and this consciousness has assuaged U.S. human rights concerns and somewhat allayed suspicions about Sino-Russian strategic cooperation. The sharing of counterterrorist intelligence has been fairly substantial, resulting in expressions of mutual appreciation. The Russians and Chinese clearly do not share the Americans' categorization of Iran and North Korea as places of state-sponsored terrorism and hence constituents of an "axis of evil," and they have publicly opposed further U.S. preemptive military activity or UN sanctions against either country (in which both have economic stakes); however, both also oppose the proliferation of nuclear weapons and support UN inspection efforts toward that end. Thus the Chinese have been very helpful in establishing and hosting the six-party talks to facilitate a solution to the North Korean nuclear problem, in which the Russians have also participated (see chapters 8 and 9 in this volume).

Although the strategic threat from the United States has driven China and Russia into a closer partnership, both have a major stake in cooperating with the United States, and a softer U.S. line has the potential to prize them apart. Early in the George W. Bush administration, it appeared that his objective was to charm Putin into the American camp while isolating China, but then China became indispensable in dealing with North Korea. Meanwhile, the U.S. failure to give Putin any quid pro quo for rescinding the ABM Treaty or for allowing basing rights in Central Asia caused Russo-American relations to fall into disrepair. None of the European powers have posed any major challenge to the Sino-Russian relationship, cultivating good relations with both partners as the Euro-American connection has cooled, but both Japan and India have the potential (hitherto unexploited) to split the two partners. Japan, still the world's second largest and most advanced economy, even after a decade of stagnation, has been a problem for both Russia and China, but for different and apparently unrelated reasons. Although Japan has a great deal to offer Russia in terms of capital and technology, without raising immigration or territorial anxieties, Japan's relations with Russia remain in a relatively deep freeze. The two never even signed a peace treaty to end World War II. The reason for this long-standing enmity is a dispute over four tiny islands north of Hokkaido: Etorofu, Shikotan, Kunashiri, and the Habomais. The Russians occupied these islands during the war, later forcing the 17,000 Japanese inhabitants to evacuate the islands and resettling them with Russian fishermen and military personnel. Meanwhile, Sino–Japanese relations have also deteriorated seriously as a result of historical grievances (symbolized by Prime Minister Koizumi's annual visits to Yasukuni Shrine), as well as a maritime border dispute involving the small island of Senkaku (Diaoyu). Although the northern islands issue has thus far blocked Japanese involvement in Russian development, if the Japanese could either reach a political compromise (e.g., revive the 1958 agreement of two islands now, two later) or disregard the issue for the sake of compromise on larger issues of bilateral economic and political coordination, Russo–Japanese cooperation could give Moscow an alternative route to the Pacific for development. There are signs that this might occur in the form of Japanese investment in Sakhalin oil and in the pipeline deal from Angarsk to Nahodka. Japan has become the third largest aid donor to Russia (after the United States and Germany), and Japanese trade with the Russian Federation increased 40 percent from 1992 to 1995, surpassing US$20 billion in 2007, making Japan the Russian Federation's biggest Asian export market, although investment has not followed trade.[20] This may be a missed opportunity from Tokyo's perspective, in view of the still cool relations between Japan and China spurred by rising nationalism and an implicit contest for leadership of East Asia.

The Indo-Russian friendship antedates Sino-Russian reconciliation, and although it was somewhat neglected by Yeltsin in the immediate aftermath of the Cold War, the strategic relationship has endured. Indian arms purchases from Russia from 1990 to 1996 totaled US$3.5 billion, and a great majority of India's military hardware is Russian made or of Russian origin, although the nonmilitary trade relationship has remained relatively anemic. India and Russia signed a Declaration of Strategic Partnership and other important agreements during Putin's October 2000 visit; they pledged to work together for the establishment of a multipolar world and expressed their "determined opposition to the unilateral use or threat of force in violation of the UN Charter, and to intervention in the internal affairs of other states, including under the guise of humanitarian intervention."[21] In September 2002 the foreign ministers of India, Russia, and China—Yashwant Sinha, Igor Ivanov, and Tang Jiaxuan—met on the sidelines of the UN General Assembly to underscore their interest in cooperation, at the same time denying any interest in confronting the United States (whose invasion of Iraq they all opposed). The reasons are clear: Although India has a close defense relationship with Russia, Indo–Russian trade is barely 1.5 percent of the commercial flow between

India and the United States, and China's trade with India is a fraction of Sino-American trade. Still, all share a desire for greater distance from the U.S. approach to the war on terror (which they all support in principle). Yet, at the end of the day, the Indo-Russian relationship is warmer than the Indo-Chinese relationship; India and China still have an unsettled border dispute (though a bilateral security dialogue has been started, and a joint working group has been set up to negotiate the issue), and they have long been rivals for leadership among newly emerging powers. Pakistan, China's "all-weather friend" and principal military patron and arms supplier, also remains a source of Indian grievance. Yet Russia has no current interest in exacerbating these differences to block the slowly improving relationship between India and China. Thus, a lateral expansion of the partnership for a more adequate balance of power is possible, although the notion of a Chinese-Russian-Indian triumvirate first suggested by Primakov in 1996 has not gained much diplomatic momentum.

Acutely aware of the precariousness of an Asia policy relying predominantly on a "partnership" in which its partner's relative power in East Asia threatens to eclipse Russia's own (and whose interests may diverge), Moscow has also sought to expand ties with other Asian powers. Russia's noninvolvement with the Asian Pacific region before 1992 has been replaced by much greater openness to multilateral trade and investment, and it has sought membership in all the existing regional forums, including the Asia Pacific Economic Cooperation (APEC), Association of Southeast Asian Nations (ASEAN) Regional Forum (ARF), Asian Development Bank, and World Trade Organization (WTO). The Russian Federation has also attempted to reactivate its Soviet-era relationships with North Korea, Vietnam, and Iraq—all now in Beijing's sphere of interest. Just as China's grand design for the region tends to leave Russia out and focus on the Chinese-Japanese-American triangle, Russia's historical interest in a multilateral grand design diverges from the Chinese preference for bilateral power balancing. Gorbachev first pushed the idea of an Asian collective security treaty in the late 1980s, and Foreign Minister Andrei Kozyrev revived the idea in January 1994, advocating step-by-step movement toward a "security community" open to every country in the region; for these purposes, Russia proposed to establish an Asian-Pacific Center for Conflict Prevention and an Asian-Pacific Institute on Security Problems. In the late 1990s Russia promoted the counter ballistic missile (CBM) and demilitarization agreements signed in 1996–1997 by the (then) "Shanghai five" as a security model applicable to the Asian region, and it has held meetings promoting this idea with various countries (e.g., India's December 1996 agreement with China was modeled on the five-nation CBM agreement). Despite China's own increasing interest in multilateralism, as witnessed by its involvement in the ARF, SCO, six-party talks on Korea, and ASEAN+3, it has shown little interest in seeing Russia's initiatives progress further; Japan, however, has shown considerable interest in this type of multilateral forum.[22]

Conclusion

One of the hallmarks of the end of the Cold War was the disintegration of the communist bloc, triggered in part by the May 1989 Tiananmen Square protests. In view of the erstwhile "polar" status of the Soviet Union in a bipolar system, this threw the structure of international politics into considerable disarray. Since the 1960s, strict bipolarity was made somewhat more flexible by the rise of the nonaligned bloc on the one hand and by the ideologically based secession of China from the bloc on the other. The latter, more relevant to the contemporary Asian Pacific, gave rise in the 1970s to the "strategic triangle," which permitted a manipulation of the balance of power to facilitate Soviet-American strategic arms control and reduction, as well as China's policy of reform and opening to the outside world. Triangularity essentially meant that the three players arranged their bilateral relationships to take into account their respective relationships to the third player; it began with Washington playing the pivot to mediate Sino-Soviet hostility (and advance the American interest in détente), permuting during the Reagan era to permit Beijing to take advantage of the revived Soviet-American arms race to pursue an independent foreign policy (and cut its own defense budget). The consensus impression of strategic analysts has been that the triangle collapsed at the end of the Cold War for at least two reasons: First, the USSR bowed out of the game because its national heir, the Russian Federation, repudiated communism and disclaimed any further interest in pursuing worldwide revolution, and it lost the economic, demographic, and national wherewithal to sustain a bipolar confrontation in any case (e.g., Russian arms spending abruptly dropped to one-fourth its former total in 1992 and remained there). Second, the ideological deradicalization that proceeded simultaneously in the two revolutionary powers since the 1960s, particularly in the wake of China's Cultural Revolution, deprived them of a credible pretext for the use of nuclear weapons (except for deterrence), thus negating much of the triangle's strategic raison d'etre. Yet despite these blows to the relevance of this conceptual device, the spirit or ghost of the triangle lingers, breathing life into such diplomatic documents as the 1996 strategic partnership and the 2001 friendship treaty. That spirit is the notion that these three powers, despite the worldwide transformation that followed the collapse of the communist bloc, can still tilt the international balance of power. To repeat, this is only the ghost of the triangle and not the triangle itself, because triangular relationships are no longer mutually exclusive; there is now extensive socioeconomic inter-penetration, and in any event, the members no longer represent distinctive approaches to political reality. Yet all three are permanent members of the UN Security Council and major powers on the world stage, and if they cannot tilt the balance, who can? This means that the ghost of the triangle is the functional artifact of a dialectical antithesis to the specter of global unipolarity and U.S. unilateralism. It is a singularly weak dialectic because of the unwillingness of any member to allow the antithesis to come to a point, but until a more plausible counterforce emerges (the European Union?), the triangular ghost may continue to be invoked by this functional need for geopolitical alternatives.

The future of the Sino-Russian strategic partnership entertains three contrasting scenarios: First, the partnership is a snare and a delusion, an elaborate diplomatic pretense undermined by continuing suspicions and divergent national interests whose future is very bleak indeed. Second, the partnership is real, a successful diplomatic effort to craft international co-operation, but it will have limited relevance to bilateral relations without significant strategic implications for the West, Japan, or the Asian Pacific region. Third, the partnership is real and can be expected to affect not only bilateral relations but also strategic relations among the major powers of the world and certainly within the Asian Pacific region, perhaps in a way adverse to Western interests. The most realistic possibility, in my judgment, is the second, although the ultimate choice is not an analytical but a political one, to be decided by the actors involved and depending on a host of incalculable future international developments. In essence, the partner-ship represents the attempt of two large and precarious multiethnic conti-nental empires to form a mutual relationship useful to them in a potentially hostile international environment. Both countries have traditionally been "garrison states" or "developmental dictatorships" ruled by a hierarchically disciplined national security apparatus (though this tradition was temporarily broken in the Russian case, it seems to be returning to the mold). And in a post–Cold War world lacking strategic structure or balance, both feel threatened by de facto American hegemony. Without international help, they fear being ostracized, sanctioned by international regimes, torn asunder by ethnic cleavages, and possibly assaulted by national or international expeditionary forces engaged in humanitarian intervention.

Although the strategic partnership represents a challenge to specific American ideological objectives (such as human rights) and foreign policies (such as missile defense), it is not necessarily a threat to world peace or to vital U.S. national interests. The partnership is not a Comintern pact organized around a programmatic vision for a new world hierarchy, but it is essentially defensive, designed to enhance the national interests of the two participants. Each partner has demonstrated a willingness to use violence to achieve those interests, but the threat to peace that this entails is, for the most part, localized (e.g., Chechnya, Xinjiang, Tibet).[23] And beyond endorsing, in principle, their right to use violence on behalf of sovereign interests, neither partner necessarily feels obliged to come to the aid of the other toward that end. For example, the limits to Chinese efforts to prevent NATO expansion, to persuade Japan to forfeit the four northern islands, or to include Russia in any resolution of the Korean embroilment are fairly clear. And Russian interest in blocking the post-1997 expanded definition of the Japanese-American security alliance or in forcing Taiwan to negotiate reunification on Chinese terms has been mostly rhetorical. Neither partner has either an ideology or a coherent international vision beyond the endorsement of multipolarity. It remains to be seen whether the relationship will evolve in a direction conducive to the realization of more ambitious objectives, but for now, it is limited not only by implicit conflicts between specific national priorities but also by the predominant interest each partner retains in closer relations with the center of international economic and political gravity in the West.

Notes

1. M. I. Sladkovskii, *History of Economic Relations between Russia and China,* trans. M. Roublev (Jerusalem: Israel Program for Scientific Translations, 1966).
2. See the massive study of this period by Dieter Heinzig, *Die Sowjetunion*

und das kommunistische China 1945–1950: Der beschwerliche Weg zum Buendnis (Baden-Baden: Nomos Verlagsgellschaft, 1998).

3. Shu Guang Zhang, "Sino-Soviet Economic Cooperation," in *Brothers in Arms: The Rise and Fall of the Sino-Soviet Alliance, 1945–1963*, ed. O. A. Westad (Washington, D.C.: Woodrow Wilson Center Press, 1998), 189–225.

4. For example, Jiang Zemin himself was trained at Moscow's Stalin Autoworks, a showcase of Soviet industry. Li Peng was a graduate of the Moscow Power Institute, and Admiral Liu Huaqing, a prominent advocate of increased purchases of Russian weaponry, was trained at the Voroshilov Naval Academy in Leningrad. Jennifer Anderson, *The Limits of Sino-Russian Strategic Partnership*, Adelphi Paper no. 315 (London: International Institute for Strategic Studies, n.d.), 197.

5. For comparisons of the Soviet and Chinese approaches to reform, see Peter Nolan, *China's Rise, Russia's Fall: Politics, Economics and Planning in the Transition from Stalinism* (New York: St. Martin's Press, 1995); Mark Lupher, *Power Restructuring in China and Russia* (Boulder, Colo.: Westview Press, 1996); Minxin Pei, *From Reform to Revolution: The Demise of Communism in China and the Soviet Union* (Cambridge, Mass.: Harvard University Press, 1994); Lowell Dittmer, *Sino-Soviet Normalization and Its International Implications* (Seattle: University of Washington Press, 1992).

6. It is fairly clear that Gorbachev's visit played some role in exacerbating the Tiananmen protest (by encouraging journalists who came to record the summit to stay, thereby giving the protesters a false sense of security); however, China may have played a role in the collapse of Soviet and Eastern European communism, first by contributing a "demonstration effect" to European protesters, and second by discountenancing mass repression as a politically feasible option. See Nancy Bernkopf Tucker, "China as a Factor in the Collapse of the Soviet Empire," *Political Science Quarterly* 110, no. 4 (winter 1995): 501–19. The negative impact of the Chinese "solution" should not be overstated, however. Gorbachev had already begun to back away from his Eastern European commitments after Reykjavik and the intermediate nuclear force agreement revived détente in December 1987. The significance of the agreement was to remove American power from Western Europe (where U.S. Pershing IIs could pulverize Moscow in less than ten minutes), enabling Gorbachev to dismantle Soviet security forces there and put the relationship on a cash basis. In March 1989, in a meeting with Hungarian premier Grosz, Gorbachev stated his opposition to Soviet intervention in Warsaw Pact members' affairs, in effect rescinding the Brezhnev Doctrine. Richard C. Thornton, "Russo-Chinese Détente and the Emerging New World Order," in *The Roles of the United States, Russia, and China in the New World Order*, ed. Hafeez Malik (New York: St. Martin's Press, 1997), 221–38.

7. Admitted to the Council of Europe, a loose confederation of future candidates for the European Union, were Hungary, the Czech Republic, Slovenia, Romania, and the Baltic republics of Lithuania and Estonia.

8. Personal interview, Chinese Academy of Social Sciences, Beijing.

9. Li Jingjie, "Pillars of the Sino-Russian Partnership," *Orbis* (fall 2000): 527–39.

10. The Institute of the Far East in the Russian Academy of Sciences, previously led by Oleg Rakhmanin and now headed by his former deputy Mikhail Titorenko, is the largest research center for Chinese studies in Moscow. It has shifted from its critical stance toward Maoist ideology to an ardent embrace of it, largely because the CCP has avoided privatization and political reform while successfully regenerating socialist economic performance. Alexander Lukin, "Russia's Image of China and Russian-Chinese Relations," *East Asia: An International Quarterly* 17, no. 1 (spring 1999): 5 ff.; see also Evgeniy Bazhanov, "Russian Perspectives on China's Foreign Policy and Military Development," in *In China's Shadow: Regional Perspectives on Chinese Foreign Policy and Military Development*, ed. Jonathan Pollack and Michael Yang (Santa Monica, Calif.: Rand Corporation, 1998), 70–91.

11. The Sino-Soviet border was some 7,000 kilometers (4,340 miles) long. Since the disintegration of the USSR, it contracted to 3,484 kilometers (2,160 miles). The Chinese border with Kazakhstan stretches for about 2,000 kilometers (1,240 miles); with Kyrgyzstan, for 1,000 kilometers (620 miles); and with Tajikistan, for about 500 kilometers (310 miles).

12. See Richard Lotspeich, "Perspectives on the Economic Relations between China and Russia," *Journal of Contemporary Asia* 36, no. 1 (2006): 48–74.

13. Li Jianmin, ["Russian Efforts to Attract FDI: The Current Situation"], *Russian, Central Asian and East European Markets* 2 (2004): 8–14.

14. Lotspeich, "Perspectives," 55 ff.

15. SIPRI 2004 arms transfer database, as cited in Lotspeich, "Perspectives."

16. Sharif M. Shuja, "Moscow's Asia Policy," *Contemporary Review* 272, no. 1587 (April 1998): 169–78; Jamie Dettmer, "Russian-Chinese Alliance Emerges," *Insight on the News* 16, no. 13 (April 13, 2000): 20; Jyotsna Bakshi, "Russia-China Military-Technical Cooperation: Implications for India," http://www.idsa-india.org/an-jul-100.html.

17. A. Kotelkin, former head of the main Russian arms exporter Rosvoorne-zhenie, as cited in Alexander A. Sergounin and Sergey Subotkin, "Sino-Russian Military Cooperation: A Russian Perspective," *Regional Studies* 15, no. 4 (1997): 24; Associated Press, Moscow, February 15, 2001.

18. Compare Peggy Falkenheim Meyer, "Russia's Post–Cold War Security Policy in Northeast Asia," *Pacific Affairs* 67, no. 4 (winter 1994): 495–513.

19. Sherman W. Garnett, ed., *Limited Partnership: Russia-China Relations in a Changing Asia* (Washington, D.C.: Carnegie Endowment for International Peace, 1998), 22–23.

20. During Prime Minister Obuchi's November 1998 visit, the two countries signed the joint Moscow Declaration on Building a Creative Partnership between Japan and the Russian Federation, which provided for the establishment of two

subcommittees—one to discuss border demarcation, the other to study joint economic activities on the four disputed islands without prejudice to either country's legal claims. They also agreed to establish a joint investment company, strengthen economic cooperation, and promote intellectual and technical cooperation and exchanges. Japan has also facilitated Russian entrance into APEC. See Peggy F. Meyer, "The Russian Far East's Economic Integration with Northeast Asia: Problems and Prospects," *Pacific Affairs* 72, no. 2 (summer 1999): 209 ff.

21. John Cherian, "A Strategic Partnership," *Frontline*, October 13–27, 2000, as cited in Julie M. Rahm, "Russia, China, India: A New Strategic Triangle for a New Cold War?" *Parameters* 31, no. 4 (winter 2001): 87–98.

22. Anderson, *Limits of Sino-Russian Strategic Partnership*, 68.

23. The Taiwan issue, in the Chinese case, is a conspicuous exception but is far too complex to be reviewed here.

6. The European Union and China
Partnership with Competition
Xinning Song

China's relationship with the European Union (EU) is the best external bilateral relationship it has—better than that with the United States, Japan, and Russia. Politically, EU-China relations have matured and become institutionalized, with annual summits between China and the EU, as well as with EU member states such as Great Britain, Germany, France, and Spain. Most of the top Chinese and European leaders have paid mutual visits in the last few years, and more than two-thirds of the European commissioners have been to China. Dialogues have taken place between representatives of almost every level of government, covering most of the issues related to EU-China relations.

Economically, the EU-China relationship is vital to both partners. Since 2004, the EU has been China's most important trade partner, and China is the EU's second most important, after the United States. In 2006, EU-China trade totaled US$272.3 billion, accounting for 15.5 percent of China's total foreign trade and 18.8 percent of China's total exports (see table 6.1).

By the end of 2006, the EU member states had established more than 20,000 enterprises in China, with 25,418 projects and nearly US$100 billion of contracted foreign direct investment (FDI). Although the total amount of FDI from the EU ranked fourth in China, the average investment in each project was greater—about US$3.85 million each, compared with US$2.38 million by American investors and US$2.02 million by the Japanese.

The EU is the number-one supplier of technology to China. By the end of 2004, the technological transfer from the EU amounted to more than 24,108 projects totaling US$100 billion, or about 50 percent of China's total technology imports. At the same time, the EU is China's most important partner in the field of high technology, cooperating in such areas as the Galileo project and the EU-China agreement on the peaceful use of nuclear energy.

115

Table 6.1. China's Foreign Trade, 2006

| | TOTAL | | | EXPORTS | | IMPORTS | |
	US$ Billions	%	± % from 2005	US$ Billions	± % from 2005	US$ Billions	± % from 2005
China	1,760.68	100	23.8	969.07	27.2	791.61	20.0
EU 25	272.30	15.47	25.3	181.98	26.6	90.32	22.7
EU 15	256.36	14.56	24.1	169.02	25.4	87.34	21.7
USA	262.68	14.92	24.2	203.47	24.9	59.21	21.8
Japan	207.36	11.78	12.5	91.64	9.1	115.72	15.2
Russia	33.38	1.90	14.7	15.83	19.8	17.55	10.5
Hong Kong	166.17	9.40		155.39	24.8	10.79	−11.8
ASEAN	160.86	9.14		71.33	28.6	89.54	19.4
South Korea	134.38	7.63		44.56	26.9	89.82	16.8
Taiwan	107.88	6.13		20.74	25.3	87.14	16.7

The EU is also the biggest donor to China in terms of foreign aid. There have been more than thirty EU–China cooperative programs in the fields of political, economic, and social development in China. From 1996 to 2006, the EU donated nearly 600 million euro to China as free aid.

Internationally, the EU and China have similar ideas about world affairs, including the value of multilateralism and the peaceful resolution of disputes. Unlike the Sino–American and Sino–Japanese relationships, there is no geopolitical or strategic conflict between the EU and China. The relationship is not problem free, however. There have been disputes between China and different EU member states involving trade, human rights, arms embargo, market economy status, and so forth. But most of these issues are manageable, and both the EU and China are working hard to solve the problems through negotiation and dialogue.

The EU–China Strategic Partnership

The discussion of an EU–China strategic partnership started in 2003. It first appeared in a report on European security strategy (known as the Solana report):

> The transatlantic relationship is irreplaceable. Acting together, the
> European Union and the United States can be a formidable force

for good in the World. Our aim should be an effective and balanced partnership with the USA. This is an additional reason for the EU to build up further its capabilities and increase its coherence.

We should continue to work for closer relations with Russia, a major factor in our security and prosperity. Respect [for] common values will reinforce progress towards a strategic partnership.

Our history, geography and cultural ties give us links with every part of the world: our neighbours in the Middle East, our partners in Africa, in Latin America, and in Asia. These relationships are an important asset to build on. In particular we should look to develop strategic partnerships, with Japan, China, Canada and India as well as with all those who share our goals and values, and are prepared to act in their support.[1]

In an October 2003 report, the European Commission defined the EU-China relationship as a "maturing partnership."[2] From the Chinese side, there was no mention of a strategic partnership in a policy paper issued by the Chinese Ministry of Foreign Affairs on October 13, 2003.[3]

In a joint statement issued after the Sixth EU-China Summit, the two sides officially mentioned a strategic partnership:

The two sides agreed that their high-level political dialogues had been fruitful and the dialogues and consultations at other levels had also further expanded in intensity and scope and such multi-layered structure of China-EU relations is an indicator of the increasing maturity and growing strategic nature of the partnership.

Leaders welcomed the recent issuing of policy papers on China-EU relations by both sides. . . . They also noted the draft European Security Strategy Paper, in which China features as one of the key partners for the EU's strategic security relationships.

Leaders expressed their satisfaction with the positive outcome of this Sixth Summit meeting. They stressed their resolve to further expand and deepen China-EU relations, guided by the two policy papers, which promote the development of an overall strategic partnership between China and the EU.[4]

Chinese leaders openly referred to the EU-China comprehensive strategic partnership in May 2004 when Wen Jiabao visited Europe and delivered a speech entitled "Vigorously Developing Comprehensive Strategic Partnership between China and the European Union." He stated:

By "comprehensive" is meant that cooperation between both sides is all-round, wide-ranging and multi-level, it covers economy, sci-technology, and politics and culture; both bilateral and multilateral; and both governmental and non-governmental. By "strategic" is meant that bilateral cooperation is of an overall, long-term and stable nature, transcends the differences in ideology and social system and is free from the interference of a single event that occurs in a certain period of time. By "partnership" is meant that the cooperation between both sides is of equality, mutual benefit and win-win result and, on the basis of mutual respect and mutual trust, the two sides seek common ground on major issues while shelving differences on minor ones and endeavor to expand common interests. The development of such a relationship between China and the EU not only conforms to the mutual interests of China and the EU, but also contributes to peace, stability and common progress in our respective regions and the world at large.[5]

During the Seventh EU-China Summit in December 2004 in the Hague, there was no official statement on EU-China relations, but according to the European Commission, the "two sides stressed the importance of further deepening their relation, turning it into a strategic partnership."[6]

From the European side, there has been no further explanation of the EU-China strategic partnership. The European Policy Centre, a think tank based in Brussels, mentioned the following in a working paper:

The term strategic partnership has not been defined by the Union and there is little that the countries identified in the European Security Strategy have in common apart from their size. Yet few have questioned the decision to include China as a strategic partner.

First and foremost, the parties must be clear about their objectives. A single, common objective is not essential, but the overarching objectives cannot be in conflict with each other. The EU's objective is, or should be, to help China to be a peaceful, stable, democratic (although not necessarily in the full western sense), internationally responsible country, internally consensus-seeking and externally multilateral, sharing broadly similar values and goals. A similar objective is in China's interests. The two parties should expressly define their strategic objectives in any agreement.

Within the overarching objectives of the strategic partnership, the main goals should be:

- To promote mutual understanding
- To promote respect for the rule of law, including human rights
- To increase economic and social sustainability
- To promote regional and global security
- To strengthen international cooperation and global governance.[7]

From 2005 to 2007, the EU and China continued to talk about the strategic partnership. During the Eighth EU-China Summit in September 2005 in Beijing, Chinese and European leaders discussed the importance of deepening and boosting the China-EU comprehensive strategic partnership.[8] In a joint statement, the strategic partnership was mentioned three times. Importantly, the statement pointed out that "the leaders now wished to look ahead to the future, developing the strategic relationship through concrete actions."[9] In September 2006, when leaders met in Helsinki, Finland, for the Ninth EU-China Summit, both sides emphasized that EU-China relations had matured and deepened into a "comprehensive strategic partnership." The resulting joint statement declared:

> Leaders of the two sides agreed that the past decade had seen significant changes in the EU and in China and a progressive deepening of the relationship, which was maturing into a comprehensive strategic partnership.
>   In order to reflect the full breadth and depth of today's comprehensive strategic partnership between the EU and China, the two sides agreed to launch negotiations on a new Partnership and Cooperation Agreement which will encompass the full scope of their bilateral relationship, including enhanced cooperation in political matters.[10]

In November 2007, the Tenth EU-China Summit was held in Beijing. The joint statement noted, "Leaders expressed their satisfaction with the comprehensive cooperation between the two sides in broad fields and at all levels, and with the growing maturity of the China-EU comprehensive strategic partnership."[11] But still there was no clear definition of the EU-China strategic partnership. As Fraser Cameron argued, owing to the lack of shared values and their very different political systems, the EU-China strategic partnership could hardly go beyond commercial and economic interests.[12]

China's Strategic Interests

When we talk about a strategic partnership between two countries (or regions), we have to define the strategic interests of each partner. These strategic interests encompass essential elements of political, economic, and social development, not just traditional military and national security issues, and not just international affairs. Strategic interests are related to fundamental national interests.

Why is its relationship to the EU so important to China? Many observers emphasize the economic ties, but that is not the whole story. For China, there are two important aspects: domestic development, and China's role in the international community. Obviously, the EU–China relationship is very important for China's economic development, but its economic development also has implications for China's political and social development.

Economic Development and China's Political and Social Stability

Economic development is the precondition for both political and social stability in China. And political and social stability are the key elements in China's smooth transition to a market economy.

When we look at the domestic politics of China, the rule of the Communist Party is the most important issue. It directs the development of China's foreign policy. Today, many Chinese believe that the legitimacy of the Communist Party's rule is experiencing a major challenge. In the first forty years of the People's Republic of China, the basis of the party's legitimacy was neither public participation nor social or economic welfare but rather the personal charisma of leaders such as Mao Zedong and Deng Xiaoping, the ideology of communism plus nationalism, and the centralized political system.

After the beginning of domestic reform and opening up to the outside world, the ideology of communism lost it base. Very few people in China care about the communist future.[13] Nationalism is still important because of Sino-American and Sino-Japanese disputes on various issues, but it too is a challenge to the current leadership.[14] Along with the market economy system, decentralization has become a common demand at the local level. Jiang Zemin came into power under special circumstances and had no choice but to follow the direction taken by Deng Xiaoping. He was not a very popular leader among the ordinary Chinese people. Hu Jintao came into power under a more normal process, although he was selected by Deng Xiaoping many years ago.

Even though the communist leadership is facing a huge challenge, most

Chinese still believe that no any other political force should usurp its ruling position. It was the Communist Party that started the process of reform and opening up, and it has benefited the Chinese people. However, for the Communist Party of China to keep its ruling position, it must keep the Chinese economy developing constantly.

To maintain and solidify the legitimacy of the Communist Party, the Chinese leadership put forward the idea of "socialism with Chinese characteristics."[15] The major feature of this concept is to make economic development rather than class struggle the priority of the Communist Party. To have everything revolve around the core of economic development is the essence of the so-called Deng Xiaoping theory, which Jiang Zemin and Hu Jintao have continued and expanded. Jiang Zemin put forward his "three representations," and Hu Jintao has coined the phrases "harmonious society" and "socialist new rural society."

For the Chinese leadership, foreign policy is a continuation of domestic politics. Because of the Communist Party's legitimacy problem, political and social stability is regarded as the most important issue. But how to maintain political stability is open to debate: by strengthening the so-called people's democratic dictatorship, or by enhancing economic development and economic welfare? I believe the answer is the latter. Economic development is necessary not only to strengthen China's national capabilities but also to maintain the ruling position of the Communist Party. That is the most important issue in China's domestic politics.[16] And EU-China economic relations provide a solid foundation for China's political and social stability.

The EU Model and China's Domestic and Social Stability

Currently, China is facing some major challenges resulting from tensions between the people and the Chinese Communist Party, between the developed (coastal) and the less developed (inner) regions, and between the rich and the poor. China would like to learn from (not copy) the European model to deal with these political and social issues.

The European model has two parts: political development, and social and economic development. In the political realm, Chinese scholars have been debating the issue of democratic socialism since the 1990s. Recently, some scholars have openly argued that the Chinese Communist Party should follow the example of European social democracy in order to improve its position in Chinese society.[17] In the social and economic realm, Chinese scholars started to study the European model of social welfare in the 1980s, with a particular interest in the Nordic model.[18] Since the late 1990s, when European studies became one of the hot topics in international studies, many Chinese have paid special attention to the European welfare state, the social welfare and social security system, and EU regional policy. Many Chinese scholars believe that if China establishes its own social security system to solve social problems in the transitional period, the state will play an essential role. The European social security model is more relevant than the American model, although both have problems.[19]

China's International Role

China is gradually integrating into the world economy and the international community. One of the major goals of the EU policy toward China has been to integrate China into the world economic system. Because of its domestic reform, rapid economic growth, and opening up to the outside world, China has become one of the major world powers, and how to deal with China has become an issue among the other major powers, including the United States and the European Union. China itself has been working hard to become a responsible world power and to play a constructive international role. Since the Sixteenth Party Congress of the Communist Party in 2002, cooperation with developed countries, especially the United States and the EU, has been a priority in Chinese foreign policy. Economic cooperation not only helps China maintain its economic growth but also makes China and the EU, as well as China and the United States, more economically interdependent.

Both the Chinese government and the Chinese public accept the concept of effective multilateralism advocated by the EU. Although many European scholars have argued about the various meanings of multilateralism between the EU and China, the similarities outweigh the differences.[20]

The Chinese are using European-style regional integration and patterns of external relations as a model for dealing with the outside world. Although European regional integration is regarded as a special European phenomenon, it embodies certain universal values, such as functional cooperation and the processes of institutionalization and legalization. The European model is also a good example of peaceful rise. It is cited by some Chinese scholars as proof that China's peaceful rise is not a historical exception. After World War II, the countries of Europe formed the European Community and later the European Union, becoming an important world power through the process of peaceful rise. Some Chinese have argued that the European peaceful rise has been accepted by the international community because the EU established good relationships with neighboring countries through the process of regional integration, maintained good relationships with the hegemonic power (the United States) through political and military alliances, and played an active role in the world community through cooperation with international institutions and developing countries.[21]

From both the domestic and the international perspective, the EU is strategically very important to China. It is easy to understand why China would like to work with the EU and have a strategic partnership with it. But what is the EU's main objective in establishing a strategic or cooperative partnership with China? Although we can find some answers in official EU documents, in terms of policy implementation, the answer is less clear.

The EU-China Competitive Partnership

Both the EU and China would like to deepen their relationship to the level of a strategic partnership. However, the two sides have not reached a common understanding of the elements of that partnership. Since 2005, when it became clear that issues such as the arms embargo and the status of the market economy could not be solved easily or quickly, the EU and China have realized the difficulties of developing a strategic partnership and have become more realistic and pragmatic. Both sides emphasized in September 2005 the need "to look ahead to the future, developing the strategic relationship through concrete actions."[22]

In September 2006, at the Ninth EU-China Summit, both the EU and China worked on concrete issues rather than principles, resulting in a joint statement with thirty-six sections referring to many substantive points.[23] In 2007, the Tenth EU-China Summit went even further, compiling a joint statement that listed forty-seven issues the EU and China had discussed and would like to cooperate on, including the following: Taiwan, arms embargo, nonproliferation and disarmament, human rights, multilateral international system with the United Nations as the core, antiterrorism, Darfur, Myanmar, North Korea, Iran, Israeli-Palestinian conflict, Kosovo, Asian regional cooperation, Beijing Olympics, sustainable economic and social development, environmental and climate change, energy, market economy status, macroeconomic policy cooperation, exchange rate, small and medium-size enterprises, science and technology, customs matters, transportation, civil aviation, cultural relations,

World Health Organization, employment and social affairs, legal and judicial cooperation, youth affairs, and higher education.[24]

In October 2006, the European Commission issued new policy papers on China, including "EU-China: Closer Partners, Growing Responsibilities" and "Competition and Partnership." It stated:

> To better reflect the importance of their relations, the EU and China agreed [to] a strategic partnership in 2003. Some differences remain, but are being managed effectively, and relations are increasingly mature and realistic. At the same time China is, with the EU, closely bound to the globalisation process and becoming more integrated into the international system.
>
> The EU's fundamental approach to China must remain one of engagement and partnership. But with a closer strategic partnership, mutual responsibilities increase. The partnership should meet both sides' interests and the EU and China need to work together as they assume more active and responsible international roles, supporting and contributing to a strong and effective multilateral system. The goal should be a situation where China and the EU can bring their respective strengths to bear to offer joint solutions to global problems.[25]

Still, the real meaning of the EU-China strategic partnership is not clear. The European Commission has mentioned only one concrete issue: nonproliferation. It stated, "Non-proliferation represents a key area for the strategic partnership."[26]

In December 2006, the Council of the European Union even used "EU-China Strategic Partnership" as the title of the conclusion of a report on EU-China relations. It declared:

> The Council is strongly committed to the maturing of the EU's comprehensive strategic partnership with China. For this partnership to develop to its full potential, it must be balanced, reciprocal and mutually beneficial. The partnership is increasingly focused on addressing global challenges, and China plays a key role in the effective international response to these issues. The EU and China have important commitments and responsibilities, and must both work hard to deliver them, in the interest of wider international security and stability and to strengthen an effective, fair, just and rules-based multilateral international system, with the United Nations at its centre.[27]

Obviously, both the European Commission and the Council of the European Union believe that the comprehensive strategic partnership with China involves only global issues, or only European and global security issues that include both traditional and nontraditional security. They continue to follow the basic strategy of the 2003 Solana report.

For most bilateral issues, China is regarded not only as a partner but also as a competitor of the EU. As a European Commission policy paper on trade and investment indicated, "China is the single most important challenge for EU trade policy."[28] Thus, although the EU and China are close partners in political, economic, social, and cultural affairs, they are also competitors in various fields.

Economic Partnership and Competition

Europeans are becoming increasingly worried about Chinese economic competition. According to the European Commission, the EU's open market has been a large contributor to China's export-led growth. The EU has also benefited from the growth of the Chinese market: EU exports to China have more than doubled in the past five years, competitively priced Chinese products have helped keep inflation and interest rates in Europe low, and European companies have gained from their investments in China. However, competition from China has posed some serious challenges in some important European manufacturing sectors, and Chinese products compete with EU products not just at home but also in emerging markets in Asia, Africa, and Latin America.

One crucial issue is the complaint from the EU side about unfair trade practices that hinder access to the Chinese market. These obstacles include tariff and nontariff barriers, government procurement, investment restrictions, and issues involving intellectual property rights. The Chinese side complains about protectionism from the Europeans, especially the unfair antidumping measures due to China's not being granted market economy status. The EU insists that trade defense measures are instrumental to ensure fair trade conditions between the EU and China. The EU is actively working with China to create the conditions that would permit an early granting of market economy status. Yet at the same time, the EU has stated that an improving bilateral trade relationship will help create the environment in which this can happen. China's policy of reform will be instrumental in fulfilling the technical criteria for market economy status.

Political Partnership and Competition

China has a more mature political relationship with the EU than with any other global actor. The EU and China have had productive political dialogues on various domestic, regional, and global issues. The EU-China political competition is not as obvious as the economic one. Also, very few people debate this issue, concentrating instead on political differences such as ideology, the political system, human rights, and the rule of law.

Since 1995, when the European Commission issued its first China policy paper, the basic strategic objectives of EU policy have been to integrate China into the international system, support and encourage China's internal political and economic reform process, and promote China's transition toward a more open and plural society. Although China welcomes this European support, it does not always follow the European approach. For instance, the Chinese leadership put forward the concept of the "harmonious society," in contrast to the European concept of the "plural society."

The Chinese are willing to learn from the European model for China's political, economic, and social development, as well as its foreign policy and external relations. But at the same time, the so-called China model, or Beijing consensus, has great attraction for other developing countries in the world, especially in Africa. During a June 2007 conference in Brussels organized by the European Commission, entitled "Partners in Competition? The EU, Africa, and China," some African participants openly challenged the European model and welcomed the Chinese way (if not to say the Chinese model) of development and its relevance to other developing countries.

The Competition for Other Partners

Neither China nor the EU regards the other as its *most* important partner. The United States is the most important ally for the EU and the first priority for the Chinese foreign policy agenda.

The United States is China's most important partner not only strategically but also economically. Although the EU is China's number-one trade partner based on the official statistics of China and the EU, according to official U.S. statistics, the United States is China's number-one trade partner (with bilateral trade of US$343 billion, including US$287.77 billion in Chinese exports and US$55.22 billion in Chinese imports, in 2006). China is the fourth largest export market and the second largest import market for the United States.[29]

Japan may be another factor in EU-China economic relations. Along with the gradual improvement in Sino-Japanese political relations, people are ex-

Table 6.2. China's Trade Relations with the European Union, United States, and Asia, 2006

	TOTAL		EXPORTS		IMPORTS	
	US$ Billion	%	US$ Billion	%	US$ Billion	%
China	1,760.68	100	969.07	100	791.61	100
EU 25	272.30	15.47	181.98	18.78	90.32	11.41
USA	262.68	14.92	203.47	21.00	59.21	7.48
East Asia	776.64	44.07	383.66	39.60	392.98	57.56
Japan	207.36	11.78	91.64	9.46	115.72	14.62
ASEAN 10	160.86	9.14	71.33	7.36	89.54	11.31
South Korea	134.38	7.63	44.56	4.60	89.82	11.35
Hong Kong	166,17	9.40	155.39	16.04	10.79	9.27
Taiwan	107.84	6.12	20.74	2.14	87.11	11.01
APEC	1227.30	69.71	644.66	66.52	582.64	73.60

pecting better economic cooperation between the two countries. Another important element is the impact of Sino-Japanese cooperation on regional cooperation in East Asia. Actually, China's current level of trade with Japan, South Korea, and the ten members of the Association of Southeast Asian Nations (ASEAN) is much higher than that with either the European Union or the United States. In 2006, the trade between China and Japan, South Korea, and ASEAN totaled US$776.64 billion (44.07 percent of the total), with US$383.66 billion in exports (39.60 percent of the total) and US$392.90 billion in imports (57.56 percent of the total). Between China and Asia Pacific Economic Cooperation (APEC) countries, the total trade was US$1,227.3 billion (69.71 percent of the total), with US$644.66 billion in exports (66.52 percent of the total) and US$582.64 billion in imports (73.60 percent of the total). In other words, China's economic relations with East Asia and APEC countries are more important than its economic relations with any other region, including Europe (see table 6.2).

The third potential competitor is Russia, due to its rich oil and gas resources. Both China and the EU are keen to have a good relationship with Russia, although this has caused no direct conflict between them.

Since 2006, Africa has become a factor in EU-China relations. From the Chinese point of view, there are more opportunities for cooperation than for competition with the EU in Africa. For the Europeans, however, many of whom regard Africa as the backyard of Europe, China's activity in Africa is seen as undermining European influence in the continent.

Conclusion

Since 1995, when the European Commission published "A Long Term Policy for China-EU Relations," the EU-China relationship has developed smoothly and successfully. The 2003–2004 period was regarded as the "honeymoon" between the two. Since 2005, however, the honeymoon has been over, and both China and the EU have experienced the normal ups and downs of a bilateral relationship and have become more pragmatic and realistic.

Although the EU-China strategic partnership is a debatable concept, the two have a solid base to strengthen their partnership and their cooperation.[30] First, China and the EU have no conflicts over fundamental interests and no outstanding historical issues. There is no major political obstacle standing in the way of the relationship. At the same time, some people argue that the EU-China relationship cannot exceed the U.S.-China relationship strategically. The EU-China relationship is, however, much easier to manage than more troublesome relationships such as China-Japan or even China-Russia.

Second, China and the EU follow similar principles in addressing international issues. Both China and the major EU member states are key participants in the international community and are influential in determining international trends and shaping the international system. If both sides want to play a more active and responsible role in world affairs, they must cooperate with each other.

Third, China and the EU are both in a crucial stage of development, and their interests often overlap. They can offer more opportunities to each other through their development, and their cooperation is mutually beneficial. Despite growing economic competition, economic interdependence is increasing rather than decreasing.

Fourth, China and the EU need to work together to deal with global challenges such as climate change, energy, security, antiterrorism, and nonproliferation. Cooperation between China and the EU in responding to these challenges not only serves the interests of both sides but also conduces to international peace, stability, and development.

Fifth, both sides are attracted to the other's culture. Blessed with time-honored and rich cultural heritages, China and the EU have much to learn from and offer each other. A good example is the fact that there are more Confucius Institutes—institutions for the teaching of Chinese language and culture—in Europe than anywhere else in the world.[31]

In summary, we can expect a bright future for EU–China relations, characterized by partnership with competition.

Notes

1. Javier Solana, "A Secure Europe in a Better World: European Security Strategy," June 20, 2003, http://ue.eu.int/ueDocs/cms_Data/docs/pressdata/EN/reports/76255.pdf. The report was officially approved by the Council of the European Union on December 12, 2003.

2. European Commission policy paper, "A Maturing Partnership: Shared Interests and Challenges in EU-China Relations," October 9, 2003, http://eur-lex.europa.eu/LexUriServ/site/en/com/2003/com2003_0533en01/pdf.

3. China's EU policy paper, October 13, 2003, http://www.fmprc.gov.cn/eng/wjb/zzjg/xos/dqzzywt/t27708.htm.

4. Joint press statement of the Sixth EU-China Summit, http://europa.eu.int/comm/external_relations/china/summit/jpss_301003.htm.

5. *China Daily*, May 7, 2004.

6. See http://europa.eu.int/comm/external_relations/china/intro/index.htm.

7. Fraser Cameron, Axel Berkofsky, and Stanley Crossick, "EU-China Relations: Towards a Strategic Partnership," EPC Working Paper no.19, July 14, 2005, 32–33. There is no evidence that the European Policy Centre's argument has been accepted by any European institution.

8. *China Daily*, September 5, 2005.

9. See http://ec.europa.eu/external_relations/news/barroso/sp05_478.htm.

10. See http://www.consilium.europa.eu/ueDocs/cms_Data/docs/pressData/en/er/90951.pdf.

11. See http://www.eu2007.pt/UE/vEN/Noticias_Documentos/20071202CHINA.htm.

12. Fraser Cameron and Yongnian Zheng, "Key Elements of a Strategic Partnership," in *China-EU: A Common Future*, ed. Stanley Crossick and Etienne Reuter (Singapore: World Scientific Press, 2007).

13. Since 2002, the Chinese Communist Party Charter has referred to communism as just "an idea" rather than "an idea as well as an institution."

14. One good example is Qiang Song and Zangzang Zhang, *China Can Say No* (Beijing: Zhingguo Gongshang Lianhe Chubanshe, 1996). Many people regarded it as a nationalist challenge to the United States, but it was actually a challenge to China's policy toward the United States. The logic was that if China had become strong enough to say no to the United States, why didn't the Chinese government do so?

15. Many Chinese define "socialism with Chinese characteristics" as capitalism led by the Communist Party or as capitalism in economics (market economy) and socialism in politics (one–party system).

16. See Xinning Song, "The Impact of Domestic Politics on Chinese Foreign Policy," in *Leadership in a Changing China,* ed. Weixing Chen and Yang Zhong (New York: Palgrave Macmillan, 2005), 147–68.

17. See Tao Xie, "Minzhu Shehui Zhuyi moshi yu Zhongguo de qiantu" [The model of democratic socialism and the future of China], *Yanhuang Chunqiu* 2 (2007). The left wing in China has criticized the "three representations" for attempting to change the Chinese Communist Party into a kind of European social democratic party.

18. See Fanzhang Huang, *Sweden: The Practice and Theory of Welfare State* (Shanghai: Shanghai Renmin Chubanshe, 1987); Anmiao Huang and Xiaojin Zhang, *Analysis of the Swedish Model* (Harerbin: Heilongjiang Renmin Chubanshe, 1989); Xiaojin Zhang and Tianqing Li, *From Functional Socialism to Funding Socialism: Theory and Practice of Swedish Social Democratic Party* (Harerbin: Heilongjiang Renmin Chubanshe, 1989); Yunling Zhang, ed., *Nordic Social Welfare System and Reform of China's Social Security System* (Beijing: China Social Sciences Press, 1993); Ping Zhang, *Sweden: Good Example of Social Welfare Economy* (Wuhan: Wuhan Chubanshe, 1994).

19. See Yuanlun Qiu and Hongbo Luo, eds., *Comparative Studies on Employment Policy in the EU and China* (Beijing: China Economics Press, 1998); Peng Du, *The European Aging Issues and Policies* (Beijing: China Population Press, 2000); Jianhua Zhang, *European Integration and the EU Economic and Social Policy* (Beijing: Shangwu Yinshuguan, 2001); Keyun Zhang, *Regional Economic Policy: Theoretical Basis and the Practice of the EU* (Beijing: China Light Industry Press, 2001); Dewen Tian, *European Social Policy and European Integration* (Beijing: Social Sciences Document Press, 2005); Hong Zhou, *Whither the Welfare States?* (Beijing: China Social Sciences Press, 2006). For a more detailed discussion of the EU as a model, see Xinning Song, "China's View of European Integration and Enlargement," in *China-Europe Relations: Perceptions, Policies and Prospects,* ed. David Shambaugh et al. (London: Routledge Press, 2008), 174–86.

20. See Gudrun Wacker and Xinning Song, "Same Bed, Different or Compatible Dreams? Commonalities and Differences," in Crossick and Reuter, *China-EU: A Common Future.*

21. Xinning Song, "China's Rise and the European Experience," *Teaching and Research* 4 (2004); Xinning Song, "China's View of European Integration and Enlargement," in Shambaugh et al., *China-Europe Relations.*

22. See http://ec.europa.eu/external_relations/news/barroso/sp05_478.htm.

23. For the English version, see http://www.consilium.europa.eu/ueDocs/cms_Data/docs/pressData/en/er/90951.pdf. For the Chinese version, see http://www.fmprc.gov.cn/chn/wjb/zzjg/xos/gjlb/EuropeanUnion/smgb/t271095.htm.

24. See http://www.eu2007.pt/UE/vEN/Noticias_Documentos/20071202CHINA.htm.

25. See http://ec.europa.eu/external_relations/china/docs/06–10–24_final_com .pdf, p. 2.

26. Ibid., p. 11.

27. See http://register.consilium.europa.eu/pdf/en/06/st16/st16291.en06.pdf, p. 6.

28. See http://trade.ec.europa.eu/doclib/docs/2006/october/tradoc_130791.pdf.

29. Data from the Ministry of Commerce of the People's Republic of China; see http://countryreport.mofcom.gov.cn/assay/qikan.asp?id=325.

30. See Yang Jiechi's speech at the Royal Institute of International Affairs, United Kingdom, December 5, 2007, at http://www.fmprc.gov.cn/chn/wjb/wjbz/zyhd/ t387184.htm.

31. According to the Office of Chinese Language Council International, there had been 170 Confucius Institutes or classes in the world as of July 2007—50 of them in Europe, and more than 40 in the EU member states. See also http:// www.hanban.org/cn_hanban/kzxy_list.php?state1=Europe.

7. China's Japan Policy

Beijing's View of the U.S.-Japan Alliance

Quansheng Zhao

Chinese foreign policy toward Japan can be analyzed from many different angles. The U.S.-Japan alliance has been the foundation of Japanese foreign policy in the postwar era, so this chapter uses Beijing's changing view of that alliance to examine the major factors influencing China's Japan policy.

When analyzing how Chinese foreign policy has affected Beijing's attitude toward the U.S.-Japan alliance over the past several decades, one can discern three different foreign policy approaches: the history-embedded approach, the national interest–driven approach, and the co-management of international crises approach. Until recently, the People's Republic of China (PRC) emphasized the first two approaches, but it now seems to be gradually moving toward the comanagement approach. To illuminate the significance of the comanagement approach, I address here two flash points in East Asia—the Korean peninsula and the Taiwan Strait—as empirical evidence. The discussion that follows includes an analysis of these two cases, as well as developments in China's view of the U.S.-Japan alliance.

The alliance was formed during the American occupation of Japan after World War II and was formalized by the signing of the U.S.-Japan Security Treaty in 1951. From the Chinese perspective, the U.S.-Japan alliance was originally regarded as a hostile tool of the U.S.-led Western camp in the Cold War era, but those views have evolved over time. Four elements have directly affected Beijing's view of the alliance: (1) the overall relationship between China and the United States, (2) the changing international environment, (3) the dynamics of the political situation in Japan, and (4) China's changing status as a world power.

The History-Embedded Approach

Chinese foreign policy toward both Japan and the United States has been greatly influenced by history. China's view of the U.S.-Japan alliance over the past half century has gone through several stages. The first stage began with the inception of the alliance in the 1950s and ended with the rapprochement between China and the two allied countries in the early 1970s, signified by Richard Nixon's visit to Beijing and Tanaka Kakue's normalization trip to China. This was the Cold War era, and several regional wars, such as the Korean War and the Vietnam War, also occurred during this period. China's view of the U.S.-Japan alliance was enormously influenced by its own conflict with the United States and the changing international environment. By and large, Beijing's basic attitude toward the alliance was confrontational.

The second stage covered the early 1970s to the late 1980s. During this time, China's relations with the Soviet Union continued to deteriorate until the latter's collapse. China's perspective toward the U.S.-Japan alliance was increasingly colored by the strategic triangle consisting of Beijing, Washington, and Moscow, and its approach seemed ambivalent. Although it was still wary of the containment aspect of the U.S.-Japan alliance, it also saw the alliance as an instrument to deter the expansionist policies of the Soviet hegemon. Therefore, Beijing expressed a more tolerant attitude.

The post–Cold War era ushered in the third stage, during which the world power structure experienced what I call the "two ups, two downs" shift.[1] That is, China and the United States rose in power (two ups), while Russia and Japan experienced a reduction in power status (two downs). Of course, this is only in relative terms, as Japan remains the second largest economy in the world. At the beginning of the twenty-first century, the key relationship in the Asian Pacific, and therefore a key element in Beijing's foreign policy, is the relationship between the rising power (China) and the dominant superpower (the United States). China's perspective toward the alliance has been significantly affected by this new power configuration. To secure a peaceful and stable international environment for its continued modernization drive, Beijing has adopted a more conciliatory and cooperative approach toward Washington. At the same time, however, China's political relations with Japan deteriorated considerably during the Koizumi era despite the deepened economic interdependence between the two powers. This seemingly contradictory trend in Chinese foreign policy has certainly influenced China's approach toward the alliance.

The U.S.-Japan Security Treaty was signed during the Korean War, which involved a direct military confrontation between China and the United States. During this period, China made it very clear that it opposed the alliance in the name of preventing Japanese remilitarization. This was connected to the Cold War reality that, as in Europe, there were two camps in the Asian Pacific: the U.S.-led Western camp, and the Soviet-led communist camp. Therefore, the alliance was viewed as an effort by Washington to establish a dominant position in the Asian Pacific.

China's view of the U.S.-Japan alliance began to change in the late 1960s and early 1970s because of the changing international environment. Just as Beijing's relations with Moscow were deteriorating, Beijing and Washington began their process of rapprochement in 1971. With the drama of the Beijing–Washington–Moscow triangle unfolding, Beijing began to view the alliance in a more positive way.[2] China's attitude toward the alliance also vacillated with the changing dynamics of domestic politics in Tokyo, growing more accepting during more conciliatory prime ministerships and less accepting during the reign of prime ministers with less tolerance.

After Nixon's visit to Beijing in 1972, China took a more positive view of the alliance when Mao Zedong decided that a close relationship between Japan and the United States was preferable to one between Japan and the Soviet Union. The Soviet threat was a significant security concern for China from the late 1970s to the early 1980s. Thus, Japan's alliance with the United States came to be seen as a brake on "Japanese expansionism and militarism."[3] This was confirmed during Prime Minister Yasuhiro Nakasone's visit to Beijing in April 1980 and his meetings with Premier Hua Guofeng and Wu Xiuquan, deputy chief of the Chinese army's general staff. China's positive attitude toward Japan's defense expenditures lasted until the mid-1980s.

The year 1989 was a watershed in Sino-Japanese relations owing to several important events. First, China's rapprochement with the Soviet Union and the later collapse of the Soviet empire decisively removed the Soviet security threat to both China and Japan and significantly shifted their defense priorities. Second, the Tiananmen incident prompted U.S.-led sanctions against China, which Japan joined. Although Japan was the first country in the Western camp to remove the sanctions, the event itself reversed the positive perceptions of China among the Japanese and has had a lasting impact on China's image.

That year also marked the beginning of a slow shift toward a more assertive Japanese foreign policy. Japan has gradually become less cautious and less sensitive with regard to the concerns of its Asian neighbors, particularly China and South Korea. Increasingly, Japanese politicians, and even the Japanese public, have advocated a more active political and military role in international affairs. This new momentum may well include a change in the Japanese Constitution and a revision of Article 9. Other sources of tension include Japan's textbook revisions, former prime minister Koizumi's visits to Yasukuni Shrine, and Japan's recent changes in its Taiwan policy (discussed later). Therefore, Beijing has been much more irritated with Tokyo than with Washington.

Relations took a positive turn in 2006 with the successful visit of the next Japanese prime minister, Shinzo Abe, to China. This resulted in a pledge to move forward in China-Japan strategic relations and triggered a series of cooperative gestures aimed at declaring a new era of cooperation on North Korea, intellectual property rights, energy development, and the environment. During this period, Abe said that Japan "must build future-oriented and stable Japan-China relations,"[4] and Premier Wen Jiabao toned down Beijing's usual criticism of Japan's wartime actions and focused instead on optimistic, forward-looking statements about the Sino-Japanese relationship.[5] Yet relations are still fragile and wary. Wen warned that issues such as competition over energy, territory, and regional influence still need to be resolved.[6]

Since then, the reconciliatory momentum between the two countries has trickled down from the top level to the governmental and people's levels. In May 2007, the first round of the Japan–China–Republic of Korea Senior Foreign Affairs Officials' Consultation was held in Beijing. In June, the Ninth Japan-China Consultation concerning the East China Sea was held in Tokyo. In July 2007, a group of thirty-two Chinese students returned to their country after spending eleven months attending school in Japan (twenty schools in sixteen places) as part of the Japan-China Twenty-first Century Friendship Program. Another forty Chinese students were scheduled to arrive in Japan in September 2007.[7] Both sides hope that such consultations and learning experiences will enhance understanding between the two countries.

Korea Policy

From Beijing's perspective, both Taiwan and Korea have been crucial to China's security concerns and national interests since the early nineteenth century. The link between these two vital areas emerged early in 1950 when the People's Liberation Army (PLA) prepared to take over Taiwan. This attempt was prevented by the outbreak of the Korean War,[8] at which time the PLA's main target switched from Taiwan to Korea and its engagement by the United States. The Korean War also prompted President Harry Truman to order the U.S. Seventh Fleet into the Taiwan Strait to guarantee Taiwan's security, thereby internationalizing the issue of Taiwan and making it a focus of future conflict between Beijing and Washington.

Historically, China and Korea have shared complex and intimate relations symbolized by a hierarchical tributary system. Korea often acted as a buffer between China and far-away nations, Japan being the prime example.[9] Tributary relations between China and Korea came to an end when China was forced to sign the Treaty of Shimonoseki with Japan in 1895. As part of that treaty, the Qing government agreed to cede Taiwan to Japan. Further confirmation of Japan's leading position in the region came with its victory in the Russo-Japanese War of 1904–1905, which also introduced American intervention into Northeast Asian geopolitics. Japan has also had a historical role in the Korean peninsula, particularly its colonization of Korea from 1910 to 1945. When Japan was defeated in World War II and withdrew from Korea, the peninsula was once again divided as a result of the onset of the Cold War.

The Korean War served as another historical reminder of the importance of Korea to China's national security. China's reentry into the Korean peninsula began in October 1950, when the new Beijing leadership made the momentous decision to cross the Yalu River and get involved in the war, thereby engaging in direct military confrontation with the United States. The war had important strategic implications for East Asian international relations. Korea has historically been known as a place of *bingjia bizheng* (a strategic stronghold for military conflict) among the major powers, and this is still true today. All four major powers—China, Japan, Russia, and the United States—have vital stakes in the dynamics of the Korean peninsula. Japan is the most important U.S. military ally in the region. Any settlement of the Korea issue will definitely require positive Japanese participation, although the leadership role will be assumed by China and the United States.

Taiwan Policy

With regard to its relationships with Washington and Tokyo, a central locus of concern for Beijing is the issue of Taiwan. Indeed, Beijing sees the United States as a major obstacle to its goal of reunification with Taiwan. This issue can be traced back historically to the Chinese civil war (1946–1949), when the

United States supported the Chiang Kai-shek regime. Then, when the Korean War ended in the early 1950s, the United States signed a mutual defense treaty with Taiwan that effectively prevented the PRC from taking over the island. In the late 1960s and early 1970s, both Beijing and Washington were willing to normalize their relations primarily because of the threat of the Soviet Union.

The PRC's dilemma with regard to Taiwan is twofold. First, Beijing would like to achieve national reunification with Taiwan through peaceful means, but it must be prepared for war if Taiwan insists on independence from the mainland. Second, there has been a consensus among China's elite since 1978, when Deng Xiaoping began his reform and openness policy, that economic development should be the top priority for China. The modernization drive, however, has promoted greater nationalist sentiment among the Chinese people, making a compromise with Taiwan's demand for separation virtually impossible for any leader to grant.

China's fundamental concern is that Taiwan's prolonged separation may in fact promote its eventual independence. Thus, the PRC State Council issued a white paper on Taiwan in February 2000 stating that if Taiwan indefinitely delayed negotiations with the mainland, it would prompt military action.[10] Beijing's fears of indefinite delays were fanned by the victory of the pro-independence Democratic Progressive Party (DPP) candidate Chen Shuibian.[11] Chinese leaders became increasingly concerned about developments leading to independence and involvement by the United States and Japan.

In sum, the two hot spots of Taiwan and Korea have been contentious issues for the major powers for more than a century. The history-embedded analysis illuminates internal tensions and their effects on international relations, including triggering wars among the major powers in the region.

The National Interest–Driven Approach

China's policy toward Japan and its alliance with the United States have also been influenced by national interests. Since the normalization of relations between Tokyo and Beijing in 1972, which constructed the so-called 1972 System, Japan has emphasized its friendly relationship with China. Changes in China's Japan policy were motivated by a greater awareness of its national interests. In this case, China's modernization drive required close economic ties with industrialized societies, including Japan. Japan has become increasingly important as a trading partner for China. In 2004, China became Japan's largest trading partner, surpassing Japan's trade with the United States.[12]

The significance of the financial ties between China and Japan is evidenced by the fact that Japan is the main provider of official development assistance (ODA) to China; this aid started in 1979 and has helped China tremendously in its modernization drive, especially in meeting its infrastructural needs.[13] Japan's economic assistance was so influential in the late 1980s that China stopped mentioning Japan's military buildup until the revitalization of the U.S.-Japan security alliance and the release of its joint declaration in 1996. Beijing's perceptions began to change in 1997 with the release of the new "Guidelines for the U.S.-Japan Defense Cooperation," replacing those issued in 1978. China's key concern was the enlargement of the defense scope from the "Far East" to the "surrounding areas of Japan." In these circumstances, Japan promised to provide logistical support to American troops.[14]

According to Liao Xuanli, among think tanks in Beijing, there are three perspectives on this redefinition of the U.S.-Japan alliance.[15] First, military think tanks tend to take a negative view, arguing that the new guidelines would enable the Japanese self-defense forces to play a greater military role in the region; they also see the potential for U.S. and Japanese codomination in the Asian Pacific. The second group takes a more liberal view of the alliance. They think that the new guidelines serve a twofold purpose: they enhance Japan's military role, but they also contain Japanese military development and prevent Japan from becoming independent of the United States. The third group has adopted a more pragmatic view of the alliance. They see no threat in Japan's enhanced military role; they believe that Japan's role is defensive in nature—namely, providing logistical rather than frontline support. Furthermore, they emphasize the fact that economic interdependence is better than having an arms race in the region. Although there are differing opinions about the evolution of the alliance and the revised guidelines, the Chinese side has rarely cited the revival of Japanese militarism as a criticism, focusing instead on historical issues and the Taiwan Strait.

In general, the perception in China is that the new guidelines and the U.S.-Japan Security Treaty set up a "two-against-one" framework. The new guidelines alarmed Beijing because they touched on China's core national interest: Taiwan (elaborated on later). Therefore, from the national interest–driven approach, the U.S.-Japan alliance might be viewed as a threat. There are, however, different perspectives within Beijing's foreign policy apparatus, ranging from a negative, zero-sum assumption to a more pragmatic and positive win-win viewpoint.

The dynamics of Chinese foreign policy have been fundamentally influenced by changes in its domestic politics,[16] most importantly by the rising influence of nationalism. Since the beginning of the Deng era in 1978, Beijing has adopted reform-oriented and increasingly practical policies both internally and externally. Focusing on its drive toward modernization, China has completely changed its attitude toward such previously labeled "capitalist practices" as joint ventures, foreign investment, and foreign loans. With this change from a foreign policy based on ideology to a more national interest-driven approach, China has significantly improved its relations with the U.S.-led Western camp, including both Japan and South Korea.

Korea Policy

Changes in China's Korea policy were motivated by a greater awareness of its national interests. In this case, China's modernization drive required close economic ties with industrialized societies as well as with South Korea, Singapore, Taiwan, and Hong Kong. Beijing's first official step to enhance bilateral relations with Seoul was an agreement to set up trade offices in each capital in October 1990, leading to the normalization of relations between the two countries the next year.[17] South Korea has become increasingly important as a trading partner for China. In 2004, China became South Korea's largest trading partner for the first time, with bilateral trade reaching US$79.3 billion.[18] In the same year, China's trade with North Korea was a mere US$1.4 billion, despite a 35 percent increase over the previous year.[19] The difference in China's economic relations with the two Koreas is striking.

Beijing has strong incentives to develop better relations with Seoul, including the possibility of increasing China's leverage in dealing with the Korea problem and with East Asia as a whole. Despite being a long-time ally of the United States, Seoul has indicated that it would remain neutral in the event of a military confrontation between Beijing and Washington. As one U.S. official suggested, "Having good relations with both [Koreas] puts China in the best possible situation" in terms of world politics as well as regional affairs.[20] Since the beginning of the Deng era, Beijing's desire to avoid another major military conflict has given it a keen interest in maintaining a peaceful and stable environment on the Korean peninsula. China must take balanced actions toward the two Koreas.

Taiwan Policy

China's national interest in Taiwan takes at least two forms. First, since unification issues relating to Hong Kong and Macao were resolved in 1997 and 1999, respectively, reunification with Taiwan has become a top national goal. Second, ever since China's policy of reform and openness began in 1978, modernization has been a national priority, and Taiwan, as one of the four East Asian tigers, has the capacity to provide China with capital, technology, and markets. Further, because of their shared culture, Taiwan is in a position to provide the mainland with capitalist know-how to help China develop a market economy and integrate itself further into the world economy. Beijing thus considers Taipei critical not only to its national interests in terms of sovereignty and legitimacy but also to its economic drive.

To achieve its goal of national unification, Beijing has always maintained two different approaches—peaceful means and military force—to prevent Taiwan from gaining independence (*Taidu*). Cross-strait relations have been highly uncertain since Taiwan's presidential election in March 2000. But instead of political and military pressure to promote integration with Taiwan, as was the case in 1996, Beijing has increasingly relied on economic means. Whatever the outcome, Beijing's overall strategy remains clear. Over the years, the mainland has attracted significant levels of Taiwanese investment, and the total value of bilateral trade has increased dramatically. It is Beijing's hope that it can use economic means to promote bilateral exchange and integration, thus demonstrating its conciliatory position.

Beijing's reaction to the change of government in Taiwan from late 1999 to early 2007 can be characterized as a pendulum swinging between alarm and conciliation.[21] The highly publicized visit of Taiwan's two opposition party leaders, Lien Chan and James Soong, in 2005 indicated the beginning of a new stage in cross-strait relations. It clearly demonstrated Beijing's renewed conciliatory efforts to pursue unification through economic cooperation. Given the complicated nature of cross-strait relations, one cannot be overly optimistic, but it is clear that the danger of an all-out war across the Taiwan Strait has been significantly reduced.

To better understand this pendulum, one needs to analyze both hard- and soft-line views on national interests within the Beijing leadership.[22] Among hard-liners, there are general and genuine worries that Taiwan's pursuit of independence is likely to become more active under the new DPP regime. This deep suspicion has been strengthened by a series of official actions in Taiwan to emphasize its new identity. Some Beijing observers view these actions as incremental steps toward independence that can be stopped only by nonpeaceful means. From this perspective, a military takeover of Taiwan is seen as the likely approach and outcome, even if it risks intervention by the U.S.-Japan alliance.

In contrast, soft-liners generally believe that sufficient pressure has been placed on Taiwan—including the military means indicated in the February 2000 white paper—to ensure that Taipei will not make an official declaration of *Taidu*. Therefore, the PRC should emphasize economic integration and avoid making military threats toward Taiwan. In this way, China's modernization drive will continue, and economic development, particularly along the east coast, will not be damaged. Soft-liners tend to believe that the mainstream DPP leadership may have to modify its more radical positions and move toward the center. Soft-liners also believe that China's national sovereignty is the major principle at stake and that China would use military force if that sovereignty were violated. However, they emphasize the importance of first engaging Taiwan peacefully.

The Comanagement Approach

On a theoretical level, cooperation among states with regard to international relations requires three basic elements. First, there must exist a coalition of willing nations. Robert Keohane and Henry Kissinger both emphasize that willing countries must have overlapping national interests so that it is mutually beneficial for all to engage in cooperative efforts.[23] Second, there must be incentives to overcome differences in interests among countries, since cooperation is so hard to maintain.[24] Third, both Keohane and Stephen Krasner state that mechanisms and institutions must be established to act as vehicles to facilitate comanagement among major powers[25]—in this case, between China and the U.S.-Japan alliance.

Korea Policy

Since the inception of the six-party talks in August 2003, it has been clear that the governments of the United States, China, and North Korea are the major players. Tokyo and Moscow, though important, have played only minor roles, and Seoul has helped facilitate the dialogue between North Korea and the United States. The agreement made in February 2007 indicates a certain breakthrough and compromise primarily between those two nations. According to the joint statement issued on July 20, 2007, "North Korea confirmed its agreement to disclose all nuclear programs and disable all facilities related to its nuclear programs."[26]

Although it is still an uncertain, ongoing process, the result has demonstrated the usefulness of the six-party talks. As Christopher Hill indicated in February 2007, the framework of the six-party talks may continue to evolve into a more permanent mechanism for dealing with security issues and crisis management in Northeast Asia.[27] This development has vast implications for China's policy toward Japan and requires closer examination.

There is much common ground between Beijing and Tokyo in terms of the North Korean nuclear crisis. First, both governments would prefer a peaceful and stable international environment, especially on the Korean peninsula. As mentioned earlier, Beijing's top priority in the new century will continue to be economic modernization, which requires a peaceful environment. Moreover, the Chinese government would prefer to focus its energy and resources on settling the Taiwan issue and does not want a potential military confrontation on the Korean peninsula to jeopardize its position in Taiwan, as happened during the Korean War.

Second, both insist on a nuclear-free Korean peninsula. For Beijing, the main concern is not a nuclear threat to its own security; however, it may be concerned that a nuclear North Korea will encourage the Japanese to develop nuclear weapons. Tokyo, in contrast, has genuine security concerns about a possible nuclear attack by North Korea, given the long, hostile relationship between the two countries. Thus, neither the Chinese nor the Japanese want an arms race on the Korean peninsula.

Third, both governments view the six-party talks as an excellent vehicle not only for raising their international profiles in the region but also for solving their individual problems by simultaneously conducting bilateral negotiations with Pyongyang. For example, in preparation for the talks in late October 2005, President Hu Jintao visited Pyongyang and held lengthy meetings with Kim Jong Il.

Fourth, both governments have recognized the United States' special role in the region as a stabilizer. Neither country wants to challenge this U.S. position or withhold cooperation as long as the U.S. stance is in accordance with its own interests. Further, all the participants in the six-party talks recognize that this format is the only multilateral security forum led by both Washington and Beijing and that it may evolve into a new security framework (discussed later).

Despite their common ground, China and Japan differ on certain points. First, Beijing is much less inclined to agree with U.S. hard-liners that a regime shift in Pyongyang will completely solve the problem of North Korea. Tokyo is more or less in agreement with Washington in this regard. Beijing, however, has made it clear that it does not favor a quick regime change, which could lead to the total collapse of the government in Pyongyang.

The Chinese government fears that such a collapse would push even more refugees across the border into China, causing a security problem. As a result of the widespread famine in North Korea since the late 1990s, hundreds of North Koreans have already made their way over the Sino-Korean border.[28] Unfortunately, the refugees have little legal protection, and allegations of widespread abuse are common. Incidents related to the refugees have created diplomatic tension in the region.[29] Beijing does not want the situation to deteriorate further due to a regime collapse.

Tokyo has its own grievances with Pyongyang—namely, the North Korean abduction of Japanese citizens over the past few decades—making a hard-line policy toward Pyongyang quite popular among the Japanese. Japanese leaders and diplomats repeatedly raise this issue whenever they have an opportunity to meet representatives from North Korea, including at the six-party talks. But because this issue has no impact on China, Beijing has openly disapproved of Tokyo's attempts to bring the issue to this forum.[30]

There are also different policy preferences in China and Japan. Beijing has advocated a more patient policy toward North Korea, while Tokyo prefers to show its solidarity with Washington in taking a hard line vis-à-vis North Korea.

Additionally, it is obvious that the governments of China and Japan have different levels of political and economic influence over North Korea. With relations rooted in the Korean War, Beijing enjoys substantial economic leverage over North Korea. Japan, historically a colonizer on the Korean peninsula, is an easy scapegoat for North Korean propaganda. Nevertheless, Japan's importance is expected to increase pending its provision of ODA to North Korea.

Despite these minor differences, circumstances indicate that the common interests of China, Japan, and the United States will prevail, and the six-party talks will continue.

There is frequent coordination among the six parties. Beijing's shuttle diplomacy has been helpful in bringing the different parties together. More difficult is coordinating different positions, stances, and concerns. Fortunately, the common ground is large enough to overcome these difference, and all the concerned parties have been relatively well coordinated by the Chinese.

There are at least five ways to coordinate between China and Japan. First, there are frequent gatherings and discussions among the leaders of the countries, providing opportunities to adjust their policies toward North Korea. Leading politicians and officials other than the heads of state continue to meet and take advantage of these opportunities to discuss the issue of North Korea. Second, Beijing has fully utilized its shuttle diplomacy to coordinate the different parties' positions. Its envoys have paid periodic visits to Tokyo to brief the Japanese Ministry of Foreign Affairs and make preparations. Third, the Chinese government recently proposed setting up a strategic dialogue between China and Japan at the deputy foreign minister level.[31] General security issues, including North Korea, will be among the major points discussed. Fourth, frequent exchanges of information have occurred through diplomatic channels, primarily between the Japanese embassy in Beijing and the Chinese embassy in Tokyo. Fifth, frequent working discussions at lower levels of the governmental hierarchy have taken place between the two countries' diplomats. Of these five coordinating mechanisms, the most noteworthy is the forthcoming security and strategic dialogue at the deputy foreign minister level, which will certainly provide a new high-level forum to discuss issues of mutual concern, including North Korea.

Taiwan Policy

Although the Taiwan issue is of a different nature, a comanagement posture can also be discerned in the interactions between Beijing and Washington (and, to a lesser degree, Tokyo). The newly emerged comanagement approach to Taiwan between China and the United States is implicit at best, yet one can observe some subtle changes in Beijing's approach that suggest it has begun to move in this direction.

The first obvious signs of a willingness to comanage the Taiwan Strait came in December 2003 when Premier Wen Jiabao met with President George W. Bush in Washington to discuss Taiwan. The other clear official signal from Washington came in October 2004, when Secretary of State Colin Powell stated, "Those who speak out for independence in Taiwan will find no support from the United States." Powell made the U.S. position even clearer by saying, "Taiwan is not independent, it does not enjoy sovereignty as a nation and the two sides should improve dialogue" and "move forward to that day when we will see a peaceful unification."[32] This view reflects a detached policy toward Taiwan. Washington's clear statement and its willingness to comanage with Beijing have had an enormous impact on Taipei, effectively curbing the island's independence campaign. This was a huge step for the United States to take, as Beijing has long regarded Washington as a major obstacle to its reunification with Taiwan.

After the United States, Japan is perhaps the next most important international player in this "Taiwan game," for two key reasons. First, the historical legacy of Japan's colonization of Taiwan from 1895 to 1945 places Japan in a fairly awkward position with China, on the one hand, and it implies a "special relationship" between Japan and Taiwan, on the other hand. Japan has been careful not to offend China by openly including Taiwan in its military alliance with the United States, not only because of Japan's past colonial history but also because it recognizes that Taiwan is key to China's national interests.

Beginning with a state visit by Chinese president Jiang Zemin to Japan in 1998, however, bilateral relations deteriorated significantly. Tokyo received the message that Beijing was uneasy about Japan's treatment of historical issues and that Japan's cultural influence may be perceived as soft power in Taiwan. Japan has nevertheless made its position on the Taiwan issue clear. The Japan–China joint statement signed by Shinzo Abe and Wen Jiabao in April 2007 states, "regarding the Taiwan issue, the Japanese side expressed its adherence to the position which was set forth in the Joint Communiqué of the Government of Japan and the Government of the People's Republic of China."[33]

The second key element has more to do with the current agenda— namely, the U.S.-Japan Security Treaty and the 1997 guidelines. These guidelines practically spell out Japan's participation in any military confrontation between China and the United States with regard to Taiwan. The nature of Japan's participation is unclear; it may be strictly logistical, or it may include military combat as well. In either scenario, Japan's participation would almost certainly invite retaliation from China. Therefore, Japan would prefer to maintain the status quo—that is, the relatively peaceful separation between the mainland and Taiwan. Nevertheless, Taiwan's strategic position may assume greater importance in the global calculations of the United States and Japan if security in the region were to quickly deteriorate.[34] Obviously, the issue of Taiwan has its own strategic significance in Sino-Japanese relations.

Conclusion

The preceding analysis of China–Japan relations and the two countries' policies toward North Korea and Taiwan has presented a comprehensive picture of the major domestic and international issues facing the two governments. It has been argued that in addition to the traditional history-embedded and national interest–driven perspectives, China—and, to a lesser extent, Japan—has moved toward a comanagement approach in dealing with North Korea and Taiwan. This new approach to these two hot spots reflects China's increasing confidence in its foreign policy and its ascending influence in the international community.

It is clear that both North Korean nuclear power and Taiwan reunification are critical to China's and Japan's national interests and overall foreign policy strategies. Both are keenly aware of the key role played by the United States in dealing with these two hot spots. The PRC is expected to intensify its efforts to gain Washington's forbearance so that the United States will not play a one-sided role in the cross-strait relationship. Beijing has also taken great pains to sway Japan to China's preferred policy on Taiwan. This effort, along with similar attempts to gain the understanding of other countries and international organizations, such as the United Nations, will remain an important focus of Chinese foreign policy in the future.

The implications for international relations in the Asian Pacific, including the effects on power relations and the future directions of security arrangements in the region, are many. In the long run, the six-party talks may go beyond merely bringing the concerned parties to the table to work out a peaceful solution; they may represent a move toward the institutionalization of a new security framework in the Asian Pacific region.

China's main concern is the United States. It is known that there are hard-liners and soft-liners within the U.S. foreign policy apparatus.[35] Some in Washington advocate a "soft landing" in Korea—a gradual process of unification while the United States helps North Korea achieve a China-style economic reform.[36] Beijing has deep suspicions, however, and does not believe that the United States truly wants to solve the Korean problem.[37] But as one China specialist pointed out, "China cannot change the U.S. forward deployment or its web of alliances in Asia in the foreseeable future. Working with the U.S. has become not a choice but a necessity."[38] Consequently, the two countries must develop confidence-building measures and coordinate routine consultations over the issue of Korea. These mechanisms are extremely important to both China and the United States. The same considerations apply to the relationship between China and Japan.

There has been speculation that Beijing may use its advantageous position as host of the six-party talks as a bargaining chip in its relations with Tokyo. For example, Beijing may appear to be cool toward Tokyo's participation in the talks in order to encourage Japan to change its attitude about China. This kind of manipulation has not yet happened, for a number of reasons. For example, the six-party talks are still ad hoc in nature, and full institutionalization is pending. Also, the leaders in the six-party talks are China and the United States; Japan has played only a marginal role. Therefore, there is not much China can do to influence Japan at this point. It may nevertheless try to prevent Japan from playing a greater role in this important international forum, particularly if the negotiations become more substantial.

North Korea and Taiwan are different problems, but there are linkages between the two hot spots, even though the connections are usually not mentioned. Beijing has recognized that its own national interests require close coordination with the United States (and, to a lesser degree, Japan) to curb a possible shift in its Taiwan policy. One incentive for China's cooperation on the North Korean nuclear issue is Beijing's desire to gain Washington's support on the Taiwan issue. Therefore, Beijing has moved from being a passive player to being an active one to demonstrate its goodwill to Washington. At the same time, however, Beijing has been cautious in using the North Korean issue as a bargaining chip to push the United States on Taiwan, as the two carry different weights in China's foreign policy calculations.[39]

It is clear that a key factor in all regional conflicts in the Asian Pacific is how to manage the U.S.-China and Japan-China relationships. As a rising power, China is quite different from the other two nations, which are status quo powers that enjoy many well-developed bilateral security arrangements. With a new approach to its security environment, Beijing is increasingly inclined to work within multilateral security frameworks. From the Chinese perspective, the six-party talks on the North Korean nuclear crisis may develop into a mechanism for dealing with Northeast Asian security issues, just as the ASEAN Regional Forum and the Shanghai Cooperation Organization address their regions' security issues. On that front, Beijing has also worked with India and Pakistan to improve relations. Indeed, China and India held their first joint naval exercises in November 2003. A month earlier, similar naval exercises involving China and Pakistan were held.[40] More recently, China and India announced plans to join forces in 2005 to meet energy needs.[41] China has also looked beyond the region, cultivating its relations with Europe. Bilateral trade with the European Union is on the rise, reaching levels that match those of China's trade with Japan and the United States.[42]

It is important to pay attention to a positive trend toward the institutional development of multilateralism in the region, including incentives and other opportunities. Major players may wish to emphasize their overlapping interests as a basis for cooperation, rather than emphasizing their conflicting interests. As demonstrated by China-U.S. relations after the midair collision of a U.S. Navy surveillance plane and a Chinese fighter jet in 2001, the two great powers have placed their common strategic interests above concrete disputes. This has prompted unexpectedly close cooperation in a multilateral direction, as in the case of the six-party talks. It has also highlighted that it is crucial for the sensible development of a regional multilateral framework to include great powers in leadership roles. Although there are still no tangible results, the very fact that the major powers have come together to deal with the North Korean crisis is itself a success, providing a base for a multilateral security framework. This has laid a foundation for cooperation among China, the United States, and Japan in dealing with critical issues in the Asian Pacific. This new development may have a significant impact on the nature of the U.S.-Japan security alliance and China's policy toward it.

Notes

1. See Quansheng Zhao, "The Shift in Power Distributions and the Change of Major Power Relations," in *Future Trends in East Asian International Relations*, ed. Quansheng Zhao (Portland: Frank Cass, 2002).

2. These changes have been well documented by Liao Xuanli, *Chinese Foreign Policy Think Tanks and China's Policy towards Japan* (Hong Kong: Chinese University Press, 2006).

3. William Burr, ed., *The Kissinger Transcripts: The Top Secret Talks with Beijing and Moscow* (New York: New Press, 1999), 83, 92.

4. Kozo Mizoguchi, "China and Japan Pledge Closer Ties," Associated Press, April 12, 2007.

5. Hiroko Tabuchi, "Wen Calls 3-Day Japan Trip a 'Success,'" Associated Press, April 13, 2007.

6. George Nishiyama, "China's Wen Seeks to Charm Japan as Ties Thaw," Reuters, April 13, 2007.

7. Ministry of Foreign Affairs, "Japan-China Relations," http://www.mofa.go.jp/region/asia-paci/china/index.html (accessed July 29, 2007).

8. There are many studies analyzing the Korean War. See, for example, Allen Whiting, *China Crosses the Yalu: The Decision to Enter the Korean War* (New York: Macmillan, 1960); Bruce Cumings, *The Origins of the Korean War*, 2 vols. (Princeton, N.J.: Princeton University Press, 1981, 1990); Sergei Goncharov, John W. Lewis, and Xue Litai, *Uncertain Partners: Stalin, Mao, and the Korean War* (Stanford, Calif.: Stanford University Press, 1993); Jian Chen, *China's Road to the Korean War* (New York: Columbia University Press, 1994).

9. For an excellent analysis of the historical legacy of China's security concerns with regard to Japan, see Thomas J. Christensen, "China, the U.S.-Japan Alliance, and the Security Dilemma in East Asia," *International Security* 23, no. 4 (spring 1999): 49–80.

10. In the Taiwan white paper, the PRC government states: "If a grave turn of events occurs leading to the separation of Taiwan from China in any name, or if Taiwan is invaded and occupied by foreign countries, or if the Taiwan authorities refuse, *sine die*, the peaceful settlement of cross-Straits reunification through negotiations, then the Chinese government will only be forced to adopt all drastic measures possible, including the use of force, to safeguard China's sovereignty and territorial integrity and fulfill the great cause of reunification." See "The One China Principle and the Taiwan Issue," *Renmin ribao* [People's Daily, Beijing], February 22, 2000. The English version was reprinted in *Issues and Studies* 36, no. 1 (January–February 2000): 161–81. Previously, the conditions for China's intervention were a declaration of Taiwan independence or foreign power occupation.

11. Julian Baum with Dan Biers, "When a Giant Falls," *Far Eastern Economic Review*, April 6, 2000, 18.

12. "China Becomes Japan's Largest Trading Partner, Replacing the U.S.; Implications Are Not Limited to Economics," Foreign Press Center Japan, http://www.fpcj.jp/e/mres/japanbrief/jb_23.html.

13. Marie Soderbergh, "The Role of ODA in the Relationship," in *Chinese-Japanese Relations in the Twenty-first Century*, ed. Marie Soderbergh (London: Routledge, 2002), 114–29.

14. "Guidelines for the U.S.-Japan Defense Cooperation," September 23, 1997, New York.

15. Liao Xuanli, *Chinese Foreign Policy Think Tanks*, 131–34.

16. For a detailed analysis, see Quansheng Zhao, *Interpreting Chinese Foreign Policy* (New York: Oxford University Press, 1996).

17. For detailed analysis of economic relations between China and Korea, see Chae-Jin Lee, *China and Korea* (Stanford, Calif.: Hoover Institution, 1996), especially chap. 5.

18. Trade statistics are from the Korea Customs Service, 2004, available at http://english.customs.go.kr/kcshome/jsp/eng/PGAS301.jsp.

19. "North Korea-China Trade Surges," *Chosun Ilbo,* January 31, 2005, http://english.chosun.com/w21data/html/news/200501/200501310009.html.

20. Nayan Chanda, "Chinese Welcome North Korea's Kim, But Relations Are Subtly Changing," *Asian Wall Street Journal Weekly,* October 21, 1991, 24, 26.

21. For a detailed analysis of the evolution of China's policy toward Taiwan, see Quansheng Zhao, "Beijing's Dilemma with Taiwan: War or Peace?" *Pacific Review* 18, no. 2 (June 2005): 217–42.

22. This impression is based primarily on my participation in a number of international conferences held in the PRC between 2002 and 2005, during which I had the opportunity to discuss Taiwan with high-ranking government officials. In this chapter, I have kept the identities of these officials and scholars confidential. My knowledge of official lines on both sides of the Taiwan Strait has also been strengthened by my experience as an observer of presidential elections in Taiwan in 2000 and 2004.

23. See Robert Keohane, *International Institutions and State Power* (Boulder, Colo.: Westview Press, 1989), 138; Henry Kissinger, *Does America Need a Foreign Policy?* (New York: Touchstone, 2001), 152–53.

24. See Kenneth Waltz, *Theory of International Politics* (Reading, Mass.: Addison-Wesley, 1979), 106; John Mearsheimer, *The Tragedy of Great Power Politics* (New York: W. W. Norton, 2001), 373.

25. See Robert Keohane, *After Hegemony* (Princeton, N.J.: Princeton University Press, 1984), 244; Stephen Krasner, *Problematic Sovereignty* (New York: Columbia University Press, 2001), 182.

26. See "Six-Party Talks," http://en.wikipedia.org/wiki/Six-party_talks (accessed July 29, 2007).

27. Briefing by Ambassador Christopher Hill, assistant secretary of state, February 22, 2007, Brookings Institution, Washington, D.C.

28. Mary Jordan, "Fearing Deluge, Political Fallout, China Spurns Fleeing N. Koreans," *Washington Post,* April 14, 1997, A14.

29. David Kruger, "Diplomatic Chaos," *Far Eastern Economic Review,* May 23, 2002, 11.

30. "No Role for Japan at Six-Party Talks—Pyongyang," *China Daily,* http://www.chinadaily.com.cn/english/doc/2005-2007/20/content_461843.htm.

31. *Asahi Shimbun,* February 8, 2005, 2.

32. Colin L. Powell, "Interview with Mike Chinoy of CNN International TV"

and "Interview with Anthony Yuen of Phoenix TV," October 25, 2004, www.state.gov/secretary/rm/37366pf.htm.

33. Ministry of Foreign Affairs, "Japan-China Relations."

34. Robert Sutter, "Recent Convergence in China-U.S. Views—Rethinking U.S. Policy Options" (paper presented at an international conference on U.S. Taiwan Policy and the Dynamics of the Taipei-Beijing-Washington Triangle, American University, Washington, D.C., January 28, 2005).

35. For a detailed analysis and debate over U.S. foreign policy toward North Korea, see Victor D. Cha and David C. Kang, "The Debate over North Korea," *Political Science Quarterly* 119, no. 2 (2004): 229–54.

36. Selig Harrison, "Promoting a Soft Landing in Korea," *Foreign Policy* 106 (spring 1997).

37. Yu Meihua, "Xin shiqi Me-Ri dui Chaoxian bandao zhengce tedian jiqi zoushi" [The Korea policies of the United States, Japan, and Russia in the new era and future directions], *Contemporary International Relations* (January 1997): 33.

38. Suisheng Zhao, "China's Periphery Policy and Its Asian Neighbors," *Security Dialogue* 30, no. 3 (September 1999): 345.

39. Conversation with Chinese Deputy Minister of Foreign Affairs Zhou Wenzhong, Beijing, March 9, 2005.

40. "China Briefing," *Far Eastern Economic Review*, November 22, 2003, 29.

41. Diane Francis, "China, India in Innovative Power Play," *Financial Post*, September 8, 2005.

42. David Murphy, "It's More Than Love," *Far Eastern Economic Review*, February 12, 2004, 26–29.

Part III

CHINA'S REGIONAL RELATIONS

8. The Korean Peninsula

A Chinese View on the North Korean Nuclear Issue

Yufan Hao

History and geography have combined to make the Korean peninsula important to China's security. This importance lies not only in the peninsula's long common border with China's industrial heartland in the northeast but also in the convergence—and often the clash—of the interests of Russia, Japan, and the United States in Korea. For the last century, Korea has served as an area of conflict and an invasion corridor for these three powerful states. The Chinese were involved in the Korean War from 1950 to 1953, supporting North Korea after the United States intervened on behalf of South Korea. This, together with the close ties between the leadership of the Chinese Communist Party and the Korean Workers Party, which can be traced back to the 1930s, has reinforced the importance of Korea in China's policy calculations.

North Korea's recent development of a nuclear program has introduced elements of unpredictability and dilemma into Beijing's foreign policy concerns. Uncomfortable with Pyongyang's nuclear program, China joined the United States and other neighboring countries in an effort to stop the North Korean nuclear weapons program. North Korea's explosion of a nuclear device on October 9, 2006, put its relationship with China to a serious test, with Beijing publicly opposing North Korea's action. But just as people were becoming pessimistic about the denuclearization of the Korean peninsula, the United States and North Korea suddenly hammered out an agreement to freeze Pyongyang's nuclear program on February 13, 2007, in Beijing. According to the pact, North Korea would receive fuel oil, economic assistance, and humanitarian aid in return for shutting down and sealing its nuclear facilities within sixty days. However, when the April 14 deadline passed and no action had been taken by North Korea, people began to question its sincerity. What are the prospects for the denuclear-

155

ization of the peninsula? What are China's interests in this issue and in the region? How much can Beijing do to push for the nonproliferation of North Korean nuclear technology?

This chapter answers these questions by examining the North Korean nuclear issue and its implications for Chinese interests as well as Chinese policy toward the Korean peninsula. I argue that although there are still many uncertainties on the road to denuclearization, the pact signed on February 13 represents an important step toward that goal.

Background

To better understand the chances of actually implementing the deal reached on February 13, 2007, a brief review of the historical development of the issue, as well as China's role in it, is in order.[1]

North Korea's efforts to acquire nuclear weapons and develop ballistic missile capabilities can be traced back to 1980, when U.S. intelligence detected the construction of a new research reactor at the Yongbyon Nuclear Research Center, located about sixty miles north of Pyongyang. U.S. experts believed that this reactor could be used to produce plutonium for a nuclear weapon. With the help of the Soviet Union, the United States successfully pressured Pyongyang to accede to the Non-Proliferation Treaty (NPT) on December 12, 1985, and to allow the International Atomic Energy Agency (IAEA) to inspect its facilities. In return, Moscow promised to sell North Korea four light-water reactors for the generation of nuclear energy. However, Pyongyang found various reasons to delay the implementation of the agreement and later requested a reduction in U.S.–North Korean tensions as a prerequisite to its abiding by the agreement.

Meanwhile, North Korea quickened the pace of its nuclear program with the operation of a five-megawatt graphite-moderated reactor in 1986 and the construction of a fifty-megawatt graphite-moderated reactor at the end of the 1980s. President George H. W. Bush adopted a balanced approach of inducement and pressure when he announced that all land- and sea-based U.S. tactical nuclear weapons would be removed from overseas locations, including South Korea. In the wake of Bush's initiative, North and South Koreans announced the North–South Denuclearization Declaration in December 1991, which banned the development and possession of nuclear weapons, as well as enrichment and reprocessing facilities, and called for a North–South inspection regime to verify the agreement. Washington subsequently suspended its annual joint military exercises with South Korean troops to reward the relaxed situation on the peninsula. Soon after that, North Korea signed a comprehensive safeguard agreement with the IAEA, which took effect on April 10, 1992.

However, tension between the IAEA and the North Korean government mounted when the former attempted to inspect two underground sites that it suspected of containing waste from undeclared reprocessing. The North Koreans viewed these two sites as "military related" and thus beyond the IAEA's jurisdiction. In March 1993, North Korea suddenly announced its withdrawal from the NPT, claiming that its national interests were being jeopardized by U.S. military threats as well as U.S. efforts to manipulate the IAEA to gain access to North Korea's military sites.

Washington finally agreed to resolve the dispute through direct meetings with Pyongyang. Beginning in June 1993, the United States and North Korea entered into a seventeen-month negotiation that eventually produced the October 1994 Agreed Framework. Under its terms, North Korea would immediately freeze its reactors and related facilities and put them under IAEA monitoring. In return, the United States would organize an international consortium to finance and supply the light-water reactor project and supply heavy fuel oil to North Korea for energy use. As expected, implementation of the agreement proved to be complicated and difficult, with a delay in the light-water reactor project. In April 1996, the United States proposed a series of four-party talks—involving the United States, China, North Korea, and South Korea—to discuss the possibility of confidence-building measures on the peninsula and to conclude a treaty to replace the 1953 armistice. Little progress was made in several rounds of talks. However, North–South relations substantially improved after Kim Dae Jung was elected president of South Korea; he advocated a "sunshine" policy, with an emphasis on inducements when dealing with Pyongyang.

The historical summit in Pyongyang between Chairman Kim Jong Il and President Kim Dae Jung in June 2000 helped ameliorate tensions and gave North Korean leaders the confidence to cope with the missile proliferation issues raised by the United States. North Korea claimed that it would freeze the development, production, deployment, and testing of missiles with a greater than 500-kilometer (310-mile) range if the United States promised to launch a few North Korean civilian satellites every year at no cost. Although some progress was made during the discussions between North

Korea and the United States, there were major differences over a number of key issues. Pyongyang suggested that President Bill Clinton come to North Korea to discuss these issues, but domestic politics prevented Clinton from making the trip.

When George W. Bush took office in January 2001, there were divergent views on North Korea within the new administration. Many incoming officials disliked the 1994 Agreed Framework; they saw it as paying blackmail to a rogue regime that could not be trusted to honor its commitment. The neoconservatives in the administration argued that the United States should adopt a strategy of containment and isolation, hoping to remove the root of the problem by quickening the collapse of the Pyongyang regime.

Although no major policy change was made at the beginning of the Bush administration, the events of September 11, 2001, helped shift Washington's North Korean policy. The terrorist attacks galvanized fear of a new threat posed by the combination of international terrorism and the proliferation of weapons of mass destruction. Even though North Korea had not been linked to terrorism, Bush included it in the "axis of evil." This resulted in a deepening of Pyongyang's suspicions about U.S. intentions and led to the death of the Agreed Framework.

Soon, the United States began to suspect that North Korea was developing a plan to produce enough weapons-grade uranium for two or more nuclear weapons. After a successful summit between Japanese prime minister Koizumi and Kim Jong Il in Pyongyang, Washington sent Assistant Secretary of State for East Asia and Pacific Affairs James Kelly to North Korea to make it clear that the United States could not improve bilateral relations with North Korea until it dismantled its clandestine uranium enrichment program. To Kelly's surprise, his North Korean counterpart, Vice Minister Kang Sok Ju, angrily acknowledged the enrichment program and justified it as a reasonable response to the Bush administration's threats and hostility. Washington demanded that North Korea abandon its nuclear weapons program as a condition for any further bilateral discussions on improved relations. Pyongyang rejected that demand and made three counterdemands as prerequisites for negotiation: that the United States recognize the sovereignty of the Democratic People's Republic of Korea (DPRK), that it assure the DPRK of nonaggression, and that it not hinder the economic development of North Korea.[2]

As it had done a decade earlier, North Korea ordered the IAEA to remove all surveillance cameras and seals on the five-megawatt reactors and the other reprocessing facilities in December 2002, and it formally withdrew from the

NPT on January 10, 2003. As a result, Washington reportedly sent additional bombers and stealth aircraft to the region and put its long-range bombers on alert for possible deployment in the Korean peninsula.

Six-Party Talks

In the midst of these rising tensions and the obvious death of the Agreed Framework, Beijing stepped in. Having a vested interest in regional stability, China called for three-party talks in Beijing to resolve the issue. The talks were held on April 24–25, 2003, but they went badly. North Korea asked for a series of actions from the United States, including the resumption of oil shipments, a nonaggression pact, and normalization of relations between Pyongyang and Washington and Pyongyang and Tokyo as preconditions. Americans viewed these demands as totally unacceptable.

In July 2003, China joined with Russia to block action by the UN Security Council against North Korea. At the same time, Beijing tried to find a formula for multilateral talks concerning the North Korean nuclear issue. Finally, China persuaded North Korea to agree to six-party talks (involving the United States, China, Russia, Japan, North Korea, and South Korea) with the inducement of extra food and oil supplies.

The first round of six-party talks was held in Beijing in August 2003, and two other rounds were held in February 2004 and June 2004. In June, there were finally positive signs that the large gap between the United States and North Korea might be reduced. Yet before the fourth round resumed in July 2005, the North Koreans declared, "The DPRK had become a full-fledged nuclear weapon state, [and] the six-party talks should be disarmament talks where the participating countries negotiate the issue on an equal footing."[3] After a fruitless fifth round in November 2005, Pyongyang boycotted the six-party talks.

In July 2006, Pyongyang tested its ballistic missiles, including one Taepodong-2 missile. On October 9, 2006, the DPRK undertook its first test of a nuclear device, in open defiance of repeated warnings by the other five parties and the international community. This reflected a purposive, long-term commitment and the dedication of substantial resources to the development of nuclear weapons by a small, isolated, economically vulnerable, and self-referential regime.[4] It pushed China and Russia to agree to a UN Security Council resolution condemning the tests and threatening sanctions.

Even though the quantitative and qualitative characteristics of North Korea's capabilities remained to be determined, its possession of nuclear weapons had become a fact. Most international observers believed that North Korea would never agree to dismantle its entire nuclear inventory and weapons potential. Pyongyang, however, indicated its willingness to "trade," or to limit some of its nuclear activities in return for guarantees and commitments from external powers. Then on February 13, 2007, Pyongyang suddenly signed a pact with the United States under which it agreed to shut down and seal its nuclear facilities in Yongbyon within sixty days. The world was surprised at this news, and various speculations emerged. When the April 14 deadline for North Korean action passed, there was widespread pessimism in the world, with many believing that this was just another North Korean stalling tactic.

China's Interests

What are China's regional objectives and interests? How will China pursue its interests in the context of recent developments? Chinese policy toward the Korean peninsula is largely a function of its overall foreign policy concerns, which at present are based on the following five premises:

1. As the only superpower in the world, the United States is potentially a major security concern. Although direct military confrontation with the United States is unlikely in the near future, the issue of Taiwan—with the historical involvement of the United States and the current independent-minded leaders in Taiwan—represents a major challenge to bilateral relations and to the security interests of the People's Republic of China.

2. China needs a fairly long period of peace to develop its economy, solve its social problems, upgrade its industrial and defense capacity, and become strong enough to defend itself from external threats. For these purposes, Beijing needs to maintain internal political stability and harmony and a peaceful external environment.

3. Russia is not a threat to China and, in fact, is a potential strategic partner in the face of U.S. military and political pressure. Maintaining good relations with Russia is important to China's national interests.

4. Having a good, healthy relationship with Japan is important for the stability of East Asia, particularly at a time when Japan is readjusting to the

rise of China and is seeking political influence in the world. At the same time, China does not want to see the Japanese rearm themselves rapidly, because a militarily strong Japan is not in China's best interests.

5. Having a good-neighbor policy is important to let surrounding countries adjust to an ascendant China. At the same time, exploring economic opportunities with all its neighbors will benefit China's economic development.

These foreign policy calculations require China's policy toward the Korean peninsula to have three basic objectives: (1) to maintain regional peace and stability, (2) to denuclearize the peninsula to avoid a chain reaction of nuclearization in the region, and (3) to maintain the historically shaped special strategic relationship with the DPRK.

China's principal interest is maintaining peace along its border so that it can concentrate on its economic development and modernization program. Chinese leaders believe that China's future lies in sustained economic growth and in social and political improvements. In a carefully prepared speech at the Bo'ao Forum in April 2004, President Hu Jintao stated that China's goals for the first twenty years of the twenty-first century are to "quadruple the 2000 GDP to US$4 trillion with a per capita GDP of US$3,000" and to "further develop the economy, improve democracy, advance science and education, enrich culture, foster greater social harmony and upgrade the texture of life for the people."[5]

Accordingly, China has tried to cultivate good relations with the outside world, particularly because its growing economic and military capabilities have aroused so much apprehension. Indeed, within the span of a single generation, China has moved from near isolation to the hub of a globalized economy, from military obsolescence to a high-tech, professional force, and from hostility toward global institutions to active participation in multilateral organizations. As China's economic and military power has grown, it has expanded its influence not only within Asia but also in other regions of the world. People are beginning to wonder what kind of international behavior an increasingly powerful China will exhibit in the foreseeable future.

According to President Hu Jintao, "China will promote the steady growth of relations with major countries, stick to the principles of building friendship and partnerships as well as security and prosperity with neighbors while combining bilateral friendship with regional cooperation."[6] Since the United States has great influence on China's external environment, Beijing has sought every opportunity to develop a cooperative relationship with Washington.

In terms of Northeast Asia, China requires a peaceful relationship between the United States and the DPRK, even though it might be a cold peace with occasional problems. China does not want to see any trouble between the United States and the DPRK that might undermine its own relationship with the United States. Any developments in and around the Korean peninsula that might lead to instability would be regarded as adverse to China's interests. The reasons are obvious. A military conflict in the region would place China in an extremely uncomfortable position. Bound by its traditional relationship with North Korea, China would be faced with a dilemma: should it assist the DPRK if a conflict occurred without provocation by Pyongyang? If China chose to assist North Korea, it would inevitably damage China's cooperative relations with the United States and Japan and could compromise its economic modernization program. Therefore, the primary objectives of China's regional policy are to maintain the status quo and reduce tensions on the peninsula.

China believes that the best way to maintain regional stability is through inter-Korean dialogue and multilateral talks. China sees the improvement of inter-Korean relations as essential to increase regional stability and eventually create a relaxed environment for resolving the North Korean nuclear crisis. China's top priority in Northeast Asia is to actively engage in or even lead the regional security dialogue so as to make the six-party talks a security mechanism for maintaining regional peace and stability.

China's second greatest concern is the potential spread of nuclear weapons to Japan, South Korea, and ultimately Taiwan. China views this possibility with the utmost seriousness. North Korea's first nuclear test on October 9, 2006, sent a security shock wave across Northeast Asia. Regional powers such as Japan and South Korea scrambled to respond in the form of sanctions. In particular, China worries that an unstoppable North Korean nuclear program may push Japan to develop a nuclear program of its own. It is widely believed that Japan has nuclear weapons technology and enough uranium for hundreds of nuclear weapons. However, Tokyo prefers not to go nuclear for political reasons.

China is concerned that among the current non–nuclear weapon states in Northeast Asia, some "reversal" or "threshold" states might be provoked by North Korea to embark on their own nuclear weapons programs. As noted, Japan might be the first to reconsider its nuclear option, followed closely by

South Korea; this might lead Taiwan to develop an interest in gaining nuclear weapons capacity.[7] President Bush has indicated his concern and expressed confidence that Japan will not go nuclear. However, there is some willingness in the United States to exploit the so-called Japan card—that is, encourage Japan to break its nonnuclear stance as a means of punishing China for its failure to pressure North Korea to halt its nuclear program.[8] If Japan took that step, it would force China to reconsider the upgrading of its nuclear capabilities and doctrine in reaction to a nuclearized Japan and Korean peninsula. It would trigger an arms race in East Asia, which would be a nightmare for China's national security. Therefore, dismantling the North Korean nuclear program is in China's best interests.

Beijing's overriding security interests in Korea cannot be fully protected without a good relationship with Pyongyang. Even if regional stability were maintained, if North Korea (like Vietnam in the late 1970s) became hostile toward China, the consequences would be adverse to China's interests. In addition, the collapse of North Korea might result in millions of impoverished people pouring into northeastern China, which would upset China's domestic stability.

Among China's objectives, the most difficult one to achieve is maintaining its relations with North Korea in such a way that Sino-America and Sino–South Korean relations are not circumscribed. Twenty years ago, the cornerstone of China's regional policy was its relationship with the DPRK.[9] Today, the strategic importance of North Korea has declined. Beijing has also lost much of its leverage over Pyongyang due to its policies toward the United States and South Korea. Regardless of assurances by the Chinese leadership, North Korean leaders always cast a wary eye on Beijing's dealings with Washington, Seoul, and Tokyo. Fortunately, Pyongyang no longer has the Soviet card to play, as it did some twenty years ago. Yet the nuclear program gives North Korean leaders some bargaining power in dealing with China.

Therefore, Chinese national interests require Beijing to be actively involved in the North Korean nuclear crisis. China does not want to see nuclear weapons in the Korean peninsula; at the same time, it does not want to see any kind of destabilizing change in North Korea. Beijing would like to maintain its "brotherly friendship" with Pyongyang and continue to have the DPRK as a buffer state on China's border. To achieve that objective, the North Korean nuclear issue must be resolved in a peaceful manner that does not undermine the stability of the region.

Beijing's basic objectives on the Korean peninsula mesh well with those of Washington, Moscow, Tokyo, and Seoul. They all desire regional stability and have no interest in allowing tensions to escalate or radical changes to occur. However, Beijing and Washington differ on how to achieve stability. Before 2002, Beijing's position was to support a nuclear-free Korean peninsula achieved through peaceful dialogue. China opposed any U.S. policies that would topple communist control in North Korea. Privately, Chinese officials urged Washington to solve the dispute directly with North Korea and complained that the U.S. policy toward North Korea was too harsh and counterproductive. At the request of Secretary of State Colin Powell during his February 2003 visit, Beijing advocated three-party talks in April of that year. China's only role, however, was to play host while representatives of the United States and North Korea talked to each other in Beijing.

China has always advocated the resolution of international problems through multilateral cooperation and international organizations. As former vice premier Qian Qichen put it in 2004, "We should opt for multilateralism and give full play to the important role of the UN. Our world is one big family. Naturally, family affairs should be handled by all its members through consultations." The United Nations, Qian said, is "the core of the collective security mechanism and the best venue for multilateral interchanges." It therefore "should continue to play its important role in international affairs."[10]

It is widely believed that China has more leverage over North Korea than do any other countries in the world. Indeed, North Korea has close economic ties with China. From 2000 to 2005, North Korea's imports from China (including oil, pork, electronic gadgets, and machinery) more than doubled, totaling US$1.1 billion in 2005, while its exports to China (fish, low-grade steel, and minerals) increased more than tenfold, from US$37 million to US$499 million; this constituted more than half of North Korea's total exports and imports in 2005. Japan had been North Korea's largest trade partner in 2000, but it fell to the third in 2005, with a total of only US$200 million—far below the North Korean–Chinese total of US$1.6 billion. China supplied about 80 percent of North Korea's energy and more than 90 percent of the 576,582 tons of cross-border food aid to Pyongyang in 2005.[11]

However, China's influence over North Korea is a bit overstated. Although China holds certain economic leverage, Beijing gradually lost its influence after it established diplomatic relations with Seoul without insisting that the United States recognize North Korea first. In addition, Beijing has reduced its economic assistance to North Korea, forcing Pyongyang to appeal to the United Nations for emergency food aid.[12]

Prospects for the February 13, 2007, Pact

On February 13, 2007, a joint document was issued in Beijing. The DPRK agreed to shut down and seal, for the purpose of eventual abandonment, its Yongbyon nuclear facility, including the reprocessing facility, and it agreed to invite back IAEA personnel to conduct all the necessary monitoring and verifications. In return, North Korea and the United States would resume bilateral talks aimed at resolving outstanding issues and moving toward full diplomatic relations. The United States would begin the process of removing North Korea's designation as a state sponsor of terrorism and terminating the application of the trade-with-the-enemy act with respect to the DPRK. In addition, North Korea and Japan would start bilateral talks aimed at normalizing their relations in accordance with the Pyongyang Declaration, and the parties agreed to provide 50,000 tons of heavy fuel oil within sixty days as the initial phase of the provision of energy assistance to North Korea.[13]

This was indeed a significant step toward the denuclearization of the Korean peninsula—if it could be implemented. However, the international community had reason to be skeptical. Was the goal of denuclearization realistic or achievable in light of recent developments? Was North Korea's promise a mere stalling tactic, or did it herald the beginning of a strategic adjustment?

As the April 14 deadline passed, a new complication arose. According to the pact, North Korea would take action only after it had received its $25 million that was being held at the Banco Delta Asia in Macao. Technically, because no money had been withdrawn from those accounts, Pyongyang had not reneged on its agreement. The United States would permit the bank to release North Korea's US$25 million only in cash, but North Korea insisted that the money be transferred into other financial institutions so that it could be used internationally. Obviously, North Korea wanted a lifting of the financial sanctions imposed by the United States, but Washington was willing to release only the US$25 million in frozen funds that belonged to North Korea. Because of these differences, the transfer of the $25 million was delayed, turning into a test of mutual trust. At the time of this writing, North Korea had not taken any action to move the money and had expressed its willingness to have the money transferred to a bank in Russia, Italy, or the United

States. Washington, though reluctant to allow the North Koreans to use American banks, extended the deadline to the end of the year for North Korea to implement the deal. Significantly, however, North Korea demolished the cooling tower for its main nuclear reactor in Yongbyon on June 28, 2008, aiming to show that it was sincere about dismantling its nuclear weapons program. North Korea and the United States are following what diplomats call "action for action," a series of reciprocal concessions. On June 26, North Korea submitted a sixty-page report detailing the scope of its nuclear program, a step that the Bush administration had demanded as a prerequisite for removing North Korea's designation as a sponsor of terrorism. The controlled implosion of the reactor took place twenty hours after Bush announced the easing of sanctions against North Korea. "That will not be the end of the story," Secretary of State Condoleezza Rice said cautiously. "We also must deal with proliferation. We must deal with highly enriched uranium. We must verifiably end all of North Korea's programs."[14]

The key to the current impasse is in the hands of Pyongyang and Washington. North Korea claims that the justification for its nuclear weapons program is the perceived American threat and that its sole purpose is to deter a U.S. attack. Part of the reason for Pyongyang's pursuit of a nuclear weapons program is that its conventional weapons lag behind those of South Korea. Since an American attack would likely trigger a second Korean war, North Korea alleges that its nuclear program protects all Koreans on the peninsula. Kim Jong Il has argued that if the United States had signed a nonaggression pact and a peace treaty and normalized its diplomatic relations with the DPRK, Pyongyang would not have pursued the nuclear deterrent.

It seems that the primary reason for North Korea's agreement to reopen the six-party talks and sign the pact is to resolve its economic predicament by ending the financial sanctions imposed by the United States. In this sense, it may be a stalling tactic. But there is no practical need to seek a strategic change.

It is well known that North Korea has various economic difficulties. Because of its suspicions about China's reform and openness policy, North Korea missed a chance at the end of the Cold War to concentrate on economic reform. Instead, it focused on improving relations with the South and sought peaceful reunification of the peninsula. The nuclear issue raised by the United States slowed down the progress of Pyongyang-Seoul contact and forced Pyongyang to put security before economic development.

Since Kim Jong Il took full control, North Korea has pursued a policy of "military first," which has speeded up its economic plunge.

Of course, Washington's policy toward Pyongyang is an important factor in North Korea's economic stagnation. At the beginning of the twenty-first century, there were signs that North Korean leaders might consider changing their economic policy. Kim Jong Il visited China on an unofficial basis to study its economic achievements. Pyongyang actively sought diplomatic relations with European countries, demonstrating its eagerness to look outward, and some reform policies were introduced. However, the Bush administration's hostile attitude toward Pyongyang made it impossible for North Korea to adjust its development strategy. After that, the nuclear deterrent became the primary focus for North Korea's survival.

Therefore, a final resolution of the nuclear issue may present an opportunity for Pyongyang to effect positive changes in its internal and external environments. That is why Pyongyang's major objectives in the six-party talks are to obtain a formal nonaggression guarantee from and normalize relations with the United States. To Kim Jong Il, trading his nuclear program for the normalization of U.S.–North Korean relations may be a feasible strategic choice.

Now the question is whether the United States is willing to give North Korea a chance. Having rejected Clinton's engagement policy, the Bush administration adopted a high-handed policy toward Pyongyang. This has done nothing to solve the nuclear issue; it only makes North Korea more vigilant and hostile toward the United States, and it keeps Beijing in the difficult position of trying to deal with both countries.

At this point, there seems to be an equally important incentive for the Bush administration to bring the North Koreans back to the negotiating table. Obviously, Bush's war against terrorism has not gone well. The turmoil in Iraq led to the defeat of the Republicans in the midterm elections. The Democratic-controlled Congress passed a resolution calling for a timetable to withdraw U.S. troops. With the rising tension over Iran, Bush needs an agreement with North Korea to avoid being confronted with two nuclear standoffs at the same time. Bush needs some concrete results from North Korea, and in this context, North Korea's initiatives have paved the way for a U.S. policy change.

The major stumbling block in the talks so far has been that both the United States and North Korea have made extreme demands but failed to demonstrate good faith by considering a compromise. Confidence building is essential for both sides at this time. A settlement of the issue is needed, but it must be recognized that dismantling the North Korean nuclear program is a complex process.

China's options are limited. There are basically four instruments at China's disposal in dealing with the North Korean nuclear issue: (1) bilateral diplomatic persuasion of both North Korea and the United States to reach a peaceful settlement; (2) multilateral negotiations as exemplified by the six-party talks, in which China's prestigious position and its working relationships with all five parties make it a unique and effective leader; (3) leverage over North Korea as the most important supplier of energy and food to that country; and (4) the presentation of itself as a model of economic reform for North Korea.

China will continue to exert its influence and encourage Pyongyang to talk with the other parties on the nuclear issue and to open its economy to the world, as China has done. Beijing noted with approval the DPRK's recent plan to reform its economic system and to set up special economic zones. Even though Pyongyang is reluctant to give up its strategy of self-reliance, leaders in Beijing seem confident that they can influence North Korea's future economic orientation if China's own modernization program proves to be successful.

Conclusion

China opposes North Korea's pursuit of nuclear weapons, and it is likely that Beijing will remain active in resolving the North Korean nuclear issue. A sense of urgency to do so has been reflected in Chinese initiatives since 2003. Although there is a strategic consensus among all six parties on the goal of a nuclear-free Korean peninsula, most Chinese analysts believe that the key to the nuclear issue remains in the hands of the United States.

American hard-liners have never trusted North Korea and have always accused diplomatic give-and-take of rewarding bad behavior. They argue that Kim Jong Il duped President Clinton by halting the North Korean plutonium program while starting a covert uranium enrichment program. However, most Chinese observers believe that the United States bears the major responsibility for the current impasse. It is the United States that first reneged on the 1994 Agreed Framework, failing to reward North Korea's good behavior. Washington managed to freeze Pyongyang's plutonium program, which, if it continued to operate, would have generated enough plutonium for at least fifty bombs. Yet Washington failed to live up to its end of the bargain. Since Republicans gained control of Congress after the accord was signed in the mid-1990s, Clinton did little to ease the sanctions until 2000. Although the United States had pledged to provide two nuclear power plants by a target date in 2003, the concrete for the first foundation was not poured until August 2002. In addition, the delivery of heavy oil was seldom on schedule. Above all, the United States did not live up to its promise to move toward full normalization of political and economic relations.

In the mid-1990s, there was an illusion among Washington policy makers that the North Korean regime might not last very long. Therefore, many people in the Washington Beltway preferred economic sanctions and a naval blockade when dealing with Pyongyang. Yet neither China nor Russia nor South Korea nor Japan under Koizumi would go along; they all knew that such pressure would only provoke the North Koreans to arm rather than to collapse.[15] Therefore, changing the course in Washington was the key to resolving the issue, and only the United States' willingness to reconcile would alter North Korea's course.

However, there are some good reasons to look beyond what should have happened and focus instead on what is likely to happen with regard to the February 13 pact. Considering the domestic political climate in the United States and Bush's status as a lame duck, the president may have to make some difficult political concessions to escape his self-imposed policy corner with regard to North Korea. Obviously, President Bush has realized that his hardline strategy has failed, and he is ready to engage in diplomatic give-and-take. Since Pyongyang insists on the United States taking genuine actions to end the enmity, releasing the US$25 million from the Macao bank might give Kim a sense that the United States has indeed changed course.

Kim Jong Il may also have an interest in changing course, as the North Korean domestic situation continues to worsen. Nothing seems to be more important to Kim than the regime's survivability in a highly fluid situation. A change of course may help him ameliorate both internal and external threats. So far, North Korea remains committed to its promise, but the road to its implementation may be a series of zigzags. The prospect of successful denuclearization of the Korean peninsula in a peaceful manner is still within reach. The joint pact signed on February 13 has provided the guiding principles for further negotiations and implementation.

Because of the strategic importance of North Korea, China cannot treat

Pyongyang too harshly. North Korean leaders may not like some of the Chinese policies, but they recognize that they are largely dependent on China both economically and militarily; more important, China is the principal counter to U.S. pressure. This unavoidable dependence may breed frustration and resentment. However, China will continue to encourage North Korea to reaffirm, rather than renege on, its commitment to abandon its nuclear program. Yet, owing to the special nature of the relationship, China may be very cautious in handling the DPRK and may concentrate on its own domestic economic development. The success of China's modernization program would not only increase its economic leverage on North Korea but also have a significant effect on North Korea's international economic orientation and its foreign relations.

Notes

1. For a useful review of the North Korean nuclear issue, see *Disarmament Diplomacy with North Korea* (London: International Institute of Strategic Studies, January 21, 2004).

2. Ibid., 8.

3. Ralph C. Hassig and Kongdan Oh (for the Foreign Policy Research Center), *Prospects for Ending North Korea's Nuclear Weapons Program* (Philadelphia: Orbis, October 17, 2006).

4. Jonathan Pollack, "North Korea's Nuclear Weapons Program to 2015: Three Scenarios," *Asia Policy* 3 (January 2007): 105–23.

5. "Full Text of Hu Jintao's Speech at BFA Annual Conference 2004," Bo'ao, April 24, 2004, http://www.china.org.cn/english/features/93897.htm.

6. Ibid.

7. Christopher W. Hughes, "North Korea's Nuclear Weapons: Implications for the Nuclear Ambitions of Japan, South Korea and Taiwan," *Asia Policy* 3 (January 2007): 75–104.

8. Jim Lobe, "U.S. Neo-Conservatives Call for Japanese Nuke, Regime Change in North Korea," *Japan Focus*, October 17, 2006.

9. Yufan Hao, "China and Korean Peninsula," *Asian Survey* 27, no. 8 (August 1987): 862–84.

10. "Multilateralism, the Way to Respond to Threats and Challenges: Statement by H. E. Mr. Qian Qichen, Former Vice Premier of China at the New Delhi Conference," July 2, 2004, http://www.fmprc.gov.cn/eng/wjdt/zyjh/t142393.htm.

11. Jian Yang, "A Matter of Lips and Teeth: China and North Korea and the Prospect of the Six Party Talks," in *Whither the Six Party Talks?* ed. Yongjin

Zhang, NZAI Regional Analysis 2006/1 (Aukland: New Zealand Asia Institute, 2006), 27–34.

12. Antonaeta Bezlova, "Politics—China: Beijing's Influence over North Korea Overstated," Global Information Network (N.Y.), January 10, 2003, 1.

13. See http://www.state.gov/r/pa/prs/ps/2007/february/80479.htm.

14. *Los Angeles Times,* June 28, 2008, 1.

15. Leon V. Sigal, "North Korea to Suspend Plutonium Production," http://www.alternet.org/story/48617.

9. China's Dilemma over
the North Korean Nuclear Problem
Shi Yinhong

The history of the North Korean nuclear problem, from October 2002 to the present, is full of puzzles, many of which concern China's behavior. No one, not even policy makers themselves, can solve these puzzles before all the relevant data are available. However, careful observation, a historical and empathic perspective, and a strategic perception can help our understanding of the situation. If the primary task in studying China's foreign policy is to develop a preliminary formula for interpreting or even predicting China's policy orientation, the main target of this research is to identify the fundamental parameters of China's diplomatic behavior, consisting of three categories: perceived national interests, the dynamic situation, and the means available for policy implementation.

China's National Interests

The first of China's vital interests is peace—a cold peace (perhaps a very cold one) on the Korean peninsula and between North Korea and the United States, and an absolute peace between China and the United States in relation to the peninsula. These two great and increasingly interdependent powers cannot allow the North Korean nuclear problem to provoke any direct or indirect confrontation, which would have terrible consequences for bilateral relations. Thus, China's goal is to prevent the North Korean situation from deteriorating and forcing China to make a choice between one or another of its vital national interests.

China's second vital interest is the denuclearization of North Korea to prevent a dangerous chain reaction of nuclear proliferation and the possibility of a U.S. military strike against a North Korea armed with a "primitive" offensive nuclear capability. That would be a nightmarish situation for Japan and South Korea, which, stimulated by the nuclear "breakthrough" of North Korea, would sooner or later have to consider "going nuclear" themselves. That, in turn, would likely provoke North Korea to engage in nuclear "blackmail" against some other country in the region, causing great diplomatic and strategic problems for China. In addition, such an action by North Korea might lead to the collapse of its regime and massive chaos owing to severe economic hardship and international isolation.

Third, China has a vital interest in keeping its historically and geographically shaped "strategic relationship" with the Democratic People's Republic of Korea (DPRK)—a most "entangled alliance"—in today's dynamic and not so benign regional security environment. China would like to maintain the DPRK as a "strategic buffer zone," or at least it would prefer not to have a hostile and troublesome DPRK at its border. In other words, China must prevent the denuclearization process from seriously damaging China-DPRK relations, which would make China a loser in a major geopolitical game. A closely connected issue is China's concern about the possible collapse of the North Korean regime and the ensuing mass chaos in the northern part of the peninsula. This would force China to deal not only with a massive influx of refugees but also with a number of complex strategic and diplomatic problems. In summary, to Beijing, the best solution to the North Korean nuclear problem is peaceful denuclearization in such a way as to avoid losing its relationship with the DPRK or creating a highly unstable or even chaotic neighbor across the Yalu.

The Dynamic Situation

It is not difficult to identify and define China's three vital national interests. However, attempting to practice and pursue them simultaneously is a challenge. Therefore, Chinas must prioritize its interests, which is by no means an easy task, partly because of the dynamic nature of the situation in North Korea and the larger strategic environment. Strictly speaking, peace is China's top priority because of the enormous stakes involved. However, identifying peace as the first priority does not help in prioritizing China's other interests, particularly given the dynamic situation and the necessarily changing requirements. Moreover, although peace on the peninsula is an absolute demand by Beijing, preserving it an all-or-nothing proposition that permits no flexibility, achieving denuclearization and maintaining its strategic relationship with the DPRK have a more flexible room for definition and different possible "bottom lines." This means that China must try to balance the complex and changeable relationship between ends and means, desirability and feasibility.

During China's search for a peaceful solution to the North Korean nuclear problem, another important interest has emerged: to promote China's international prestige and diplomatic role. By organizing the six-party talks in Beijing, China has assumed a significant role in the United States' global strategy and increased Washington's dependence on China both multilaterally and bilaterally, acting as a leader and an indispensable middleman between the United States and the DPRK. This has been the most prominent manifestation of China's new proactive foreign policy style and its increasingly constructive role in regional security affairs and world politics. The international response to China's efforts has been quite positive, and during the second half of 2003 and the early months of 2004, China's critical role as the organizer and the main promoter of the six-party talks was met with worldwide appreciation.

However, three points should be emphasized here. First, China's interest in prestige and diplomacy is a by-product of its search for a peaceful solution to the North Korean nuclear crisis, which originated from the desire to avoid danger rather than obtain benefits. Second, until February 2007, the six-party talks produced no major breakthroughs. Even if the denuclearization of North Korea might be achieved, there surely will be enormous difficulties and uncertainties, so it is still too early to determine the overall effect on China's international prestige and other diplomatic and strategic interests. Third, since early 2006, from China's nearly absentminded involvement in the U.S. financial sanctions against North Korea to the Berlin talks between the United States and the DPRK in January 2007 and thereafter, China has largely lost its position as a leader and middleman owing to its deteriorating relations with North Korea.

Means of Implementation

China's policy has been shaped by Beijing's perception of the means available to pursue a peaceful solution to the North Korean nuclear problem. Four of these means have been recognized for a long time and are well known to every experienced observer of the problem: (1) Bilateral diplomatic persuasion of both North Korea and the United States to implement peaceful denuclearization. China's special relationship with North Korea has facilitated this effort (until 2006, as discussed later). (2) Multilateral talks among all the concerned parties, using the six-party talks as the institutional framework. China's prestige, reasonable policy position, and effective working relationships with the other five powers have been critical in these negotiations. (3) China's position of strength as the most important supplier of aid to North Korea, one of the major diplomatic partners of the United States, and the only available bridge between the two main antagonists. (4) Rare or limited use of leverage to discourage North Korea's dangerous behavior (generally before North Korea's nuclear arms test on October 9, 2006) and the use of massive economic pressure as a last resort.

Besides these four well-known means of pursuing a peaceful settlement, a fifth one emerged in 2004 (coinciding with the end of the second round of the Beijing six-party talks). Observers still do not have a rich understanding or a keen sense of this strategy, which can be called a "reformist" approach. The basis of this approach is the use of increased economic aid as a stimulant to encourage, assist, and tactfully induce or facilitate slow, cumulative economic reform in North Korea. The hope is that this will gradually change the DPRK's outlook on domestic and foreign policy, thereby increasing the stability of the regime and solidifying China's long-term influence on that country. Ideally, North Korea would voluntarily end its nuclear arms program or at least agree to a "rational and responsible" suspension of the program if the DPRK could not be assuredly denuclearized.

Up to now, the Chinese government has maintained a rigid stance, limiting the use of its substantial leverage to force the DPRK to denuclearize or to punish its provocative nuclear behavior—even after the nuclear test, which the Chinese angrily denounced as a "flagrant" or "brazen" action. China voted in favor of the UN Security Council's resolution against North Korea's nuclear test, but it has largely continued to provide economic assistance to North Korea, especially the oil supply that is indispensable to North Korea's military maintenance. However, withholding or substantially reducing the supply of materials not covered by the sanctions could be very effective in persuading North Korea politically.

Any good strategy, regardless of other imperatives for success, should (1) define its end in accordance with the available means, and (2) fully mobilize the available means to serve its end. To many observers (especially those outside China), what has been left to be desired most in Beijing's policy toward the North Korea nuclear problem is the latter, and this point of view is definitely plausible. More people have come to understand Beijing's weighty considerations in terms of protecting its third vital interest—its relationship with North Korea. Yet China's stakes in denuclearization, as well as its increasingly significant "joint stakeholder" cooperation with the United States and its regional diplomatic actions, have pushed China's policy behavior with similar force in a generally opposite direction. At the bottom there is an almost perennial strategic paradox: the need to balance opposing imperatives and deal with them using less efficient half-measures.

Actions and Sanctions

After a three-year stalemate in dealing with the North Korean nuclear problem (with the exception of the ambiguous joint statement issued on September 15, 2005), dramatic changes began to take place. On July 5, 2006, North Korea conducted a missile test, despite the inevitable international condemnation and China's advance warning.

Diplomatically speaking, the Chinese and South Korean governments were most affected by the ensuing crisis. Their policies toward North Korea suffered extraordinarily, and their relations with the DPRK dropped drastically to their lowest points in years. At the same time, it was obvious that neither Pyongyang nor Washington were heeding their longtime advocates in Beijing and Seoul (though on the part of Washington, limited respect remained), and their influence on these two main antagonists was remarkably reduced. In Japan, Prime Minister Koizumi's cabinet and hawkish forces within his Liberal Democratic Party headed by Shinzo Abe (the leading nationalist candidate to succeed Koizumi) fully exploited this "gift from Pyongyang." They used the "North Korea threat" argument— now much more plausible—to obtain political advantage at home and to promote Japan's military "normalization." The United States also benefited from North Korea's missile launching, but on a different front. Diplomatically, the United States was recognized as the international leader in dealing with North Korea for the first time since early 2003. Hard-liners in the Bush administration, who had long advocated hard pressure against North Korea, suddenly seemed to be proved correct.

In fact, U.S. financial sanctions against North Korea, imposed only four

days after the issuance of the joint statement on September 15, 2005, constituted the primary and direct cause of this missile crisis. The sanctions deeply
injured North Korea's ability to develop military technology, and undoubtedly they also hurt Kim Jong Il's personal feelings and probably his prestige
within the regime. As a result, extremists and hard-liners outnumbered any
would-be moderates ("moderate" in a very limited, North Korean sense) who
might prefer to conduct the diplomatic game for the purpose of "having their
cake and eating it" with regard to the nuclear matter.

The U.S. sanctions also affected China's capacity to influence Pyongyang's behavior and China–DPRK relations overall. Owing to U.S. persuasion and probably mild pressure, along with China's grave concerns about
North Korea's behavior, China was involved in these sanctions. Unfortunately, it did not foresee all the future political and strategic consequences
of its involvement, and as a result, China's use of economic leverage on
North Korea in this case was decidedly unstrategic. It would have been a
real coup if China had been able to reverse the ineffective policy of diplomatic persuasion, but to be successful, its strategy would have required the
following three elements: unilateral action, rather than collaboration with
the United States or any other countries; unpublicized diplomatic efforts,
rather than efforts publicized by other parties; and parallel pressure on the
United States for peaceful resolution, rather than pressure against only
North Korea. Because China did not follow this course of action, its exer-
tion of economic leverage had too high a cost: China lost its diplomatic
persuasiveness over Pyongyang and thereby indirectly and unintentionally
produced unwanted political effects and strategic consequences. On the
positive side, China's involvement in the U.S. financial sanctions and its
endorsement of the UN Security Council resolution substantially benefited
Sino-American relations.

Having totally ignored Beijing's advice to show restraint, the extremist
dynamics and gambling mentality in Pyongyang continued to drive North
Korea along the road of provocation. On October 9, 2006, North Korea
tested its nuclear bomb, followed immediately by grave consequences. The
nuclear test dramatically escalated the confrontation between the DPRK
and the United States and the DPRK and Japan, and it encouraged and
validated the hard-liners in those two countries. It gave the United States
and Japan perfect justification to dramatically tighten their squeeze and
expand their individual sanctions into collective international sanctions in
the form of the UN Security Council resolution. At the same time, North

Korea's extremist behavior and the shock of the nuclear test discredited the "soft" and extremely patient approach persistently taken by China and South Korea—both in international circles and among the Chinese and South Korean people. The nuclear test stimulated the right-wing forces in Japan and strengthened the Japanese nationalist orientation. (It even encouraged some prominent people to speak publicly and openly about Japan's possible "nuclear option" in the future.)

For China, the most negative effect of North Korea's nuclear test was the worsening of Pyongyang's attitude toward Beijing. China-DPRK relations fell to their lowest point in recent history; China lost almost all its diplomatic influence on Pyongyang, which was now nearly hostile toward Beijing. In a sense, however, China's extraordinarily angry and strong reaction was a short-lived aberration, lasting only ten days until Kim Jong Il hosted China's state councilor Jiaxuan Tang in Pyongyang on October 19 and said that he had no plans to conduct a second nuclear test.

Divergence in the fundamental approaches of the concerned parties rapidly reemerged after the UN Security Council resolution was passed on October 15. The hawkish and aggressive policies of the United States and Japan continued, as did the soft, appeasement policies of China and South Korea. Roughly speaking, a four-year-old pattern of fundamental strategic mismatch became even clearer. On the one hand, the United States and Japan had an essentially clear strategic end—forcing Kim Jong Il's regime to either surrender its nuclear arms program or collapse.[1] However, they lacked the minimal means to realize this goal because they had no control over North Korea's oil and rice supply. On the other hand, China and South Korea had sufficient means to force North Korea to abandon its nuclear arms program, but they lacked a clear strategic end—or, more accurately, they were unable to prioritize their competing strategic ends.

Developments in 2007

The situation in North Korea was clearly in a highly dynamic phase of drastic changes and surprising events. The next dramatic development occurred in January 2007 when the Bush administration reversed its position and held direct bilateral talks with North Korea in Berlin. This was quickly followed by the first major breakthrough in the crisis: the six-party accord of February 13, 2007. This agreement firmly and concretely obligated

North Korea to shut down and seal its nuclear facility at Yongbyon within sixty days and allow inspections by the International Atomic Energy Agency; in return, North Korea would receive certain economic, financial, and political rewards. The pact also included ambiguous and multiple-conditioned stipulations about the denuclearization of North Korea. For instance, it mentioned "discussion" with other parties about "a list of all its nuclear programs . . . including plutonium extracted from used fuel rods, that would be abandoned," but existing nuclear arms were not referred to.

Remarkably, the United States had suddenly become eager to reach an agreement—any agreement—with North Korea. It quickly lifted the financial sanctions, started diplomatic talks about normalization, and made optimistic statements about the prospects of achieving resolution. Some have even speculated that the United States is preparing to abandon the objective of the assured denuclearization of North Korea. What prompted this turnaround?

The only possible answer, or at least the primary one, is the domestic political situation faced by President Bush and his administration. Because of the terrible strategic failure in Iraq in particular and the Middle East in general, they are desperate to show the American people that they are still capable of successfully dealing with major foreign affairs issues. They hope to win public support for a possible conflict with Iran in the near future and for the Republican Party in the 2008 presidential election. The decline of neoconservative forces within the administration, brought about by the strategic failure in Iraq, undoubtedly makes this turnaround much easier than it otherwise would have been.

Why did North Korea also suddenly change its posture and language in Berlin in January 2007? Why was it suddenly so willing to reach an agreement on its nuclear program after declaring both domestically and internationally that it had become a nuclear power? Up to now, many seemingly overly optimistic people, especially those in the U.S. government, have avoided providing a plausible explanation. However, one of North Korea's purposes is to eliminate the justification for the collective and individual sanctions imposed by the United Nations and various states. In addition, North Korea hopes to induce, encourage, and strengthen the United States' inclination to find a way out of this difficult situation and finally abandon its quest to denuclearize North Korea.

North Korea's second and third purposes are related to China and South Korea, respectively. Pyongyang wants to demonstrate to Beijing that it is willing to soften its confrontation with the U.S. superpower and even pursue (and make Washington pursue) some rapprochement with Washington, even as it continues its semihostile attitude toward Beijing. Perhaps it is also trying to undermine an increasingly likely prospect—Sino-American comanagement of the North Korea problem. By suddenly changing its nuclear posture, North Korea also hopes to reduce the appeal of the Grand National Party— and its hard-line attitude—to South Korean voters. If the Grand National Party loses in the upcoming general election, the Pyongyang regime can be assured of Seoul's ongoing policy of excessive tolerance and appeasement. North Korea also intends to extract as much economic and energy assistance as possible, with minimal "strategic cost."

Conclusion

The major changes discussed here have already produced important consequences. One is that the North Korean nuclear problem has become, in essence (and also in form), a bilateral issue between North Korea and the United States, with the roles of China and South Korea remarkably reduced. China seems to have lost (at least temporarily) any leverage it had over North Korea, and the United States has in fact marginalized China since the two-party talks in Berlin. Because of this action on the part of Washington, the China-U.S. "joint stakeholder" relationship that emerged so rapidly and vigorously has been hurt with regard to one of the most critical issues—the Korean peninsula. We will have to wait and see how great and lasting this damage might be.[2] It should also be noted that U.S.-Japan relations may have been undermined to some degree, because Washington did not consult Tokyo in advance on its nuclear trade-off with Pyongyang and did not raise with any seriousness (if at all) Japanese concerns over the abduction of its citizens.

After the long stalemate, there has finally been progress in resolving the North Korean nuclear problem. This is a welcome development. But from a broader and geopolitical Chinese perspective, China is, in a sense, a loser, at least at present. (And the same might be said about the goal of denuclearization itself.) The poor state of China's relations with the DPRK is due in part to the basic nature of the Pyongyang government and its unjustifiably hostile attitude toward China. However, China's North Korea strategy—or, rather, the nonexistence of such a strategy—also deserves some of the blame. China should act accordingly and develop a sound strategy to deal with this problem, which is so important to its security, its diplomatic influence, and its people's national honor.

Notes

1. The primary difference between the United States and Japan is that the U.S. government is very much concerned with getting China "on board" by making some compromise or concession to China's position, whereas the Japanese government has no such concern and is preoccupied with winning public support through its hard-line posture toward North Korea.

2. Broader observations might lead one to conclude that the United State is inclined to weaken China's diplomatic influence in Northeast Asia. With the newly accomplished U.S.–South Korea Free Trade Agreement, if the pro-American Grand National Party can win the general election (and, based on current indications, it probably can), this inclination might be strengthened even further.

10. Changes in South Asia since 9/11 and China's Policy Options

Du Youkang

Since the end of the Cold War, and especially since the terrorist attacks of September 11, 2001, and subsequent developments, South Asia has witnessed significant and profound changes. These changes and their implications go beyond the region. China is closely connected with the South Asian subcontinent, so the situation there has a direct bearing on the security and stability of China's border areas and may even affect its whole peripheral environment. This chapter reviews the major post-9/11 changes in South Asia, analyzes China's opportunities and challenges related to these developments, and presents some possible policy options for China's dealings with South Asia in the near future.

Developments in South Asia since 9/11

In the wake of Operation Enduring Freedom launched by the United States in Afghanistan, a series of important changes have taken place in the international relations and geostrategic structure of South Asia.

U.S. Influence
The United States' ability to intervene in South Asian affairs has increased to an unprecedented level. After 9/11, U.S. military forces entered the South Asian subcontinent for the first time in history. The U.S. Central Command established and was permitted to use about ten military bases in Afghanistan and the surrounding area, which laid the foundation for the long-term stationing of U.S. troops in South Asia. With the Taliban regime dismantled and the operational base of al Qaeda's network destroyed,

183

the United States has become the dominant power in Afghan affairs. In addition to having access to military facilities, the United States has predominated in Afghanistan's peace and reconstruction process by providing resources and expertise in the areas of economic assistance, security needs, and infrastructure projects and by supporting the creation of a framework for a civil society and a democratic government. As a reasonable result of these developments, U.S. president George W. Bush and Afghan president Hamid Karzai jointly announced the creation of a U.S.-Afghanistan strategic partnership in May 2005.

Meanwhile, the Bush administration, in the name of fighting terrorism, lifted the sanctions imposed by the Clinton administration against India and Pakistan after their nuclear tests in May 1998. This removed the barriers between Washington and New Delhi and between Washington and Islamabad, pushing U.S. relations with India and Pakistan to new heights almost simultaneously:

Recent landmark agreements between the United States and India include the "Next Steps in Strategic Partnership" declared by President Bush in Washington and Prime Minister Atal Behari Vajpayee in New Delhi at the beginning of 2004. These steps expanded U.S.-India cooperation on a quartet of issues: civilian nuclear activities, civilian space programs, high-technology trade, and dialogue on missile defense. President Bush called such cooperation "an important milestone in transforming the relationship between the United States and India" and observed that the vision of a U.S.-India strategic partnership was "now becoming a reality."[1] In June 2005, U.S. defense secretary Donald Rumsfeld and India's defense minister Pranab Mukherjee signed a ten-year military agreement, indicating that their defense relationship had "entered a new era" and advanced to "unprecedented levels of cooperation."[2] One month later, President Bush and Prime Minister Manmohan Singh announced a "path-breaking U.S.-India civil nuclear cooperation agreement" that, according to Secretary of State Condoleezza Rice, "elevates the U.S.-India relationship to the new strategic level."[3]

Significant developments in U.S.-Pakistan relations since 9/11 include the signing of a ten-year "Acquisition and Cross-Servicing Agreement" in early 2002 to facilitate the reciprocal provision of logistical support and services between the two countries' armed forces, primarily during combined exercises, training, deployments, operations, or other cooperative efforts.[4] The Bush administration offered a US$3 billion five-year aid package to Pakistan when President Bush and President Pervez Musharraf met at Camp

David in June 2003. This aid was "tied to an annual review of Pakistan's cooperation in the war on terrorism, control of the spread of nuclear weapons and steps towards democracy."[5] When Secretary of State Colin Powell announced that the United States would designate Pakistan a "major non-NATO ally" during his visit to Islamabad in March 2004, it meant that Pakistan would "join an elite group of nations," including Japan, Australia, Israel, South Korea, New Zealand, and the Philippines, that "are granted significant benefits in the area of foreign aid and defense cooperation."[6]

Obviously, due to the U.S. military presence and Washington's closer bilateral relations with the major South Asian nations, the United States has achieved an unprecedented influence on the South Asia region.

South Asia's Strategic Significance

South Asia is home to about one-fifth of humanity, and it is an important region in terms of its strategic location, potential for economic development, and impressive military buildup. To some extent, it is "beginning to shift the balance of global power."[7] Since 9/11, it has become a primary theater of the global war on terrorism, thus having strategic implications worldwide.

The regional development with perhaps the most influence on the international structure is that India, as acknowledged by Rice, has become "a rising global power."[8] Since its economic reform in 1991, India's gross domestic product (GDP) has witnessed annual increases of 6 percent to 8.5 percent in recent years, amounting to 32 trillion rupees (about US$723.3 billion) in fiscal year 2005–2006.[9] Maintaining the third largest armed force in the world, India is one of the five military powers that possess both nuclear weapons and aircraft carriers. Its defense budget has increased steadily, amounting to 890 billion rupees (more than US$20 billion) in 2006–2007, a 7.2 percent increase over the previous year's budget.[10] Showing its political will to be ranked as a world power in the shortest possible time, India, together with Japan, Germany, and Brazil (constituting the G-4), formally staked its claim for permanent membership on the UN Security Council in 2004. As an emerging new power center, India may shift the balance of power in the region and remodel the existing structure of international relations.

It is interesting that the international status, reputation, and influence of Pakistan, India's longtime adversary, have also been rising visibly since 9/11. The United States has pressed for support, coordination, and cooperation from Pakistan in its fight against terrorism and extremist forces, its pursuit of the ringleaders of al Qaeda and the Taliban, its efforts to stabilize the Afghan situation, and its attempts to resolve the Iranian nuclear issue. As the second largest Muslim country in terms of population and the sole possessor of nuclear weapons in the Islamic world, Pakistan has a voice in Islamic and international affairs. In recent years, it has condemned Islamist terrorists for tarnishing the image of Islam, stating that they "need to be crushed with force."[11] Pakistan has also promoted reform of the Organization of Islamic Conferences (OIC) for a better understanding of the values of Islam within the Islamic community, and it has mediated the Iraqi problem and the conflict in Darfur, Sudan. Its strategic location also places Pakistan in a position of great significance. For instance, it is vital for the two proposed energy pipelines involving Turkmenistan-Afghanistan-Pakistan and Iran-Pakistan-India. If India plans to import energy from Central Asia or from Iran by land, Pakistan may be the only feasible route.

Indo-Pakistani Relations

Using the December 2001 terrorist attack against its Parliament building in New Delhi as an excuse, India deployed hundreds of thousands of troops along the India-Pakistan border and the Line of Control in Kashmir in an attempt to get Pakistan to stop supporting Muslim militants in Indian-held Kashmir. Unwilling to appear weak, Pakistan immediately moved its troops to the border areas. This resulted in more than 1 million troops from both sides converging along the border and exchanging frequent fire. With India and Pakistan spiraling toward conflict in May 2002, Indian prime minister Vajpayee stated during his visit to Kashmir that "the time has come for a decisive battle" and warned that the Indian army should be ready for sacrifices.[12] India and Pakistan approached the brink of war twice in 2002, and only the timely intermediation of the international community, especially the United States, defused these crises.

After nearly going to war twice, the governments of both India and Pakistan were forced to face some realities. First, with its greatly increased ability to intervene in South Asian affairs, the United States would not permit anything to hurt its core interests, especially once the war on terrorism got under way in the region. Second, a full-scale nuclear war between India and Pakistan could kill up to 12 million people and injure another 7 million.[13] With such terrible consequences, neither side would be a winner, and war was no way to resolve their conflicts. Third, their long-term confrontation—lasting more than half a century—had restrained their economic and social development, which could only have internecine results.

Based on these realizations, in April 2003, Vajpayee addressed a public meeting in Srinagar, the capital of Indian-held Kashmir, and extended "a hand of friendship" to Pakistan on his own initiative.[14] Pakistan's response was immediate and positive. Thus the two countries jointly initiated composite dialogues and a peace process. Since 2004, India and Pakistan have held several summit meetings as well as dialogues on the Kashmir dispute and other important bilateral issues. During these dialogues, the two parties have pushed the peace process from the confidence-building stage to the stage of resolving down-to-earth issues, despite their snail-paced progress in doing so.

Compared with previous ones, the current peace process reflects the political wills of both parties to settle their disputes through dialogues and achieve long-term peaceful coexistence. Doing so can only hasten their social and economic development, thereby making their respective countries more vital. However, the conflicts between India and Pakistan are deeply rooted, especially the Kashmir issue, which is closely related to their territorial disputes and their national and religious feelings and has become a sensitive domestic issue in the party politics of both countries. Because the leeway of both parties is limited, there is unlikely to be a comprehensive solution to this issue in the near future.

Nontraditional Security Issues

Since al Qaeda was routed and the Taliban regime was overthrown in Afghanistan, the war against terrorism in South Asia has entered a new stage. The main battlefield has moved to the tribal areas along the Pakistan-Afghanistan border. However, the remnants of al Qaeda and the Taliban, fleeing hither and thither in the tribal areas and beyond, put up desperate fights by colluding with local extremists and continuing their terrorist raids. Their targets include heads of state, prime ministers, military officers, government officials, and foreigners. Al Qaeda has even declared the government of Pakistan to be its main enemy, calling for its overthrow.[15] There have been several attempts to assassinate President Musharraf by terrorists who are willing to go all out to create chaos in Pakistan.

Meanwhile, revolts and violence against South Asian governments are rampant. Besides the uprising in Kashmir and the operations of violent separatists in India's northeastern states, an agrarian peasant movement called Naxalite has spread through eastern, central, and southern India in an attempt to seize political power through armed struggles, posing a serious long-term challenge to the federal government. The domestic peace in Sri Lanka, based on the 2002 cease-fire between the Sri Lankan government and the Liberation Tigers of Tamil Eelam, has been interrupted numerous times by the latter's violations, one of which resulted in the assassination of the Sri Lankan foreign minister in August 2005.[16] In addition, the acts of terrorism carried out by Jamaat ul Mujahedin Bangladesh have been escalating. In Afghanistan, more than 1,500 people were killed in terrorist attacks in 2005,[17] and Afghanistan's opium production that year totaled 4,100 tons, the income from which accounts for about 52 percent of the country's small GDP.[18] The growing problem of Afghan poppy cultivation and opium trafficking to world markets has become a major obstacle to the process of peace and reconstruction in Afghanistan and has also affected its peripheral regions and beyond.

Impact on China's Security Environment

As a neighboring country, China has been affected by the developments in South Asia since 9/11, which in general have been beneficial to China's security environment.

Improved Sino-American Relations

China is the sole big power that shares borders with South Asian countries, and it has a traditional influence in the region. Since 9/11, China has played an important role in supporting Pakistan's participation in the international antiterrorism campaign and in relaxing the tensions between India and Pakistan. Therefore, China and the United States share many common interests in South Asia, such as defeating international terrorism, preventing a clash between India and Pakistan, reconstructing Afghanistan, maintaining stability in Pakistan, and so forth. It has been encouraging to see the Bush administration paying so much attention to China's unique position and seeking its coordination and cooperation on relevant issues in South Asia; the two countries have even established consultations on the region's affairs. Given this new development, as well as the issues on the Korean peninsula, South Asian affairs have become another area of cooperation between China and the United States. These positive dynamics are likely to promote the further development of constructive and cooperative relations between the two countries.

Security and Stability in China's Western Regions

Since China began to implement its strategy of "Western development," the importance of stabilizing the peripheral regions of western China has increased. Before 9/11, there were two hot spots: Afghanistan and Kashmir. The Eastern Turkistan Islamic Movement (ETIM), a very dangerous organization that has plotted and carried out numerous terrorist attacks in the Xinjiang Uygur Autonomous Region and beyond, used to maintain major bases and special training grounds in Afghanistan.[19] Thanks to the war against terrorism in Afghanistan, the ETIM's major bases were uprooted, and the United States and United Nations both declared the ETIM to be a terrorist group in 2002.[20] Against the background of international cooperation in fighting against terrorism, the ETIM and East Turkistan terrorist forces suffered heavy losses—politically, psychologically, and in terms of personnel. This is generally conducive to stronger national solidarity, an improved public security environment, greater social stability, and enhanced economic development in China's western regions.

In addition, after 9/11 the United States played an active role in mediating and cooling down the crisis between India and Pakistan. It then implemented a series of preventive diplomatic activities and subsequently became a major promoter of the Indo-Pakistani composite dialogues on the Kashmir issue. Although the United States' purpose was clearly to protect its own strategic interests in South Asia, its actions nevertheless furthered China's general strategic goal of maintaining security and stability in its peripheral regions.

China-India and China-Pakistan Relations

After winning their independence, India and Pakistan were quite sensitive about each other's relations with third countries, especially with extraregional powers. Pakistan is China's "all-weather" friend; the China-Pakistan relationship "has withstood the test of time and the changing international environment"[21] and can be regarded as a model for contemporary state-to-state relations. The Pakistani government firmly supports the Chinese government's fight against the East Turkistan terrorist forces, and it was the Pakistani army that killed Hasan Mahsum, ringleader of the ETIM, in a joint antiterrorism raid along the Pakistan-Afghanistan border in October 2003. China and India, with their long histories and brilliant ancient civilizations, have enjoyed a friendly relationship for more than 2,000 years; yet there have been some setbacks, such as their border clash in 1962 and India's charge that the threat from China was responsible for its 1998 nuclear tests.[22] However, following Indian foreign minister Jaswant Singh's visit to Beijing in June 1999, China-India relations were back on the right track.

In the wake of improved India-Pakistan relations, China has developed its relationship with the two countries simultaneously and in parallel, yet separately. For instance, during Premier Wen Jiabao's visit to South Asia in April 2005, the Chinese and Pakistani governments signed the Treaty of Good-Neighborliness and Friendly Cooperation, laying down the legal framework for the China-Pakistan strategic partnership. A couple of days later, China and India announced the establishment of their "strategic partnership for peace and prosperity," thus raising the China-India relationship "to a new height."[23] The establishment of a Sino-Indian strategic partnership will certainly contribute to the process of building a multipolar world, enhance the developing countries' strength, and improve China's surrounding environment.

Strategic Stability in the Region

In the long-term conflict between India and Pakistan, the latter has appeared to be deficient in terms of economic and military potential and strategic depth. This situation became even worse with the imposition of sanctions by the United States and its allies after Pakistan's nuclear tests and military coup in 1999. When the Northern Alliance in Afghanistan came into power for a time, Pakistan worried about its location between the hammer and the anvil, and it was hard to give attention to both eastern and western sides, especially when India was endeavoring to strengthen its relations with the new Afghan regime and Central Asian republics. However, an unstable Pakistan is not in the best interests of any neighboring countries, including China and India, let alone the United States as it pursues its war against terrorism. Therefore, the Bush administration adjusted its South Asian policy after 9/11 by greatly promoting U.S.-Pakistan relations and pressing for the dialogues between India and Pakistan, which in turn improved Pakistan's strategic environment. This is advantageous to the peace and security of South Asia in general and to the stability of Pakistan in particular.

However, a variety of nontraditional threats to the social stability and economic development of South Asia cannot help but have some adverse effects on China by virtue of their transnational features. In addition, from a long-term perspective, there are some uncertainties about the United States' South Asia policy. So far, the United States has maintained its military presence and increased its input in the South Asia region. It seems that the U.S. objective is not only to meet its current need for antiterrorism activities but also to manage its geopolitical strategy in Asia. If so, this adds some uncertainty to China's security environment. Although Deputy Secretary of State Robert Zoellick proposed in September 2005 that China would be a "responsible stakeholder" in the international system, a series of strategic reports issued by the Defense Department shows that it still regards China as a "strong rival." In the 2006 *Quadrennial Defense Review Report*, China is exaggeratedly reckoned as having "the greatest potential to compete militarily with the United States and field disruptive military technologies that could over time offset traditional U.S. military advantages absent U.S. counter strategies."[24] Moreover, China is stigmatized as "generating capabilities that could apply to other regional contingencies, such as conflicts over resources or territory," in the Pentagon's 2006 *Annual Report to Congress: Military Power of the People's Republic of China*.[25] Meanwhile, the Defense Department has been transferring the strategic center of gravity to Asia with some major adjustments in military deployments in the Asian Pacific region. It also sponsored and presided over the Central and South Asian Regional Security Conference in January 2005, attempting to legitimize the stationing of American troops there.[26] The Pentagon's military adjustments and deployments may not necessarily be aimed at China; however, its real motivations remain ambiguous. Given this background, a long-term U.S. military presence in South Asia is likely to have a negative influence on China's security environment in the future.

China's South Asia Policy

At present, China is making use of its strategic opportunities to build a moderately prosperous society. Only in a peaceful international environment can China concentrate on its own construction and development. Therefore, a major challenge for China is how to design a judicious South Asia policy in accordance with the changing regional situation, allow itself to exploit favorable new developments while avoiding unfavorable ones, maintain a safe and stable security environment on the periphery of its western regions, and prevent damage to its strategic interests. Here, I present some options for China's South Asia policy.

First, based on the concepts of building "good neighborly relationships and partnerships with neighboring countries" and creating "an amicable, secure and prosperous neighborhood,"[27] China can continue its established South Asia policy, which has been highly effective. The essence of that policy is as follows:

- To develop good neighborly relations with all the countries in South Asia on the basis of the Five Principles of Peaceful Coexistence (or *Panchsheel*).
- To sincerely hope that the countries of South Asia can resolve their disputes and conflicts peacefully through consultation and negotiation in the spirit of seeking common ground while reserving differences, as well as seeking mutual understanding and accommodation.
- To contribute to the maintenance of regional peace, security, and stability by cooperating closely with all South Asian countries.
- To strengthen economic and trade cooperation with South Asian countries and promote common development in the region.

Second, with various kinds of nontraditional security threats increasing and becoming more transnational and interrelated, international cooperation is vital. World or regional powers such as the United States, Russia, and China, as well as the South Asian countries, have no major conflicts of interest in terms of fighting international terrorism, maintaining regional stability, preventing the proliferation of weapons of mass destruction, containing the spread of religious extremism, impelling the peace and reconstruction process in Afghanistan, eradicating arms smuggling and the drug trade, and the like. On the contrary, they must rely on one another to handle these challenges, and in fact, they have done so to a greater extent since 9/11. China could exploit these common interests and enhance the exchanges and interactions among these countries, thereby maintaining the momentum of cooperation. If so, it might be able to minimize any potentially negative impacts of a changing South Asian situation. In addition, when pursuing international cooperation, China needs to handle properly the three triangle relations: China-U.S.-India, China-India-Pakistan, and China-Russia-India. To a large extent, the security, stability, and development of the region depend on their interactions.

Third, China can take the initiative in regional cooperation among the South Asian countries. In recent years, as an active participant in and staunch supporter of regional cooperation in its peripheral regions, China has joined in such cooperative organizations as the Shanghai Cooperation Organization (SCO) and the Asia Pacific Economic Cooperation (APEC). In addition, it has participated in the Association of Southeast Asian Nations (ASEAN) plus China; ASEAN plus China, Japan, and the Republic of Korea; ASEAN Regional Forum; Summit of the Conference on Interaction and Confidence-Building Measures in Asia, East Asian Summit, and Asian Cooperation Dialogue. These groups and forums have created a web around China on the basis of multilateral cooperation in Northeast, Southeast, and Central Asia. It is noteworthy that the regular meetings of such regional organizations and forums give Chinese leaders the opportunity to get together with the leaders of other Asian countries at least once a year; this face-to-face interaction enhances communication and coordination, allows the development of more in-depth understanding, and facilitates the resolution of bilateral issues, thus improving China's relations with peripheral countries. Given the lack of such a mechanism between China and the South Asian countries, China has two options: (1) join the South Asian Association for Regional Cooperation (SAARC) as a formal member, not merely as an observer; or (2) encourage the SCO to upgrade the observer status of India and Pakistan to formal membership. Either option would establish a cooperative mechanism between China and South Asian countries—or at least the major ones—filling the vacancy of China's participation in regional cooperation on the subcontinent.

Finally, China could take advantage of its unique role in promoting the common development and common security of South Asian countries. With the overall improvement in China-India relations and the development of China-Pakistan relations, China has enjoyed its best relations with South Asia since the founding of the People's Republic of China in 1949. As part of the developing world, China and South Asian countries share the same or similar viewpoints on many international affairs; have broad and bright cooperative prospects in terms of economy, trade, and technology; and can draw lessons from one another and share their experiences with reform and opening up. Because the changes and developments in post-9/11 South Asia resulted from the interaction of internal and external factors, China and the South Asian countries would be well advised to take positive steps in advance to restrain potential threats to the region rather than reacting after the fact. China should play a more constructive role in some important issues concerning peace and development in the region.

Conclusion

It is encouraging to see successful international cooperation on many issues in post-9/11 South Asia. Changes in this region are ongoing—whether favorable or unfavorable to the relevant parties. A stable and healthy relationship among world or regional powers and among South Asian countries as well is essential for the region. China has proved itself to be a good neighbor, good friend, and good partner of the South Asian countries. It would like to cooperate with any interested countries, including the United States, to promote security, stability, and development in South Asia by adhering to the principles of consensus, equality, mutual benefit, and respect for the concerns of others. In short, China's development requires a stable and prosperous South Asia, and vice versa.

Notes

1. "President's Statement on Strategic Partnership with India," released by the White House Office of the Press Secretary, http://www.whitehouse.gov/news/releases/2004/01/20040112–1.html (accessed January 12, 2004).

2. Amelia Gentleman, "'New Era' on Defense for India and U.S.," *International Herald Tribune,* June 30, 2005.

3. Condoleezza Rice, "The U.S.-India Civilian Nuclear Cooperation Agreement," opening remarks before the Senate Foreign Relations Committee, Washington, D.C., http://www.state.gov/secretary/rm/2006/64136.htm (accessed April 5, 2006).

4. Staff reporter, "Govt Warned over [Military] Ties with U.S.," *Dawn,* February 12, 2002.

5. Anwar Iqbal and Masood Haider, "U.S. Package Tied to Certain Goals: Post," *Dawn,* June 26, 2003.

6. Shaukat Piracha, "U.S. Will Make Pakistan a 'Major Non-NATO Ally': Powell," *Daily Times,* March 19, 2004. President Bush designated Pakistan a major non-NATO ally of the United States in June 2004.

7. Richard A. Boucher, "Pursuing Peace, Freedom and Prosperity in South and Central Asia," remarks before the Senate Foreign Relations Committee, Washington, D.C., http://www.state.gov/p/sca/rls/rm/2006/61317.htm (accessed February 16, 2006).

8. Rice, "The U.S.-India Civilian Nuclear Cooperation Agreement."

9. Ministry of Finance, Government of India, "General Review," in *Economic*

Survey 2005–2006, http://indiabudget.nic.in/es2005–06/chapt2006/chap11.htm (accessed February 27, 2006).

10. Ibid.; http://indiabudget.nic.in/es2005–06/chapt2006/table1.1.pdf (accessed February 27, 2006).

11. Associated Press of Pakistan, "Terrorists Need to Be Crushed: Musharraf: Unanimity of Views on Issues with S. Arabia," *Dawn,* June 27, 2005.

12. Luv Puri, "Be Ready for Decisive Battle, PM Tells Jawans," *Hindu,* May 23, 2002, 1.

13. Ahmed Rashid, "12m Deaths in Nuclear War," *Telegraph,* May 28, 2002.

14. Shujaat Bukhari, "PM Extends 'Hand of Friendship' to Pakistan," *Hindu,* April 19, 2003.

15. Iftikhar Ali, "U.S. Report Calls Struggle against Terrorism 'Formidable,'" *Nation,* April 29, 2005.

16. E. Weerapperuma and Rohan Mathes, "Kadirgamar Assassinated," *Daily News,* August 13, 2005.

17. Office of the Coordinator for Counterterrorism, *Country Reports on Terrorism 2005,* 149.

18. Peter Holland, *Afghanistan: Counter Narcotics* (London: Afghan Drugs Interdepartmental Unit, 2006), 2.

19. Information Office of the State Council, "'Eastern Turkistan' Terrorist Forces Cannot Get Away with Impunity," *People's Daily,* January 22, 2002, 4.

20. U.S. Deputy Secretary of State Richard Armitage publicly announced in September 2002 that, after careful study, the Bush administration had "judged that the ETIM was a terrorist group and that it committed acts of violence against unarmed civilians, without any regard for who was hurt." See Zamira Eshanova and Bruce Pannier, "U.S. Adds to Its Terrorist List; China Benefits," *Daily Times,* September 3, 2002.

21. Ministry of Foreign Affairs of the People's Republic of China, "Premier Wen Jiabao Accepts the Interview of the Associated Press of Pakistan," 2005, http://www.fmprc.gov.cn/eng/wjdt/wshd/t190329.htm (accessed April 4, 2005).

22. In his letter to President Clinton, Prime Minister Vajpayee implicitly identified China as the main reason for India's going nuclear. For the text of Vajpayee's letter, see "Nuclear Anxiety; Indian's Letter to Clinton on the Nuclear Testing," *New York Times,* May 13, 1998.

23. Ministry of Foreign Affairs, "Premier Wen Jiabao Accepts the Interview of the Associate Press of Pakistan."

24. U.S. Department of Defense, *Quadrennial Defense Review Report* (Washington, D.C.: U.S. Department of Defense, February 6, 2006), 29.

25. Office of the Secretary of Defense, "Executive Summary," in *Annual Report to Congress: Military Power of the People's Republic of China* (Washington, D.C.: Office of the Secretary of Defense, 2006), I.

26. Lt. Gen. David Barno, opening remarks at the Central and South Asian Regional Security Conference, Garmisch, Germany, January 11, 2005.

27. Ministry of Foreign Affairs of the People's Republic of China, "Premier Wen Jiabao Attends the Leadership Dialogue of the East Asia Summit and Delivers an Important Speech," http://www.fmprc.gov.cn/eng/topics/wjbfw/t226328.htm (accessed December 12, 2005).

11. After the Anti-Secession Law

Cross-Strait and U.S.-China Relations

Zhidong Hao

The March 2008 presidential election restored the Kuomintang (KMT) to power in Taiwan. Since the KMT is sympathetic to improving relations with mainland China, and since it was voted back into power based on that platform, one wonders what this means for the future of cross-strait relations. Just three years earlier, on March 14, 2005, the National People's Congress of the People's Republic of China (PRC) adopted an anti-secession law with regard to Taiwan. The party in power at the time, the Democratic Progressive Party (DPP), had some fairly strong reactions to the law and continued to follow policies that would move Taiwan further away from the PRC. Does this most recent development mean that the DPP's course will be reversed and that the military threat contained in the anti-secession law will be eliminated?

The answer to that question is: not yet. Xu Caihou, one of the three vice chairmen of the Central Military Commission of the Chinese Communist Party (CCP), says that China will not change its current military strategy because a hostile relationship still exists between the two sides of the Taiwan Strait.[1] In other words, until a peaceful accord is reached, the CCP will not remove the military threat, and such an accord will not be easy to achieve. In fact, an examination of developments after passage of the anti-secession law leads to the same conclusion.

This chapter answers the following questions: (1) What has transpired since the PRC's passage of the anti-secession law. In particular, what were the effects of Hsu Wen Lung's statement and the visits of Chiang Bing-kun, Lien Chan, and James Soong to the mainland? (2) What does passage of the law mean for the status of relations among the major parties involved—China, Taiwan, and the United States? What cannot change, what can change, what is difficult to change, and why? (3) What are the possibilities for the future, considering all the developments in the past three years?

Whether there is war or peace across the Taiwan Strait concerns not only the involved parties but also the international community. It is thus important to examine developments occurring after the anti-secession law and to analyze what future prospects might look like.

Reactions to the Law

The anti-secession law created storms of protest in the days following its passage. The pan-Green camp in Taiwan, which is led by the DPP and favors distance from the mainland, staged a large-scale demonstration on March 26, 2005, to protest the law. The U.S. government declared that the law was not helpful.[2] The Japanese government indicated concern about developments across the Taiwan Strait, something it had not done before.[3]

At the same time, Hsu Wen Lung, a business tycoon, renowned adviser to the Taiwanese government, and longtime supporter of the pan-Green camp, made a statement supporting the anti-secession law. Hsu had just retired as chairman of the board of trustees of the Chi Mei Group, a large corporation with massive investments in China. In announcing his approval of the law, he said that Taiwan and the mainland were both part of China and, contrary to his previous stance, he was against Taiwan independence because it would only lead to war. He did not want to see the disastrous consequences of war befall the people across the Taiwan Strait, and he did not want his colleagues at Chi Mei to lose their homes.

On March 28, Chiang Bing-kun, vice chairman of the KMT, led a high-ranking delegation to Beijing for discussions about exchanges with the mainland; the issues covered included agriculture, mass media, and education. The pan-Green camp criticized Chiang for doing the wrong thing at the wrong time. Some even called him a traitor.

Meanwhile, another government adviser and business tycoon, Shi Chen-jung, resigned from his government post on April 1, 2005, saying that he wanted to remain neutral on the Taiwan-mainland dispute. This indicated that there might be a chain reaction of businessmen switching their political allegiance or at least remaining politically neutral—not a good sign for the pan-Green's cause of de jure independence.

Chiang's visit to Beijing was only preparatory to that of Lien Chan,

chairman of the KMT. Lien's visit in April 2005 marked a formal reconciliation between the CCP and the KMT after some fifty years of hostility.
The KMT hoped the visit would accomplish several things: the mainland's
recognition of the existence of the Republic of China (ROC), its acknowledgment that the PRC and ROC are different political entities, and its willingness to sign a treaty with Taiwan guaranteeing peace across the Taiwan
Strait for a period of thirty or fifty years. The actual visit yielded only
moderate, albeit significant, results. In the joint communiqué issued by
Lien and Hu Jintao, mention of the ROC was nowhere to be found. The
two sides stated only that they would pursue further exchanges and would
promote peace across the Taiwan Strait. Partly because Lien was afraid of
being accused of meddling in issues that could be decided only by the government, which would be against the law in Taiwan, the CCP and KMT
merely outlined their wishes for the future.

James Soong, chairman of the People First Party (PFP), made a visit to
the mainland in May 2005, almost immediately following that of Lien. He
was initially more ambitious, hoping to make China acknowledge in words
the existence of the ROC. During the first few days, he made a number of
speeches in which he mentioned by name the "Republic of China." However,
he soon stopped doing so, sensing that the CCP was not yet ready to make
any official changes. As it turned out, the six-point agreement between Soong
and Hu did not mention the ROC, either. In their joint communiqué, the two
sides outlined their positions: the Taiwan side had a different interpretation
of "one China," and the mainland side agreed not to talk about the political
meaning of "one China" while discussing other business. This is the so-
called 92 consensus (based on the positions of the two parties at talks held in
1992). Soong and Hu came up with another phrase to summarize the spirit of
the agreement: "two sides of the strait, one China." Although Soong said that
it meant "one China, two interpretations," implying recognition of the ROC,
people in Taiwan were not so sure, since the mainland government never
formally acknowledged the ROC.

What was the pan-Green's response, and especially the government's response, to these developments? First, to counteract the storms created by Hsu
Wen Lung and Chiang Bing-kun, the government issued a statement in April
that can be summarized as follows: (1) the DPP government would not retreat
from the position that the ROC was a sovereign state; (2) the government was
against the use of force to resolve the dispute across the Taiwan Strait; (3) the
various political forces in Taiwan should speak with one voice when talking to

Beijing; and (4) any changes should take place in the Beijing government—
that is, a change from an authoritarian state to a democratic one.

But there were two things the statement did not address: (1) If the DPP
government believed that the ROC was a sovereign state, did it acknowledge the ROC Constitution, which would include both Taiwan and the
mainland as part of China? If it did, there would be no problem initiating a
political dialogue between the two, since that was the only condition set by
the PRC for the resumption of talks. (2) In the April statement, the PRC
was referred to as "China," "Beijing," and "the other side of the Taiwan
Strait." But in his six-point statement issued soon after passage of the anti-
secession law, President Chen Shui-bian used the term "Chinese Communist Party" eight times and "China" only twice. The term "CCP" has been
used since the civil war, implying that the two sides are still one country. In
the ten-point agreement between Chen and Soong in February, neither
"CCP" nor "China" was used to refer to the PRC—just "the other side."
Did this mean that the Chen administration's China policy had vacillated?

The answers to these two questions are important because they indicate whether the two sides have any common ground on which to start political negotiations. This vacillation on Chen's part became even more
obvious in his reaction to Lien's and Soong's visits to Beijing. At first, he
was supportive of their visits and stated that he was using them to test the
waters. He even asked Soong to take a message to Hu. When Lien and Hu
made the agreement to promote cross-strait relations, Chen indicated that
the agreement was within the boundaries of the law. Chen's comments
came as a surprise to the pan-Green camp, which launched a campaign to
criticize Chen. Wang Xing-nan, a senior DPP legislator, observed that the
president should consider leaving the party if he did not agree with its ideology of Taiwan independence and with those who supported it.

Under vehement criticism from the pan-Green camp, Chen changed
course. He began to criticize Lien for siding with the communists against
Taiwan. He said that the 92 consensus of "one China, two interpretations"
was a lie and that Lien was not identifying with the ROC when he talked
about "identifying with this country." Chen also ratcheted up his criticism of
Soong, saying that it was wrong for Soong to say that he was against Taiwan
independence, because he was depriving the Taiwanese people of a choice.
He even wrongly accused Soong of meeting with Chen Yunlin, director of
the State Department's Taiwan Affairs Office, when they were both in the
United States. Such a meeting would be an indication of mainland China's

meddling in Taiwan's affairs. Though critical of Lien and Soong for not asserting Taiwan's sovereignty, Chen did say that he was willing to talk with President Hu Jintao about peace across the Taiwan Strait.

What did Chen's changes mean, then? Were they merely for the purpose of influencing the election for the special parliament on May 14? What do they imply for the future of cross-strait relations? These and related questions are discussed in the next sections.

The Possibility of Change in Cross-Strait and U.S.-China Relations

What do developments in Taiwan mean to China, Taiwan, and the United States? In this section, I discuss what changes can and cannot occur, and why.

China's Bottom Line and the Possibility of Change

When Wu Bangguo, chairman of the Standing Committee of the National People's Congress, announced the passage of the anti-secession law, the applause lasted for two minutes. This indicates the degree of support for the law among the delegates and the extent of mainstream Chinese nationalism.

The anti-secession measures—including both peaceful and nonpeaceful means—might be viewed as a response to the Taiwanese independence movement. In the decade before 2005, the independence movement made much headway under the leadership of Lee Teng-hui and Chen Shui-bian. In the 2004 presidential elections, the pan-Green side again won the presidency, and the DPP began to prepare for long-term rule over Taiwan. Plans were made to change the Chinese names of streets, corporations, and other entities into Taiwanese names. The Ministry of Education was proceeding to eliminate any references that Taiwan had ever belonged to China. These changes were under way even though Chen had stated both in 2000 and again in 2004 that during his term he would not declare independence, change the name of the country, revise the constitution, have a referendum on independence or unification, or abolish the committee on national unification or its guidelines. Thus, everything in Taiwan was changing, except for Chen's stated position—at least not until later. It was under these circumstances that China decided to push for the legislation against secession.

For many years, during the Deng Xiaoping and Jiang Zemin eras, the mainland Chinese government did not have an effective policy toward Taiwan except for the "one country, two systems" formula, which apparently would not work in Taiwan. Along with this fairly rigid policy was a rigid means of implementing it. For example, people still remembered former Chinese premier Zhu Rongji, who had warned Taiwanese voters in the 2000 presidential election to be careful what they did. His stern, dry face had been shown again and again on television. People also remembered men such as Sha Zukang, who had accompanied Wu Yi to the World Heath Organization meeting in 2003. Their stern faces and cruel words had also been shown repeatedly on television in Taiwan. They had rebuked the Taiwanese media's request for an explanation of why Taiwan could not even be an observer at the World Health Organization and had answered their questions with short, stiff, callous, undiplomatic words, such as "Who cares about you?!" "Didn't you see the voting results?"

Whatever Zhu or Sha (later appointed undersecretary-general of the United Nations) was thinking at the time, we do not know. But the result was that the Chinese policy toward Taiwan was not only unhelpful but also counterproductive. However, the four points made by Hu Jintao at the National People's Congress in March 2005 and the ensuing anti-secession law have made a difference. First, Hu made it clear that both Taiwan and the mainland are part of China. There will be no question of who devours whom. Second, the PRC would like peaceful unification with Taiwan on an equal basis. Third, the PRC would like to institute all kinds of exchanges with Taiwan, including the sale of Taiwanese agricultural products to the mainland and direct flights of passenger and cargo planes. Fourth, despite the previous three points, the PRC will not compromise on the issue of Taiwanese independence and will firmly defend its national sovereignty and territorial integrity. The anti-secession law further outlines the possible exchanges between the two sides. But at the same time, it states that if Taiwanese independence becomes a fact or is imminent, or if there is no possibility of a peaceful solution, the PRC will resort to nonpeaceful means to protect its national sovereignty and territorial integrity.

What does all this mean for China? One thing is unlikely to change: China will not tolerate Taiwan's independence and is prepared to go to war if necessary. This is true not only because of Taiwan's strategic location but also because of Chinese nationalism. The strategic importance of Taiwan is obvious from the following quote from the U.S. Department of Defense: "Many Chinese strategists and analysts view Taiwan as occupying a critical geostrategic location whose control would enable the PLA [People's Liberation Army] Navy to move its maritime defensive perimeter further seaward and improve Beijing's ability to influence regional sea lines of communication. Alternatively, according to some observers, permanent separation of Taiwan from the mainland would constrain China's ability to project power and provide the United States with a strategic foothold adjacent [to] China's coastal economic centers."[4]

Chinese nationalism will not allow Taiwan independence without a fight, either. Elsewhere, I recently analyzed two different kinds of nationalism: individualistic ethnic nationalism and collectivistic ethnic nationalism.[5] The former emphasizes individual as well as ethnic group interests, such as individual freedom, human rights, equality, and democracy; the latter emphasizes ethnic group interests as opposed to individual interests, including national interests such as sovereignty and territorial integrity. These two nationalisms exist in just about every nation, although one type may dominate. For example, in mainland China, collectivistic ethnic nationalism is now dominant. In Taiwan, both are emphasized. In the United States after 9/11, collectivistic ethnic nationalism seems to have gotten the upper hand as well. Even if China further democratizes, nationalism will still exist. For many, Taiwan is the last symbol of China's humiliating 150-year history. This is unlikely to be erased from the Chinese memory, so collectivistic ethnic nationalism will continue to be strong. The strategic location of Taiwan and the domination of this strand of Chinese nationalism will make it almost impossible for the PRC to give up Taiwan.

Although the Chinese view of Taiwan independence is unlikely to change, the way to unify the two sides may. In fact, the mainland has already experienced some changes—from the "liberation of Taiwan" in the 1950s and 1960s to the "peaceful unification of Taiwan" in the 1980s and 1990s. In 2000, the Chinese government was still claiming that there was only one China in the world, that Taiwan was part of China, and that the PRC was the only legitimate government of China. In the anti-secession law of 2005, a new principle was adopted: "there is only one China in the world, both the mainland and Taiwan are part of that China, and China's sovereignty and territorial integrity cannot be divided." Under this new principle, Taiwan and the mainland have equal status. "China" is used rather than the "PRC," implying that this will be a new and different China.

Nonetheless, there are still difficulties in China's efforts to unify the country. First of all, what will the future China look like? Will it be the same as the PRC? Should the ROC be recognized? What will its status be? Because the Chinese side has not clearly defined this future China, the Taiwan Solidarity Union, which is adamant about Taiwan independence, is able to claim that the PRC wants to devour Taiwan and that the future China will be the PRC. Former president Chen believed that the 92 consensus really meant "one country, two systems," or the model applied to Hong Kong and Macao, even though China has stopped using such language with regard to Taiwan.

The second difficulty is the mainlanders' lack of understanding of and empathy with the Taiwanese. They do not really comprehend Taiwan's political system and history over the past 100 years, in spite of apparent attempts to do so. Because of the various problems encountered in the Taiwanese democracy, for example, some on the mainland think that democracy is not so good after all.[6] They do not believe that people can have a different kind of nationalism, and they demonstrate prejudice and arrogance toward the Taiwanese. For instance, in March 2005, Foreign Minister Li Zhaoxing told Taiwanese reporters at the National People's Congress that he did not know who Hsieh Chang-ting (Frank Hsieh, former premier of Taiwan's Executive Yuan and the DPP's 2008 presidential candidate) was and that he was unaware that Taiwan even had a constitution. His face was shown repeatedly on TV ads rallying people to attend the March 26, 2005, mass protests against the anti-secession law.

Likewise, some people use derogatory words to refer to the new policy of working with those who are in favor of independence. They exhibit intolerance and arrogance and imply that there is only one way of thinking. It is certainly not democratic, and the lack of democracy has been one of the obstacles to China's unification. If Chinese mainlanders cannot overcome such negative attitudes toward Taiwan and the Taiwanese, whatever their political convictions, and learn to be tolerant of different opinions, peaceful unification will be difficult.[7] The cloud of war will still be hanging over the strait. The same applies to the Taiwanese.

Taiwan's Bottom Line and the Possibility of Change

There are at least two things that Taiwan is unlikely to give up: democracy and the ROC. It seems that once democracy has been experienced, it is hard to go back to authoritarianism or dictatorship. Since the 1990s, Taiwan's democracy has developed to such an extent that it would be impossible to revert to one-party rule. There are many indications that no single political force can decide the major issues in Taiwan without considering what others think. After the DPP won the presidential election in 2004, it claimed to be preparing for long-term rule, implying that it could do whatever it wanted, just like in a one-party system. The pan-Green camp thought that once it had the majority in the Legislative Yuan, it would be able to change the constitution and realize the goal of independence. But it did not win the majority there in the November 2004 election. And it lost the 2008 presidential election.

The storms created by Hsu Wen Lung, Chiang Bing-kun, Lien Chan, and James Soong were handled within the democratic political framework. President Chen and the pan-Green camp were not overly critical of Hsu, in spite of pressure from the opposition parties. In a democratic polity, people are supposed to be able to express their views on an issue, either for or against. Chiang Bing-kun faced legal charges for betraying his country, but the case was never tried. It would have posed a dilemma for the administration if it had been. If the Chen administration adhered to the ROC Constitution, which claims that Taiwan and the mainland are both part of China, visiting the mainland or even signing an agreement with it would not be a crime. But if the court interpreted the constitution to mean that these were two enemy countries, this would risk the use of nonpeaceful means by the mainland, since it would amount to a legal declaration of Taiwan independence. This may illustrate the limits of democracy, but it is democracy nonetheless. That brings us to the next common denominator, the ROC.

It is true that the majority of the pan-Green camp does not like the ROC, but many still think that it is at least useful in their negotiations with the mainland. The majority of the pan-Blue camp (represented by the KMT) not only identifies with the ROC but also believes in its role in cross-strait negotiations. When he was competing for the post of KMT chairman in 2005, Ma Ying-jeou announced that his candidacy stood for protection of the ROC from the military threat of the PRC and from the political threat of the Taiwan independence movement. One can safely assume that the majority of the people in Taiwan would like to maintain the ROC, for whatever reasons.

It is thus fairly clear that both democracy and the ROC are the bottom lines for Taiwan, just as unification is the bottom line for the PRC. If they want to develop a peaceful relationship in the future, both sides have to come to terms with the other's bottom line. If those bottom lines are unlikely to change, something else must, but what?

It seems feasible that the two sides could talk about their future political arrangement based on their respective understandings of the 92 consensus. In 1992, the two governments held talks through two semiofficial organizations: the Straits Exchange Foundation (SEF) in Taiwan, and the Association for Relations across the Taiwan Strait (ARATS) in mainland China. These two organizations actually reached a consensus on agreeing to disagree: one China, two interpretations. But with the Taiwan side claiming that the one China was the ROC, and the China side claiming that the one China was the PRC, the Chen administration did not recognize this as a consensus. However, it expressed a willingness to work out a way to start political talks between the two sides. President Chen proposed in 2004 that the talks be based on the 1992 Hong Kong negotiations, which was equivalent to agreeing to the 92 consensus without using those exact words. So a change in Taiwan's position on the one-China policy might be possible, even within the pan-Green camp—toward a position of one China, two interpretations—as long as the ROC polity is maintained.

Hsieh Chang-ting, 2008 contender for the presidency, said he believed in the "constitutional one China," a term that neither the PRC nor the DPP and President Chen would agree with, he claimed. In his campaign to obtain the DPP's nomination, however, Hsieh tried to negate his earlier comment. What he really meant, he said, was that he wanted to change the one-China constitution, but his defense sounded insincere. So, it seemed that Hsieh was more pragmatic about cross-strait relations. In addition, he has advocated the slogan "coexistence and reconciliation." Analysts in both the PRC and Taiwan predicted that Hsieh's pragmatism would win him votes in the 2008 election, since the moderates, even those in the pan-Green camp, would probably identify with him on these issues.[8] If he had won the presidential election, it is likely that the two sides would have started to talk about many things, just as President Ma Ying-jeou is doing now. Agreeing to the one-China principle was what the mainland required to open talks with the pan-Green camp, even if the PRC stressed "one China" while Taiwan stressed "two interpretations."

However, even if the two sides could find a way around the one-China principle, there are other difficulties. They come mainly from two quarters. First, as on the mainland, there is evidence of prejudice and discrimination in Taiwan. Second, there are some people who truly believe in Taiwan independence.[9] Several examples illustrate these difficulties.

One instance of prejudice occurred during the farewell press conference by Chiu Tai-san, deputy chair of the Mainland Affairs Council of Taiwan. Journalists jokingly asked Chiu whether the council planned to open jobs in the "eight professions" (i.e., the sex industry) to mainland spouses, since they would suit Taiwanese men's tastes very well. This can be viewed as offensive not only to Chinese women but also to mainlanders in general. In fact, mainlanders married to Taiwanese have to spend more years in Taiwan before they can get their resident identification cards than do spouses from other parts of the world; even then, they might still be watched. It is understandable that a country has to do everything possible to safeguard its national security, but to suspect every scholar, spouse, laborer, and even prostitute of spying for China is a bit too much. Hsieh Chang-ting would even go so far as to say that foreign spouses have lowered the quality of the Taiwanese. (Many wives of Taiwanese men are from the mainland.)

Such beliefs and acts of discrimination are easily translated into government policies, which may further impede negotiations and communication between the two sides. Like former secretary of defense Donald Rumsfeld (also mentioned in the next section), some Taiwanese believe that the mainland Chinese are not yet civilized. Chuo Jung-tai, former spokesman of the Executive Yuan of Taiwan, said that if China did not pass the anti-secession law, it might still have a chance to enter the civilized world. But once the law was passed, what was the point of talking with barbarians?

In Taiwan, the independence movement still has some potency, as shown by the reaction to Chiang Bing-kun's visit to Beijing in March 2005. Chiang was dubbed a "traitor," and the KMT was called "the representatives of the CCP" and "a party from outside Taiwan." The criticism of Lien and Soong by the pan-Green camp was less sharp, probably due to Chen's vacillation over the issue (discussed earlier), and it lasted only a short time. But these men have consistently been viewed by some as helping the communists take over Taiwan.

There are some people who truly believe in Taiwan independence, and in a democracy, one must allow people to have different beliefs. The task of respecting these different beliefs and devising a system that can accommodate the interests of most of the people most of the time is still a challenge for the politicians across the Taiwan Strait.

The United States' Bottom Line and the Possibility of Change
The United States has been a crucial factor in cross-strait relations, and we could not fully understand what is happening there without examining the

U.S. role. First, as in Taiwan, democracy and human rights are prominent U.S. values, although the United States may compromise if these values conflict with its other national interests. These values were especially prominent during the Carter and Clinton administrations.[10] But even in the current Bush administration of neoconservatism and political realism, one can see such idealism. For example, the U.S.-China Economic and Security Review Commission made the following recommendation in its 2004 report: "Congress should consult with the administration on developing appropriate ways for the United States to facilitate actively cross-Strait dialogue that could promote the long-term, peaceful resolution of differences between the two sides and could lead to direct trade and transport links and/or other cross-Strait confidence-building measures. The administration should be directed to report to Congress on the status of cross-Strait dialogue, the current obstacles to such dialogue, and, if appropriate, efforts that the United States could undertake to promote such a dialogue."[11]

In 2007, Thomas J. Christensen, deputy assistant secretary of state for East Asian and Pacific affairs, stated in September and December that the United States respected Taiwan's democracy and would like to see it prosper. In his September speech entitled "A Strong and Moderate Taiwan," Christensen said that the United States has "acquired deep admiration for [Taiwan's] achievements under difficult circumstances and a special concern for [its] democracy, freedom from coercion, and prosperity." He emphasized that the United States would like to see the two sides sit down and work out their differences in a peaceful and mutually acceptable way.[12]

Second, the United States is unlikely to give up its other national interests across the Taiwan Strait. Just as Taiwan is strategically important to China, it is also strategically important to the United States. Indeed, Taiwan played a major role in the Cold War and has been used by the United States as, in the words of General Douglas MacArthur, an unsinkable aircraft carrier and submarine base—in reality at one time, and figuratively now.[13] It continues to play a crucial role today, and the United States is unlikely to give up its sphere of influence. But for now, a peaceful and prosperous Taiwan is the United States' major interest. As Christensen said in his September speech, "As a Pacific power with global interests and obligations, the United States has a natural interest in peace throughout Asia." Indeed, with its hands full in other parts of the world, the United States would hate to get caught in a military conflict across the Taiwan Strait. That is why it keeps pressuring Taiwan and urging China to exercise caution and not provoke the other side by hostile measures. In his two speeches, Christensen almost pleaded with the Taiwanese people and the Chen administration not to rock the boat.

One might argue that the United States' primary objective is to keep the status quo across the Taiwan Strait. That way, it can use China to constrain Taiwan and Taiwan to constrain China for purposes of its own international and national interests. The United States certainly does not want confrontation in the region; however, it may not be happy with the prospect of an association between the mainland and Taiwan either. But if the two sides want to reconcile, the United States will have to accept it. Any association or reunification will have to be peaceful, and it will have to respect human rights and democracy. As long as these requirements are met, the United States cannot object—these are, after all, U.S. values. Just as the United States might sacrifice human rights for its other national interests, it might also sacrifice other national interests for human rights and democracy.[14]

Some things will be more difficult to change. For example, some hawks among the neoconservatives think that China is a potential "hostile hegemon."[15] They believe that China will seek to replace the United States and become the dominant force in the Far East. They are convinced that China's political and religious underpinnings, so different from those of the United States, will make it "a new evil empire."[16] Some are already thinking about how to fight China in the future. It is difficult to convince them that China will not become a competitor and that its rise will be strictly peaceful.[17] It is hard, too, for China to convince the world that it will not become a hostile hegemon.

These views also reflect the anxiety among ordinary Americans that China will become a serious problem, a threat, or an enemy state.[18] Indeed, "with the events in Tiananmen Square in 1989, public attitudes toward China changed from favorable to divided, leaning toward unfavorable— where they have stayed for over a decade."[19] Even the U.S.-China Economic and Security Review Commission stated the following in its 2004 report: "*Based on our analyses to date, as documented in detail in our Report, the Commission believes that a number of the current trends in U.S.-China relations have **negative implications** for our long-term economic and national security interests, and therefore that U.S. policies in these areas are in need of urgent attention and course corrections.*"[20] The commission recommended that Congress and the administration work jointly to assess developments across the Taiwan Strait and in Hong Kong and that Congress enhance its oversight role in the implementation of the Taiwan Relations Act. It also suggested a reassessment of the United States' one-China policy, "given the changing realities in China and Taiwan."

It will be very difficult to change the views of U.S. officials who see China as a potential enemy state and to change the negative views of ordinary Americans. China's reform and development will not be fast enough to change these opinions. Meanwhile, the United States will continue to base its policies, such as arms sales to Taiwan, on the belief that China is a potential enemy. The situation is not helped by comments such as those by Rumsfeld, who said that China is not a civilized country.[21]

Future Prospects

Having analyzed the bottom lines of each of the parties involved in cross-strait relations, it is now possible to speculate about what might transpire in the future. Will the parties be able to reconcile, and if so, how?

Elsewhere, I discussed the possibility of a hybrid of federation and confederation—a political entity in which both Taiwan and mainland China would share Chinese sovereignty and thus each lose some of it. For example, the PRC has to agree to the ROC's seat in the United Nations, which would be characteristic of a confederation, with each state maintaining its own sovereignty. But the ROC has to promise, constitutionally, not to break away from China, which would be characteristic of a federation, with each state being part of the nation and sharing sovereignty.[22]

This means that the PRC has to clearly define China primarily as a historical and cultural entity, and it has to recognize the ROC. On that basis, the two sides can negotiate a hybrid of federation and confederation that is democratic and that respects human rights. The mainland has to realize that the two major obstacles in cross-strait relations are the lack of democracy in the PRC and its nonrecognition of the ROC's existence. Both give the Taiwan independence movement an excuse to persist. It is ironic that both the PRC and the Taiwan independence movement want to get rid of the ROC. Even if only for that reason, the PRC should recognize the ROC. By doing so, the mainland Chinese would go a long way toward fighting prejudice and discrimination. By doing all these things, the PRC would give substance to its statement that both the mainland and Taiwan belong to one China and that anything can be discussed under that principle.

On the Taiwanese part, reconciliation would mean that both the pan-Blue and pan-Green camps recognize the ROC as their common denominator, and they define China as a cultural and historical entity. Or they could simply acknowledge the ROC's constitutional China, as Hsieh Chang-ting has done. On that basis, they could negotiate a hybrid of federation and confederation that would be democratic and respectful of human rights. This would be in line with the Taiwanese adherence to the ROC. And it would be in line with the pan-Green's claim that it wants to build Taiwan into a democratic, sovereign, and great country, even if it is a "country within a country." In future negotiations with China, whichever party is involved, it needs to make clear what it wants out of the relationship. In addition, the Taiwanese have to overcome their prejudices against the mainlanders. Only when they have done these things will there be a possibility of reconciliation.

For the United States, it is important that the administration adhere to the principles of human rights, democracy, and peaceful resolution. It has to be prepared to give up its scheme of using Taiwan to contain the mainland if Taiwan and the mainland unify to the satisfaction of both parties. Although eliminating U.S. prejudices against China depends, to some extent, on improvements by the Chinese, Americans have to realize that this is a problem that must be dealt with.

Conclusion

The anti-secession law might have led to crisis, but there is opportunity as well. The bottom line of each party has become clearer, and political entrepreneurs have an opportunity to build a peaceful relationship based on those bottom lines.

In Taiwan, the independence movement seemed to have picked up momentum after passage of the law. The government abolished the National Unification Council and the Guidelines for National Unification in early 2006. In early 2007, President Chen asserted that Taiwan wanted independence, name rectification, a new constitution, and development. Some of Chiang Kai-shek's statues were removed or demolished, and the Chiang Kai-shek mausoleum in Taipei was turned into a democracy memorial hall. Despite the opposition of the United States—as embodied in the repeated pleas by Christensen, as well as by chairman Raymond Burghardt and director Stephen

Young of the American Institute in Taiwan—the Chen administration insisted on a referendum on UN membership under the name of Taiwan.[23]

On a positive note, further exchanges between the KMT and the CCP have softened the hostility inherent in the mainland's anti-secession law. The KMT has continued to have economic forums with the CCP government every year, and many Taiwanese attend the annual symposium on cross-strait issues. Other exchanges, academic or otherwise, have also allowed the two sides to better understand each other. In addition, the KMT won the 2008 presidential election. Even the DPP has been conciliatory on occasion, and the contradictions and uncertainties of its policies have already been discussed. In Taiwan, although the forces pushing Taiwan away from China and the forces pulling Taiwan toward it may be equally strong, the tendency may favor reconciliation, despite the various provocative initiatives of the independence movement.

In China, after passage of the anti-secession law, the CCP government sped up its efforts toward reconciliation. As promised in the law, the CCP government is prepared to do anything to promote peace and prosperity across the Taiwan Strait. For example, it bought agricultural products from Taiwan when the latter had a problem selling them. After its talks with the KMT, the CCP implemented various beneficial policies toward Taiwanese seeking jobs in China, and it decided to allow its citizens to visit Taiwan and study in its universities.

Most important, ongoing exchanges between the two sides have changed the mainlanders' attitude toward Taiwan; hostility has been reduced. For example, according to a national survey, before KMT representatives visited the mainland in 2005, 13 percent of respondents thought that violence should be used to take Taiwan. After Lien's and Soong's visits and the ensuing exchanges, only 5 percent thought so.[24] In addition, government officials no longer make statements, like those of Li Zhaoxing or Sha Zukang, that appear to be insensitive to Taiwanese feelings.

Nonetheless, difficulties still abound in cross-strait relations. The anti-secession law reveals the bottom line of the Chinese government and stipulates that force is still possible. Events of the past three years seem to indicate that the Taiwan independence movement is still strong, so war is still possible, as I stated at the beginning of this chapter. In short, the controversial anti-secession law has created an opportunity of reconciliation as well as a crisis of war. War or peace, however, still depends on the will and skills of the political entrepreneurs on both sides of the strait, as well as the role of the United States. We will just have to wait and see what happens now that the KMT is in power.

Notes

1. See "The Vice Chair of the Military Committee of the Central Party Committee: China Will Not Lower the Military Force against Taiwan," *United Daily*, July 3, 2008, http://udn.com/.

2. Scott McClellan, President Bush's chief spokesman, said, "We view the adoption of the anti-secession law as unfortunate. It does not serve the purpose of peace and stability in the Taiwan Strait." See Jim Yardley, "U.S. Is Displeased with China's Taiwan Bill," *New York Times*, March 14, 2005. I consulted a number of newspaper reports on developments across the Taiwan Strait. The electronic versions of these articles can be found at www.nytimes.com/, taiwandaily.com.tw/ (the newspaper no longer exists), www.libertytimes.com.tw/, udn.com/, and news.chinatimes.com.tw/.

3. See Yong Xue, "Is the Empire Striking Back?" *New York Times*, March 16, 2005, op-ed.

4. See U.S. Department of Defense, "Annual Report on the Military Power of the People's Republic of China," May 28, 2004, http://www.defenselink.mil/pubs/d20040528PRC.pdf (accessed January 28, 2005).

5. See Zhidong Hao, "Between War and Peace: The Role of Nationalism in China's U.S. Policy-Making with Regard to Taiwan," in *China's Foreign Policy Making: Societal Force and Chinese American Policy*, ed. Yufan Hao and Lin Su (London: Ashgate Publishing, 2005).

6. For the distrust of democracy, see Chen Ping's interview with Cheng Siwei, vice chairman of the Standing Committee of the National People's Congress, broadcast on Sun TV on August 5, 2006. Chen Ping is the host of a program called *The Economist* on Chinese TV.

7. For the same point, see Zhidong Hao, "Obstacles to Integration: What Would It Take to Reconcile People on the Two Sides of the Taiwan Strait?" *Issues and Studies* 1 (March 2006): 47–80.

8. See Ong Hwee Hwee, "Frank Hsieh: Taiwan's Comeback Kid," and Clarissa Oon, "Chinese View Pragmatic Hsieh as Someone They Can Work With," *Straits Times*, May 19, 2007, 14.

9. I make the same points in "Obstacles to Integration."

10. See Su Ge, *Meiguo Dui Hua Zhengce yu Taiwan Wenti* [The United States' China policy and the Taiwan issue] (Beijing: Shijie Zhishi Chubanshe, 1998), 400–402, 651–55.

11. See http://www.uscc.gov/researchreports/2004/04reportpage2.pdf (accessed October 10, 2004).

12. See Thomas J. Christensen, "A Strong and Moderate Taiwan," September 11, 2007, and "Roundtable Briefing with Taiwan Media," December 6, 2007, at the State Department's Web site: http://www.state.gov/p/eap/rls/rm/2007/.

13. See Su Ge, *Meiguo Dui Hua Zhengce yu Taiwan Wenti*, 146.

14. In the latter part of the 1990s, the United States decided to give China most-favored nation status in trade relations, in spite of protests from human rights groups. In the annual debates on this issue in Congress, human rights groups would call for greater freedom in China, and this usually yielded some results, such as the release of one or two political prisoners. But the U.S. government decided to give up this practice due to trade considerations. In this case, human rights were sacrificed for other national interests.

15. Pan Yining, "Shixi Meiguo Jiduan Baoshou Sixiang dui Zhongmei Guanxi de Yingxiang" [On the influence of radical conservatism in China-U.S. relations], in *Baoshouzhuyi Linian yu Meiguo Waijiao Zhengce* [Conservatism and U.S. foreign policy], ed. Ren Xiao and Shen Dingli (Shanghai: Sanlian Press, 2003), 325–44.

16. Ibid., 336.

17. See Robert D. Kaplan, "How We Would Fight China: The Next Cold War," *Atlantic Monthly*, June 2005; Benjamin Schwarz, "Managing China's Rise, or How National Interests and Threats Can Be Redefined," *Atlantic Monthly*, June 2005.

18. See Pan Yining, "Shixi Meiguo," 338; Shi Yinhong, "Zhongguo de Waibu Kunnan he Xin Lingdao Jiti Miandui de Tiaozhan" [China's external difficulties and the challenges facing the new collective leadership], *Zhanlue yu Guanli* [Strategy and Management] 3 (2003): 34–39.

19. See http://www.americans-world.org/digest/regional_issues/china/ch_summary.cfm (accessed January 30, 2005).

20. See http://www.uscc.gov/researchreports/2004/04annual_report.htm (accessed October 10, 2004); emphasis in original.

21. Rumsfeld stated: "The People's Republic of China is a country that we hope and pray enters the civilized world in an orderly way without the grinding of gears and that they become a constructive force in that part of the world and a player in the global environment that's constructive. . . . They've got competing pressures between the desire to grow, which takes a free economy as opposed to a command economy, and their dictatorial system, which is not a free system. And there's a tension there, and I don't know how it'll come out, but I quite agree with you that we need to be attentive to it." Pentagon spokesman Lawrence Di Rita later said that Rumsfeld did not mean to say that that China was not a civilized nation; he only meant that China was inward looking. See Eric Schmitt, "Rumsfeld Warns of Concern about Expansion of China's Navy," *New York Times*, February 18, 2005.

22. For a list of works that envision future cross-strait relations, see Zhidong Hao, "Obstacles to Integration."

23. Apparently, China did not think the U.S. stand would make a difference in Taiwan. When asked about Christensen's remarks, Foreign Ministry spokesper-

son Jiang Yu's response was that they had noticed the repeated efforts on the part of the United States. She emphasized the importance of Taiwan to China and hoped that the United States would honor its commitment to China on the issue and join hands with China to maintain stability in the region. See http://www .china-embassy.org/eng/fyrth/t362589.htm (accessed December 16, 2007),

24. See Liu Fang, "Mindiao Xianshi: Lian Song Fangwen hou Dalu Yingpai Xianzhu Jianshao" [Poll shows that the number of hawks in the mainland dwindles significantly after Lian's and Song's visits], *Zhongguo Shibao,* April 26, 2007.

12. Hong Kong and Macao

In between China and the West

Ting Wai

Even though Hong Kong was a British colony for 155 years, it has always been "useful" to China. The city played a very important role in the economic, societal, and even political development of China. Every Chinese knows that Hong Kong was the cradle of the revolutionary thoughts of Sun Yat-sen, who was educated in medicine in Hong Kong and later founded the Republic of China. During the 1930s and 1940s, cadres and intellectuals of the Chinese Communist Party (CCP) were sent to Hong Kong to propagate revolutionary ideas and establish "united fronts" to fight against the Japanese as well as the Kuomintang (KMT).

Starting in the 1950s, during the Cold War, China was isolated from the international community, while Hong Kong remained free and open under the British administration. Due to the clairvoyant policy of Mao Zedong and Zhou Enlai, the newly created People's Republic of China (PRC) decided to keep the status quo in Hong Kong; that is, Beijing did not seek to resume Chinese sovereignty over the colony. Instead, under the policy of *Changqi Dasuan Chongfen Liyong* (planning for the long term, benefiting the most),[1] the Chinese leaders sought to promote the stability and prosperity of Hong Kong and gave their tacit consent to British rule, although Beijing never recognized Hong Kong's status as a colony. Maintenance of the status quo in Hong Kong was perceived to be beneficial to the Chinese mainland, which suffered from a trade embargo imposed by the United States during the Korean War, as well as isolation resulting from Washington's containment policy. According to Chinese leaders and analysts, the Chinese policy vis-à-vis Hong Kong reflected a perfect combination of "a high degree of principle and a high degree of flexibility." The principle (maintenance of Chinese sovereignty and nonrecognition of Hong Kong's status as a colony) and the practice (tacit consent to British rule) could coexist in a dialectic way, and this was perceived as fulfilling the Chinese national interests. As a result, although it was squeezed between the Western powers—mainly the United Kingdom and the United States—and China during the Cold War period, Hong Kong remained prosperous and stable under British rule and Chinese "collaboration." Hong Kong's Federation of Workers' Unions, an umbrella institution for the vast number of trade unions under Beijing's control, was even ordered not to disrupt the stability and prosperity of Hong Kong by launching strikes against the capitalists and the colonial government. So, apart from the riots and social unrest launched by local Chinese communist leaders instigated by the Cultural Revolution in 1967, Hong Kong after 1949 remained a free and liberal capitalist enclave. It became a paradise for many refugees from China as well as for the wealthy from other parts of Asia—a vast continent torn between totalitarian communist rule and the authoritarian rule of anticommunist regimes.

Even during the Mao era, reflections on Hong Kong and the decision to keep Hong Kong under British rule were very much related to Chinese foreign policy as well as Chinese domestic development. After the Chinese resumption of sovereignty in 1997, when Hong Kong became part of China, Hong Kong remained a highly autonomous special administrative region (SAR) under the formula of "one country, two systems." Deng Xiaoping, paramount Chinese leader during the open-door and reform period, believed that keeping Hong Kong a free capitalist society would be beneficial to China. But once the Cold War was over and Hong Kong—once considered part of the West—had, geopolitically speaking, become part of China, how would the changing dynamics of the international political order influence the role of Hong Kong? It is clear that, in the past, Hong Kong served primarily Western interests, yet it served Chinese national interests as well. This was the fundamental reason why Hong Kong survived so well between the East (China under CCP rule) and the West, even though they were constantly in ideological opposition. As part of China, Hong Kong obviously must serve primarily Chinese interests, but the Western countries have a stake in maintaining Hong Kong as it is; they need a base in Asia for expansion in mainland China and other parts of Asia. The question is, will Hong Kong still be able to fulfill the interests of both China and the West in a world influenced by globalization and neoliberal ideas? While people around the world consider the challenges and opportunities of the rise of China (Chinese leaders seem to prefer the term "peaceful development" to "peaceful rise"), the questions arise: What role will Hong Kong and its neighboring sister city, Macao, play in the foreign policy of China? Further, what impact will Chinese foreign policy in this age of peaceful development have on Hong Kong and Macao?

The Recent Historical Development of Hong Kong

Despite its position between ideologically opposed China and the West, Hong Kong managed to prosper and remain stable from the 1950s to the 1980s. Thus, there is no reason to be pessimistic about the international status and role of Hong Kong—a pioneer of capitalism—in this age of globalization. In reality, Hong Kong's unique status, as well as its own path of development since the 1950s, has been the result of a strange geopolitical environment and Beijing's geostrategic considerations. During China's period of isolation from the early 1950s until the early 1970s—isolation either imposed by the West after the Korean War or self-imposed in the 1960s—Hong Kong under British rule served as China's window to the outside world. It was through this open capitalist enclave that the PRC learned how the outside world operated, collecting information and intelligence on countries that had no diplomatic relations with China, purchasing Western products, and acquiring Western technology. What is more important, Hong Kong was the place where Chinese officials could meet delegates from other countries and conduct secret negotiations. The British colony was the place where China could break through the isolation and maintain contact with the international community. As long as these functions continued to be performed, the PRC had no interest in disrupting the status quo, and its tacit consent to British rule continued.

China's open-door and reform period started in December 1978, and it led to a new era for Hong Kong as rich Chinese entrepreneurs in the colony became the leaders in providing capital, technology, and expertise to China. As of the end of 2004, official statistics placed the total value of outward direct investments from Hong Kong to mainland China at US$155 billion, but this figure does not include funds channeled to the British Virgin Islands (US$180 billion) and Bermuda (US$17 billion) before being invested in the mainland.[2] These offshore financial centers make it difficult to assess the actual amount of funds originating from Hong Kong; in addition, some of the funds invested in China originate from the mainland but pass through Hong Kong and the British Virgin Islands. In any case, Hong Kong and Taiwan have invested the greatest amount in the mainland during the past twenty-five years. In Guangdong province alone, 77,000 factories were established by Hong Kong entrepreneurs.[3] So during China's reform period, Hong Kong also contributed to China's economic development. Hong Kong is an international and cosmopolitan city fully integrated into the system of global capitalism, and it is a definite asset to China as it seeks to enter the global capitalist market while deepening its reforms.

The result is clear: whether China is isolated or opening up to the world, Hong Kong contributes a lot to its national interests. That is why Deng Xiaoping decided to favor Hong Kong with a lenient policy of one country, two systems, and that is why, even under the red flag of China, Hong Kong's socioeconomic system should remain unchanged. Although it was obvious that many Hong Kong citizens were not happy with the one country, two systems guarantee of the CCP, whose trustworthiness has always been suspect, this was the most Beijing could offer. In any case, the government of Hong Kong must be responsible and accountable to the central government.

Whether Hong Kong can maintain its superiority in socioeconomic development depends not only on the goodwill of Chinese leaders and the intelligence and diligence of the Hong Kong people but also on Western perceptions. If Westerners think that Hong Kong has changed, and if their participation and investments decline as a result, the international character and cosmopolitan nature of Hong Kong will be lost. Hong Kong's raison d'etre would be gone, and the principle of one country, two systems would be meaningless; if Hong Kong is no longer international, it cannot provide as many benefits to China. Therefore, it is in Beijing's interest to maintain Hong Kong's unique international character, even though Hong Kong will inevitably become more Chinese.[4]

Since 1997, Hong Kong has become an even more significant international financial center (third, after New York and London). This is not due to the SAR's aspirations but due to the fact that more Chinese enterprises from the mainland have been using Hong Kong to raise funds for expansion. Hong Kong has truly become the most important Chinese financial center owing to its maturity in the development of related institutions (legal and financial), strong supervisory mechanisms, and enforcement of transparency in corporate governance. China is grateful to have the SAR in this role, but Hong Kong businesspeople have mixed feelings because they would like to see Hong Kong become a truly international financial market, attracting the interest of companies from all over the world, rather than just a Chinese financial center. The crucial question is, has the inevitable growth in Hong Kong's Chinese character led to a decline in its international character? Indeed, it is in the interests of both Hong Kong and China to maintain Hong Kong's uniqueness and international character, despite the fact that it is a Chinese city. However, China seems eager to fill the ideological vacuum left by the decline of communism with nationalism.

Globalization and Regionalism versus Nationalism

An analysis of the relationship between Hong Kong and mainland China from the perspective of the international political economy reveals some interesting and meaningful details about Hong Kong's role in China's integration into the international community. The realists in China would like to see a strengthening of the comprehensive national power of China through the addition of Hong Kong to its territory. It is no coincidence that, starting in the late 1990s (when Hong Kong and Macao were returned to the motherland in 1997 and 1999, respectively), China began to think about "great-power diplomacy" in relation to debates about its "rise." The growing confidence of the Chinese people also helped boost the nationalistic spirit, as evidenced by the reaction to the U.S. bombing of the Chinese embassy in Yugoslavia in May 1999 and the EP-3 plane incident in April 2001. The liberals in China also welcomed the return of Hong Kong to Chinese sovereignty. The capitalist enclave can assist China's integration into the global capitalist economy, and it can play a crucial role in facilitating China's connection to the world (*Jiegui*). For example, in the early 1990s, the border city of Shenzhen simply copied the property and administrative laws of Hong Kong to encourage people from Hong Kong to invest in Shenzhen's property market and set up businesses there. China also learned a lot from Hong Kong's massive reform of its economic, financial, and legal institutions, as well as its banking sector. So it is no exaggeration to say that Hong Kong plays a significant role in encouraging Western enterprises to invest in China and in helping China integrate into the world economy. It can be said that Hong Kong "shortens" the distance between China and the world and promotes better understanding between them.

In terms of regional cooperation, Hong Kong's role cannot be ignored. Washington has urged Beijing to become a "responsible stakeholder" in the international community,[5] and China has been actively cultivating better relations with its neighbors. China has been successful in promoting friendly and mutually beneficial relations with its neighbors in Southeast Asia in particular. Chinese analysts estimated that by 2005, China would be the largest importer in the world; by 2010, the largest exporter; and by 2020, the largest trading nation.[6] They are optimistic that members of the Association of Southeast Asian Nations (ASEAN) will benefit from the rapid growth of China. Bilateral trade between China and ASEAN reached US$106 billion in 2004 and surged to US$130 billion in 2005.[7] It is estimated that by the year 2010, mutual trade will reach US$200 billion.[8] The eventual establishment of the ASEAN-China Free-Trade Area (ACFTA) in 2010 will reinforce the growing trend in mutual trade exchanges and become a driving force in strengthening the competitiveness of enterprises in both China and ASEAN. Hong Kong stands to benefit from this surge in ASEAN-China trade, since a lot of goods pass through Hong Kong. The busiest port in the world could benefit from increased demand for transportation, logistics, and processing fees. In 2005, exports from the mainland to ASEAN countries that passed through Hong Kong amounted to US$17 billion (5.8 percent of Hong Kong's total exports), while imports from ASEAN to the mainland were valued at US$38 billion (12.7 percent of Hong Kong's total imports).[9] When the ACFTA is established in 2010, these goods will travel back and forth directly between ASEAN and China, without passing through Hong Kong; as a result, Hong Kong will lose a significant amount of reexports. Thus, the economic rise of China, in parallel with improved relationships with its neighbors, means that Hong Kong will lose the benefits of its "middleman" role between China and the outside world.

In response to these developments, Hong Kong has to come up with new ways to survive. First, the Hong Kong government is keeping a close eye on the fast-growing commercial exchanges between ASEAN and China. It envisages signing free-trade agreements with ASEAN countries so that Hong Kong is not marginalized by the continued opening up of the mainland. Second, some believe that Hong Kong should participate in the ASEAN+1 mechanism, either as a direct participant or as part of the Chinese delegation. It is difficult to envision Hong Kong as a sovereign state with an equal partnership in the ASEAN+1 mechanism, but the central Chinese authorities as well as the Hong Kong government have to devise ways to involve Hong Kong in the evolving free-trade area. Moreover, there are reports that Taiwan wants to participate in the ACFTA. In a speech at the National University of Singapore on May 8, 2006, Ma Ying-jeou, the KMT candidate who was elected president of Taiwan in 2008, urged ASEAN to accept Taiwan on an equal footing with the PRC. He would like the ASEAN+3 (China, Korea, and Japan) dialogue and free-trade area to become ASEAN+4—including Taiwan as well. Apparently, this message has been transmitted by senior Singaporean politician Lee Kuan Yew to the Beijing authorities.[10] China probably would not accept Taiwan as a full member in the ASEAN dialogue, but it would definitely welcome the participation of Hong Kong and Taiwan in the Chinese delegation. Taiwan does not want to be excluded in the regionalization process in East Asia, and Hong Kong, which used to have very close economic relations with neighboring countries, is certainly anxious to join in any community-building efforts that involve China.

In brief, Hong Kong facilitates China's integration into the international community and assists China's participation in the globalization processes. The distance between China and the world is "shortened" because of Hong Kong. Hong Kong also provides badly needed capital for the mainland's modernization through its investments in China and through the raising of funds by Chinese enterprises in the Hong Kong capital market. Hong Kong is interested in participating in the Pan–Pearl River Delta economic cooperation project, which involves nine southern provinces and Macao. However, it is clear that regional cooperation between China and its neighbors poses new challenges for Hong Kong as well. The SAR must worry about being marginalized due to the rapid development of the mainland, which is becoming more open to the outside world. Hong Kong businesspeople are skeptical about the future of Hong Kong's middleman status, and its function as a bridge between the world and China seems to be weakened.

Bridgehead, Gateway, and Middleman

Great Britain was never interested in colonizing Hong Kong. It simply wanted to use Hong Kong as base in Asia to facilitate political, military, and economic actions in the vast Asian Pacific region in general and China in particular. When China was weak, the British could use Hong Kong as a bridgehead to fight against China. If China became strong and prosperous, they could use Hong Kong as a gateway to enter the vast Chinese market. In fact, the former British consul general in Hong Kong used the word "gateway" to characterize the significance of Hong Kong for British enterprises.[11] By the same token, for several centuries, Macao has been used as a stepping-stone by foreigners who wished to enter China. If China was closed to the outside world, Westerners stayed in Macao and waited for an opportunity to cross into China in the future. Missionaries, most notably the Jesuits, entered China through Macao. It is not surprising that after all the turmoil and chaos in China since the Opium War, the Jesuits have returned to Macao and set up the Ricci Institute there, now that China has become relatively peaceful and prosperous.

In the 1980s, although mainland China had already instituted its reform and open-door policies, it still lacked diplomatic relationships with some anticommunist Asian nations such as South Korea and Indonesia. Hong Kong became the most important venue for countries that wanted to initiate contact with Beijing. Starting in the mid-1980s, Seoul sent its best China experts from the Foreign Ministry to Hong Kong; the Korean consul general at that time had previously been director of the Bureau for Asian Affairs within the ministry. The objective was clear: to pave the way for normalization of the relationship with China. Indonesia also started discussions with Chinese officials in Hong Kong regarding the normalization of their relationship. The free and liberal environment and the unique status of Hong Kong made the city an ideal place for contact between Chinese authorities and the outside world. Needless to say, Hong Kong has also played an extremely significant role in cross-strait relations. The refusal of *Santong* (three direct linkages: direct transport, direct mail, and direct trade) by the Taiwanese authorities meant that Hong Kong was a crucial bridge for multiple linkages at all levels between the mainland and Taiwan. Many "official" unofficial contacts and "unofficial" official contacts between Beijing and Taipei have been accomplished in Hong Kong.

Hong Kong's role is also unique in terms of Sino-Japanese relations. The Japanese business sector in Hong Kong is still optimistic about the intermediary role of Hong Kong. This is especially true among those small and medium enterprises attempting to enter the Chinese market for the first time. Hong Kong employees have the ability to break through the cultural and linguistic barriers between China and the outside world and serve as a kind of "lubricant" or catalyst for commercial and economic transactions. This know-how is very much appreciated by Japanese entrepreneurs. In brief, Japan wants Hong Kong to continue its success not only economically but also politically. Hong Kong is considered a gateway to China by the Japanese, and it can play an important role in improving Sino-Japanese relations, as emphasized by then consul general of Japan, Takanori Kita-mura, in early 2005.[12] Hong Kong, which is less nationalistic and more in-fluenced by Japanese popular culture, could act as a facilitator in ameliorating the relationship between Japan and China. The close linkage between Japan and Hong Kong was demonstrated by the granting of visa-free status to Hong Kong citizens in January 2004. And in 2005, the "Japan–Hong Kong Cultural Year" was baptized with a series of cultural events. Hong Kong, as an open and liberal city, is seen as a frontier for the future of Greater China. A more open and democratic society in Hong Kong will act as a showcase for the development of China in the future.

Hong Kong can be proud of its status as the most cosmopolitan and in-ternational city in China, and it has dubbed itself Asia's "world city." This is demonstrated by the 107 consulates general or consular offices of other na-tions in Hong Kong. In comparison, New York has only ninety-three consul-ates general.[13] For many nations, their consuls general in Hong Kong have a higher status than other consuls general in Chinese cities and even higher status than many of their ambassadors in other countries. In addition, con-sulates general in Hong Kong are directly responsible to their respective Ministries of Foreign Affairs, not to their embassies in Beijing. Thus, the one country, two systems formula also has an effect on the diplomatic representa-tion of other nations in China and Hong Kong. Many nations wish to have representation in Hong Kong and Macao, which rely on the Western pres-ence for their livelihood. But these nations also want to use the open, liberal environment of Hong Kong to study the domestic politics of the mainland; Greater China issues, especially those relating to Taiwan; and China's rela-tions with the outside world, especially its Asian neighbors.

Hong Kong's importance as a regional hub with links to all parts of Asia is reflected by the vast number of regional headquarters and regional offices established by multinationals in Hong Kong. The total number as of June 1, 2005, was 3,798, with 1,167 regional headquarters and 2,631 regional offices.[14] But Hong Kong's status as a regional hub is being threatened by other cities—notably, Shanghai and Singapore, which have induced some companies to establish their China or Asian Pacific headquarters there. Al-though both the mainland and Hong Kong would like to maintain the lat-ter's international status and profile, many foreign companies would prefer to move their China or regional headquarters to the mainland to be closer to production bases and also to the market. Moreover, the economic envi-ronment of the mainland has become quite open and has gained the confidence of foreign enterprises. Despite the superiority of Hong Kong's infrastructure and telecommunications, the high costs of operating in Hong Kong and the lack of talent have raised concerns about whether Hong Kong's role as a regional hub can be maintained.

In any case, whether Hong Kong can continue to be prosperous and stable, whether it can perform useful functions in fulfilling Chinese national interests as well as the interests of other nations, and whether its socioeconomic system can remain intact as it marches toward democracy will be a test of the theory and practice of the one country, two systems principle. Other nations usually measure the "successes" of Hong Kong and Macao according to economic and political progress. If political progress toward democratization remains stagnant, and if Hong Kong cannot find its own developmental model that involves a fundamental restructuring of its economy, Hong Kong after 1997 may be deemed a failure.

Thinking in Quadrangles: United States, Europe, China, and Hong Kong–Macao

Although Hong Kong and, to a lesser extent, Macao have linked China to the world, the two SARs are inevitably under the influence of Chinese foreign policy. This is especially true as Beijing is becoming a more assertive regional power and thus more influential in regional affairs. Indeed, it is clear that the Beijing government wants to maintain Hong Kong's status as the most international and cosmopolitan city in China—a position being challenged by Shanghai. Beijing also wants to maintain Macao as a Chinese city with Portuguese characteristics and a Mediterranean flavor so that it can serve as an attractive entertainment and tourist resort and, more important, a bridge to the Portuguese-speaking world. To keep an open and international atmosphere in these two cities, foreign participation is inevitable. However, Chinese leaders since the 1990s have emphasized that although economic internationalization is permitted, political internationalization is impossible under Chinese sovereignty.

Under the theory of one country, two systems, Hong Kong and Macao have no jurisdiction over national defense and foreign policies, but Chinese foreign and security policies certainly have a significant impact on the two SARs. China deploys about 7,000 soldiers in Hong Kong, under the control of the Guangzhou Military Region.[15] Although this military presence is largely symbolic, Beijing has to be prepared to defend this international city in the event of a conflict with Taiwan, which has threatened to target missiles at both Hong Kong and Shanghai. The two local SAR governments have no input in situations involving the United States and China, such as the containment policy. During and after the Korean War, embargoes against China caused serious economic problems in Hong Kong, even though the city belonged to the Western camp at the time. Fortunately, due to the one country, two systems formula, Washington treats Hong Kong differently from the mainland (a result of the 1992 United States–Hong Kong Policy Act), provided that the guarantees given by the Chinese are valid.[16] Moreover, despite serious setbacks, such as the U.S. bombing of the Chinese embassy in Yugoslavia and the EP-3 plane incident, China continues to seek integration into the international community. China eventually joined the World Trade Organization in 2001, as well as other international institutions, demonstrating Beijing's willingness to abide by various international norms even though they are based on Western values and worldviews. China's active move toward regionalization and its desire to benefit from globalization provide a favorable atmosphere for Hong Kong and Macao to find their niches and their proper paths of development. From a structural realist point of view, change in the domestic behavior of a nation such as China causes a restructuring of the international system, not only because of China's rise to power but also because of its attitude (whether receptive or not) toward the international political order that is still dominated by the Western powers, especially the United States. Hong Kong and Macao, long part of the Western world, definitely welcome the opening up of China and its tendency to abide by international norms.

However, the question today is whether China seeks to modify or transform the existing norms in international institutions or at least influence the formulation of new ones. The two SARs have no say regarding Chinese security and foreign policy matters such as arms control, but as a mature capitalist market and financial center, Hong Kong could exert some influence over China in international economic and financial matters. Within the international system, the not so equidistant triangular relationship among United States, Europe, and China would become the determining factor in world development.[17] Since the socioeconomic development of Hong Kong and Macao has always been largely affected by Europe and the United States, what are the implications of Sino-European and Sino-American relations for the two SARs?

China's policies vis-à-vis Europe are dictated by two considerations. On the one hand, the realpolitik in Chinese diplomacy determines that China has to appease its neighbors while seeking friendly relationships in other continents, especially the very influential global actor Europe. It has even been said that a Europe-China axis is being formed to counter the U.S.-Japan alliance.[18] On the other hand, the idealism in Chinese foreign policy determines that Beijing must seek to establish a new international political and economic order that reflects China's ideas and visions. According to Chinese scholars who specialize in the study of the European Union (EU), the EU's views regarding the future of the international order differ from those of the United States but are close to Chinese thinking. The decision-making process of the EU "emphasizes common interests, sharing of power, and abiding by the restrictive common rules of the games," and the EU favors "multilateralism" in solving international problems.[19] Therefore, from both the realist and the idealist points of view, Europe is considered a major factor in the formulation of a new order.

In terms of the economic relationship, renewed restrictions on Chinese exports of garments and shoes starting in early 2005, despite the abolishment of the global quota scheme, have raised serious concerns among Hong Kong entrepreneurs who invest in the relevant industries on the mainland. Sino-European negotiations have to take into consideration Hong Kong's interests. In fact, Hong Kong, long a champion of free trade, is sympathetic with China's criticism of the protectionist measures of both the EU and the United States. It is hypocritical for countries whose products enjoy a competitive edge in the world market to talk about free trade while restricting those few products from developing countries that have a competitive edge.[20]

Regarding social and cultural aspects, Chinese scholars point out that Europeans are attempting to transform China based on the European value system; Europeans still possess the mentality that they are the "teachers" or "saviors" of these "backward" Asian nations. Nonetheless, the EU and China have been engaged in a series of dialogues on human rights since 1997. The European Commission is hopeful that this will help in "improving the human rights situation on the ground by encouraging China to respect and promote human rights and fundamental freedoms and to cooperate with international human rights mechanisms."[21] Such dialogues are considered progress by Chinese analysts, as the EU now tends to treat China as a real and equal partner.

However, the usefulness of China's joining the two existing covenants on human rights is questionable. China signed the International Covenant for Social, Economic, and Cultural Rights in October 1997 and the International Covenant for Civil and Political Rights in October 1998, creating hope around the world that China would eventually abide by these two international agreements and protect its citizens' human rights. The first document was ratified by the National People's Congress in March 2001, but the second one, which is obviously more important, has not yet been ratified. The EU is not satisfied with the human rights conditions in China, where freedom of expression, religion, and association are not guaranteed. As noted by the European Commission, "a significant gap still exists between the current human rights situation in China and international accepted standards."[22] China signed the International Covenant for Civil and Political Rights to show that it is committed to "joining the world" and abiding by international norms, but the delayed ratification denotes that China is not yet ready to fully accept international standards.

Paradoxically, human rights in Hong Kong and Macao are guaranteed by the Chinese authorities, who have promised to respect the one country, two systems formula. Hong Kong is still treasured by European companies as a gateway to China owing to its supremacy in providing professional and managerial talent, its robust legal and financial institutions, and its excellent banking facilities. Recent statistics show that 1,083 EU companies have their regional headquarters (376) and regional offices (707) in Hong Kong.[23] The EU is China's biggest trading partner, and Hong Kong benefits from this relationship because about one-fifth of Sino-EU trade passes through Hong Kong.[24] The existence of these two SARs acts as both a cohesive and a lubricating agent in the relationship between China and Britain as well as between China and Portugal.

The United States has many interests in Hong Kong and an increasing number in Macao as well, due to the active American participation in Macao's booming entertainment and casino industries. So far, Washington has expressed grievances only on issues relating to democratic development and the possible deterioration of human rights conditions in Hong Kong, notably during the controversial debate in 2002–2003 on the implementation of Article 23 of the Basic Law. The "institutional pillars" of Hong Kong (rule of law, competent and noncorrupt civil service, clear rules of the market economy, and freedom of speech) have been consolidated, and the multiple roles played by Hong Kong as an international financial, commercial, services, and media hub and a free entrepôt have largely been fulfilled. Judging from the imperatives of U.S. foreign policy, Washington's major concerns are law enforcement and export control by Hong Kong and Macao.

The U.S. government seems to be satisfied with Hong Kong's law enforcement against drug trafficking, money laundering, alien smuggling, credit card fraud, violations of intellectual property rights, and organized crime. In 1987, Washington listed Hong Kong as one of the major narcotics-producing or -transiting countries, but in November 2000, Hong Kong was removed from that list.[25] Cooperation between the law enforcement agencies of Hong Kong and Washington has in fact deepened and broadened since 1997. The United States is expanding its law enforcement presence in Hong Kong, which now includes the Secret Service, Immigration and Naturalization Service, Internal Revenue Service Criminal Investigations Division, Customs Service, Drug Enforcement Administration, Federal Bureau of Investigation, Export Enforcement Bureau of the Commerce Department, and Department of State.[26] The Hong Kong SAR government is able to exercise its law enforcement functions without interference from central Chinese authorities. With continual cooperation from the United States in this regard, Hong Kong has upgraded its law enforcement performance to a level equivalent to that in the West. Washington is also grateful to Hong Kong for its global actions against terrorism, especially now that Hong Kong has assumed the leading role in the multilateral (twenty-nine-member) Financial Action Task Force, created to uncover the financial networks of terrorists.[27]

In the case of Macao, Washington is keeping a close eye on the situation. It is no secret that for several decades Macao has been the base for a company owned by the Pyongyang government and used to buy luxurious products for party elites in North Korea. In September 2005, the U.S. Treasury disclosed the misdeeds of Banco Delta Asia (located in Macao, but headquartered in Hong Kong), which helped the North Korean regime in a money-laundering and counterfeiting scheme. The Macao government will not tolerate this kind of activity, which can adversely affect its international status as a free port and a commercial center. The government immediately started an investigation and took control of the bank. Under pressure from Washington, the bank cut its ties with North Korean entities.[28] With the increasing American participation in Macao's entertainment business, some analysts are concerned that the United States might exercise even more political influence in the future. The new casinos opened in Macao after the breakup of the monopoly of Stanley Ho are all heavily invested in by Americans. Since the Chinese government has forbidden its people to gamble in the casinos of neighboring countries, there is a massive flow of Chinese tourists into Macao. This has brought prosperity to Macao—enormous incomes for the casinos, and a rapid increase in tax revenues for the Macao government.

The issue of export control is a heritage of the Cold War, when Hong Kong served primarily Western interests. Based on the 1955 Import and Export (Strategic Commodities) Ordinance, Hong Kong does not allow the trading of weapons or strategic materials, thus assisting U.S. efforts against the proliferation of weapons of mass destruction.[29] Due to its effective export control, Hong Kong has been allowed to import high-technology dual-use items, even after 1997. For instance, powerful supercomputers can be used in Hong Kong, but they cannot be reexported to China. Hong Kong's Customs and Excise Department has been highly praised for its effective pre- and postshipment checks of strategic goods to ensure that they are properly used.[30] The U.S. secretary of commerce and the Hong Kong secretary of trade and commerce have even conducted semiannual meetings since 1997 to exchange information on export control. The stringent export control exercised by Hong Kong authorities is necessary because the city is forging ahead to become a services and business hub equipped with the latest in high technology. Washington's policy vis-à-vis Hong Kong puts the latter in an advantageous position, permitting its continued importation of state-of-the-art high-technology products.

The discovery of an armored vehicle in a Chinese cargo ship passing through Hong Kong from Thailand in late August 1997 and a similar case of five armored personnel carriers from Ukraine discovered on March 31, 2000—both shipments headed for ports in China—demonstrated the effectiveness of Hong Kong's export control mechanisms.[31] In both cases, the China Ocean Shipping Company (the largest in China) and the ship captains were penalized and fined. Beijing treated the matter as a minor foreign trade issue rather than an issue of diplomacy and national defense. If China had insisted on taking the latter stance, Hong Kong, as a port of China, would have been powerless to stop the shipments, since it has no jurisdiction over diplomatic and defense matters. Fortunately, the goodwill and foresight of the Chinese leaders prevailed. A similar case occurred in April 2006 when a Mig-29 fighter being transported from Ukraine to the United States passed through Hong Kong without an import license.[32] This was again adjudicated according to Hong Kong law, and it is impossible to know whether this case was related to China.

In brief, although China appears to be more "measured" in terms of export control, especially after passing its own series of laws in 2002 on the export of weapons of mass destruction, Washington remains watchful of China's behavior in this crucial area. Hong Kong is still operating under a 1955 ordinance, which means that the Chinese authorities and Chinese companies cannot use Hong Kong to import or export weapons of mass destruction or related strategic materials. Thus, it can be argued that Macao and Hong Kong are still being regulated by the Western powers to match the international or Western standard, even though the two cities are under Chinese rule. It may seem paradoxical that the increasingly powerful China still has to submit to foreign pressure in governing these two peculiar enclaves, but keeping the two SARs free and open by maintaining the original institutional pillars is extremely important for China in this age of globalization, not only because of its commitment to one country, two systems but also because China needs a model for its future development.

Conclusion

It is interesting to note the intertwining forces that are shaping the new Hong Kong and the new Macao, and it seems somewhat misleading to claim that the status quo of these two cities should be maintained. Macao's future is easier to determine, because the government decided right after 1999 that Macao should become a holiday resort with entertainment and gambling. Once the Chinese people had money to spend, many casinos opened in neighboring countries to attract rich Chinese tourists, but the Chinese government forbade its citizens to go to those casinos. Now they can go to Macao instead, thus helping the SAR to become very prosperous in the last few years. The Macao government has used the tax revenue to create many new programs, including a free fifteen-year education for all children.

Hong Kong is embarking on a somewhat difficult journey. It seems to be losing its competitive edge in comparison to other great cities such as Shanghai and Singapore, which are now seeking to become financial centers as well as commercial and industrial centers. In addition, Hong Kong is encountering difficulties in economic restructuring. It needs to find a niche in the fast-growing market of China. Hong Kong's role as a gateway or a bridge has always been beneficial in the past, but with China opening up, this role can only be diminished.

Hong Kong's political move toward democratization can serve as a model for the mainland in the future. The reform of Hong Kong's political institutions will lead Western nations to believe that it is possible for the CCP to allow democratization under Chinese sovereignty, even though it has always insisted that Western democracy is not suitable for the Chinese. This will help narrow the epistemological gap between the West and China. It will also soften the skepticism of many people concerning the rise of China, illustrating that the strengthening of economic and military capabilities can be accompanied by political progress in the way of governance. Political development in Macao, though not identical with that in Hong Kong, would closely follow the latter's achievements.

The two SARs can by no means be exempted from the influence of Chinese foreign policies. As China continues to open up its market, Hong Kong and Macao can only benefit from multiple linkages at all levels between China and the outside world. This will help maintain Hong Kong's status as a regional hub and international city. It is hoped that China's increasing interest in its neighbors will empower the two SARs. However, the two cities still need to work hard to consolidate their uniqueness and to prevent marginalization or provincialization.

Notes

1. See Xuan Yuan Lu, *Xinhuashe Toushi* [Perspectives on new China News Agency of Hong Kong] (Hong Kong: Wide Angle Press, 1987), 35.
2. See *External Direct Investment Statistics of Hong Kong 2004* (Census and Statistics Department, Government of Hong Kong SAR, 2005), 18.
3. See *Ming Pao* (Hong Kong), May 19, 2006, A23.
4. The balance between the so-called international character and Chinese character of Hong Kong is treated in Ting Wai, "The International Status and External Relations of Hong Kong" (Occasional Papers/Reprint Series, University of Maryland School of Law, 139, no. 2, 1997).
5. See the famous speech by Deputy Secretary of State Robert Zoellick, "Whither China: From Membership to Responsibility? Remarks to National Committee on U.S.-China Relations," September 21, 2005, http://www.ncuscr.org/recent-remarks-and-speeches.
6. Zhang Bin, "The Economic Relations and Prospects between China and East Asia," in *Guoji Wenti Yanjiu* [International Studies] 4 (July 2003): 55.
7. See http://www.newsflash.orf/2004/02/be/be003329.
8. *People's Daily* (Beijing), October 22, 2005.
9. See *Ming Pao* (Hong Kong), May 15, 2006, A6.

10. See *Ta Kung Pao* (Hong Kong), May 16, 2006, A16.

11. See the interview of Sir James Hodge, British consul general in Hong Kong, in *Britain in Hong Kong* 14, no. 6 (January–February 2001): 3.

12. See *Ming Pao* (Hong Kong), February 27, 2005, A14.

13. See Pi Jiachao, "Hong Kong's Headquarters Economy Also Has Crisis," *Ta Kung Pao* (Hong Kong), May 22, 2006, A7.

14. See Ting Wai and Ellen Lai, "Hong Kong SAR and the World," in *Contemporary Hong Kong Politics: Governance in the Post-1997 Era*, ed. Lam Wai Man et al. (Hong Kong: Hong Kong University Press, 2007), 265–82.

15. See *Military Balance, 2005–2006* (London: International Institute for Strategic Studies, 2005), 272.

16. See Ting Wai, "An East-West Conundrum: Hong Kong in between China and the United States after the Chinese Resumption of Sovereignty," in *One Country, Two Systems in Crisis: Hong Kong's Transformation since the Handover*, ed. Wong Yiu-chung (Lanham, Md.: Lexington, 2004), 187–208.

17. See Ma Zhengang, "The Increasingly Important China Element in the World Order," *Guoji Wenti Yanjiu* [International Studies] 3 (May 2005): 1.

18. See Chalmers Johnson, "No Longer the 'Lone' Superpower: Coming to Terms with China" (Japan Policy Research Institute Paper 105, March 2005).

19. See Feng Zhongping, "Looking at Sino-European Relations from a Strategic Highground," in *Qiu Shi* [Seeking Truth], September 2002, 58–60. This monthly magazine is the party organ published by the Central Committee of the Chinese Communist Party.

20. See the interview of Chinese minister of commerce Bo Xilai in *Ta Kung Pao* (Hong Kong), May 7, 2005, A11.

21. Communication from the European Commission to the Council and the European Parliament, "EU Strategy towards China: Implementation of the 1998 Communication and Future Steps for a More Effective EU Policy," May 15, 2001, 10.

22. European Commission policy paper for transmission to the Council and the European Parliament, "A Maturing Partnership—Shared Interests and Challenges in EU-China Relations," September 10, 2003, 12.

23. Thomas Roe (head of the European Commission office in Hong Kong), "World's Largest Market Still Growing," *Standard* (Hong Kong), May 8, 2006, A11. In 2004, the number of regional headquarters of American companies totaled 256, and regional offices totaled 557; for Japanese companies, the totals were 198 and 515, respectively. See *Survey of Regional Representation by Overseas Companies in Hong Kong 2004* (Census and Statistics Department, Government of Hong Kong SAR, 2004).

24. Roe, "World's Largest Market Still Growing."

25. See *Ta Kung Pao* (Hong Kong), November 3, 2000, A15, and January 3, 2001, A10.

26. See *United States–Hong Kong Policy Act Report, as of April 1, 2000* (Wash-

ington, D.C.: Bureau of East Asian and Pacific Affairs, U.S. Department of State, April 25, 2000), 5; Doug Bereuter, *Eighth Report on the Hong Kong Transition* (Washington, D.C.: House of Representatives, August 1, 2000), 4.

27. See *U.S.-Hong Kong Policy Act Report, as of March 31, 2002* (Washington, D.C.: Bureau of East Asian and Pacific Affairs, U.S. Department of State, April 11, 2002), 2.

28. See http://news.bbc.co.uk/1/hi/business/4718922.stm.

29. For an earlier analysis of this issue, see Ting Wai, "China, the United States, and the Future of Hong Kong," in *Hong Kong SAR: In Pursuit of Domestic and International Order,* ed. Beatrice K. F. Leung and Joseph Y. S. Cheng (Hong Kong: Chinese University Press, 1997), 243–57.

30. See *United States–Hong Kong Policy Act Report, as of April 1, 2000,* 15.

31. See Ting Wai, "Hong Kong in between China and the Great Powers: The External Relations and International Status of Hong Kong after the Chinese Resumption of Sovereignty," in *Hong Kong Special Administrative Region in Its First Decade,* ed. Joseph Y. S. Cheng (Hong Kong: City University Press, 2007), 261–304.

32. See *Ming Pao* (Hong Kong), April 5, 2006, A10.

Part IV

CHINESE DIPLOMACY WITH
CHINESE CHARACTERISTICS

13. Between Rhetoric and Pragmatism

Nationalism as a Driving Force of Chinese Foreign Policy

Suisheng Zhao

During the standoff that occurred after a U.S. spy plane collided with a Chinese jet fighter and landed on Hainan Island in 2001, the *Washington Post* ran a front-page story headlined "New Nationalism Drives Beijing."[1] Such a warning reflects the roiling sense of anxiety in many Asian and Western political capitals: Has a virulent nationalism emerged from China's "century of shame and humiliation," making its rise less than peaceful? Has the Chinese government exploited nationalist sentiments to gain leverage in international affairs, or has nationalism driven Chinese foreign policy in a more irrational and inflexible direction?

This political concern is also apparent among scholars. Although some scholars have been cautious in exploring the limits of Chinese nationalism and whether Chinese nationalism is affirmative, assertive, or aggressive,[2] others have found a reckless nationalism driven by China's traditional Sinocentrism and contemporary aspirations for great-power status.[3] For example, Peter Gries refers to China's "new" nationalism and argues that an emotionally popular nationalism empowered by "victim narratives" is "beginning to influence the making of Chinese foreign policy."[4] His argument echoes an earlier warning by Richard Bernstein and Ross Munro: "Driven by nationalist sentiment, a yearning to redeem the humiliations of the past, and the simple urge for international power, China is seeking to replace the United States as the dominant power in Asia."[5]

It is not difficult to find evidence to support these warnings. One example is the rising anti-Japanese sentiment among the Chinese people, which culminated in a dramatic campaign on the Internet in early 2005 that gathered the signatures of more than 20 million Chinese people opposed to Japan's bid to join the United Nations Security Council. Subsequently, thousands of

Chinese protesters marched through Shanghai, Beijing, and other Chinese cities, shouting slogans and throwing rocks, bottles, and eggs at the Japanese consulates to protest Japan's approval of history textbooks that whitewashed its wartime atrocities and Japan's recent pledge to help the United States defend Taiwan in the event of an attack by Beijing. The dramatic last-minute cancellation of a meeting between Japanese prime minister Junichiro Koizumi and visiting Chinese vice minister Wu Yi in May 2005, in response to Koizumi's contentious visits to the war-tainted Yasukuni Shrine, plunged relations between Beijing and Tokyo to a perilous low.

The rise of Chinese nationalism has also supported a deeply rooted suspicion of the United States in recent years. Many were certainly dismayed to witness massive anti-American demonstrations in the front of U.S. diplomatic missions after the bombing of the Chinese embassy in Belgrade by U.S.-led NATO forces in May 1999. Many observers were astonished at how quickly and automatically the Chinese people were convinced that the U.S. bombing had been deliberate.

The phenomenon of Chinese nationalism is much more complex than the expression of its emotional rhetoric on the streets, however. Although the Chinese government is not above exploiting nationalist sentiment when doing so suits its purposes, it has practiced a pragmatic nationalism tempered by diplomatic prudence. State-led and largely reactive, pragmatic nationalism does not have a fixed, objectified, or eternally defined content, nor is it driven by any ideology, religious belief, or other abstract idea. It is an instrument of the communist state to bolster the faith of the Chinese people in a troubled political system and to hold the country together during a period of rapid and turbulent transformation from a communist to a postcommunist society.

From a foreign policy perspective, pragmatic nationalism sets peace and development as China's major international goals. Economic prosperity is seen as a way for the Chinese Communist Party (CCP) to stay in power and also as the foundation for China's rising nationalist aspirations. In the meantime, political stability at home is emphasized as the necessary condition for the attainment of Chinese modernization. Pragmatic leaders, therefore, have tried to avoid confrontations with the United States and other Western powers that hold the key to China's modernization, at least in the foreseeable future. Although pragmatic leaders may use nationalism to rally support, they must be sure that nationalist sentiments do not jeopardize the overarching objectives of political stability and economic modernization on which the legitimacy of nationalism is ultimately based. It is certainly not in their interest to let Chinese foreign policy be dictated by the emotional, nationalistic rhetoric on the street. Therefore, although pragmatic leaders have consciously cultivated nationalist sentiments against the perceived containment policy by Western countries, strong nationalist rhetoric has often been followed by prudent policy actions in foreign affairs.

Nationalism as an Instrument of the Communist State

The communist state has exploited nationalism to compensate for and, to a certain extent, replace the declining communist ideology in post-Mao years. As communist ideology lost credibility, the communist state was unable to advance any new ideology as an integrative force, so it simply spouted expedient slogans, such "getting rich" by "practicing" market competition. People were urged to consume, to transform themselves into entrepreneurs by seizing business opportunities, and to compete with one another regardless of morality or equality. In this case, when reform brought about hardships such as high inflation, corruption, and unemployment, and the regime could find no way to compensate people for their losses, the communist state lacked an effective ideology or long-term vision to inspire people to endure the hard times for the sake of a better future. This situation not only greatly weakened mass support for the CCP and eroded its basis of legitimacy but also led some Chinese intellectuals to turn to Western liberal ideas and to call for Western-style democracy, leading to the massive antigovernment demonstrations in Tiananmen Square in the spring of 1989.

How to restore the legitimacy of the communist regime and build broad-based national support became the most serious challenge to the post-Tiananmen leadership. Thus, the instrument of nationalism was discovered. Deng Xiaoping and his successors Jiang Zemin and Hu Jintao wrapped themselves in the banner of nationalism, which, they found, was a reliable way to obtain the Chinese people's loyalty and the only important value shared by both the regime and its critics. Facing Western sanctions, pragmatic leaders moved quickly to position themselves as the defenders of China's national pride and interests. China's nationalist credentials have been bolstered in the battle against Western sanctions, China's entry into the World Trade Organization, the fight against Taiwan independence, and Beijing's hosting of the 2008 Olympics.

The discovery of nationalism coincided with the rise of pragmatism as the dominant thinking of the Chinese people as well as their leaders. The Chinese people were willing to use any means to become rich, and Chinese leaders were willing to adopt any approach that would further the quest for power and wealth. By definition, pragmatism is behavior that is disciplined by neither a set of values nor established principles. This was vividly expressed by Deng's "cat theory": that is, a cat, whether it is white or black, is a good cat as long as it is able to catch mice. Justified by the slogan "building socialism with Chinese characteristics," pragmatic leaders have made an all-out effort to strengthen China by gaining access to the world's most advanced science and technology and engaging in commercial and cultural exchanges with all foreign countries, including liberal democracies. In the meantime, they have rejected anything deemed to be inconsistent with Chinese characteristics, including any ideas interpreted as threatening to CCP rule.

Led by the state, pragmatic nationalism closely identifies the nation of China with the communist state. Nationalist sentiment is officially expressed as *aiguo* ("loving the state") or *aiguozhuyi* ("patriotism"); it implies love and support for China, which is always indistinguishable from the communist state. As Michael Hunt observes, "by professing *aiguo,* Chinese usually expressed loyalty to and a desire to serve the state, either as it was or as it would be in its renovated form."[6] From this perspective, Chinese pragmatic nationalism is state-centric. The communist state, as the embodiment of the nation's will, seeks the same loyalty and support that the people grant to the nation itself.

To make the maximum use of nationalism, the communist state launched an extensive propaganda campaign in the 1990s to educate the Chinese about patriotism. The campaign appealed to nationalism in the name of patriotism to ensure loyalty among a population that was subject to many domestic discontents. The core of the patriotic education campaign was *guoqing jiaoyu* ("education in national conditions"), which unambiguously held that China's national conditions were unique and that the country was not ready to adopt a Western-style liberal democracy. Instead, the current one-party rule should continue because it would help maintain political stability, a precondition for rapid economic development. The campaign thus redefined the communist regime's legitimacy on the basis of its provision of political stability and economic prosperity. When pragmatic leaders said that China was being bullied and humiliated by foreign powers, they indicated that China's backwardness in economic development shared some of the blame for its past humiliation and current weakness. Thus, pragmatic leaders called on the Chinese people to work hard to build a prosperous and strong China.

By reinforcing Chinese national confidence and turning past humiliation and current weakness into a driving force for China's modernization, nationalism has become an effective instrument to enhance the legitimacy of the communist state. The nationalist card is particularly effective when China faces challenges from hostile foreign countries. As one Chinese official said, if the Chinese people felt threatened by external forces, the solidarity among them would be strengthened, and nationalism would be a useful tool for the regime to justify its leadership role.[7] It is interesting to note that although corruption and other social and economic problems have undermined the legitimacy of the communist regime, many Chinese people side with the communist government when it is criticized by foreigners. No matter how corrupt the government is, their feeling is that foreigners have no right to make disparaging remarks about China or the Chinese people. Many Chinese have been upset by U.S. policies on human rights, intellectual property rights, trade deficits, weapons proliferation, and Taiwan because they believe the United States has used these issues to demonize China in an effort to prevent it from rising as a great power.

The Shared Dream of a Strong China

Nationalism is an effective instrument of the communist state because of the deep-rooted historical sense of injustice at the hands of foreign countries and because *qiangguomeng* ("the dream of a strong China") is sincerely shared by Chinese people from all walks of life. Nationalism can be defined as a set of modern ideas that centers people's loyalty on the nation-state, either as it exists or as it is envisioned; it did not exist in China before the nineteenth century because China was an empire, not a nation-state. Chinese political elite began to embrace modern nationalist doctrines for China's defense and regeneration only after its disastrous defeat by British troops in the 1840–1842 Opium War, which led not only to the eventual disintegration of the Chinese empire but also to the loss of national sovereignty to imperialist powers. Since then, a recurring theme in Chinese politics has been a quest to blot out this humiliation at the hands of imperialists. Almost all powerful Chinese political leaders since the early twentieth century—Sun Yat-sen, Chiang Kai-shek, Mao Zedong, Deng Xiaoping, Jiang Zemin, Hu Jintao—have shared a deep bitterness at China's humiliation and have been determined to restore China to its rightful place in the world of nation-states.

Despite their shared nationalist aspirations, Chinese leaders have offered a variety of programs designed to build a nation-state to their liking. As a result, at least three strands of nationalism have occurred in modern China. One is ethnic nationalism, which sees the nation as a politicized ethnic group and often produces a movement to create an ethnic nation-state. The second is liberal nationalism, which defines a nation as being composed of citizens whose duty is not only to support and defend their own state's national rights but also to pursue their individual rights of governmental participation. The third is state nationalism, which defines the nation as a territorial and political unit; the state speaks in the name of the nation and demands that its citizens subordinate their individual interests to those of the state.

Chinese nationalism started as an ethnic state–seeking movement led by the Han majority in an attempt to overthrow the minority Manchu dynasty. Since the fall of the Qing dynasty in 1911, both the Kuomintang (KMT) and the CCP have defined the Chinese nation as a multiethnic political community and endorsed only state nationalism. Ethnic nationalism has remained alive only among ethnic minorities in China's frontiers, such as the Tibetans and the Mongols, who are denied the right to establish separate states and therefore pose a serious threat to the unity of the multiethnic Chinese state. Ethnic nationalism has been thoroughly suppressed by both the KMT and the communist regimes.

Liberal nationalism was introduced to regenerate China through political and social reforms in the early twentieth century. Liberal nationalists identified with the Chinese state against foreign imperialism and, in the meantime, pushed for participation in the political process against the authoritarian state. Before the founding of the People's Republic of China (PRC) in 1949, liberal nationalists often came into conflict with the KMT regime, which was incompetent to resist foreign imperialist powers and repeatedly violated individual rights. Therefore, some liberal nationalists allied with the CCP, which appealed to the Chinese people's desire to build an independent and democratic new China. After the founding of the PRC, however, many liberal nationalists quickly discovered that the CCP was no better than the KMT in protecting individual freedom. Taking advantage of the Hundred Flowers Campaign in 1957 to criticize the CCP's monopoly of political power, many liberal nationalists were brutally purged.

Deng Xiaoping's call for the liberation of thought and post-Mao reform in the 1980s created new opportunities for the reemergence of liberal nationalism. However, due to the danger of criticizing the communist state, many liberal nationalists blamed China's authoritarian culture for the lack of modernization and called for the rejection of Chinese tradition and the boundless adoption of Western culture and models of development. In the wake of the end of the Cold War, liberal nationalists called for the adoption of liberal democratic ideals as the best means of promoting China's national regeneration. This was symbolized by the erection of a "Goddess of Democracy," modeled on the U.S. Statue of Liberty, during the pro-democracy demonstrations in Tiananmen Square in 1989. As noted by a Western reporter, "the pro-democracy demonstrations in Tiananmen Square began as a patriotic movement by students who wanted to strengthen China through political reform."[8] However, the mainstream Chinese intellectual discourse shifted drastically in response to the deterioration of China's relations with major Western countries, particularly the United States, and the rising advocacy for the containment of China in the Western media in the 1990s. Many liberal nationalists became suspicious that the Western powers were conspiring to prevent China from rising to the status of a great power and therefore became very critical of the United States and Japan in particular.

Liberal nationalism has often been expressed in the form of popular sentiments against the perceived infringement on Chinese national interests by foreign powers. For instance, popular nationalist sentiments propelled young anti-Japanese demonstrators into the streets in April 2005 and anti-American demonstrators in May 1999. From this perspective, popular nationalism has become an important expression of liberal nationalism. Because of the popular attack on the "evil" intentions of Western countries, some liberal nationalists are labeled "neoconservatives" by Western observers. However, this label is simplistic; although the communist state and liberal nationalists share the dream of a strong China, most liberal nationalists do not identify themselves with the communist state, nor do they refrain from criticizing the policies of the government. Qin Hui, a professor of history in Beijing, vividly expressed this split personality of liberal nationalism: it is not right to be slaves of foreign powers, nor is it right to be slaves of their own state.[9]

Holding high expectations for the government's fulfillment of its promise to safeguard China's national interests, liberal nationalists have called for popular participation in the government in general and in foreign policy making in particular—an arena that has long been monopolized by the state. In an interview with Wang Xiaodong, a leading neoconservative intellectual and popular (liberal) nationalist, a Western reporter found that "Wang's nationalism begins, surprisingly for some, with an unequivocal commitment to democracy." Wang demanded that Chinese leaders be accountable to the Chinese public. For example, he was angry at the failure of the state-controlled Chinese media to report that Beijing paid US$2.87 million for damage inflicted on U.S. diplomatic properties in China by anti-American demonstrators. According to Wang, if China was a democracy, the media would tell the truth, the government would seek the people's consent before making this kind of concession to the United States, and the Chinese people would have the right to vote out of office any leaders who inadequately defended their national interests.[10]

Taking on a tinge of populism in their criticism of China's foreign policy, liberal nationalists have routinely charged the communist government with being too chummy with Japan and being too soft in its dealings with the United States in recent years. The communist state is criticized for being neither confident enough nor competent enough in safeguarding China's vital national interests.

Foreign Policy Implications of Pragmatic Nationalism

The increasing assertiveness of popular nationalism has posed a daunting challenge to the communist state as it tries to maintain its monopoly of power. Taking a pragmatic attitude toward nationalism, Chinese leaders have been determined to prevent the nationalist sentiments of the Chinese people from getting out of control and severely damaging China's foreign relations.

Historically, nationalism has influenced Chinese foreign policy in different ways. Nationalism has produced xenophobia. It has also inspired generations of Chinese intellectuals to resist imperialism and to modernize by emulating the West. These different orientations came about because Chinese nationalists have been divided on how to revive China and, as a consequence, developed at least three different nationalist perspectives: nativism, antitraditionalism, and pragmatism. Each perspective is rooted in a unique assessment of the sources of national weakness and advocates a distinctive approach to revitalize China.

Nativism regards the impact of imperialism on Chinese self-esteem and the subversion of indigenous Chinese virtues as the root of China's weakness and calls for a return to Chinese tradition and self-reliance. In contrast, antitraditionalism identifies Chinese tradition as the source of China's weakness and calls for the boundless adoption of foreign culture and models of economic and political development. Pragmatic nationalism takes a middle road. Since the lack of modernization made China an easy target for Western imperialism in the first place, pragmatic nationalism advocates the adoption of whatever approach will help modernize China.

The three types of Chinese nationalism have different foreign policy implications. Nativism is often linked with confrontational antiforeignism, hypersensitivity to perceived foreign insults, and militant reactions to them. The most extreme acts of nativist antiforeignism in modern China have been the xenophobia of the Boxer Rebellion in 1900 and the Cultural Revolution of the late 1960s. Nativism lost its momentum in the 1980s but regained some ground among elites who reacted militantly to the so-called Western hegemony and cultural colonialism of the 1990s.

Antitraditionalism is an accommodation to a "progressive" or "modern" international system. In the 1950s, China was willing to adopt the Soviet model and conform to a Soviet-led communist world. Liberal antitraditionalists in the 1980s called on the Chinese people to rejuvenate the nation by adopting and assimilating Western models of modernization and accommodating to the capitalist world system. For this purpose, they demanded a fundamental change in the Chinese mind-set by acquiring the spirit of science and democracy.

Pragmatic nationalism involves adaptation to the changing world. It is a doctrine driven by national interest; it is ideologically agnostic, having little or nothing to do with either Marxism or liberalism. In Mao's final years, such adaptation took the form of the noncommunist strategy of the Three Worlds. Since the end of the Cold War, Beijing has envisioned a multipolar community of sovereign nations mutually respecting the principle of noninterference, and it has worked hard to promote and adapt to this multipolar world, despite those who speculate about a unipolar world. In the process, pragmatic leaders have recognized that the failure of the Soviet Union was largely due to its strategy of confrontation against the United States in a competition for superpower position, which exhausted its economic and military capacity. The author of a popular Chinese book, *China Does Not Want to Be Mr. No*, suggested that, as one of the weaker poles in the multipolar world, China should not become the second "Mr. No" by following in the footsteps of the former Soviet Union and engaging in conflict with the United States. Instead, China should defend its national interests by conducting a shrewd diplomacy, which "requires rationality and calmness."[11] Pragmatic adaptation thus seeks to defend China's national interests by developing cooperative relations with major powers. Pragmatic nationalists are flexible in their tactics, subtle in their strategies; they avoid appearing confrontational, although they are uncompromising when it comes to foreign demands that involve China's vital interests or trigger historical sensitivities, such as Taiwan independence and territorial disputes with Japan.

Since the inception of market-oriented economic reform, pragmatic nationalism has prevailed in China, although nativism and antitraditionalism continue to lurk in the background. In the sense that pragmatic leaders appeal to nationalism in response to perceived foreign pressures that could erode, corrode, or endanger China's national interests, pragmatic nationalism is more reactive than proactive in international affairs. It is not hard for pragmatic leaders to realize that nationalism is a double-edged sword: both a means to legitimate the CCP rule and a means for the Chinese people, particularly the Chinese liberal nationalist elite, to judge the performance of the communist state. As Nicolas Kristofor observed, "All this makes nationalism a particularly interesting force in China, given its potential not just for conferring legitimacy on the government but also for taking it away."[12] Indeed, if Chinese leaders cannot deliver on their nationalist promises, they will be vulnerable to criticism. Nationalism thus could become a Pandora's box. Without constraints, it could release tremendous forces with unexpected consequences. It is possible that if the Chinese people repudiate the communist government in the near future, it could be for nationalistic reasons after a conspicuous failure in foreign policy or economic development.

Balancing the positive and negative aspects, pragmatic leaders have been cautious to prevent the nationalist sentiments of the Chinese people from turning into a criticism of Chinese foreign policy. Although popular nationalists have called on the government to take a hard line against perceived provocations from the United States and Japan, pragmatic Chinese leaders know that China's economic success depends on integration with the outside world and, particularly, on cooperative relations with advanced Western countries. Therefore, they have emphasized the principles of peaceful coexistence, peaceful orientation, peaceful rise, and peaceful development as China aspires to the status of a great power.

Acting on these principles, pragmatic leaders have described nationalism as a force that must be "channeled" in its expression, including restraining or even banning students from holding anti-American and anti-Japanese demonstrations. Indeed, officials in Beijing watched the anti-Japanese demonstrations early in 2005 with great alarm; they knew that this was a volatile situation, risking not only a confrontation with foreign powers but also the possibility of turning the protesters' passions against the government. Walking on a tightrope, Beijing ordered a stop to the demonstrations in late April when leaders discovered a campaign on the Internet for even larger-scale protests on May 4. The date was significant: the May Fourth Movement had been triggered by anger over the Versailles Treaty of 1919, which gave Japan control over parts of China's Shandong province. It was a symbol of social reform, individual emancipation, and resistance to foreign aggression—almost the Chinese equivalent of the Boston Tea Party.

To stop the demonstrations, the government sent a blizzard of text messages to mobile phone users in major cities warning against "spreading rumors, believing rumors or joining illegal demonstrations." Several organizers of online petition drives and popular protests were detained. In Shanghai, one major state-run newspaper published a viciously worded editorial warning that anti-Japan protests were a cover for an "evil conspiracy" to undermine the government. Police in main cities throughout the nation went on full alert to prevent a recurrence of anti-Japan protests on the sensitive May 4 anniversary and for months thereafter. Busloads of riot police were stationed outside the Japanese embassy in Beijing, while scores of police patrolled nearby streets. Tiananmen Square was closed to the public for a government-organized coming-of-age ceremony for eighteen-year-olds in another apparent attempt to thwart any protests. Shanghai authorities closed the area around the Japanese consulate to traffic, using metal shipping containers to create a barrier. Hundreds of police stood guard around the building.

In fact, this was not the first time Chinese leaders had used heavy-handed tactics to ban antiforeign demonstrations. Beijing had learned its lesson the hard way during the crisis caused by the U.S. bombing of the Chinese embassy in Belgrade on May 8, 1999. Afterward, a highly emotional nationalism burst forth. University students gathered in front of the U.S. embassy in Beijing and consulates in other cities, throwing eggs and stones to express their anger at the U.S. action. The Chinese government encouraged or tolerated such demonstrations for the first couple of days. Then they quickly spiraled out of control, not only threatening damage to Sino-American relations but also provoking domestic criticism that the leadership was unwilling to confront the United States. Two days after the bombing, Vice President Hu Jintao made a televised speech in which he expressed government support of the students' patriotism but also warned against extreme and destabilizing behavior. In the meantime, the *People's Daily* reported that various Western countries had issued advisories against traveling to China, hurting tourism and foreign investment. Meeting with foreign visitors on May 11, President Jiang Zemin stated that life in China should now return to normal and that it was time to turn a new page in the name of economic necessity.

When a U.S. EP-3 and a Chinese jet fighter collided over the South China Sea on April 1, 2001, pragmatic leaders were determined to avoid a repeat of the anti-American demonstrations two years earlier. In response to rising nationalist sentiments, Chinese leaders talked toughly, and they followed a two-pronged policy. On the one hand, Beijing's public stand was uncompromising in stating that the American crew would be released only after a formal apology by the U.S. government and its promise to stop military spying and other provocative activities along China's coast. On the other hand, internally, Chinese officials made a point of separating the issue of the airplane from the issue of the crew members. When Secretary of State Colin Powell used the words "very sorry" with regard to the missing Chinese pilot and aircraft, Beijing accepted that as the equivalent of an apology for the whole incident and released the crew the next day. It was a testimony to the Chinese leaders' pragmatic tactical flexibility that they instructed the official Chinese media to translate Powell's expression of "very sorry" as *baoqian*, which is nearly identical to *daoqian*, the Chinese expression of "apology" that Beijing had initially demanded. This was a face-saving solution for Chinese leaders. They did not alter their tough rhetoric for domestic reasons, but they did everything they could from their perspective to avoid confrontation and maintain the framework of cooperation with the United States during the crisis.

Conclusion

The seemingly contradictory strategy of talking tough but acting in a calculated manner shows that pragmatic nationalism rather than emotional nationalism has influenced China's foreign policy. The rise of nationalism has not made Chinese foreign policy particularly uncooperative or irrational; however, this does not mean that China's commitment to cooperation is endless. Although China has remained a communist authoritarian state, it is no longer headed by charismatic leaders such as Mao Zedong or Deng Xiaoping, who had the authority to arbitrate disputes among the leadership or personally set the country's course. Current Chinese leaders must cater to a range of constituencies and will be increasingly constrained by the rise of Chinese nationalist sentiments. As a result of reform and opening up, they have become far more accountable to public opinion than in earlier years. Even average Chinese citizens now have access to information via telephone and the Internet and have found ways to express their views, including their nationalist feelings. Although pragmatic leaders have remained in full control and nationalism has not gotten out of hand so far, it remains to be seen how long this type of authoritarian control can last.

Notes

1. John Pomfret, "New Nationalism Drives Beijing: Hard Line Reflects Popular Mood," *Washington Post*, April 4, 2001, A01.

2. Erica Strecker Downs and Philip C. Saunders, "Legitimacy and the Limits of Nationalism: China and the Diaoyu Island," *International Security* 23, no. 3 (winter 1989–1990): 114–46; Allen Whiting, "Assertive Nationalism in Chinese Foreign Policy," *Asian Survey* 23, no. 8 (August 1983): 913–33; Allen Whiting, "Chinese Nationalism and Foreign Policy after Deng," *China Quarterly* 142 (June 1995): 295–316; Michael Oksenberg, "China's Confident Nationalism," *Foreign Affairs* 65, no. 3 (1986–1987): 504.

3. Ying-shih Yu, "Minzu zhuyi de jiedu" [Interpretation of nationalism], *Minzhu Zhongguo* [Democratic China] 35 (June–July 1996); Samuel P. Huntington, *The Clash of Civilizations and the Remaking of World Order* (New York: Simon and Schuster, 1996), 229; James R. Lilley, "Nationalism Bites Back," *New York Times*, October 24, 1996; Richard Bernstein and Ross H. Munro, "The Coming Conflict with America," *Foreign Affairs* 76, no. 2 (March–April 1997): 19.

4. Peter Gries, *China's New Nationalism* (Berkeley: University of California Press, 2004), 12, 134.

5. Bernstein and Munro, "The Coming Conflict with America," 19.

6. Michael Hunt, "Chinese National Identity and the Strong State: The Late Qing-Republican Crisis," in *China's Quest for National Identity*, ed. Lowell Dittmer and Samuel S. Kim (Ithaca, N.Y.: Cornell University Press, 1994), 63.

7. Liu Ji, "Making the Right Choices in Twenty-first Century Sino-American Relations," *Journal of Contemporary China* 7, no. 17 (1998): 92.

8. Henry Chu, "Chinese Students Renew Emphasis on Patriotism," *Los Angeles Times*, June 2, 1999, 1.

9. Qin Hui, "Zhiyou zhuyi yi minzu zhuyi de qihedian zai nali?" [Where is the convergent point between liberalism and nationalism?], in *Zhishifengzhi lichang: minzu zhuyi yu zhuanxingqi Zhongguo de mingyun* [The positions of intellectuals:

nationalism and China's future in the transitional period], ed. Li Shitao (Changchun: Shidai Wenyi Chuban She, 2000), 385.

10. Susan V. Lawrence, "China—The Say No Club," *Far Eastern Economic Review,* January 13, 2000, 16.

11. Shen Jiru, *Zhongguo Budang Bu Xiansheng: Dangdai Zhongguo de Guoji Zhanlue Wenti* [China does not want to be Mr. No: problems of international strategy for today's China] (Beijing: Jinri Zhongguo Chubanshe, 1998), 62.

12. Nicolas D. Kristofor, "Guess Who's a Chinese Nationalist Now?" *New York Times,* April 22, 2001.

14. Engagement or Sanction?

U.S. Economic Diplomacy toward China since the Cold War

C. X. George Wei

Economic policy is the "soft power" that has been employed in international history since the Athenian era in the late fifth century B.C.[1] Up until World War I, U.S. foreign policy makers, whether following an isolationist or an open-door policy, believed that free trade and commerce would promote peace.[2] That changed, however, when Woodrow Wilson declared in 1919 that "a nation boycotted is a nation in sight of surrender. Apply this economic, peaceful, silent, deadly remedy and there will be no need for force."[3] After World War II, U.S. foreign policy makers, due to their Cold War mentality, increasingly used economic "soft power" in a negative way to achieve diplomatic goals that military "hard power" could not. This tendency continued after the Cold War ended as the Soviet Union collapsed and the United States became the most powerful nation in the world. Confidence in its military and economic supremacy has motivated even greater U.S. use of this soft-power option. The United States is the country that has most frequently employed economic sanctions in pursuit of its foreign policy goals. It applied sanctions 115 times between World War I and 1999; sanctions were imposed 104 times from the end of World War II to 1999, and nearly one-third of the total sanctions occurring from 1919 to 1999 were imposed in the four-year period from 1995 to 1999. For example, in 1994–1998, the U.S. government authorized sixty-one unilateral sanctions covering thirty-five countries and 42 percent of the world's population.[4] In 1998, the United States had more than fifty unilateral sanctions on seventy-five countries, in addition to twenty unilateral sanctions under consideration. The United States has had sanctions against Algeria, Angola, Bahrain, Egypt, Kuwait, India, Pakistan, China, Russia, Saudi Arabia, Venezuela, and Burma, to name a few.[5]

Have economic sanctions been effective and achieved their goals? The conclusion of most scholarly works in response to this question is negative. Research on economic sanctions has been dominated by case studies that "have presented conspicuous examples of failure."[6] Richard N. Haass, director of foreign policy studies at the Brookings Institution, titled an article on the policy "Sanctioning Madness: A Rotten Core." After chairing a Council on Foreign Relations study group on economic sanctions, he concluded that, "with a few exceptions, the growing use of economic sanctions to promote foreign policy objectives is deplorable."[7] Adlai E. Stevenson, U.S. ambassador to the United Nations (1961–1965), spoke out against sanctions, observing that "punitive measures would only provoke intransigence and harden the existing situation." In 1985, Deputy Secretary of State Kenneth W. Dam told Congress, "Sanctions . . . would be counter-productive: they are more likely to strengthen resistance to change than to strengthen the forces of reform."[8] Gregory A. Fossedal pointed out that "failure to generate growing incomes in developing countries would certainly threaten to undermine democracy by fostering or exacerbating harsh and divisive conditions of zero–sum social conflict."[9] According to Richard Green Lugar of Indiana, chairman of the Senate Foreign Relations Committee and named one of America's ten best senators by *Time* magazine in 2006, studies conducted by think tanks, trade groups, the business community, the U.S. government, and foreign governments in the late 1990s all reached similar conclusions about the use of unilateral economic sanctions as a foreign policy tool:

1. When utilized to achieve foreign policy objectives, economic sanctions rarely succeed in doing so.

2. Economic sanctions seldom help those we seek to assist.

3. Economic sanctions often penalize the United States more than the target country.

4. Economic sanctions may weaken our international competitiveness and economic security.

5. Economic sanctions have increasingly become a foreign policy of first choice, even when other alternatives exist.[10]

Thus, significant numbers of scholars, diplomats, and policy makers, today and in the past, have opposed the use of sanctions as a means of diplomacy. Why, then, is U.S. economic diplomacy so often conducted in this negative way rather than more positively? It seems to me that this policy orientation is largely attributable to the Cold War ideology or mind-set of American policy makers, which has politicized, misconstrued, and distorted the implications of U.S. economic diplomacy. From its inception, the Cold War forged a certain mentality among many U.S. policy makers, who in turn prioritized the political goals of U.S. foreign policy and misinterpreted and mishandled U.S. economic and diplomatic relations with socialist countries. This mentality has been the predominant factor in U.S. foreign policy since the Cold War era, and it lingers today. As long as U.S. policy makers perceive diplomatic relations with socialist countries through the lens of the Cold War, economic sanctions will naturally be seen as a better alternative to a "hot war," and it will be very difficult to consider using economic means to reduce the political hostility between the United States and its socialist "enemy." The postwar U.S. economic policy toward China clearly reflects this phenomenon and illustrates how U.S. economic diplomacy deviated from its initial engagement orientation to disengagement and eventually sanctions.

The Politicization of U.S. Economic Policy toward China

As early as the spring of 1945, the United States' postwar economic policy toward China was formed, with two objectives: to develop China into an American international market, and to establish China as a political ally that would be a major force in stabilizing the Far East. The former was economic and the latter was political, but the two objectives were closely interrelated and interdependent. U.S. foreign policy makers believed that establishing a capitalist, liberal economic system in China would lay the basis for stability and U.S. interests in China and Asia. In the postwar global strategic structure designed by American policy makers, "the need for China to be a principal stabilizing factor in the Far East is a fundamental requirement for peace and security in that area." Thus, the United States' long-range goal was to help China become "a strong, united, and democratic" country that "would be a bulwark for peace in the Pacific and in the world."[11] However, a strong and democratic China, American policy makers believed, required a firm economic base.[12] President Harry Truman stated in April 1946 that "the roots of democracy . . . [would] not draw much nourishment in any nation from a soil of poverty and economic distress."[13] Thus, the postwar economic policy of the United States should "aid in achieving the broad objective of a strong, more united and increasingly democratic China."[14] The dual objectives of the U.S. economic policy toward China were consistent with U.S. foreign economic policy in general. "The international economic interests of the United States," Assistant Secretary of State William L. Clayton explained, "are part and parcel of its international interests in general. Our paramount international interest is peace."[15]

In the early stage, U.S. diplomatic efforts were concentrated mainly on the economic aspects of the U.S.-China policy. The Americans tried to persuade the Chinese to adopt a capitalist, liberal economic policy and attempted to use economic assistance as the bait to induce the gigantic Chinese fish to swim in that direction. Economic assistance to China was considered a direct contribution to China's economic development as well as a means to force the Nationalist government to carry out political and economic reforms to achieve a stable and democratic China.

By 1947, however, the Cold War broke out. The conflict between the Kuomintang and the Chinese Communist Party (CCP) within the Cold War context and the uncertainty of China's future made American diplomats reconsider their economic policy toward China from a more expedient and political perspective. President Truman sent Secretary of State George Marshall to China, and Edwin A. Locke Jr. recalled that Marshall "was preoccupied with the political and military aspects and had no time and little interest for the economic"; as a result, the "opportunities were pretty much lost by that time in the economic area."[16] Although Marshall persuaded the Nationalist government to adopt some liberal economic policies, his main purpose was to prevent the pending large-scale civil war in China.

The failure of the Marshall mission further diminished the economic aspects of U.S. economic policy toward China and led to a China aid program. The U.S. Congress passed the China Aid Act in 1948,[17] and many scholars claimed that the Truman administration had been forced by public and congressional opinion to support the legislation.[18] John H. Feaver, however, has persuasively refuted this claim, stating that the China lobby was not responsible for Truman's decision to forward the bill to Congress; instead, the president did so to prevent a swift change of power from the Nationalists to the Communists, which, it was believed, would lead to a dominant Soviet influence in East Asia.[19] Indeed, the China Aid Act derived mainly from the State Department's pessimistic and passive political view of the Nationalist government. According to Roger Lapham, chief of the Economic Cooperation Administration's mission to China, when the secretary first advocated the Marshall Plan, "he was thinking not of China, but of Europe, as his public statement of January 7, 1947, made at the time he left China, clearly indicates how hopeless he felt the Chinese political situation then was, and seems to imply that he felt that our best policy would be to let the Chinese people work out their own salvation."[20]

Once civil war broke out in China in 1948, the U.S. government became more concerned about the effect of the civil war on U.S. economic assistance programs rather than the actual economic needs of China. U.S. officials stressed that "so long as serious political instability continued in China, the requirements for economic aid must necessarily depend upon decisions as to specific political objectives to be attained thereby."[21] To prevent U.S. dollars from being wasted, the Americans preferred to strive for a limited but substantial achievement rather than institute an ambitious program that might become the victim of the civil war.[22] An assistance plan that assumed full responsibility for China's stability became inconceivable because it was too expensive; in addition, it might lead to increased Soviet assistance to the CCP, which could eventually involve the United States in a confrontation with the Soviet Union.[23] Nevertheless, cutting off assistance to China entirely and immediately was inconsistent with the Cold War atmosphere and with rhetoric advocating a U.S.-Europe policy, and it would put the State Department in the position of being blamed for the failure of the Nationalists. The National Security Council report of March 26, 1948, concluded that limited economic assistance to China meant that "the military responsibility for the survival of the National[ist] Government would be clearly placed upon Chinese shoulders" and "would limit the drain on U.S. resources and avoid a complete underwriting of the National[ist] Government," yet it would not be "a reversal of past U.S. policy."[24] Marshall insisted on limited assistance to China,[25] and he repeatedly emphasized that without an adequate self-help effort by the Nationalist government, the United States could do nothing to reverse the tide in China, regardless of how much aid China received.[26] Based on Marshall's experience with and knowledge of the Nationalist government, he apparently thought that it was incapable of initiating any effective self-help measures.[27] Thus, his statements were hypocritical; he was, in effect, asking the Nationalist government to take the entire blame for its forthcoming failure and allowing the United States to withdraw its commitment to China. It was a deliberate and smooth transition of the U.S.-China policy that maintained the United States' "freedom of action" in China.[28] The China Aid Act of 1948 was purely a product of political concern and calculation. On October

13, 1948, the State Department enunciated its new China policy in another report, where it predicted that if the Nationalist government disappeared, China would be a chaotic and undependable factor in the Far East for some time to come. Thus, it concluded, the United States must not become irrevocably committed to any one course of action or any one faction in China.[29] The State Department preferred to wait and see what happened once the dust settled in China. This was a passive policy of disengaging and distancing the United States from China. In undertaking this new policy, the State Department and the White House did not consider economic interests (either China's or the United States') but only the strategic needs of the Cold War. American economic policy toward China was largely politicized.

The Economic Cooperation Administration's Engagement Approach

The Economic Cooperation Administration (ECA) was established in part because of the outbreak of the Cold War.[30] Under the China Aid Act of 1948 (Title IV of the Foreign Assistance Act of 1948), the ECA's mission to China, which took place between early May and late June 1948, was to concentrate on commodities programs, industrial reconstruction and replacement projects, and rural reconstruction. As a governmental agency concerned more with the humanitarian and economic aspects of U.S. foreign policy, the ECA took a very different approach toward China. It instituted an engagement approach, trying to prevent economic aid from being blockaded by ideological conflicts or considerations.

In 1948, Harlan Cleveland, director of the ECA's China program, urged the State Department to find "means whereby economic activity in the area might be further stimulated and international economic cooperation strengthened . . . , giving the peoples concerned a larger stake in economic development in collaboration with the democratic nations, and fortifying and extending economic ties with the United States and the western European democracies."[31] This is the epitome of the goal and means of an engagement policy, which puts strong faith in the economic, cultural, and humanitarian effects of U.S. aid on a foreign country. Cleveland believed that the Chinese could be pulled away from communism and the Soviet Union, and to achieve this long-term purpose, the most effective and important means was to build economic bonds and friendship between the United States and China. Cleveland stressed that the United States should not get out of China and "let the Chinese Communist[s] beat their heads against some of the insoluble problems of China." Rather, the United States should continue the commodity portion of its present aid program during the takeover and thereafter, thus competing with the Soviets for the hearts and minds of the Chinese people. "Our objective," he remarked, "should be to demonstrate to the Chinese people that we are on their side in any event, and the ECA is not a program of American imperialism."[32] If the communists permitted U.S. commodities to be distributed in the areas they controlled, Cleveland calculated, progress could be made in demonstrating the Americans' continuing friendship for the Chinese people, thus counteracting a trend toward domination by Moscow to some extent. If the communists rejected American assistance, they would make it clear who had brought down the Iron Curtain.[33] Winning over the Chinese people was the key to preventing China from leaning toward the Soviet Union. Many other ECA officials shared Cleveland's view. Roger D. Lapham believed that no one could sell Moscow ideology to a people like the Chinese, nor should the United States go to the extreme of using military means or economic blockade to oppose the Chinese communists. Rather, the Americans should focus on their countless Chinese friends—people of education and capability—"whom the Chinese Communists will need to employ. Their position can be immeasurably strengthened if our skill is great enough and our patience enduring."[34]

In 1948–1949, while Nationalist and Communist forces were fighting a fierce war that would decide China's future, the ECA was engaged in a political battle with the State Department over the ECA's role in China. W. Walton Butterworth, director of the State Department's Office of Far Eastern Affairs, told Cleveland on September 17, 1948, that it was highly unlikely that "the Secretary would change the position on China he has consistently taken, particularly the strong desire not to get involved in Chinese affairs too deeply." Given this tough stand, Cleveland suggested that the ECA should develop some sensible proposals while "keeping the State Department informed at all stages but not expecting State to take any initiative on these proposals."[35] On December 30, 1948, however, President Truman (no doubt influenced by the State Department) approved Butterworth's memorandum, which repudiated the ECA's policy recommendation that the U.S. government maintain flexibility for a "foot in the door" approach.[36]

Truman's decision did not stop the efforts of the ECA. Paul Hoffman, overall head of the agency, continued to claim that the ECA's opinion was supported by 95 percent of the people he had talked to in China. Hoffman insisted that the development of Western trade and economic contact with the communists in China was the best way to take advantage of American economic power in combating communism. The core of the disagreement was that the State Department wanted to "walk out" of China and the ECA wanted to be "thrown out" of China.[37] ECA officials felt that its administrator had the right, under Section 118 of the Foreign Assistance Act, to determine when or whether the United States should terminate assistance to a country.[38] Cleveland suggested that the United States should exercise its influence through the following efforts: (1) encourage any potential deviation of Chinese policy from a Soviet orientation and strengthen those within the CCP who advocated a more Chinese policy; (2) preserve the goodwill of the Chinese people toward the United States; (3) protect American investments and promote American commercial interests in the Far East; (4) emphasize the advantages that would accrue to China through U.S. technical assistance and economic development; (5) give encouragement or assistance to anticommunist elements; and (6) retain access to valuable resources and markets in China for other Far Eastern areas in which the United States was interested, especially Japan. Charles L. Stillman, head of the Technical Mission of the ECA, included these recommendations in a memorandum for use by ECA officials testifying before Congress in support of an amendment to the China Aid Act of 1948 that would cover the period from April 3 to June 30, 1949.[39]

Nevertheless, Truman approved a National Security Council report on March 3, 1949, that ruled out the possibility of aiding and developing economic relations with China in the near future and insisted that the United States threaten to impose economic sanctions, if necessary, as a means of influencing Chinese behavior.[40] ECA officials were very upset by this report. At a meeting on March 10, 1949, attended by Butterworth and Secretary of State Dean Acheson, ECA officials reviewed a memorandum on China policy prepared by Lapham point by point. The memo stated that "the interests of the U.S. are best served by continuing further economic aid to Shanghai, Canton or Swatow as long as those areas remain in non-Communist hands" (even though it was obvious that Shanghai would soon fall to the communists). Lapham urged that "no matter what State may later decide to do I feel that ECA should now be prepared to advance an affirmative program and state its position publicly" for further aid to China.

He noted that "merely asking for this amount" of aid to China would "have a great psychological effect." It would "give heart not only to those Americans and foreign interests who would be greatly affected if ECA aid was exhausted before Shanghai, Canton and Swatow fell, but it would also strengthen the morale of those Chinese who are not anxious for Communist control." Above all, the memo emphasized, further aid "would give notice to the world that we are still interested in the Chinese people."[41] ECA officials believed that the humanitarian, economic, and cultural effects of aid to China would promote "the real friendship of many high-class and truly patriotic Chinese" and that this friendship would grow "slowly with every individual and group with whom the Mission organization came in contact, for the honesty of purpose and complete integrity of the organization" and the United States would be apparent.[42]

After the communists took over Shanghai, Lapham wrote to Hoffman in July 1949 to urge that the United States not impose an economic blockade against China but "continue to at least give moral encouragement to all Americans now in Communist territory to hang on as best they can and keep the door a little ajar, waiting for the breaks." He continued, "One thing the year has taught me [is that] you cannot afford to hold to fixed ideas. You must keep fluid, face things as they are and not as you would like to have them."[43] In September 1949, Lapham recommended that the United States (1) continue private business dealings with the Chinese, to the extent possible; (2) extend all possible help to American-endowed enterprises—educational, medical, and missionary—and continue the private support these enterprises had received in the past; (3) keep its embassy and consulates in China open; and (4) be prepared to recognize the CCP government.[44] Such views remained strong among ECA officials until the outbreak of the Korean War,[45] which eventually terminated any engagement policy.

Sanction or Engagement? A Historical Assessment

The preceding analysis reveals that there was a strong element of engagement in U.S. economic diplomacy toward China at the end of World War II and early in the Cold War. Unfortunately, the Cold War environment, growing anticommunist sentiments, and political pressure prevented American policy makers from keeping that policy orientation and trying the strategy of engagement. The outbreak of the Korean War totally eliminated that possibility.

In the late 1940s and early 1950s, there was much talk in the United States about whether the Truman administration had "lost" China to the communists. This evolved into a scholarly debate from the late 1960s to the early 1980s.[46] Scholars such as Warren I. Cohen believed that the CCP was "open to relationships with the United States" and that "the Truman administration had sought accommodation." A consensus developed among students of U.S.-China relations that the communist leaders were interested in contact with the West to avoid dependence on the Soviet Union; however, they had to move cautiously because Stalin was suspicious of their loyalty. Although an overt political alliance with the United States was impossible because China could not afford to be weaned from the Soviet Union, civil political contacts and modest economic relations between the two countries were conceivable. But this opportunity was lost in 1949–1950 because of domestic political restraint in the United States and misperceptions and miscalculations in both Beijing and Washington.[47] Based on Soviet advice and the desire to protect information about communist military maneuvers in Manchuria, the CCP forced British, American, and French diplomats out of Shenyang in November 1948; tried to seize the radio transmitters in the Western consulates in Shenyang; and placed U.S. consul Angus Ward and his staff, who refused to hand over their radio equipment, under house arrest on November 20. Nevertheless, the CCP issued several orders in January–March 1949 to protect the life and property of American and British personnel and to prevent people from trespassing at Western embassies and institutions in China. Mao Zedong, leader of the CCP, instructed his subordinates to separate economic affairs from politics and try to do business with capitalist countries.[48] When John Leighton Stuart, the U.S. ambassador to China, started a series of meetings in May and June 1949 with Huang Hua, director of the Foreign Affairs Office under the Nanjing Municipal Military Control Commission, the communist leaders showed an interest in the possibility of establishing a relationship with the United States.[49] However, this was not feasible once the Korean War broke out.

In examining the United States' postwar economic policy toward China, the Korean War makes the analysis more complex. The hostilities in Korea brought an abrupt end to any engagement policy and altered the course of history and U.S.-China relations. Had the Korean War not broken out, would the engagement policy of the ECA have been feasible? Would the CCP have responded positively to the ECA's economic and people-to-people diplomacy even though political relations with the United States were in jeopardy? History cannot answer these questions. However, one example of how the CCP dealt with U.S. aid reveals the possibility of collaboration between the CCP and the ECA. When the ECA was wrapping up its mission in China in 1949, it distributed yards of cotton cloth worth US$4 million to the Shanghai Federation of Emergency Relief (SFER), the Church World Service, and the China Welfare Fund. It seems that the ECA purposely distributed these goods mostly to SFER, which the CCP controlled or at least trusted. Interestingly, these goods were not confiscated by the communists when they seized Shanghai. The CCP demanded only that all the ECA supplies be transferred from the Church World Service and the China Welfare Fund, which they did not trust, to the SFER for distribution.[50] Clearly, the CCP did not mind receiving economic assistance from its ideological antagonist the United States.

Since history cannot be rerun and replayed under another set of conditions, it is difficult to assess the possible impact of continuing U.S. aid to China. In pondering this question, the following story may be helpful. During an interview with a senior Chinese engineer and general manager of a large factory in Henan province in the 1970s, I asked, "Why don't you like communism?" This man, who had been a victim of the antirightist movement in the 1950s, answered, "It's because I had learned the nature of communists as early as in the civil war, when I was a kid starving to death. My life was saved by a small bag of grain supplied by the ECA and labeled 'Made in America.' I did not know what American imperialism was, but I knew that while the so-called 'American evils' were trying to save thousands of Chinese lives, the Chinese, both the Communists and the Nationalists, were busy with killing each other. I don't like the CCP simply because they don't like American imperialists, whom I like."[51] This plain and sincere expression of an educated Chinese is definitely worth digesting. It shows that the ECA's approach could have worked, at least on the level of people's diplomacy.

The effect of the ECA's approach in combating the influence of communism was more evident on the global level. Ironically, the end of the ECA's China mission led to the implementation and strengthening of programs in other parts of Asia, such as Taiwan, South Korea, Indonesia, Indochina, Thailand, Burma, and the Philippines, which gave the ECA more field laboratories to test its approach.[52] Although the situation in each of these countries was unique and complex, the ECA's approach toward China was relevant and became a pattern for its operations in the region. From the outset, the ECA clearly reported to Congress that the goal of its economic and cultural missions in Asia was the promotion of "confidence, good will, friendship for the United States among the governments concerned and among the masses of the people."[53] As a result of this approach, as Harry Bayard Price concluded in his authoritative research on the Marshall Plan, the governments and the peoples of Southeast Asia were brought to "a better understanding of the United States aims and policies," and they straightforwardly refuted the Soviet charges of U.S. "imperialism."[54]

Thus, the ECA's China policy reflected its general approach toward Asia as a whole. As Price noted, the ECA fully realized that "communism was only one aspect of the dilemma confronting the underdeveloped areas. Their fundamental problem lay in the condition that made communism possible and that would be a potential source of danger whether communism existed or not." The ECA had to prevent Asian communists from taking advantage of nationalism, and it had to advance Asian countries' capacity to deal with their own problems and the communist threat without inviting suspicion and resistance.[55] This is the very point ignored by the State Department. In terms of U.S. aid to other parts of Asia, the ECA's approach encountered much less opposition from the State Department, mainly because there was no imminent threat from the communists in these countries, except for Vietnam. Thus, the ECA's experience in China had broader significance in the context of Asia, but the economic opportunity that the ECA failed to capitalize on in China was unique.

Sanction or Engagement? A Historical Comparison

In assessing U.S. economic policy toward China, a brief summary and comparative analysis of U.S.-China relations after the postwar era will be helpful. The U.S. economic policy toward China since the Korea War can be divided into three phases. The first phase began when engagement was replaced by the economic embargo of UN Resolution 500 on May 17, 1951, for which the United States was the main impetus. After these multilateral sanctions against China disintegrated in the late 1950s, the U.S. embargo continued until 1972, when the United States began to normalize its political and economic relationship with China.[56] Did the embargo policy work? What were its effects and consequences? If the embargo achieved its goals and the results were positive, we could assume that the opposite policy of engagement during the postwar era probably would have failed. However, history tells us that twenty years of sanctions against China brought about nothing but a more defiant, isolated, consolidated, and dangerous communist regime in China and the loss of huge potential profits for the United States from U.S.-China trade and great economic opportunities for American businesses in China. I am not aware of any empirical study that supports this view of the embargo's impact on the U.S. economy, but studies of other cases bolster my point and offer a rough idea of the possible effects. According to Gary C. Hufbauer and coauthors, in 1995, the United States lost about 200,000 high-paid jobs and nearly US$1 billion in export-sector wage premiums because of sanctions. This latter number would actually be much higher if the impact on U.S. exports to third parties was included. For instance, Jianwen Yang and associates estimated that the U.S. export loss averaged more than US$15 billion per year between 1989 and 1998.[57] Taking into account that China is a large country and that none of the targeted countries in 1995 was comparable in terms of size, the negative impact of the embargo against China on the U.S. economy in the 1950s and 1960s was certainly not insignificant.

A few scholars hold the view that international economic sanctions have been and can be successful if one defines the concept of success appropriately and pays more attention to the relatively modest or indirect long-term goals.[58] It seems to me that the main problem with this argument is that it uses war and military force as references for comparison and the assessment of success. Of course, if economic sanctions could replace war or the use of military force or even postpone their occurrence, they would be considered a success. In making this kind of comparison, one can surely identify cases in which some type of sanction was relatively more successful than others. Yet if one uses engagement as a measure for comparison, one may find that sanctions are always a worse option because engagement increases economic and social intercourse, which in turn reduces hostility, distrust, and misunderstanding; in contrast, sanctions sever normal channels of interaction, communication, and understanding, which creates and intensifies confrontation and exacerbates tension, mistrust, and animosity. Some scholars have argued that the embargo against China was successful because it led to "the collapse of Sino–Soviet economic cooperation" and the eventual Sino–Soviet rift.[59] It seems to me, however, that the conclusion should be the opposite: what led to the Sino–Soviet rift was not the embargo but engagement. As a result of British-led efforts, the elimination of the China differential in 1957 and the scaling back of multilateral sanctions gave China an alternative to economic reliance on the Soviet Union. Therefore, it lifted the lid that had long suppressed Beijing's smoldering anger at Moscow and significantly contributed to Mao's triumphant attitude, romantic and unrealistic domestic policies, and increasing defiance of Moscow, which eventually led to the Sino-Soviet rift.

The second stage of U.S.-China relations since the Korean War started when President Richard Nixon visited China in 1972. Afterward, U.S.-China relations normalized and trade greatly increased, especially after China initiated its economic reform. This trend, however, suffered a significant setback when the Chinese government cracked down on dissidents in June 1989, beginning the third stage of U.S.-China relations. At that point, discussions about the use of sanctions against China were loud and widespread. There was worldwide condemnation of the Chinese government's methods of suppressing students' demands for democracy and an outcry from American politicians, human rights activists, and the press. Nevertheless, the end of the Cold War and the weakening of anticommunist ideology allowed the U.S. government to maintain an engagement policy toward China. Although relations between the two countries were rocky, and the U.S. government imposed some sanctions against China during the 1990s, the overarching nature of U.S. economic policy toward China during that period was engagement: to promote political and economic liberalization within China, integrate China into global institutions, and pursue U.S. commercial interests there.[60] The most important point is that the U.S. government did not revoke China's most-favored nation (MFN) status, believing that the ensuing retaliation would only hurt American exports while doing little or nothing for human rights.[61] Presidential candidate Bill Clinton criticized the China policy of President George H. W. Bush during the 1992 campaign, but as president, Clinton signed an executive order in 1993 to extend MFN until 1994, and he recertified China's MFN status in 1995 and 1996. Many prominent Republicans also supported the extension of China's MFN status on the grounds that Washington's annual threat not to do so only increased tension and harmed U.S.-China relations without accomplishing anything positive. There is no doubt that this engagement policy has paid off and has led to significant improvements in the relationship between the two countries.

Today, U.S.-China trade has reached unprecedented levels, and the two countries have become indispensable economic partners. U.S. economic diplomacy toward China since the Korean War has clearly demonstrated that engagement is a much better option than sanction. As Senator Richard Green Lugar correctly concluded, "American interests are better advanced through engagement and active leadership that afford us an opportunity to influence events that threaten our interests. In some cases, unilateral sanctions restrict our ability to take advantage of changes in other countries, because trade embargoes impose a heavy bias against dialogue and exchange. Unilateral sanctions may create tensions with friends and allies—including democratic countries—that jeopardize cooperation in achieving other foreign-policy priorities, including multilateral cooperation on the sanctions themselves."[62]

Conclusion

In the post–Cold War era, military and political confrontations between the East and West have ended, and cultural and economic issues have come to the forefront of international relations. It is imperative, however, to recognize the history of economic interaction between China and the United States during the Cold War—namely, the essential problems existing between developed and undeveloped countries that were once colored, distorted, and mishandled through political and diplomatic relations within the context of the Cold War. Today, China is the forerunner in a trend of worldwide reform, as well as the last "socialist" stronghold. Although U.S.-China economic relations have dramatically changed since the late 1980s, some old patterns of interaction remain. The recent political and military tension involving China, Taiwan, and the United State demonstrates that there are still hostilities and conflicts between democratic America, where the free economy is a dominant force, and communist China, where the government still has great power to interfere in the economy. Conflicting political views and trade disputes between the United States and China in the twenty-first century may have an adverse effect on their economic relations. Thus, it is very important to reexamine U.S.-China economic relations of the late 1940s, when they moved from a planned economic partnership to a state of decreasing economic intercourse and growing political and ideological involvement. The political and economic relations between China and the United States today may well reflect that older pattern. The fundamental nature of U.S.-China relations is well characterized by the words of Henry Kissinger, with which I conclude this chapter: "China remains too important for America's national security to risk the relationship on the emotions of the moment . . . geopolitical realities will dictate a rapprochement between the United States and China."[63]

Notes

1. Hrach Gregorian, "Economic Sanctions as a Tool of Foreign Policy: A Short History of the U.S. Experience," in *Private Property and National Security: Foreign Economic Sanctions and the Constitution*, ed. Richard J. Ellings, Hrach Gregorian, Monroe Leigh, and Jo Anne Swindle (Washington, D.C.: National Legal Center for the Public Interest, 1991), 2.

2. Ibid.

3. Gary Clyde Hufbauer and Barbara Oegg, "Economic Sanction," *Quill*, January–February 1999.

4. Testimony by Undersecretary of State Stuart Eisenstat before the House International Relations Committee; see Richard G. Lugar, "Does Economic Sanctions Make Good Policy?" *The World and I* 14, no. 3 (March 1999): 283.

5. Kenneth T. Derr (chairman of the board and chief executive officer, Chevron Corporation), "Engagement—A Better Alternative," speech to the Commonwealth Club of California, San Francisco, November 5, 1998.

6. Shu Guang Zhang, *Economic Cold War: America's Embargo against China and the Sino-Soviet Alliance, 1949–1963* (Stanford, Calif.: Stanford University Press, 2001), 7, 265; Diance B. Kunz, *Butter and Guns: America's Cold War Economic Diplomacy* (New York: Free Press, 1977), 328–29.

7. Richard N. Haass, "Sanctioning Madness: A Rotten Core," *Foreign Affairs* (November–December 1997).

8. Jagdish Bhagwati, "Democracy and Development," in *Capitalism, Socialism and Democracy Revisited*, ed. Larry Diamond and Marc F. Plattner (Baltimore: Johns Hopkins University Press, 1993), 35. See also Ali M. Farfer, "Sanctions and Development: Some Hypotheses," in *Economic Sanctions and Development*, ed. Hans Köchler (Vienna: Studies in International Relations, International Progress Organization, 1997), vol. 23.

9. Gregory A. Fossedal, "Sanctions for Beginners," *New Republic* 193 (October 21, 1985): 18–21. See also Farfer, "Sanctions and Development."

10. Lugar, "Does Economic Sanctions Make Good Policy?"

11. John D. Sumner, "American Economic Policy toward China," Papers of John D. Sumner, Folder 1, "Chungking Conference," Box 1, China File, 3, 9, Harry S Truman Library, Independence, Mo. (hereafter HTL); "Memorandum by Mr. Everett F. Drumright of the Division of Chinese," March 2, 1945; Carl H. Boehringer (in charge of Commercial Section), April 3, 1945; "Memorandum

Prepared in the Office of Far Eastern Affairs," April 18, 1945; letter from Joseph C. Grew to James Forrestal, May 21, 1945; letter from George C. Marshall to William D. Leahy, November 30, 1945; John D. Sumner, "Memorandum Prepared in the Department of State: U.S. Policy towards China," all in *Foreign Relations of the United States: Diplomatic Papers*, ed. Department of State, 9 vols. (Washington, D.C.: U.S. Government Printing Office, 1969), 7:249–53, 82–84, 93–95, 878–82, 747–51, 754–57.

12. "Basic Considerations in Planning American Aid for China's Postwar Economy," April 23, 1945, enclosed in the correspondence between General Hurley and Mr. Nelson, 893.50/5-1245, Record Group (RG) 59, National Archives (hereafter NA).

13. "Address by Mr. John Carter Vincent, Director of Far Eastern Affairs, Department of State, before the Thirty-third Convention of the National Foreign Trade Council," Arthur N. Young Papers, Box 98, Archives of the Hoover Institution on War, Revolution, and Peace, Stanford, Calif. (hereafter AHI).

14. "Basic Considerations in Planning American Aid for China's Postwar Economy"; Harry S Truman, *Memoirs by Harry S Truman*, vol. 2, *Years of Trial and Hope* (Garden City, N.Y.: Doubleday, 1956), 67–72.

15. "Fourth General Session, Chamber of Commerce of the United States," Atlantic City, N.J., May 2, 1946, Chamber of Commerce of the United States Records, Accession 1960, Box 9, 127, Hagley Museum and Library, Wilmington, Del.

16. Georgia Valdosta, interview with Edwin A. Locke Jr., April 5, 1967, Oral History, HTL.

17. "Legislative History of the China Aid Program," R. Allen Griffin Papers, Box 2, AHI.

18. William Whitney Stueck Jr., *The Road to Confrontation: American Policy toward China and Korea, 1947–1950* (Chapel Hill: University of North Carolina Press, 1981), 54–58; William Whitney Stueck Jr., "The Marshall and Wedemeyer Missions: A Quadrilateral Perspective," in *Sino-American Relations, 1945–1955: A Joint Reassessment of a Critical Decade*, ed. Harry Harding and Yuan Ming (Wilmington, Del.: Scholarly Resources, 1989), 96–118; Kenneth C. Kan, "The Diplomacy of Foreign Aid: China, the United States and Marshall Plan Assistance, 1947–1949" (PhD diss., Miami University of Ohio, 1983), 48–76; Lewis M. Purifoy, *Harry Truman's China Policy: McCarthyism and the Diplomacy of Hysteria* (New York: New Viewpoints, 1976), 17–18, 57, 66–69; Ross Y. Koen, *The China Lobby in American Politics* (New York: Octagon Books, 1974), 198–99; Tang Tsou, *America's Failure in China, 1941–1950* (Chicago: University of Chicago Press, 1963), chap. 11; H. Brandford Westerfield, *Foreign Policy and Party Politics: Pearl Harbor to Korea* (New Haven, Conn.: Yale University Press, 1955), 260–68; John H. Feaver, "The China Aid Bill of 1948: Limited Assistance as a Cold War Strategy," *Diplomatic History* 5, no. 2 (spring 1981).

19. Feaver, "The China Aid Bill of 1948."

20. Roger D. Lapham, "The Chinese Situation as I Saw It," address before the Commonwealth Club of California, September 8, 1949, San Francisco, Folder 21.0, "General Policy & Procedures," China Subjects Files, Box 3, RG 286, Washington Records Center, Suitland, Md. (hereafter WRC).

21. "U.S. Policy toward China," (1947) 360.001; "United States Assistance to China," May 21, 1947, State-War-Navy Coordinating Committee 360 and 360/1, (1947) 400.5; John Carter Vincent, "JCS Paper on Military Assistance to China," June 20, 1947, Box 12, RG 59, NA.

22. George F. Kennan, "Memorandum for Mr. Lovett," June 23, 1947, U.S. Department of State Decimal "Lot" File, Box 13, Records of the Policy Planning Staff, RG 59, NA.

23. "U.S. Policy toward China"; Vincent, "JCS Paper on Military Assistance to China."

24. National Security Council (NSC) 6, "Note by the Executive Secretary to the National Security Council on the Position of the United States Regarding Short-Term Assistance to China," March 26, 1948, U.S. Department of State Decimal "Lot" File, Box 13, Country and Area Files, RG 59, NA.

25. U.S. Congress, Senate Committee on Foreign Relations, *Foreign Relief Assistance Act of 1948: Hearings Held in Executive Session,* 80th Cong., 2d sess., Historical Series (Washington, D.C.: U.S. Government Printing Office, 1973), 348–51.

26. U.S. Congress, House Committee on Foreign Affairs, *Hearings on United States Foreign Policy for a Post-War Recovery Program,* 80th Cong., 1st and 2d sess. (Washington, D.C.: U.S. Government Printing Office, 1948), vol. 2, 1545–47; U.S. Congress, House Committee on International Relations, *United States Policy in the Far East, Selected Executive Session Hearings of the Committee, 1943–1950,* Historical Series (Washington, D.C.: U.S. Government Printing Office, 1976), vol. 7, pt. 1, 160–61, 165–68.

27. Lapham, "The Chinese Situation as I Saw It"; J. Leighton Stuart to the Secretary of State, May 26, 1948, *FRUS,* 7:231–32, 257–59.

28. Letter from George C. Marshall to J. Leighton Stuart, February 9, 1948, *FRUS,* 8:13.

29. "A Report to the National Security Council by the Department of State on United States Policy toward China," NSC 34, October 13, 1948, U.S. Department of State Decimal File, Box 13, RG 59, NA II; "Memorandum by the Policy Planning Staff (PPS 39)," September 7, 1948, *FRUS,* 8:146–55.

30. "China—1947 (only)," General File, Box 418, Papers of Harry S Truman, HTL.

31. Harlan Cleveland, "Study of Economic Potentialities in the Far East," Countries: China, 1948, Box 13, Subject Files, 1948–1950, Assistant Administrator for Programs–Assistant Administrator, RG 469: Records of U.S. Foreign Assistance Agencies, 1948–1961, NA II.

32. Harlan Cleveland, "Memorandum: Aid-to-China Policy," R. Allen Griffin Papers, Box 4, AHI.

33. Ibid.

34. "Reappraisal of ECA Policy," Paul H. Johnstone to Robert Allen Griffin and Norman J. Meiklejohn, February 21, 1949, China Subjects Files, 1947–1950, Box 5, RG 286, WRC; "A Study of Future China Aid—Emphasis Propaganda," attached to letter to Roger D. Lapham, "Comments on Future Plans for ECA," February 8, 1949, China Subjects Files, 1947–1950, Box 5, RG 286, WRC.

35. Harlan Cleveland, director of the ECA's China program, to Paul Hoffman, administrator of the ECA, September 19, 1948, Robert Allen Griffin Papers, Box 2, Subject File: Correspondence, Harlan Cleveland, AHI.

36. "Comment on Your Covering Draft for Congressional Presentation," Harry Price to Harlan Cleveland, January 12, 1949, China Subjects Files, Box 25, RG 286, WRC. The president's decision was as follows:

(1) That this Government would continue to support through the implementation of the China Aid Act the present Chinese Government or a legal successor Government which pursues an anti-Communist policy. However, should a government come into power which comes to terms with the Chinese Communists, all aid should cease irrespective of whether the Communists are in numerical ascendancy or not. (2) When the Chinese Communists either directly or indirectly through a coalition government take control over any area, all ECA supplies ashore or in the process of being unloaded can be distributed under conditions similar to those new prevailing. However, ECA supplies which have not yet reached such ports should be diverted elsewhere.

See "China: Effect of Further Communist Expansion on the ECA China Program," January 25, 1949, 500.3, U.S. Department of State Decimal File, Box 15, RG 59, NA II; "Memorandum Prepared in the Office of Far Eastern Affairs," January 25, 1949, FRUS, 9:616–17; W. Walton Butterworth, December 30, 1948, FRUS, 8:667–68.

37. Harlan Cleveland to Roger D. Lapham, January 7, 1949, FRUS, 9:610–13.

38. A. I. Henderson, general counsel of the ECA, and Harlan Cleveland, director of the China Division, ECA, "Continuance of Assistance to Peripheral Areas in China," February 1, 1949, 500.3, Aid to China (General) and ECA Program, U.S. Department of State Decimal File, Box 15, RG 59, NA II.

39. Charles L. Stillman, "Draft of Suggested Statement on China," February 28, 1949, Charles L. Stillman Papers, Box 1, Folder: China, 1949, AHI.

40. This report is NSC 41. See Sidney W. Souers, March 3, 1949, FRUS, 9:834.

41. "Memorandum of Conversation—Subject: Future of the China Aid Program," March 10, 1949, Robert Allen Griffin Papers, Box 1, Folder: Correspondence, Roger Lapham, AHI.

42. Roger D. Lapham to Paul Hoffman, June 30, 1949, Charles L. Stillman Papers, Box 1, Folder: ECA Personal, AHI.

43. Ibid.

44. Lapham, "The Chinese Situation as I Saw It."

45. Raymond T. Moyer, chief ECA representative in China, Taipei, Taiwan, "Important Considerations in an Approach to Aid to Taiwan under Present Condition," July 12, 1950; "Budget Recommendations for Formosa for Fiscal Year 1951," RG 469: Records of U.S. Foreign Assistance Agencies, 1948–1961, Countries: China, 1948, Box 27, Subject Files, 1948–1950, Assistant Administrator for Programs–Assistant Administrator, NA II.

46. Warren I. Cohen, "Symposium: Rethinking the Lost Chance in China— Introduction: Was There a Lost Chance in China?" *Diplomatic History* 21, no. 1 (winter 1977): 71–75.

47. Ibid., 73–74.

48. He Di, "The Evolution of the CCP's Policy towards the United States, 1945–1949," in *Sino-American Relations, 1945–1955: A Collaborative Reassessment of a Troubled Time*, ed. Yuan Ming and Harry Harding (Beijing: Peking University Press, 1989), 90–91.

49. Chen Jian, "The Myth of America's 'Lost Chance' in China: A Chinese Perspective in Light of New Evidence," *Diplomatic History* 21, no. 1 (winter 1977): 77–80.

50. John B. Nason, director of ECA China Mission, to Philip D. Sprouse, chief of the Division of Chinese Affairs, Office of Far Eastern Affairs, State Department, June 14, 1950, Box 27, Countries: China, 1948, Subject Files, 1948–50, Assistant Administrator for Programs–Assistant Administrator, RG 469: Records of U.S. Foreign Assistance Agencies, 1948–1961, NA II.

51. For his political safety, I have concealed the identity of this man.

52. Harry Bayard Price, *The Marshall Plan and Its Meaning* (Ithaca, N.Y.: n..p., 1955), 179–80, 402, chap. 10.

53. Economic Cooperation Administration, *Twelfth Report to Congress* (1951), 64. See also Price, *The Marshall Plan and Its Meaning*, 205–6.

54. Price, *The Marshall Plan and Its Meaning*, 218.

55. Ibid., 14–15, 203, 371, 374–76.

56. Shu Guang Zhang, *Economic Cold War*, chap. 7, appendix.

57. Gary C. Hufbauer, K. A. Elliott, T. Cyrus, and E. Winston, *U.S. Economic Sanctions: Their Impact on Trade, Jobs and Wages* (Washington, D.C.: Institute for International Economics, 1997); Jianwen Yang, Hessein Askari, John Forrer, and Hildy Teegen, "U.S. Economic Sanctions: An Empirical Study," *International Trade Journal* 18, no. 1 (spring 2004): 25, 58.

58. Shu Guang Zhang, *Economic Cold War*, 9, 268–69; Gregorian, "Economic Sanctions as a Tool of Foreign Policy," 9; Gary C. Hufbauer and Jeffrey J. Schott, *Economic Sanctions Reconsidered: History and Current Policy* (Washington, D.C.:

Institute for International Economics, 1985), 27–69; Hufbauer and Oegg, "Economic Sanction."

59. Shu Guang Zhang, *Economic Cold War*, 258.

60. Marcus Noland, "U.S.-China Economic Relations," Working Paper 96–6, Institute for International Economics, 1996.

61. Under the Jackson-Vanik amendment to the Trade Act of 1974, most-favored nation (MFN) status can be extended to nonmarket economies only if the president grants a waiver certifying that the country does not impede emigration. China first gained MFN status in the U.S. market in 1980, and its annual renewal was routine until the Tiananmen Square incident of 1989. See Noland, "U.S.-China Economic Relations."

62. Lugar, "Does Economic Sanctions Make Good Policy?"

63. Henry Kissinger, *Washington Post*, August 1, 1989, A21.

15. The Rupture of the Sino-Soviet Alliance

An Assessment of the National Intelligence Evaluation

Shen Zhihua

In October 2004, I was invited to attend a special academic conference in Washington, D.C., on U.S. intelligence during the Cold War. Some valuable original files, known as the National Intelligence Evaluation (NIE), had recently been deciphered by the U.S. National Intelligence Council. These files, consisting of evaluations and forecasts by the Central Intelligence Agency (CIA), purportedly represent the most authoritative intelligence obtained by the U.S. government regarding the situation, government policies, and stages of development in mainland China from 1948 to 1976. There are many more or less reasonable comments and accurate inferences in these documents, but what interests me is the assessment of the Sino-Soviet relationship and American comments on the eve of its rupture, because these judgments proved to be wrong.

Wrong Judgments and Predictions by the CIA

Before the second Taiwan Strait crisis, the CIA stated in a May 1958 report: "They [the Chinese] will probably not resort to overt military aggression as long as they believe it would involve them in military action with the U.S. . . . A decision to initiate military action to seize these Islands would probably be contingent on an estimate that the U.S. would not intervene militarily."[1] In fact, three months later, Mao Zedong gave the order to bomb the island of Jinmen (Quemoy). Although Mao considered the possibility of U.S. intervention, he cleverly took advantage of the Sino-Soviet alliance and used it as a deterrent to achieve his aims—a move that was obviously not expected by the CIA.[2] After the crisis, in July 1959, the CIA reckoned that the Chinese communists were unlikely to maintain a state of calm in the Taiwan Strait. The CIA believed that although the communists would not attack the main islands, they would continue to exert scattered military pressure on the region, such as occasional navy or air exercises. In time, they would likely take some action in the Taiwan Strait to test U.S. intentions. In addition, an attack on one or more of the smaller islands controlled by Kuomintang was possible at any time.[3] However, there was no further military conflict in the Taiwan Strait that could cause a crisis in the Far East until the death of Mao Zedong. One of the main reasons was that China had lost the strong backing and support of the Soviet Union, which the Americans did not take into account.

Let us now look at the issue of nuclear weapons. During 1958–1959 the CIA observed, "It is impossible for the Soviet Union to transfer nuclear weapons to the control of the Chinese communists. Nevertheless, they might provide . . . some surface-to-surface missiles (SSM) carrying nuclear weapons and having a range sufficient to reach Taiwan. And the warheads of these missiles are likely to be placed in the Communist Party of China's territory. If so, it is almost sure that they will be under the supervision of the Soviet Union." Even if the nuclear warheads were not placed in China, "they could be quickly used."[4] In reality, the Soviet Union provided China with a lot of assistance regarding nuclear technology and nuclear facilities, but the Chinese, adhering to the principle of self-reliance, were unlikely to allow the Soviets to control the nuclear button. Similarly, Moscow was unwilling to risk using nuclear weapons for the common interests of China and the USSR.[5]

The crux of the problem for the CIA was that, in its forecasts, it never considered the real possibility of a Sino–Soviet split. In the summer of 1958, before Mao Zedong revolted against Moscow over the "joint fleet" issue and the Taiwan Strait crisis, the CIA reported that China would surely maintain its firm alliance with the Soviet Union and continue to recognize Moscow as the leader of the communist world. With the strengthening of China's status, some friction would inevitably arise in the future, but the CIA believed that this was unlikely to damage Sino–Soviet cooperation.[6] Although the CIA recognized that China's Great Leap Forward and the People's Commune plan caused some discord between China and the Soviet Union, U.S. intelligence reported in February 1959 that these issues were not serious enough to threaten the Sino–Soviet solidarity against the Western world.[7] At the end of July 1959, Mao Zedong decided during the Lushan meeting to split with Nikita Khrushchev and all those who were unsupportive of the Great Leap Forward. Meanwhile, the CIA still judged that the Chinese and the Soviets would cooperate closely in their stand against Western countries, with the Soviet Union continuing to be the leader in the alliance. Even though there were differences between China and the Soviet Union, the CIA believed that the two countries had no choice but to maintain the status quo. It reported that the main result of these differences was that China and the Soviet Union gave each other lee-way when formulating policies; it did not detect a weakening of the alli-ance.[8] Even in August 1960, when the Soviet Union announced the withdrawal of all Soviet experts from China, bringing the Sino-Soviet split to public attention, the CIA estimated that within five years, "the cohesion in [the] Sino-Soviet relationship will be stronger than the centrifugal force." Facing the obvious fact that Sino-Soviet differences were growing daily, the CIA admitted that it was "unable to assess how these fundamen-tal conflicts of interest will influence Sino-Soviet relations," but it insisted that China and the Soviet Union did not want to push the conflict to the extent that there would be irreparable damage to their bilateral relations.[9]

Obviously, the Americans' analysis was in error, for their conclusion has little resemblance to the historical facts.

Breakup of the Sino-Soviet Alliance

Beginning in the second half of the 1950s, the viewpoints and policies of China and the Soviet Union became more divergent, leading to frequent dis-putes between the leaders of the two countries. The existence of differences is a prevalent and unavoidable phenomenon in any alliance. However, this does not necessarily mean the inevitable rupture of the alliance; disintegra-tion can be avoided if the two sides can reach a compromise and resolve con-tradictions. Only when both sides find the other's views and policies intolerable and both are unwilling to alter their own positions will there be a breakdown of the alliance. What are the problems that made China and the Soviet Union decide that they could no longer tolerate each other?

In the past, people generally thought that the Sino-Soviet abruption began with the Twentieth National Congress of the Communist Party of the Soviet Union (CPSU). In fact, this point of view was first advanced by China during the Sino-Soviet polemic. Some researchers still believe this to be the case, calling the Twentieth National Congress "the first historical turning point in the history of Sino–Soviet relations."[10] This is a myth. In fact, there was no fundamental divergence between the new guidelines proposed in the Twentieth National Congress of the CPSU and the party line of the Eighth National Congress of the Chinese Communist Party (CCP).[11] Therefore, the Twentieth National Congress had no negative influence on the Sino–Soviet relationship; on the contrary, Sino–Soviet relations became more solid.

Later, in the process of resolving the October crisis in Poland and Hungary, as well as its aftermath, Khrushchev invited China to participate in the handling of European affairs, and the CCP helped mediate relations between Moscow and Eastern Europe. Thus, China and the Soviet Union cooperated more closely.[12] In 1957, on the issue of removing the Molotov antiparty clique in the Sixth Session of the CPSU Central Committee, Mao Zedong expressed support for Khrushchev. On October 15, Khrushchev reciprocated by endorsing the Pact on the New Technologies of National Defense, under which the Soviet Union would provide real assistance to China's development of nuclear weapons. Sino–Soviet relations were thus in ascendance. They peaked at the Moscow conference in November 1957, when the Sino–Soviet alliance was at the height of its power and influence. Mao's speeches and behavior during this conference reflected the reality that the CCP and the CPSU were on equal footing in the international communist movement.

Yet at this time, the divergences between the two sides began to manifest. At the Moscow conference, Mao made his famous assessment that "easterly wind overpowers westerly wind." Mao had long been dissatisfied with the Soviet Union's diplomatic line, which tended to smooth over relations with the United States. At this time, he publicly declared his judgment that the power of the socialist camp had exceeded that of the West. He was, no doubt, answering the question, who is afraid of whom in the world? And he was advising the Soviet Union to change its diplomatic line toward the United States. Mao also announced that in fifteen years, China's economy would surpass that of the United Kingdom; this was directed against the Soviet Union's plan to surpass the U.S. economy in fifteen years. In fact, Mao's real goal was to surpass the Soviet Union in terms of speed of socialist construction. He had been considering the possibility of taking a different path from the Soviet Union and spreading his ideas throughout the communist movement, which soon became a reality. Thus, China and the Soviet Union were obviously following different strategies in both external and internal policies.

In the summer of 1958, the leaders of China and the USSR had a serious quarrel over the so-called long-wave radio and joint-fleet incidents. The Soviets wanted to establish a long-wave radio station in China to facilitate the movement of its nuclear submarines in the Pacific Ocean. Meanwhile, in response to China's request that the Soviet Union provide the technology for the Chinese to build their own nuclear submarines, the Soviet Union proposed a joint Chinese-Soviet fleet instead. For a long time, many historians believed that this conflict was the last straw in the rupture of Sino-Soviet relations; the argument was that the Soviet Union had infringed on China's sovereignty and that Khrushchev had attempted to control China.[13] However, my research indicates that this view lacks foundation. First, the USSR's actions in these incidents were taken in response to China's demand for assistance and were aimed against their common enemy the United States; thus, this was entirely in keeping with the existing Sino-Soviet military alliance and involved no infringement on China's sovereignty. Second, Mao resented only the manner in which the Soviets addressed the issue. His towering rage indicated his hurt nationalist feelings and the damaged amour propre of the leader of a country that had long suffered oppression and humiliation at the hands of foreign powers. Khrushchev later somewhat regretted the situation, made a proposal that the Chinese side rejected, and the Soviets acquiesced. This indicates that the bifurcation of the two sides was generally a difference in opinion on how the military alliance should operate: Khrushchev required common action, while Mao needed only unidirectional aid. In any case, the result was compromise rather than disruption—the Soviet Union made concessions and reached an agreement on China's terms.[14]

At the time, Mao Zedong was dissatisfied with the foreign policy of the USSR. Recently released Czech archives reveal that before the Political Consultative Conference of the Warsaw Pact countries in 1958, the Soviet Union had decreed that the goal of the meeting was "to work out new common measures to relieve international tensions" and had prepared a draft declaration. Based on the suggestions of the Soviet Union, the conference reached an agreement on several issues: the Warsaw Pact unilaterally disarmed 419,000 persons, Soviet troops withdrew from Romania, and the Warsaw Pact and the North Atlantic Treaty Organization (NATO) signed a nonaggression treaty.[15] These measures were diametrically opposed to those desired by Mao Zedong, who got angry but did not mention the policy problem. Since Khrushchev tolerated Mao's anger, there were no ill effects. Only later did the great divergence between China and the Soviet Union become apparent and cause sharp confrontation.

On August 23, 1958, shortly after Khrushchev and his delegation had left China, the CCP suddenly undertook the military action of bombing Jinmen, which caused the United States to intervene. The situation in the Far East became tense. This incident angered Moscow, and Khrushchev found China's action intolerable for four reasons. First, China did not disclose its intentions to the Soviet Union beforehand. Mao Zedong explicitly admitted that when he had met with Khrushchev, there had been "no talk about the issue of Jinmen."[16] Later, Mao proudly stated that the Americans "thought we [China and the Soviet Union] had reached an agreement on the issue of bombarding Jinmen. In fact, our two sides did not discuss this issue at that time."[17] An irritated Khrushchev questioned Mao face-to-face and complained that the Soviet Union, China's supposed ally, did not know what China would do next.[18] According to Khrushchev, China's violation of the rules was an act of defiance and an insult to the Soviets.

Second, the intentional concealment of this military action from the Soviet Union was undoubtedly designed to show that China had the ability to act independently. China's position was that resolving the Taiwan issue was an internal matter, and it would not consult with outsiders. The Soviets had some experience with this inclination, as noted in a report emanating from the Soviet embassy: "The Chinese people [have] shown a tendency to solve problems in Asia [on] their own. They do not consider it necessary to discuss their plan of action with us. Although when the situation [gets] out of control they will count on our support."[19] Khrushchev repeatedly stressed to Mao that although the Taiwan issue was a Chinese matter, it had a bearing on the overall international situation. Further, he observed, allies should exchange information on major issues to coordinate their policies. During their talks, Mao was unwilling to compromise and put on airs to challenge Moscow's leadership status.[20]

Third, the bombing itself showed that China disapproved of the Soviet policy of easing international tensions. The Soviet embassy's report criticized China's actions, which could lead to "the deterioration of the international situation," and it urged the United States to adopt a "brink-of-war-policy."[21] According to the Soviet leader, the tense international situation was not conducive to the common interests of the socialist camp. But Mao believed that China could also pursue a "brink-of-war policy" because "international tension" was harmful to the United States; he hoped that this tension would "mobilize the people of the world" in a struggle against the United States.[22]

Fourth, China's delay in providing the Soviet Union with U.S. "Side-winder" missiles acquired in the air fight during the Taiwan Strait crisis made Khrushchev furious. To retaliate, he decided not to provide China with data on the P-12 intermediate-range ballistic missile. A few months later, when China was forced to deliver a U.S. missile that had already been disassembled many times, Soviet researchers found that one critical component was missing—the infrared sensors of the warhead. In Khrushchev's view, that was not the behavior of an ally.[23]

Khrushchev, who was impulsive, could not tolerate China's actions, which to him indicated that Sino-Soviet relations had changed. Therefore, in June 1959 he decided to suspend the provision of technological materials for China's development of nuclear weapons. Moscow's violation of their agreement angered Mao, but obviously Khrushchev did not care about China's response. However, it was not this action by Moscow but a public speech by Khrushchev one month later that led Mao to break with the Soviet Union.

After their Moscow meeting, Mao Zedong became very eager to bring about an economic upswing in China that could "surpass the United Kingdom and catch up with the United States." Mao asked, since "the Soviet Union and China are both socialist countries, can we build socialism in a way that is efficient, faster, better with more economic results?" He noted, "We have more people, and with different political conditions. With the objective conditions, we can be faster than them."[24] According to Mao, it seemed that "the Marxist mainstream" had come to the Orient.[25] So, half a year later, China's goal to surpass the United Kingdom in fifteen years had changed: Mao intended to catch up with Britain in three years, with the Soviet Union in five years, and with the United States in seven to ten years.[26] In the Second Session of the Eighth National Congress, Mao stated with confidence, "the newcomer precedes," by which he meant that "our communism probably will arrive ahead of the Soviet Union."[27] Therefore, not only the speed of construction but also the means of production had to surpass the Soviet Union. As a result, the People's Commune movement was launched on a large scale. Mao believed that the People's Commune system was a "specific way to transition to communism" and that the commune was "the best grassroots unit of communism's social structure."[28] Thus, in November 1958, speaking with the authority of the international leader of the communist movement, Mao Zedong said that China would soon be on the doorway of a communist society, waiting for the Soviet Union to reach that threshold.[29] According to Mao, China's economic strength would soon surpass that of the Soviet Union, and he pointed out a bright path that would lead to communism. If all these plans gained the support of socialist countries—particularly the Soviet Union— that would be tantamount to acknowledging the CCP's leading position in the socialist camp.

However, Mao was quite disappointed with the actual results. Although the Chinese people were praised by the Soviet press for their enthusiasm and energy, Soviet cadres and experts continually expressed skepticism about the practices and goals of the Great Leap Forward.[30] About the People's Communes, the Soviet media remained silent. Among the hundreds of articles and broadcasts commemorating the ninth anniversary of China's National Day, only six articles acknowledged the communes in passing. Moreover, in a speech given by the Soviet ambassador to commemorate the Soviet Union's October Revolution, the People's Commune movement was not even mentioned.[31] The CPSU Central Committee believed that the People's Commune movement had been instigated by a leftist faction, but because negative comments would affect Sino-Soviet relations, they decided "neither to praise nor to criticize."[32] Later, many local Soviet cadres and some leaders of Eastern European countries showed great interest in the People's Commune movement, and some even believed that China had found a road leading to communism. The Soviet Union, however, did not take this path. To discourage people from "blindly following" China, Khrushchev criticized the People's Communes in his report for the Twenty-first National Congress of the CPSU.[33] A few months later, Khrushchev gave a speech at a rally on a collective farm in Poland; in that speech, he recalled the mistake of establishing rural communes in the Soviet Union in the 1920s, although he did not mention China specifically.[34] The Polish newspaper that published the speech omitted the part about communes. *Pravda*, however, printed the full text on July 21—unfortunate timing. Mao Zedong was already in a bad temper because of a critical position paper written by Peng Dehuai, and Khrushchev's speech made him furious. He was determined to publicly lash out at Khrushchev.

With the Great Leap Forward, many CCP cadres believed that "the center of the communist movement had been transferred to China."[35] This was largely a reflection of the mentality of Mao Zedong and the CCP. Mao hoped that his initiative would receive recognition at home and abroad, particularly in socialist countries. What Mao did not want was a downturn in the economic situation in 1959 and widespread criticism from cadres at all levels.[36] First, Peng Dehuai's paper stirred up a hornet's nest, and Mao was determined to strike back at those who made frivolous remarks about his masterpiece in communist experimentation. Then some grassroots cadres submitted data reproaching the Great Leap Forward and the People's Communes. They criticized that "steelmaking by whores" was a "waste of manpower and money"; that it would result only in political, not economic, gain; and that the People's Commune was an "artificial product" and "impulsive." Then the Ministry of Foreign Affairs announced rumors of problems in China that were widely circulated among Soviet cadres, who believed that the CCP had made mistakes. Finally, the text of Khrushchev's speech was sent to Lushan on July 28. The Lushan meeting was held against this backdrop.

Mao Zedong tried to maintained his composure. The next day, he issued a directive to print these materials and distribute them to the conference delegates.[37] He instructed his comrades to investigate and determine whether "the once collapsed commune of the Soviet Union and the People's Commune are similar to each other or not; and if the People's Commune will collapse." On August 1, Mao stated that "the split is designed to refute Khrushchev. In the future I plan to draft texts to propagandize the superiority of the People's Commune. The Policy of Letting a Hundred Flowers Blossom, the People's Commune, and the Great Leap Forward, these three were opposed . . . by Khrushchev." On August 19, Mao said, "To refute the attacks, defamation, and suspicion on the People's Commune" by "enemies at home and abroad and rightist opportunism inside the Party," it would be necessary "to combat all people" and "to break opposition and skeptics among comrades of the Soviet Union." On September 4, Mao sent several letters and requested that *People's Daily* publish Khrushchev's speech on the commune to "make him more passive, to make people more aware of Khrushchev's anti-commune position." Mao further instructed the newspaper to publish stories from Czechoslovakian and East German newspapers that praised and propagandized the Lushan meeting, which "could strengthen morale and check and challenge some people in the Soviet Union."[38] All these acts showed that Mao Zedong was determined to turn against Moscow.

The Taiwan Strait crisis showed the major differences between the foreign policies of China and the Soviet Union. Khrushchev found these differences intolerable and was determined to put the fear of God into the CCP. The commune question reflected serious differences in domestic policy that Mao Zedong found intolerable as well, and the CCP decided to openly criticize Moscow. In October 1959, after the leaders of the two countries engaged in a heated argument, China and the Soviet Union separately established the same principles to deal with Sino–Soviet relations. Mao Zedong believed that the fundamental interests of China and the Soviet Union were the same; any differences were only "partial, temporary." However, Khrushchev was naïve and did not understand Marxism-Leninism; "if he did not admit his mistakes, he would be completely bankrupt in a few years." Mao believed that the truth was on the Chinese side: "the great development of Marxism-Leninism was in China," and the main task of the CCP was to criticize revisionism.[39] Therefore, at the CCP Central Committee meeting in December, it was decided that in dealing with the Soviet Union, there should be "firmness of principle and flexibility of strategy."[40] Similarly, the CPSU Central Committee believed that the Sino–Soviet friendship was important for both parties and essential for the entire socialist camp and the international communist community. However, because of the personality cult of Mao Zedong, the CCP's domestic and foreign policies contained some shortcomings and errors. Hence it needed to "overcome the difficulties of mutual relations under the conditions of upholding our principles."[41] At this point, the Sino–Soviet split was inevitable unless at least one party was willing to compromise.

Beginning in 1960, each side started to publish articles expounding its ideas in newspapers and periodicals, with the intention of persuading the other side to adopt its point of view. This persuasion was ineffective, and at the meeting of the World Federation of Trade Unions in early June, the CCP distributed material critical of the Soviet Union, trying to press the Soviets to correct their mistakes. At a meeting in Bucharest in late June, the CPSU organized a siege of the CCP delegation, attempting to force the CCP to back down. Neither side was willing to make a concession.[42] Finally, Khrushchev had had enough, and he announced a deadline for the withdrawal of all Soviet experts working in China. Divisions between the Chinese and the Soviets were thus unfurled. Despite attempts by both China and the Soviet Union during 1961–1962 to ease the conflict and repair their relations, neither was willing to be the first to admit its mistakes. The outcome of their talks in July 1963 once again showed that there was no room for compromise,[43] and the breakdown of the Sino–Soviet alliance became irretrievable.

Yet the CIA continued to dismiss the possibility of a collapse of the Sino–Soviet alliance, based on the following two presumptions: the CCP would continue to accept Moscow's leading position in the international communist movement, and, ultimately, both the Chinese and the Soviets would be mindful of their common interests and act accordingly. But the Americans misunderstood the situation between Beijing and Moscow on precisely these two issues.

The Internal Logic of the End of the Sino-Soviet Alliance

The CIA's conclusion was reasoned, and its inference was completely logical. According to the Americans, China and the Soviet Union had a common ideology of Marxism-Leninism, a common goal of a communist society, and common security interests, in that they both considered the United States and the Western world their main enemies. The only differences between them involved details such as means, procedures, risks, and so forth. Therefore, although the divergence between China and the Soviet Union might continue for a long time and even deepen, the CIA believed that with their common fundamental beliefs and interests at stake, the two sides would adjust their policies to strengthen the alliance and eliminate any trend that might do permanent damage to bilateral relations. The existence of such an alliance had not only greatly enhanced the military forces of the whole socialist camp but also improved the respective positions of China and the Soviet Union in international affairs. Furthermore, because China's increase in power and influence was due to its reliance on the Soviet military and economy, the Soviet Union was thought to play a decisive role as the current developer of armaments standards and the arbiter of military modernization in the future. Therefore, the CIA believed that China had no choice but to continue its alliance with the Soviet Union. It seemed to be a reasonable conclusion, given the U.S. intelligence analysis.

Thus, there was quite a gap between reasonable inferences and the historical fact of Sino-Soviet relations. One reason was that U.S. intelligence came from a limited number of sources. Research indicates that the CIA had already withdrawn all its staff from the Chinese mainland by June 1949. And in 1956, due to constant failures in dispatch, the CIA had closed the overseas action center that handled China exclusively. Meanwhile, according to a CIA intelligence analyst who attended the 2004 seminar, to avoid prejudice and the influence of Taiwanese ideology, the United States did not accept intelligence from the information organization of the Kuo-mintang. Therefore, the majority of the CIA's intelligence came from pub-lic Chinese reports, and its quality inevitably suffered because of this limitation. However, the main reason for the CIA's lack of knowledge of strategic decision making by communist countries was that its method of analysis was wrong. The CIA analyzed and inferred the relationships of Eastern communist camps according to the norms of country relations common to the Western capitalist world; it did not expect there to be nu-merous irrational factors that ran counter to traditional international rela-tions theory. Intelligence staffs that were familiar with Western diplomatic principles could not grasp the decision-making procedures of socialist countries. Obviously, if they had been able to research communists' think-ing with regard to special country relations, it would have helped them correctly interpret not only the development of the Sino–Soviet alliance but also the reasons for its rupture.

People cannot help but ask why Mao and Khrushchev did not consider the common benefits of their countries' alliance. Why did both sides reach a dead end? And having done so, why was neither side willing to turn around and try another way? In terms of socialist alliances, this was not an unusual phenomenon, so we must seek answers based on common princi-ples of socialist country relations.

There are two references in our study of the fate of Sino–Soviet rela-tions. One is internal relations among the Western allies during the same time, and the other is national relations inside the socialist political camp. The Sino–Soviet alliance was entirely different from the former but a typi-cal example of the latter.

Although there may be differences and contradictions—and sometimes even fierce battles—among Western capitalist countries, the Western alli-ance has never suffered a long-term rupture. We can explain that phenom-enon using the logic of the CIA: Western countries maintain their mutual relations based on the principle of national interests. During the Cold War, the best way to protect the national interests of each individual nation was to ensure the whole security system of the Western world in its struggle against the communist world. Toward this end, each country was willing to give up short-term gains and personal profits. That is, the continuous existence of the alliance was achieved through mutual compromises.

Among the socialist countries, things are quite different. For one, there is an obvious lack of any kind of compromise system. A common phenomenon is cohesion among the socialist countries if they are on friendly terms; they think of themselves as brothers, and all differences and contradictions can be overcome by the high-minded spirit of proletariat internationalism. If they are not on friendly terms, they fight as one possessed; they discard the essential principles and conventions of international communication and may even resort to weapons. Therefore, they are either close friends or enemies unable to coexist in peace. The Sino-Soviet relationship is not the only one to illustrate the latter. In Europe, after the rupture of Soviet-Yugoslav relations, Soviet troops were stationed along the border of Yugoslavia, and they even plotted to assassinate Tito. When the politburo of the Polish Labor Union Party dismissed some members who were too intimate with the Soviets, Warsaw incurred the aggression of Soviet forces. Leading members of the Hungarian government who wanted to explore a new way to construct socialism were hanged by the Soviets. Just when economic reform in Czechoslovakia had shown that the Czechs could get rid of the Soviet model, Soviet troops ruined the Prague spring. Such things also happened in Asia, in Sino-Korean and Sino-Japanese relations. They are "bosom friends," "comrades," and "brothers," but they will calumniate each other or even fight at close quarters. In short, alliance relations among countries in the socialist political camp have never been stable. They have been characterized by constant unrest and frequent ruptures and reshuffling.

Why have the socialist allies been unable to compromise when faced with differences among them? Why have relations become so frangible during periods of growth? First of all, these problems cannot be blamed on the temporary failure of policies. Even if Tito had not decided to stop supplying economic information to the Soviets, Stalin would have exerted pressure on Yugoslavia for other reasons. Even if Rokossowski had not been made Polish secretary of defense,Gomulka would have accused the Soviets of infringing on the sovereignty of Poland. Even if Khrushchev had approved of the principle of the People's Commune, Moscow would not have stood by as Mao took further measures to assume the leadership of the communist movement. Even if Khrushchev had not recalled the Soviet experts from China, the inexorable trend of the rupture of the Sino-Soviet friendship could not be reversed. Second, these problems cannot be adequately explained without mentioning the personalities of the leaders. There is no doubt that personal character plays a role in international communications. No matter what, Tito was stubborn and unruly, Stalin was fond of conflict, Khrushchev was moody, and Mao was inconsistent. Such personalities add complexity to bilateral relationships, but they are not the substance of the problem. Because instability is a common phenomenon in the relationships of socialist countries, there must be a critical element that causes these unbalanced constructions. To me, the substance of the problem is a constitutive evil inherent in the relations of the socialist political alliance. In other words, there is some weakness in the political customs of socialist countries.

One of these constitutive evils is the contradiction between the international ideal and nationalism. Early socialist theory idealized the future society, fancying a pantisocracy in which there was no nation and no difference between nationalities. For a long time, the communists believed in the idea that under the leadership of the working class, there would be no nations. The name of the Soviet Union typifies this belief: the Union of Soviet Socialist Republics connotes neither region nor nationality; it is a name that could be applicable to the whole world, which was the communist goal. As a revolutionary party, the communists were conscious of the nation's sovereignty before they came to power. All the various communist parties had an accordant goal and a uniform theory, but with regard to the norms of mutual relations, they had only proletariat internationalism; they gave little or no consideration to the differences between countries and regions. Once the revolution was successful and the communists commanded a nation's sovereignty, they found that the old norms were far from the practical norms. From the view of the Communist Party, they must hold the flag of internationalism; from the view of the nation, however, they needed to maintain the political and economic rights of the nation. As the representatives of a country, the communists were trapped between approving the norms of internationalism and safeguarding the national interests.

These confusions and contradictions had a significant effect on the mutual relations of the socialist countries. Generally, the countries approved of the common ideology, which inadvertently covered up the diversity among their national interests. However, when there was conflict, they had their respective means of responding, which emphasized national interests. Moreover, the implementation of their policies was inconsistent. For instance, Yugoslavia accused the Soviet Union of infringing on its national interests, yet the Yugoslavs demanded absolute obedience from Albania. Whereas the Communist Party of China accused the Russians of chauvinism and deplored the tough style of the Soviet Union, it insisted that Japan and Korea accept the party line. Furthermore, these policies were often seen in different lights, depending on time and place. For example, when the Soviet Union sent troops to Hungary in 1956, it was viewed as an act of protection; in 1978, the Soviet occupation of Prague was viewed as an invasion. Because there were neither unified norms nor consensus, when faced with crises, the socialist countries had no platforms and conditions for compromise, and relations inevitably suffered.

Historically, it is clear that the relationship between the communist parties has been intertwined with the relationship between the communist countries. In modern times, a commonly accepted principle is that of the equality of countries, regardless of size. Conflicts involving national interests are resolved through mutual consultation, based on this foundation. In contrast, the organizational principle of the communist parties is that those on the lower level subordinate themselves to those on the higher level, and the entire party obeys the central committee. The contradiction between these two principles is obvious.

Owing to the successful revolution in the Soviet Union, Moscow historically held the central position in the international communist movement, and the CPSU dominated the other communist parties. After the theory of "socialism in one nation" was proposed by Stalin, the CPSU became the overlord of the various communist parties, and supporting and executing internationalism was equivalent to guaranteeing and maintaining the national interests of the Soviet Union. Under this structural relationship (leader and adherents), equality was impossible, and it expanded from the communist parties to the socialist countries. Just after the Second World War, several communist parties grasped state power in succession, and these countries joined the socialist political camp against the background of the Cold War. During this process, each communist party that came to power used the same political customs and rules of mutual relations, and the relationships among the international communists became equivalent to the relationships among the socialist countries. As the relationships between the parties and the countries became mixed, the relationship between leader and adherents was also mixed. The point is that with such a mixture, national sovereignty and national independence cannot exist in a perfect sense. The most typical example is the case of Hungary in October 1956: to subdue the Polish crisis, the Soviet Union devised "a manifesto for equal relations among socialist countries," yet at the same time, the Soviet army seized Budapest and dismissed the legitimate Hungarian government.

The Chinese have frequently accused the Soviet Union of encroaching on Chinese sovereignty, and the Vietnamese have accused the Chinese of doing the same thing. This has been a common complaint among the socialist countries. Actually, in most situations, the political criterion is the only commonality among those in the communist political camp—namely, the relationship between leader and adherents. Since the various communist parties all agree that there must be a core of leadership, and they all recognize Marxism-Leninism as the only legitimate political principle, they have in fact given up their respective independence. With a political system that combines government and party, it is very difficult to guarantee the sovereignty and integrity of any particular country in the socialist alliance. At the same time, the national sentiments and psychology of the various countries pursuing independent development have been constrained. Differences in level of development and national interests have often been hidden by superficial political unity. Usually, these countries maintain a good relationship until their differences accumulate to such a degree that their national sentiments are revealed, and mutuality is turned into crisis. This political characteristic is responsible for the intrinsic instability of the socialist union. Once the leadership of the party (or country) is challenged, or any sovereign state is no longer satisfied with the overall benefit it receives from the alliance, the principle that the adherent obeys the leader is no longer effective, and the alliance is in danger of collapse.

Besides the aforementioned universal contradictions in the socialist alliance, Sino-Soviet relations also involved a struggle for leadership of the international communist movement, as well as for the legitimacy of its ideological status. The Soviet Union and China were the two greatest nations in the socialist political camp: one led the communist parties of the various countries in Europe, and the other directed the revolutionary movement in Asia. If they had continued this division of labor and mutual cooperation, the prospects for the socialist alliance might have been bright. However, the roles of China and the Soviet Union began to change. The CPSU called for "self-criticism" at the Twentieth National Congress; Moscow's prestige was greatly reduced, and its leadership status in the alliance fluctuated. Meanwhile, the status of the CCP rose day by day, especially when the first Five-Year Plan was smoothly completed and China's participation in the handling the Poland-Hungary crisis succeeded. Mao Zedong felt that the CCP should assume more responsibility for human development in the future. Basically, China and the Soviet Union were at different stages of social development. The Soviet Union had already entered the postwar international system and had even participated in its construction; China was still an outsider. The CPSU was already a mature incumbent party, whereas the CCP had just assumed state power and had not yet changed its revolutionary consciousness. As a result, Mao Zedong and Nikita Khrushchev had completely different cognitions of the world's events and its developing tendencies, and the policies they made were in opposition to each other. The Soviet Union requested relaxation, and China wanted intensity; the Soviet Union hoped for a peaceful environment, and China agitated the revolutionary mood. This difference had a direct effect on the mode of constructing socialism, as well as the fight against capitalism. According to communist theory, only the one who lifts the Marxist-Leninist flag and obtains legitimate ideological status is qualified to lead the international communist movement. Therefore, the concrete differences between the foreign policies of China and the Soviet Union turned into a struggle of politics and ideology.

Conclusion

The CIA's mistake was to observe and analyze relations among the socialist countries using theories applicable to nonsocialist states. Although concessions and compromises could be made in a pure contest over certain fundamental interests, this was not the case in a competition over the leadership of the international communist movement. This contest would be determined not by the balance of power and interests but by the correctness of ideological and political lines. This was a struggle for principle in which reconciliation had no place. In reality, neither the Chinese nor the Soviets departed ideologically from the Marxist-Leninist orbit, and their national interests were fundamentally in concert. What they disputed was their respective right to interpret Marxism and Leninism in the international communist movement—that is, the domination of ideological orthodoxy. This dispute would not only decide these parties' qualifications to lead the international communist movement but also affect the authority and status of their respective leaders. Therefore, the dispute assumed the magnitude of a life-and-death struggle for these parties and their leaders. The Chinese and Soviet sides were by no means ignorant of the sameness of their ideologies and the commonality of their fundamental national interests. They were like a pair of brothers who did not want to split the family, but each sought to be its head. Thus, in the contest, "Marxism" and "revisionism" could not live under the same sky, and "Leninism" and "dogmatism" were as irreconcilable as water and fire. In the final analysis, the split of the Sino-Soviet alliance was inevitable.

Notes

1. NIE 13-58, in National Intelligence Council (NIC), *Tracking the Dragon: National Intelligence Estimates on China during the Era of Mao, 1948–1976,* NIC 2004-05 (Washington, D.C.: NIC, October 2004), 124.

2. See Shen Zhihua, "Did China Inform the Soviet Union before Bombarding Jinmen in 1958?" *CPC History Research* 3 (2004).

3. NIE 13-59, July 28, 1959, 4 (copy in the author's possession).

4. NIE 13-58, May 13, 1958, in *Tracking the Dragon,* 123, 127; NIE 13-59, July 28, 1959, 3.

5. See Dai Chaowu, "The Development of Nuclear Weapons in China and the Split between China and the Soviet Union," *Contemporary China History Research* 3 and 5 (2001); Shen Zhihua, "Aids and Restrictions: The Soviet Union and the Development of Nuclear Weapons in China in the 1950s," *History Research* 3 (2004).

6. NIE 13-58, May 13, 1958, in *Tracking the Dragon,* 124.

7. NIE 13-2-59, February 10, 1959, 2 (copy in the author's possession).

8. NIE 13-59, July 28, 1959, 3.

9. NIE 100-3-60, August 9, 1960, in *Tracking the Dragon,* 218, 227.

10. See *About the Debate on the General Line of the International Communist Movement* (Beijing: Renmin Press, 1965), 55–63; Sun Qiming, *The Whole Story of the Sino-Soviet Relations* (Shanghai: Renmin Press, 2002), 239–40.

11. See the detailed exposition in Shen Zhihua, "The 20th National Congress of the Soviet Communist Party, the Non-Stalinization and Their Influences on the Sino-Soviet Relationship," in *International Cold War History Research,* ed. Li Danhui (Shanghai: East China Normal University, 2004).

12. See Shen Zhihua, "The Crisis in October 1956: China's Role and Influence— One Research of Poland and Hungary Incidents and China," *History Research* 2 (2005).

13. Han Nianlong, ed., *Contemporary Chinese Foreign Policy* (Beijing: China Social Science Press, 1988), 112; Tang Jiaxuan, ed., *Chinese Foreign Policy Dictionary* (Beijing: World Affairs Press, 2000), 727, 728.

14. See Shen Zhihua, "Khrushchev, Mao Zedong and the Sino-Soviet Unconsummated Military Cooperation," *CPC History Research* 5 (2002).

15. Report of Czechoslovak Foreign Minister David about the Political Consultative Conference of Warsaw Pact countries, June 7, 1958; see "The Czech Archives on the History of the Cold War (1954–1964)," *Modern History* 6 (2003):

145–47 [in Russian]. For the declaration passed by the conference, see *People's Daily*, May 27, 1958.

16. Wu Lengxi, *Ten Years' Debate (1956–1966): The Memoir of the Sino-Soviet Relations* (Beijing: Central Literature Publishing House, 1999), 186.

17. Feng Xianzhi and Jin Chongji, eds., *Biography of Mao Zedong (1949–1976)* (Beijing: Central Literature Publishing House, 2003), 855.

18. See minutes of the talks between Mao and Khrushchev on October 2, 1959, in *Modern History* 2 (2001): 97–98 [in Russian].

19. V. Zubok and C. Pleshakov, *Inside the Kremlin's Cold War: From Stalin to Khrushchev* (Boston: Harvard University Press, 1996), 223.

20. See minutes of the talks between Mao and Khrushchev on October 2, 1959, in *Modern History* 2 (2001): 94–98 [in Russian].

21. Zubok and Pleshakov, *Inside the Kremlin's Cold War,* 223.

22. *Mao Zedong Corpus No. 8* (Beijing: Renmin Press, 1999), 19–21; *People's Daily*, September 9, 1958.

23. N. S. Khrushchev, *Selected Memoirs* [in Russian] (Moscow: Vagrius, 1997), 334; Sergeyevich Khrushchev, *Missile and Crisis,* trans. Guo Jiashen (Beijing: Central Compilation and Translation Publishing House), 266–68; Nikita Khrushchev, *The Last Words,* trans. Zhang Jialin (Beijing: Dong Fang Publishing House, 1988), 413–15.

24. Deng Liqun, ed., *Mao Zedong du shehui zhuyi zhengzhi jingjixue pizhu he tanhua* [Mao Zedong's commentaries and talks about socialist political economics] (Beijing: Association of PRC History, 1998), 44, 715; Jilin Province Archives, vol. 1, table 1-14, no. 68, pp. 17–23.

25. *Manuscript of Mao Zedong since the Foundation of PRC*, No. 7 (Beijing: Central Literature Publishing House, 1992), 117.

26. Jilin Province Archives, vol. 1, table 1-14, no. 126, pp. 1–12; Fujian Province Archives, vol. 101, table 12, no. 223, pp. 15–17.

27. Jilin Province Archives, vol. 1, table 1-14, no. 59, pp. 6–9.

28. *Selections of Important Literature since the Foundation of PRC*, No. 11 (Beijing: Central Literature Publishing House, 1995), 450; Jilin Province Archives, vol. 1, table 1-14, no. 71, pp. 6–11, 25–28.

29. Jilin Province Archives, vol. 1, table 1-14, no. 72, pp. 1–6.

30. Xinhua News Agency, Internal Reference No. 2540, 1958, 11–14; No. 2774, 1959, 15; No. 2803, 1959, 12–14; *People's Daily*, September 6, 1958.

31. Xinhua News Agency, Internal Reference No. 2654, 1958, 24–26; *People's Daily*, November 8, 1958.

32. V. Cidikhmenov, "Conversation between Stalin and Mao Zedong," *New Era* 2–3 (1993): 40 [in Russian].

33. Ding Ming, ed., "Retrospect and Thinking: Conversation with the Witnesses of the Sino-Soviet Relations," *Contemporary Chinese History Research* 2

(1998): 31; Ma Guifan, "Memoir of Khrushchev" (selective trans. 2), CPC History Files No. 71, 200–205.

34. See Xinhua News Agency, Internal Reference No. 2831, 1959, 19.

35. Changchun Archives, vol. 1, table 1-12, no. 48, pp. 8–15.

36. B. T. Kulik, *The Sino-Soviet Split: Causes and Consequences* [in Russian] (Moscow: IDV RAN, 2000), 262, 272; *Zhou Enlai Annals II* (Beijing: Central Literature Publishing House, 1997), 238–39.

37. *Manuscript of Mao Zedong since the Foundation of PRC*, No. 8 (Beijing: Central Literature Publishing House, 1993), 366, 367, 387–88.

38. Ibid., 462–63, 504, 506–7.

39. TsKhSD, Center for the Preservation of Contemporary Documentation, f. 5, op. 49, d. 235, ll. 89–96; *Manuscript of Mao Zedong*, No. 8, 601–2; *Zhou Enlai's Military Activities Chronicle II* (Beijing: Central Literature Publishing House, 2000), 515.

40. Party Literature Research Center of the CPC Central Committee, ed., *Annals of Liu Shaoqi II* (Beijing: Central Literature Publishing House, 1996), 474.

41. TsKhSD, Center for the Preservation of Contemporary Documentation, f. 2, op. 1, d. 415, ll. 56–91.

42. See Li Danhui, "About Some Problems of Beijing Conference for World Federation of Workers: Evaluation on Kozlov's Report about Bucharest Conference," CPC History Files No. 1, 2004. Russian files on the Bucharest conference are in the author's possession.

43. Russian files on the talks between the CCP and CPSU in 1963 are in the author's possession.

16. A Misty Cold War in the Himalayas

China's Historical Temperament in International Relations

Xiaoyuan Liu

In recent years, numerous predictions about China's rise in the twenty-first century have been made based on the precedents of the great powers' ascendance in world history. These exercises, however, have overlooked what can be termed China's "historical temperament," which was affected or even re-molded by its own experiences in modern international relations. In the nineteenth century, the Euro-American–dominated international system extended into East Asia and caused the collapse of an interstate political culture rooted in the region's Sinocentric cultural sphere. Consequently, states in the region were compelled to redefine their positions in international relations, retune their outlooks about the world, and learn how to behave according to the norms of Western international society. China was central in the traditional East Asian international system and therefore could not easily repudiate its own ways for the sake of learning from others. History has bequeathed China an extraordinarily rich legacy in dealing with external relations. The renowned legalist strategy of "befriend the remote and attack the near" and the famous Confucian teaching of "delight the near and attract the remote" are just two examples of how notoriously antithetic that legacy can be.[1] In modern times, such a complex and long historical experience can be either a treasure or a burden to Chinese leaders. During the twentieth century, China entered the rank of revolutionary countries, and its alternation between "rational" and "revolutionary" diplomacies rendered its course in entering international society even more tortuous. Initially, China's "leaning to one side" during the Cold War seemed to set its international identity. For a while, the People's Republic of China (PRC) appeared to depart from the path of integrating with international society by toeing conventional lines. It wanted instead to remodel the international community according to a socialist blueprint. Yet this appearance concealed the historical fact that China continued the odyssey of remaking itself into a national state. Since the nineteenth century, China's transformation from a traditional empire to a modern national state has not wavered.

Profound historical events usually possess two types of properties. One consists of the political, moral, and economic ramifications of these events to their contemporaries; the other is the historicity of the events, which may be completely beyond the comprehension of participants. The evolution of China's historical personality in the international arena is a macrohistorical subject. The study of such a subject necessarily requires an approach free from the restraints of short-term, value-ridden perceptions. In discussing the Tibetan incident of 1959, this chapter reveals how, in the thickness of the Cold War, China continued to follow the norms of international relations in its diplomatic performance and national state building. The episode also shows how a Cold War mentality and normative international behaviors became intertwined in the foreign policy making of all the parties involved.

A Consensual Historical Agenda

In evaluating the importance of the year 1949 in Chinese history, historian Paul A. Cohen points out: "Many of the most drastic and sweeping changes that occurred in the first years of Communist rule represented the realization of what I would call a consensual Chinese agenda. That is, they were changes that would have been supported by the Kuomintang (KMT)—and even in some instances the rulers of the late Qing—as well as the Communists."[2] A conspicuous example of these changes was the Chinese government's enforcement of sovereignty in Tibet in the years following 1949.

At the beginning of the twentieth century, an important element of the new administrative policies adopted by the Qing court was to substantiate the "hollow" frontiers and centralize the frontier administrative authorities. In Tibet, measures to implement these policies were carried out under Zhang Yintang. In 1907, to prevent British influence from penetrating Tibet, Zhang suggested that the ceremonial *amban* system be replaced with an imperial commissioner who possessed real power. The commissioner would have full authority in Tibetan affairs so that "the prestige of the imperial system can be enhanced and the administrative power be substantiated." Zhang contended that in Tibet, "political power has to be recovered with military force."[3] But because the Qing government itself was on the verge of collapse, it was too weak to make an effective claim of sovereignty in Tibet.

Similarly, as the direct successor of the Qing, the Republic of China could never recover from the chronic disease of internal disturbances and external frustrations. Nevertheless, the Tibetan agenda continued. In a policy proposal dated 1941, the Mongolian and Tibetan Affairs Commission contended: "Tibet has separated itself from the central government for a considerable time, and it cannot be recovered with negotiations of empty words. In a word, aside from using virtuous affection (*de hua*), power coercion (*wei fu*) must be deployed to compel Tibet to submit." Accordingly, a plan was prepared to achieve the military occupation of Chamdo by July 1943, the first step leading to a political solution to the Tibet issue. Yet this did not materialize. In July 1949, realizing that the days of the KMT regime were numbered, Lhasa expelled all KMT personnel from Tibet in the name of preventing communist penetration.[4]

Before 1949, the Chinese Communist Party (CCP) had little influence in Tibet. In the 1920s, to gain sympathy from the frontier ethnic groups, the CCP sported a slogan of "self-determination to the Manchus, Mongols, Tibetans, and Hui."[5] In his early years, Mao Zedong advocated "assistance to the self-government and self-determination of Mongolia, Xinjiang, Tibet, and Qinghai." But he changed his mind shortly after the CCP was organized under the Comintern's guidance. At that point, he believed that Tibet was under the influence of British imperialism and that its self-determination could benefit only the British.[6] By the time of China's war against Japan, the CCP had already shelved the slogan of national self-determination and had begun to promote unity between the Han and all "minority nationalities" within the officially defined territory of the Republic of China. In 1949, the CCP's victory in China was marked not only by its defeat of the KMT regime but also by its success in abolishing the separatist movements in Inner Mongolia and Xinjiang. Thus Tibet became the sole ethnic frontier that was still estranged from Beijing, and the CCP leaders immediately set out to remedy this situation. In October 1950, the People's Liberation Army (PLA) occupied Tibet's doorway in the east—Chamdo—thereby putting the KMT's plan into effect.

Yet Beijing did not immediately achieve full sovereignty in Tibet. Political scientists define sovereignty as a compound concept. Complete sovereignty includes effective domestic control by an autonomous state authority as well as the sovereign state's legitimate status and rights in international society.[7] Historians point out that in a given national history, these elements may not have existed simultaneously nor remained intact all the time. At the beginning of the PRC, the new Chinese government failed to fully achieve the domestic aspect of sovereignty.

Before the PLA entered Tibet, the Lhasa regime strove to maintain Tibet's existence outside of Chinese authority. The only concession it was willing to make was to admit that a *tanyue* (secular sponsor–religious priest) relationship had existed between Tibet and China. Conversely, Beijing's goal in Tibet was identical with its goal in the rest of China: the PLA must occupy Tibet and then "reform Tibet into a people's democracy."[8] The battle of Chamdo left Lhasa with no hope of resisting the PLA with armed force. Negotiations over the next few months eventually produced the "Agreement between the People's Central Government and the Local Tibetan Government on the Measures of Peaceful Liberation of Tibet," signed in Beijing on May 23, 1951. The seventeen-point agreement constituted a compromise between change and continuity. Under the agreement, Beijing achieved territorial and diplomatic sovereignty over Tibet and abolished Tibet's de facto separation from China.

Yet the agreement did not genuinely accomplish Zhang Yintang's goal of "recovering the administrative power" in Tibet. As stipulated in the fourth, fifth, sixth, and eleventh articles of the agreement, "the center [meaning Beijing] will not change" the current political system of Tibet, the positions and functions of the Dalai Lama and the Panchen Lama, and "various types of affairs concerning Tibet."[9] Thus Beijing recognized the usefulness of the late Qing's policy of limiting central authority in Tibet with local ethnopolitical and ethnocultural conditions. There was, however, an important difference between the CCP and the Manchus: whereas the Manchus intended to maintain their ethnic authority over a stable, layered, multiethnic enterprise, the CCP made concessions on domestic sovereignty only temporarily for the sake of achieving the quid pro quo of Lhasa's permanent submission to China's territorial and diplomatic sovereignty.

In the next few years, the only change in the original Tibetan political structure was the presence of the PLA in the region. Beijing did not have any official administrative office in Tibet. Its connection with Lhasa was maintained by Zhang Jingwu, who traveled frequently between Beijing and Lhasa in his dual capacity as director of the General Office of the CCP Central Committee and the Central Committee's representative in Tibet. In Tibet, even the CCP's lower-level organizations under the Tibetan Working Committee had to operate in the name of PLA units.[10] Thus, in the PRC's early years, despite the seventeen-point agreement, Tibet remained the only area where Beijing was unable to exercise domestic sovereignty.

The so-called paradox of state power is a phenomenon in which the unilateral strengthening of state power may proportionally weaken its effectiveness. This occurs because the effectiveness of state power can be enhanced only through its coordination with society—that is, both the state's avoidance of arbitrary behaviors and the society's active participation in the political process. A policy enforced solely with state violence nullifies social participation and is consequently ineffective in a constructive sense.[11] In 1951, Tibet's incorporation into the PRC without undue difficulties reflected the effectiveness of China's new government. The successful reconciliation between Beijing and Lhasa in 1951 indicated that the Tibetans were active, though reluctant, participants in fashioning the first "one country, two systems" of the PRC.

Yet, in light of the Inner Mongolian model for the PRC's multiethnic system, the compromise over Tibet in 1951 was just a temporary arrangement.[12] Beijing's pursuit of complete sovereignty would sooner or later lead to an attempt to "Inner Mongolize" Tibet by extending all its programs there. Beijing was certainly not the first Chinese government that tried to reform Tibet. As mentioned earlier, it was the late Qing court that initiated center-guided reforms there. The KMT regime also held that "the slavery in Xikang and Tibet is inhuman and contradictory to the Three People's Principles, and therefore it must be abolished with formal decrees." It asserted that the ordinary Tibetan people "must be thoroughly liberated by the central government."[13]

Of course, the reforms intended by the CCP had different social connotations from those intended by its predecessors. At the beginning, however, it was the very character of the CCP revolution that postponed reform in Tibet. The CCP differed from the elitist Qing and KMT governments in that it started its revolution from the bottom of society. It viewed "mass basis" as a necessary precondition for policy implementation. This created a unique contradiction in Beijing's Tibet policies from the onset. After the seventeen-point agreement was concluded, Mao pointed out that the "material basis," "upper class basis," and "mass basis" for implementing the agreement did not exist in Tibet. Beijing was superior in military power but weaker than the Tibetan authorities in the "department of social influence."[14] In Mao's words, "They [the Tibetan people] have a much stronger belief in Dalai and in local headmen than in us. . . . They support their leaders absolutely, and hold them sacred and inviolable." In 1954, the United Front Department of the CCP held a three-month working conference on Tibet in Beijing. The conference reached this conclusion: In Tibet, "the superstructure of the feudal serfdom is a theocratic dictatorship by the clergy and autocrats. Today it rules the Tibetan nation and can still represent the Tibetan nation. . . . Thus our various policies in the Tibetan region have necessarily to serve the most important task of winning over the Dalai clique."[15]

Beijing gingerly maintained its "Dalai line" until the Lhasa revolt of March 1959. After that event, "democratic reforms" were implemented in Tibet simultaneously with military suppression of the rebels. From then on, the political life of Tibet entered a stage of mass class struggles. These developments marked Beijing's failure to use the Dalai Lama as a medium to achieve interethnic cooperation in Tibet. As pointed out by Chinese and Western scholars, both the geographic distribution of the Tibetan population and the geopolitical conditions of China's ethnopolitics made it impossible for "one country, two systems" to continue in Tibet. Although the status quo of Tibet proper was temporarily maintained, in the mid-1950s, the CCP started to push reforms in the Tibetan areas of Qinghai, Xikang, and Sichuan (Amdo and Kham to the Tibetans). These reforms caused local resistance. Soon, pressed by the PLA, members of the resistance movement retreated into Tibet proper. Such a spillover phenomenon seriously undermined the fragile political balance in Tibet and eventually contributed to the Lhasa incident of March 1959.[16]

It should be added that as of 1959, the 1951 compromise was about to run its course even in Tibet proper. Recent evidence indicates that as early as 1956 and 1957, Beijing was already encouraging its Tibetan Working Committee to initiate reforms in Tibet. However, when full-scale preparations for reforms caused strong objections among the aristocrats, Beijing ordered the working committee to beat an immediate retreat. To placate the Tibetans, Beijing promised that there would be "no reforms for the next six years." Beijing's vacillation evoked different reactions in Tibetan society. Those opposed to reforms became more audacious. They demanded "no reforms forever" to counter Beijing's no reforms for six years, and they asked all Han to leave Tibet. In reality, the apparent hesitation on Beijing's part concealed an increasingly hardened stance. In the decade after 1949, the Dalai Lama grew from a teenager into an adult. In these years, Mao Zedong, Zhou Enlai, and officials of the Tibetan Working Committee made minimal progress in reshaping his attitude. About two months prior to the Lhasa revolt, Mao lost patience with the "Dalai line," predicting that "a general showdown will be necessary." In referring to the 10,000 rebels in the Lhasa area, Mao suggested that this was a good thing "because now war can be used to solve the problem."[17] Clearly, with such thinking, the one country, two system formula had already been jettisoned.

Himalayan Dominoes

The involvement of Tibet in the Cold War could be predicted in 1949, and by the mid-1950s, it was already a fact of life. The armed conflicts in Tibet after 1956 and Beijing's suppression of the Tibetan rebellion in 1959 and 1960 not only fundamentally changed the political relationship between Beijing and Lhasa but also set off a series of fallings-out between China and other nations. In the wake of the Lhasa incident, Sino–Indian relations deteriorated rapidly, which led to a border war between the two countries in 1962. American analysts in the Central Intelligence Agency (CIA) at the time and Chinese historians today agree that the Sino–Indian war was an important reason for the Sino–Soviet split.[18] After the mid-1950s, the U.S. government also took advantage of the turmoil in Tibet and launched a secret war in the region to undermine Beijing's authority. When the Sino–Indian war broke out, Washington seized the chance to include India in its containment strategy against China. In view of these developments, Beijing's failure to achieve interethnic cooperation in Tibet toppled the first domino that had sustained the great-power balance in Eurasia since the end of World War II. In a brief span of several years, China's long and tranquil borders from northeast to southwest became perilous again. In addition to the American threat from the direction of the Pacific, the PRC was now challenged along its inland frontiers. For China, the Cold War became a two-front struggle.

The deterioration of the Sino–Indian relationship was a key event that caused drastic changes in China's immediate international environment. In *India's China War*, published in 1970, Neville Maxwell analyzes the Sino–Indian conflict over a long period and does not fall into a polemic about "responsibilities." He points out that in the 1950s, when the influence of the Chinese government reached the northern border of India, the impact on the Indian public was comparable to the impact of the Qing's new administrative policy in Tibet on the British public at the beginning of the century. What differentiated the two events was Indian independence: "With independence, all that changed. The boundaries of India ceased to be the pawns of the British in their Great Games with their imperial rivals, and became the cell walls of a new national identity. No longer could boundaries be conceived or shifted by men whose concern was not territory but strategic advantages; henceforth they enclosed the sacred soil of the motherland, and politicians could tamper with them only at their peril."[19]

Whereas India, as a new national state, was claiming a geopolitical inheritance from the fallen British empire, the PRC, with its revolutionary-state identity, inherited the geopolitical claims of the bygone Qing empire. The CCP leaders were not shy of praising the Manchu contribution to China's territorial expansion.[20] The historical background of the Sino-Indian conflict was therefore the two nations' respective modernization of territoriality. Between the two largest Asian countries lies one of the highest international divides in the world. In the past two centuries, that divide served as a buffer between two colossal empires representing, respectively, the Eastern and the Western "international relation cultures."[21] In the mid-twentieth century, however, the divide turned into a seam that stitched two national states together, both of which held territorial sovereignty sacred and inviolable and watched the other suspiciously. The ambiguous borders left by the old empires indeed created difficulties for the bilateral relationship between China and India. But more often, border disputes between states are symptoms, not causes, of their mutual distrust. As for the Sino-Indian border war between the late 1950s and the early 1960s, it was a disastrous consequence of a difficult historical legacy influenced by the Cold War.

On Beijing's side, its own cold war along the Himalayas began with its conception of establishing sovereignty in Tibet. Because the PLA's advance into Tibet was conceived as the last scene of the "Chinese people's war of liberation," the legitimacy of the central government's authority in Tibet must be embodied in the justifiability of the planned military operation. Therefore, the "liberation of Tibet" became the conclusive note of the march played by the CCP propaganda as the PLA advanced to every corner of China. But that note proved to be a rather difficult one to play. A series of CCP documents dated from February to November 1950 indicates that Beijing wavered among "imperialism," "feudalism," and "KMT reactionaries" when trying to identify the target of its liberation drive toward Tibet.[22]

After it settled on a policy of winning over the "upper strata" of Tibetan society, Beijing could no longer target the actual obstacle to PLA operations—the Tibetan government. When the seventeen-point agreement was being concluded, Beijing's criticism of the Lhasa regime was limited to the mild reproach that, in the past, it had "adopted a non-patriotic [*fei aiguo*] attitude toward the great motherland." Usually, the conceptions of *aiguo zhuyi* (patriotism, or love of one's country) and *maiguo zhuyi* (national betrayal, or the selling out of one's country) were starkly antithetical in the CCP political discourse. But this time, determined to win Lhasa over, Beijing was compelled to adopt a more ambiguous wording and awkwardly retune its propaganda.[23] In the meantime, no verbal attack on the KMT government could justify the PLA's entry into Tibet. Even if the facts could be stretched to identify the KMT regime's feeble office in Lhasa as the symbol of KMT oppression of Tibet, the Tibetans had already abolished that office in July 1949. Under the circumstances, Beijing could articulate its political logic of "liberating Tibet" only through its objection to "British and American imperialist conspiracies." In view of these Western governments' hesitant and noncommittal handling of Lhasa's appeal for help before 1951 (especially Washington's), Beijing's objection was a preemptive one. The Cold War theme in Beijing's Tibet policy was nevertheless created.

Anti-imperialist struggle was always a central theme of the Chinese revolution in the twentieth century. At midcentury, India was the successor to British imperial privileges in Tibet, but these privileges were terminated by a series of Sino-Indian agreements concluded in 1954 and 1955. By this point, imperialist influence in the traditional sense no longer existed in Tibet.[24] Thereafter, in concert with its general foreign policy in the international Cold War arena, Beijing aimed its anti-imperialist struggle in Tibet at the United States. After the Korean War began, CCP propaganda asserted that the United States' intention toward Tibet was the same as that toward Korea and Vietnam: "to encircle China militarily and to make preparations for a large-scale aggression against China."[25]

In Tibet, however, the CCP's Tibetan Working Committee understood the anti-American struggle mainly as psychological warfare intended to "use anti-imperialism and patriotism as the central themes for stabilizing the upper strata and winning the upper strata from imperialism."[26] Beijing's tactic in this psywar was to convince the Dalai Lama and his followers that neither the United States nor any other foreign government could not possibly provide any meaningful assistance to Tibetan separatism and that the only choice for Tibetan elites was to be of one heart and one mind with the PRC central government. As Zhou Enlai told the Dalai Lama during the latter's visit to India in early 1957, "the so-called American assistance is a lie. It is so far away from Tibet and cannot cross the land of Indian. So the only thing it can do is to brag."[27]

Such a judgment would not have been far off the mark in the early 1950s. When the PRC was first established, the United States did not have the ability to provide material assistance to anticommunist forces in China's interior. According to the CIA's estimate, only by airlifting could American materials be distributed to the remnant anticommunist forces scattered in different locations. This was unfeasible at the time partly because airlifting was costly, but mainly because the United States did not have an air base in the mainland that could serve as a transfer station. Furthermore, an overt U.S. air operation to aid anticommunist forces in China would be tantamount to declaring war against the PRC.[28] The situation changed drastically after the Korean War began. Through close cooperation between the U.S. military and the CIA, the United States developed an ability to carry out covert airlifting over long distances. In 1957, the U.S. government began to implement covert airdrops into Tibet. The Pakistani military helped the operation by turning over an airfield in eastern Pakistan to the Americans.[29] Therefore, after the mid-1950s, Beijing made an erroneous strategic judgment in continuing to view the United States as only an oceanic threat.

Despite the United States' newly acquired ability to take action in the Himalayas, the CIA neither manufactured nor could it control the armed rebellion in Tibet. The essence of the conflict was a struggle over sovereignty between Beijing and the Tibetan establishment at different levels. Any foreign involvement only added fuel to the dispute. To policy makers in Washington, the armed conflict in Tibet constituted a golden opportunity to undermine CCP power. In the summer of 1956, the CIA worked out a plan to train Tibetan commandos. In February 1957, the first class began in Saipan in the western Pacific. After May 1958, the training site was relocated to Camp Hale in the mountains of Colorado.[30]

Between 1957 and 1961, the CIA airdropped 250 tons of military supplies and forty-nine Tibetan agents into Tibet. Of these agents, two were captured alive, ten escaped into India, and the rest died in battle.[31] Such assistance could not change the predicament of the Tibetan rebels. A CIA study estimated that the PLA controlled three transportation lines entering Tibet and could, on average, send in 1,600 tons of materials per day over the course of a year. In comparison, the total tonnage airdropped into Tibet by the CIA was insignificant. At one point, the number of Tibetan rebels reached 30,000. The issue of how to allocate the small amount of American materials caused factional friction among the Tibetan fighters. The U.S. government contemplated using its superior air force to interrupt the PLA's lifelines over land, but the idea was quickly abandoned; Washington did not want to start a war with the PRC over Tibet.[32] Meanwhile, because American assistance was delivered to the rebels via covert operations, Washington could not take advantage of its involvement in a psywar fashion. To most Tibetan fighters, American assistance was an unverifiable rumor and had only dubious value in enhancing Tibetan morale.[33] In 1959, when the Dalai Lama split with Beijing and went into exile in India with the CIA's help, that event could have been a windfall to Washington's Cold War propaganda. Yet the opportunity to take advantage of this development did not materialize as expected by American leaders. Mindful of its general psywar strategy directed toward all communist countries, the U.S. government wanted the worldwide public to understand the Tibetan incident as the Tibetan people's spontaneous resistance against Beijing. Therefore, after the Lhasa rebellion, Washington chose to maintain a "strategic silence" about the Tibetan situation. Secretly, the CIA tried to enlist the help of the Dalai Lama, as the leader of Buddhists throughout the world, in American Cold War efforts. But during his long exile, the Tibetan leader never expressed such an inclination.[34]

Even though the CIA could not manufacture a "resistance movement" in Tibet to meet U.S. needs, its covert operations implicated Washington as the principal foreign influence interfering in Tibetan affairs. Yet, strangely, the series of events in Tibet after the mid-1950s did not cause a further decline in the Sino-American relationship. Instead, the Tibetan question became the catalyst for changing dynamics in China's relations with India and the Soviet Union. Over the next few years, the PRC's "friendly neighbor" in the southwest and "socialist brother" in the north became its enemies.

Switching Sides

In the last few years of the 1950s, the U.S. government waged a small proxy war in the Himalayas against China in utter secrecy. After 1960, on several occasions the PLA seized airdropped supplies from Tibetan rebels and captured a small number of Tibetan agents who had parachuted in. These events should have alerted Beijing to the United States' covert operations.[35] But until the end of the Cold War, the PRC government kept silent about this matter. Further research is needed to determine when Beijing discovered the CIA's operations in Tibet and why it stayed quiet. So far, CCP documents suggest that Beijing's policies contributed significantly to drastic changes in the international alignment on the Asian continent. After the Lhasa revolt, Beijing changed its U.S.-centered orientation in Tibet. India, which until then had maintained a largely friendly relationship with China, became the main target. This was the first "side switching" in China's Cold War foreign policy, setting a precedent for Beijing's switching sides between the Soviet Union and the United States more than a decade later.

On July 10, 1958, in a note to the Indian government, the Chinese Ministry of Foreign Affairs pointed out that American and KMT agents were undermining the Sino-Indian friendship by using Kalimpong as a base to launch armed rebellions in Tibet. The note asked the Indian government to stop anti-PRC activities in Kalimpong. A few days later, in a directive to the Tibetan Working Committee, the CCP Central Committee asserted that recently captured evidence indicated that, among the leaders of the Tibetan rebellions in Sichuan, Qinghai, and Gansu, "there were indeed agents of imperialism, especially American imperialism, and the counterrevolutionary clique in Taiwan." On March 21, 1959, the day after Beijing discovered the Dalai Lama's escape, the General Political Department of the PLA issued a directive on suppressing the Tibetan rebellion. It stated: "The national betrayal committed by the Tibetan reactionary clique was a planned and organized counterrevolutionary action instigated, supported, and supplied by American and other imperialisms and by other foreign reactionary forces."[36] Although these diplomatic and internal documents do not prove Beijing's knowledge of CIA activities in Tibet, they indicate that, for a while before and after the Lhasa revolt, the CCP maintained its Cold War perception in identifying the United States as China's principal foreign enemy in Tibet.

In the meantime, although PRC leaders did not conceal their unhappiness with New Delhi's stated concerns about the Tibetan situation, they expressed only mild criticism of their "Indian friends." During the Lhasa revolt, anti-Beijing protesters in the streets of Lhasa handed a "proclamation of independence" to the Indian consulate and requested help in making contact with Kalimpong and notifying the United Nations.[37] Having learned of this development at a politburo meeting on March 17, Zhou Enlai asserted: "This event involved the Indian authorities. The British and American governments were very active behind the scene and pushed the Indian authorities to the forefront. The headquarters of the rebellion is in Kalimpong of

India." Mao Zedong, however, decided that India should not be openly implicated yet; the account could be settled later, after India had done enough injustice to China. For the next month, therefore, PRC propaganda continued to promote the Chinese-Indian friendship. At most, the Chinese media expressed regret that certain quarters in India had made "statements very incompatible with the Chinese-Indian friendship."[38]

Such moderation disappeared around the middle of April. On April 18, the Dalai Lama issued a written statement at Tezpur, India, denouncing Beijing for imposing its "suzerainty" on Tibet in 1951 and then interfering in Tibet's self-government. The statement also countered Beijing's story about how the Dalai Lama had been "abducted" into India. A few days later, the Chinese media issued a rebuttal in the form of a political commentary by the Xinhua News Agency, which was revised and finalized by Mao himself. The commentary attacked the Dalai Lama's statement as an expression of imperialist aggressors' intention and will. It reasoned that because the writing exhibited a "European or quasi-European style," it had not been drafted by the Dalai Lama himself but by a treacherous group supported by the British in Tibet. Now, the commentary continued, "Indian expansionists [have] inherited this inglorious British legacy."[39] Mao thus decided that the time was ripe to launch a propaganda counterattack against New Delhi. On April 25, in written remarks to Hu Qiaomu and others, Mao explained the reorientation in propaganda: "We have used the statement for a long time that 'imperialism, Chiang Kai-shek's bandit gang, and foreign reactionaries are instigating rebellions in Tibet and interfering in China's internal affairs.' This statement is completely inaccurate and must be immediately changed into, 'acting in collusion, British imperialists and Indian expansionists openly interfere in China's domestic politics and attempt to take over Tibet.' The whole country should follow the line of the political reporter's commentary on the 18th in making statements, targeting directly Britain and India without equivocation."[40]

In the ensuing volley of verbal attacks, "British imperialism" was named to maintain an anti-imperialist rhetoric, but the real target was interference by "Indian expansionists." In the next two weeks, all China's propaganda apparatuses blasted India. On May 7, Mao called for a time-out. A few days later, at a politburo meeting, Mao explained that while criticizing the bad side of Nehru, one should also remember his good side and give him a way out. Mao appeared to demonstrate his mastery of propaganda warfare, attacking and retreating at will. But neither Mao nor other CCP leaders would be able to reverse the course of the Sino-Indian relationship, which was going downhill rapidly.

The momentary focus on India did not mean that Beijing had departed from its general Cold War orientation against the United States. Mao and his associates never viewed China's relations with India as merely a bilateral dealing between two national states. Mao was convinced that a clamorous quarrel with India over Tibet would not divert China's diplomatic direction and might even enhance its struggle against the United States. At the time, the PRC's international tactics did not differ much from the CCP's seasoned strategies in domestic politics. A united front was such a typical stratagem. As perceived by the CCP, because of its Asian identity and colonized past, India was a natural member of the international united front against Western imperialism. In April 1955, at the Bandung Conference, the Chinese and Indian governments cosponsored the Five Principles of Peaceful Coexistence designed to facilitate relations among Asian and African countries with different political systems. Bandung hence became the peak of the two governments' cooperation in international affairs. In the meantime, Beijing continued to apply its class analysis to India's international stance, which was allegedly determined by the class identity of the Indian leadership. Mao categorized Nehru as a "bourgeois middle-of-the-roader." And the CCP's established policy toward wavering middle-of-the-roaders was to gain solidarity with them through principled struggles.

After the Dalai Lama's statement appeared in India, Mao suggested that criticism of Nehru must be sharp; there was no need to fear upsetting him or falling out with him. And the struggle against Nehru must be carried to the end in order to achieve solidarity with him. Such a "struggle philosophy" had a complete set of inner logic, the crux of which was a dialectical relationship between "part" and "whole." In May 1959, Mao applied such reasoning in his final version of an important letter from the Chinese Ministry of Foreign Affairs to the Indian government. In the letter, Mao wanted to explain to New Delhi that the Sino-Indian disagreement over Tibet involved China's internal affairs and sovereignty—"issues of principles" on which China could not make concessions. Yet Mao was also conciliatory, suggesting that this disagreement was only a "temporary" and "partial" problem and should not damage the two nations' overall cooperation in international affairs.[41] It was perhaps beyond Mao's apprehension that the Indian leaders would not take Beijing's struggle against them calmly, even though it was meant to be only a "partial" struggle.

In China's Cold War diplomacy, this strategy of gaining overall solidarity through partial struggle often proved counterproductive. In its annual report for 1960, the Ministry of Foreign Affairs used Mao's idea about "part" and "whole" in discussing China's foreign relations perceived as international conflicts. The report separately identified the United States, the Soviet Union, India, and Indonesia as all being in contention with China in some way and as being the target of China's diplomatic quarrels in overall, partial, or subpartial situations. India was China's main target in South and Southeast Asia during the first half of 1960; then the struggle against India had to be subordinated to the struggles against the United States and the Soviet Union. In reality, such an orderly, stratified pyramid of international conflicts often resulted in confusion. As admitted by the report, in the execution of foreign policies, the two recurring mistakes were to confuse the relationship between "struggle" and "solidarity" and to "see trees only but not the forest."[42] In the wake of the second Taiwan Strait crisis of 1958, Sino-American relations entered what Mao called a period of "Cold War coexistence." Except for their indirect contest in the Vietnam War, China and the United States engaged each other only through mutual verbal abuse. As China's "overall" cold war with the United States became stabilized, its "partial" confrontation with India began to escalate rapidly.

The verbal clash between Beijing and New Delhi was soon followed by armed conflict along their borders. As of 1954, the Indian government had already established control over territories south of the McMahon line. In April 1959, the CCP Central Military Commission ordered the PLA units in Tibet to "seal the border immediately, control important roads and passages close to the unsettled Chinese-Indian border along the McMahon line, construct defense works, and prevent treacherous bandits from crossing the border in both directions."[43] Four months later, the first armed conflict between the two sides took place. This so-called Langjiu incident was only the first shot of a much larger border war that would break out in October 1962.

By the time of the Langjiu incident, the Beijing-Moscow alliance had been strained for some time due to a long list of disagreements.[44] In early October 1959, Nikita Khrushchev led a Soviet delegation to Beijing, where the two sides quarreled over the Taiwan Strait crisis of 1958. The Soviets accused Beijing of taking a bellicose stand at the risk of provoking an unnecessary war with the United States. They also criticized Beijing for delaying reforms in Tibet and for failing to intercept the Dalai Lama's flight into exile. They laid responsibility for the Sino-Indian border conflict squarely on Beijing, contending that the CCP's India demarche created opportunities for American imperialism.

Mao and his associates refused to swallow any of these criticisms and reciprocated by labeling the Soviets' stand as opportunism. The Chinese side stressed that both Taiwan and Tibet were China's internal affairs and that China could not possibly retreat from its principled position. CCP leaders wondered why, as a "big brother," the Soviet Union failed to make a distinction between right and wrong and took the side of bourgeois India in the Sino-Indian conflict. During the talks, Khrushchev raised the issue of "the Soviet Union as the head of the socialist camp." This was meant to implicate CCP leaders' irreverent verbal thrusts and to explain why the Soviets "said things ordinary guests would not have said."[45]

These exchanges illustrated the discrepancy between Beijing's and Moscow's internationalist rhetoric and their respective national stands. It has been suggested that by failing to support Beijing in its 1959 confrontation with India, the Soviets established a precedent of not basing Soviet foreign policies on the "class stand" principle. Three years later, during the Cuban missile crisis, Beijing would reciprocate, not only denying Moscow firm support but also sharply criticizing Khrushchev's handling of the situation.[46] After these scuffles between Beijing and Moscow, the communist monolith in Eurasia disintegrated.

As the Sino-Indian conflicts were unfolding, the foreign policies of India and the United States converged. The CIA pointed out with satisfaction that a "profound change has taken place in India's outlook." It noted, "A conviction of Peiping's [Beijing's] fundamental hostility and perfidy has emerged among virtually all levels of Indian opinion in the past few months. . . . At the same time, there is general gratification with the sympathy and support received from the U.S. and the British Commonwealth and a growing realization that the preservation of India's freedom will be heavily dependent on the West." In the Sino-Indian conflict and the Sino-Soviet rupture, Washington saw opportunities for the United States to "take a tougher stance" against China and for American-Soviet collaboration in dealing with the PRC. The CIA estimated that as of the end of 1962, the so-called Aid India Club, consisting of the West plus the Soviet Union, had committed a total of UD\$2.5 billion for India's economic development over the next two years.[47]

A few months before the Sino–Indian border war, Zhou Enlai, builder of the Sino–Indian friendship in the early 1950s, lamented that the peaceful coexistence between the two states would soon be replaced by a "long armed coexistence."[48] The October war certainly terminated Beijing's hope for a cross-Himalaya united front against U.S. imperialism. For a moment, there seemed to be an American-Indian consortium for the purpose of containing China. The Sino-Indian border war would be over shortly, but the Himalayas would remain a second front for China's cold war in the years to come.

Conclusion

Since the mid-nineteenth century, the Chinese state has gone through an arduous process of structural, territorial, and behavioral reorientation. Once China adopted the prevailing international relations culture, it began to transform into a national state with explicit sovereignty and a definite bordered territory, and it began to participate in international competition in the modern sense. As discussed in this chapter, China consolidated its modern sovereignty in Tibet at a special historical juncture, at a time when China experienced the Maoist "continuous revolution" and the world became bipolarized. A number of forces—the CCPs' ascendance to power in China, the rise of India as a newly independent national state, the continuation of Tibet's unique culture and sociopolitical system, and the entry of the United States as a destabilizing foreign influence—all converged on Tibet. The result was an extremely complex, confusing, and tangled contest. In this contest, the PRC managed to hold its bottom line of preserving sovereignty in Tibet, but in doing so, Beijing paid the price of giving up interethnic harmony in the region. Yet the ensuing deterioration of the Sino-Indian relationship over Tibet and their disputed borders can be viewed as historical progress—those vague buffer-zone arrangements of the imperialist age were replaced with clear-cut boundary claims by two sovereign national states.

After 1959, in implementing its "democratic reforms," Beijing injected communist ideology into the Tibetan Buddhist society. This communist expansion into Tibet, however, did not provoke the United States to act as it did in Korea, Vietnam, and the Taiwan Strait. Leaving aside other reasons, Washington's moderation can be understood by recognizing the fact that Beijing's consolidation of domestic sovereignty in Tibet did not violate the established international norm of differentiating domestic affairs from foreign affairs. Beijing's abrogation of the Tibetan status quo ended the last legacy of the "loose rein" policy from Chinese history. As a state entity, China thereby took one more stride in homogenizing national territories and achieving the same qualities as European or American actors on the international stage. A historical coincidence is that China's "becoming national" occurred at a time when enemies and friends in international politics were identified with supranational ideologies. Thus, ironically, it was China's supposed soul mate in the socialist camp, the Soviet Union, that directly challenged Beijing's Tibetan-Indian policies. As indicated in the Mao-Khrushchev quarrels, the so-called principled basic line of PRC diplomacy was framed by a national-state temperament that had taken shape since the nineteenth century but was not informed by the communist dogmas that became prevalent in China after 1949.

When studying the PRC's official behavior, it is often difficult to determine whether China's cultural legacies, modern nationalism, or communist ideology was predominant. A tentative depiction can be proposed for this puzzling trichotomy. In terms of China's Cold War–era international behavior, if Chinese culture was an omnipresent "gene," then Chinese nationalism was a fundamental character forged during China's adaptation to the modern international environment, and communist ideology, which did not influence China's official diplomacy until 1949, was more instrumental than characteristic in Beijing's coping with the Cold War international climate.

Both the nationalist character and the communist attire of the PRC's international behavior are imported commodities. Thus, there is no reason to believe that, despite being repressed in modern times, China's Eastern international relations culture—based on thousands of years of history—will not be able to reclaim its position in today's international society. China's confidence and influence in world affairs continue to grow. There have already been signs in the twenty-first century that China has begun to recall wisdoms from its own ancient past. It can be anticipated that in this century, the research interests of historians and political scientists in the field of Chinese foreign relations will converge more than in any previous era.

Notes

1. "Qin San: Fan Sui" [Volume 3 of Qin: Fan Sui], in *Zhan Guo Ce* [Strategies of the warring states] (Beijing: Beijing Tushuguan Chubanshe, 2002), 2:47; "The Analects: Zi Lu," in Jin Liangnian, *Lun Yu Yi Zhu* (Shanghai: Shanghai Guji Chubanshe, 2004), 153.

2. Paul A. Cohen, *China Unbound: Evolving Perspectives on the Chinese Past* (London: Routledge Curzon, 2003), 132.

3. "Zhang Yintang zoufu Xizang qingxing bing shanhou shiyi zhe (Guangxu sanshisan nian shiyi yue)" [Zhang Yintang's memorial on the Tibetan situation and measures to deal with remaining problems, November 1907], *Xizang Difang Lishi Ziliao Xuanji* [Selected materials on the local history of Tibet] (Beijing: Sanlian Shudian, 1963), 258; Su Faxiang, *Qingdai ZhiZang Zhengce Yanjiu* [A study of the Qing policy toward Tibet] (Beijing: Minzu Chubanshe, 2001), 55, 64, 81, 126–37.

4. "Xizang difang zhengfu wei quzhu Guomindang Zhengfu zhu Zang banshi renyuan zhi Guomindang Zhengfu dian (1949 nian 7 yue 9 ri)" [Tibetan government's telegram to the KMT government on expelling the personnel of its office in Tibet, July 9, 1949], in *Heping Jiefang Xizang* [Peaceful liberation of Tibet], comp. Committee on Collection of Party History Materials of the Autonomous Region of Tibet (Lhasa: Xizang Renmin Chubanshe, 1995), 237–38; Melvyn C. Goldstein, Dawei Sherap, and William R. Siebenschuh, *A Tibetan Revolutionary: The Political Life and Times of Bapa Phuntso Wangye* (Berkeley: University of California Press, 2004), 119–22.

5. "Gongnong Hongjun Disi Jun Silingbu bugao, yijiu'erjiu nian yi yue" [Public notice by the Headquarters of the Fourth Army of the Workers' and Peasants' Red Army, January 1929], in *Minzu Wenti Wenxian Huibian* [Collection of documents on the nationality question], comp. Department of United Front of the Central Committee of the Chinese Communist Party (Beijing: Zhonggong Zhongyang Dangxiao Chubanshe, 1991), 99.

6. Mao Zedong, "Zhi Cai Hesen deng, yijiu'erling nian shi'er yue yi ri" [To Cai Hesen and others, December 1, 1920], in *Mao Zedong Shuxin Xuan* [Selected correspondences of Mao Zedong] (Beijing: Renmin Chubanshe, 1983), 3; "Gongchandang dangtuan huiyi (1924 nian 1yue 18 ri)" [Meeting of the Communist Caucus, January 18, 1924], in *Lian'gong (Bu), Gongchan Guoji yu Zhongguo Guomin Geming Yundong (1920–1925)* [Communist Party of the Soviet Union (Bolshevik), the Comintern, and the Chinese nationalist revolutionary movement, 1920–1925] (Beijing: Beijing Tushuguan Shubanshe, 1997), 469.

7. Stephen D. Krasner, *Sovereignty: Organized Hypocrisy* (Princeton, N.J.: Princeton University Press, 1999), 9–25.

8. Committee on Collection of Party History Materials of the Autonomous Region of Tibet, *Zhonggong Xizang Dangshi Dashiji, 1949–1994* [Chronology of important events of the Chinese Communist Party in Tibet, 1949–1994] (Lhasa: Xizang Renmin Chubanshe, 1995), 6; "Xizang difang zhengfu guanyu hetan de wu xiang tiaojian (1950 nian 12 yue 17 ri)" [Tibetan government's five conditions for negotiations, December 17, 1950], in *Heping Jiefang Xizang*, 250–51; "Gai you Xinanju danfu jinjun ji jingying Xizang de renwu (yijiuwuling nian yi yue er ri)" [Reassignment to the Southwestern Bureau of the task for military advance into and development of Xizang, January 2, 1950], in *Mao Zedong Xizang Gongzuo Wenxuan* [Selected manuscripts of Mao Zedong on the work in Tibet], comp.

CCP Central Office of Documentary Research, CCP Committee of Tibet, and Research Center of Tibetan Studies of China (Beijing: Zhongyang Wenxian Chubanshe, 2001), 6.

9. "Zhongyang Renmin Zhengfu he Xizang difang zhengfu guanyu heping jiefang Xizang banfa de xieyi (1951 nian 5 yue 23 ri)" [Agreement on the measures for Tibet's peaceful liberation between people's central government and the local Tibetan government, May 23, 1951], in *Heping Jiefang Xizang*, 125–28.

10. Zhao Shenying, *Zhongyang ZhuZang Daibiao Zhang Jingwu* [Representative of the central government in Tibet Zhang Jingwu] (Beijing: Zhongguo Zangxue Chubanshe, 2001), 1; Danzeng and Zhang Xiangming, *Dangdai Zhongguo Xizang* [Contemporary China's Tibet] (Beijing: Dangdai Zhongguo Chubanshe, 1991), 1:180–81.

11. Victoria Tin-bor Hui, *War and State Formation in Ancient China and Early Modern Europe* (Cambridge: Cambridge University Press, 2005), 214–16; Martin Sokefeld, "From Colonialism to Postcolonial Colonialism: Changing Modes of Domination in the Northern Areas of Pakistan," *Journal of Asian Studies* 64, no. 4 (November 2005): 941–43.

12. In April 1947, the Inner Mongolian Autonomous Government was established under the CCP, marking the beginning of regional autonomy for Inner Mongolia.

13. Mongolian and Tibetan Affairs Commission, "Jiefang KangZang nubei shitiao banfa" [Ten measures for the liberation of slaves in Tibet and Xikang, August 13, 1929], 141/3136, Files of the Mongolian and Tibetan Affairs Commission, Second Historical Archives of China; Wu Zhongxin to Chiang Kai-shek, December 26, 1943, and appendix, "Dui Xizang xuanchuan dagang" [Propaganda outline for Tibet], 141/2374, ibid.

14. "Guanyu Xizang de gongzuo fangzhen (yijiuwu'er nian si yue liu ri)" [The orientation for the Tibetan work, April 6, 1952], in *Mao Zedong Xizang Gongzuo Wenxuan*, 63.

15. "Xizang zizhi jiguan de juti xingshi you Xizang daduoshu renmin de yiyuan jueding (yijiuwusi nian san yue ershisan ri)" [The concrete form of the Tibetan autonomous body should be decided by the will of the majority of the Tibetan people, March 23, 1954], in *Mao Zedong Xizang Gongzuo Wenxuan*, 104; *Zhonggong Xizang Dangshi Dashiji*, 50–51.

16. Wang Lixiong, *Tianzang: Xizang de Mingyun* [Sky burial: the destiny of Tibet] (Brampton, Ontario: Mirror Books, 1998), 171–74; Melvyn C. Goldstein, *The Snow Lion and the Dragon: China, Tibet, and the Dalai Lama* (Berkeley: University of California Press, 1997), 52–53.

17. "Zhengqu qunzhong, duanlian jundui (yijiuwujiu nian yi yue ershi'er ri)" [Win over the mass and test the troops, January 22, 1959], in *Mao Zedong Xizang Gongzuo Wenxuan*, 164.

18. Intelligence Handbook, "The Deterioration of Sino-Soviet Relations 1956–1966," 4/22/1966, CIA Freedom of Information Act (FOIA) F-2000-01330,

http://www.foia.cia.gov; Dai Chaowu, "Yindu waijiao, daguo guanxi he 1962 nian Zhong Yin bianjie chongtu" [India's foreign policy, great-power relations, and the Chinese-Indian border conflicts in 1962], in *Lengzhan yu Zhongguo de Zhoubian Guanxi* [The Cold War and China's relations with neighboring regions], ed. Niu Dayong and Shen Zhihua (Beijing: Shijie Zhishi Chubanshe, 2004), 487–556.

19. Neville Maxwell, *India's China War* (London: Jonathan Cape, 1970), 67.

20. Zhou Enlai, "Minzu quyu zizhi youliyu minzu tuanjie he gongtong jinbu (1957 nian 3 yue 25 ri)" [Ethnic regional autonomy is conducive to national unity and common progress, March 25, 1957], in *Zhou Enlai yu Xizang* [Zhou Enlai and Tibet], ed. Party History Office of the Tibetan Autonomous Region (Beijing: Zhongguo Zangxue Chubanshe, 1998), 156.

21. In *A Short History of China and Southeast Asia: Tribute, Trade and Influence* (Crows Nest, Australia: Allen and Unwin, 2003), 5, Martine Stuart-Fox suggests that "international relations culture" includes conceptions about values, behavior norms, and expected effects of international interactions commonly endorsed by states involved in such interactions.

22. "Shibajun dangwei guanyu jinjun Xizang gongzuo zhishi (1950 nian 2 yue 1 ri)" [The party committee of the 18th army's directive on the work of military advance into Tibet, February 1, 1950], in *Heping Jiefang Xizang*, 59; "Xinan Junzheng Weiyuanhui, Zhongguo Remin Jiefanjun Xinan Junqu jinjun Xizang bugao (1950 nian 11 yue 10 ri)" [Public notice on expedition into Tibet by the Southwestern Military and Government Affairs Commission and the Southwestern Military District of the People's Liberation Army, November 10, 1950], ibid., 105–6; "Zhou Enlai zai Zhongyang Minwei juban de Zangzu ganbu yanjiuban shang de baogao (1950 nian 4 yue 27 ri)" [Zhou Enlai's speech at the training class for Tibetan cadres organized by the Central Nationalities Affairs Committee, April 27, 1950], in *Zhou Enlai yu Xizang*, 111; "Guanyu shencha zangwen guangbo wenti (yijiuwuling nian wu yue shisan ri)" [On the issue of reviewing broadcasting in the Tibetan language, May 13, 1950], in *Mao Zedong Xizang Wenxuan*, 14.

23. "Zhongyang Renmin Zhengfu he Xizang difang zhengfu guanyu heping jiefang Xizang banfa de xieyi (1951 nian 5 yue 23 ri)" [Agreement on the measures for Tibet's peaceful liberation between people's central government and the local Tibetan government, May 23, 1951], in *Heping Jiefang Xizang*, 125; "Juebu runxu waiguo qinluezhe tunbing Zhongguo de lingtu—Xizang (Xinhuashe 1949 nian 9 yue 2 ri shelun)" [Foreign aggressors must not be allowed to annex Chinese territory—Tibet, an editorial by the Xinhua News Agency, September 2, 1949], ibid., 147.

24. Yang Gongsu, *Zhongguo Fandui Waiguo Qinlue Ganshe Xizang Difangshi* [History of China's opposition to foreign aggression against and interference in Tibet] (Beijing: Zhongguo Zangxue Chubanshe, 1992), 262–70.

25. "Chi Meiguo dui Xizang de yinmou (Renmin Ribao duanping)" [Refute America's conspiracy toward Tibet, short commentary by the *People's Daily*, November 22, 1950], in *Heping Jiefang Xizang*, 182–83.

26. *Zhonggong Xizang Dangshi Dashiji,* 43.

27. Li Zuomin, "Yanchuan shenjiao yi wo zhongshen" [Teaching with words and examples that have benefited me for life], in *Zhou Enlai yu Xizang,* 329–30.

28. ORE 76–49, "Survival Potential of Residual Non-Communist Regimes in China," October 19, 1949, in National Intelligence Council, *Tracking the Dragon: National Intelligence Estimates on China during the Era of Mao, 1948–1976* (Pittsburgh, Pa.: U.S. Government Printing Office, 2004).

29. John Kenneth Knaus, *Orphans of the Cold War: America and the Tibetan Struggle for Survival* (New York: Public Affairs, 1999), 46; Kenneth Conboy and James Morrison, *The CIA's Secret War in Tibet* (Lawrence: University Press of Kansas, 2002), 75; Mikel Dunham, *Buddha's Warriors: The Story of CIA-Backed Tibetan Freedom Fighters, the Chinese Invasion, and the Ultimate Fall of Tibet* (New York: Jeremy P. Tarcher/Penguin, 2004), 221–22.

30. Knaus, *Orphans of the Cold War,* 137–39, 155; Dunham, *Buddha's Warriors,* 197–99.

31. Knaus, *Orphans of the Cold War,* 153, 168, 233, 246; Dunham, *Buddha's Warriors,* 263, 300–301; Conboy and Morrison, *CIA's Secret War in Tibet,* 145–63.

32. Studies in Intelligence, "Tonnage through Tibet," April 1, 1963, CIA FOIA, CSI-2001-00018, http://www.foia.cia.gov; Conboy and Morrison, *CIA's Secret War in Tibet,* 99–100.

33. Dunham, *Buddha's Warriors,* 251, 308, 337–39; Knaus, *Orphans of the Cold War,* 148–49.

34. Knaus, *Orphans of the Cold War,* 179–81; Dunham, *Buddha's Warriors,* 217.

35. Committee on Collection of Party History Materials of the Tibetan Autonomous Region, *Pingxi Xizang Panluan* [Pacification of the Tibetan rebellion] (Lhasa: Xizang Renmin Chubanshe, 1995), 183; *Zhonggong Xizang Dangshi Dashiji,* 119, 122, 135, 213; Wang Gui et al., *Xizang Lishi Diwei Bian* [Defining Xizang's historical position] (Beijing: Minzu Chubanshe, 2003), 599.

36. "Zhonghua Renmin Gongheguo Waijiaobu guanyu yaoqiu Yindu zhengfu qudi Kalunbao Mei Jiang tewu he dangdi tewu yiji Xizang fandong fenzi dui Xizang jinxing dianfu huodong de zhaohui (1958 nian 7 yue 10 ri)" [Chinese Foreign Ministry's note that demands the Indian government to abolish the sabotage activities against Tibet conducted by American and Taiwan spies, native agents, and Tibetan reactionaries based in Kalimpong, July 10, 1958], in *Pingxi Xizang Panluan,* 125–27; "Zhongyang fu Xizang diqu keneng fasheng panluan de wenti (1958 nian 7 yue 14 ri)" [The center's reply on the question of possible rebellions in Tibet, July 14, 1958], ibid., 64–65; "Zhongguo Renmin Jiefangjun Zongzhengzhibu guanyu jianjue pingding Xizang panluan de zhengzhi gongzuo zhishi (1959 nian 3 yue 21 ri)" [Directive by the general political department of the Chinese People's Liberation Army on the political work for firmly pacifying the Tibetan rebellion, March 21, 1959], ibid., 94.

37. "Pan Zili dashi xiang zhongyang baogao ta yu Dalai tanhua qingkuang (1957 nian 1 yue 3 ri)" [Ambassador Pan Zili's report on his conversation with the Dalai Lama, January 3, 1957], in *Pingxi Xizang Panluan*, 116–17; "Disi bian: dashiji: 1959 nian" [Part 4: chronicle of important events: 1959], in *Zhou Enlai yu Xizang*, 484; "Zhonggong Xizang Gongwei xiang zhongyang bao 'Xizang fandong shangceng zhengshi gao "duli" huodong de qingkuang' (1959 nian 3 yue 11 ri)" [CCP Tibetan Working Committee's report to the center on the Tibetan upper strata's activities for formally seeking independence, March 11, 1959], in *Pingxi Xizang Panluan*, 77–78; *Zhonggong Xizang Dangshi Dashiji*, 90, 93.

38. "Disi bian: dashiji: 1959 nian," in *Zhou Enlai yu Xizang*, 478; "Buneng yunxu Zhong Yin youhao guanxi shoudao sunhuai—'Renmin Ribao' guanchajia duanping (1959 nian 4 yue 15 ri)" [Damage to the Sino-Indian friendship must not be allowed—*People's Daily* observer's commentary, April 15, 1959], ibid., 85–90; Wu Lengxi, *Shi Nian Lunzhan* [Ten-year polemics] (Beijing: Zhongyang Wenxian Chubanshe, 1999), 1:193.

39. "Dalai Lama dui baojie de shengming (1959 nian 4 yue 18 ri)" [The Dalai Lama's statement to the press, April 18, 1959], in *Pingxi Xizang Panluan*, 149–51; "Ping suowei Dalai Lama de shengming (1959 nian 4 yue 21 ri)" [Comment on the so-called Dalai Lama statement, April 21, 1959], ibid., 143–48.

40. Wu Lengxi, *Shi Nian Lunzhan*, 1:196–99; "Guanyu Xizang panluan shijian xuanchuan baodao wenti (yijiuwujiu nian si yue ershiwu ri)" [On the issue of propaganda and reporting about the Tibetan rebellion, April 25, 1959], in *Mao Zedong Xizang Gongzuo Wenxuan*, 186.

41. "Shijie shang you ren pa gui, ye you ren bupa gui (yijiuwujiu nian wu yue liu ri)" [In the world some people fear ghosts, some do not, May 6, 1959], in *Mao Zedong Xizang Gongzuo Wenxuan*, 193–94; Wu Lengxi, *Shi Nian Lunzhan*, 1:198–99; *Mao Zedong Waijiao Wenxuan* [Selected writings of Mao Zedong on diplomacy], comp. PRC Ministry of Foreign Affairs and Office of Documentary Studies of the CCP Central Committee (Beijing: Zhongyang Wenxian Chubanshe, Shijie Zhishi Chubanshe, 1994), 376–77; Wang Hongwei, *Ximalayashan Qingjie: Zhong Yin Guanxi Yanjiu* [Himalaya bond: a study of Sino-Indian relations] (Beijing: Zhongguo Zangxue Chubanshe, 1998), 148–51.

42. Information Report, "Chinese Communist Ministry of Foreign Affairs Foreign Policy Report," July 3, 1961, CIA FOIA, EO-2001-00347, http://www.fioa.cia.gov. According to its introduction, this report was disseminated by the Chinese Foreign Ministry among its missions abroad. The CIA obtained the Chinese original from a Chinese diplomat who defected.

43. "Zhongyang Junwei dui Xizang Shannan diqu pingpan ji dangqian gongzuo de zhishi (1959 nian 4 yue 23 ri)" [The Military Commission of the CCP Central Committee's directive on the rebellion pacification in Shannan of Tibet and the current work, April 23, 1959], in *Pingxi Xizang Panluan*, 99.

44. "Document 1: First Conversation of N. S. Khrushchev with Mao Zedong,

Hall of Huazhentan [*sic*][Beijing], 31 July 1958," *Cold War International History Project Bulletin* 12–13 (fall–winter 2001): 250–60 (published by the Woodrow Wilson International Center for Scholars, Washington, D.C.).

45. "Document 3: Memorandum of Conversation of N. S. Khrushchev with Mao Zedong, Beijing, 2 October 1959," *Cold War International History Project Bulletin* 12–13 (fall–winter 2001): 262–70.

46. M. Y. Prozumenschikov, "The Sino-Indian Conflict, the Cuban Missile Crisis, and the Sino-Soviet Split, October 1962: New Evidence from the Russian Archives," *Cold War International History Project Bulletin* 8–9 (winter 1996–1997): 251–56.

47. SNIE 13/31-2-62, "The Sino-Indian Conflict: Outlook and Implications," December 14, 1962, CIA FOIA, EO-1993-00513; CIA memo, "Implications of the Sino-Soviet Rupture for the U.S.," July 18, 1963, CIA FOIA, EO-1998-00565; CIA memo, "India's Economy and the Sino-Indian Conflict," December 14, 1962, CIA FOIA, EO-1997-00577; all at http://www.foia.cia.gov.

48. "Disi bian: dashiji: 1962 nian" [Part 4: chronicle of important events: 1962], in *Zhou Enlai yu Xizang*, 517. Zhou Enlai used the phrase "long-term armed coexistence" in his telegram, dated July 23, 1962, to the Chinese delegation at the Geneva Conference.

17. An Intercultural Communication Model of International Relations

The Case of China

Wenshan Jia

Most of the scholarly literature on Chinese diplomatic behavior and foreign relations, and indeed on international relations in general, is policy driven, issue focused, and short-term oriented. The predominant theoretical perspectives are largely derived from the modern disciplines of the social sciences and humanities, such as political economy, political science, and history. This is not surprising, since such academic disciplines were founded primarily in the intellectual tradition of the modern West, which has weathered and thus been shaped and reshaped by two world wars, one cold war, and now the war on terror. Winning or maximizing one's group or national interests, security, or values at the expense of those of one's counterparts has been the ultimate implicit or explicit goal of such research endeavors. A classic example is game theory and its use in international relations. In most cases, leaders of modern nation-states (presumably, agents for advancing the national good) listen to their policy wonks, who advise them how to maximize the national good in the most unilateral manner. Area studies, as branches of modern academic disciplines, are usually locally grounded scholarly instruments to gather all sorts of intelligence about specific other nation-states in order to take advantage of them or to contain, control, and ultimately conquer them. Humanistic goals such as mutual understanding, win-win solutions, coexistence, and mutual enrichment using the insights from anthropological and intercultural communication perspectives are often sabotaged and marginalized by the obsessive drive for national security, national interests, and values. Unfortunately, any champion of such humanistic goals may be regarded as dovish and foolish. However, such goals are long term and transnational; their fulfillment can not only help construct a benevolent image of nation-states but also contribute to the prosperity of humanity itself. I write this chapter with such goals in mind.

In this chapter, I render a theoretical and practical model to improve international relations—in this case, based on an analysis of the relations among China, the United States, and Japan. As a focal point, I explore the cultural supports and constraints of foreign policy and diplomatic behavior with regard to China. I argue that the cultural lens in the traditional anthropological sense should be used more often in making sense of foreign policy discourse and diplomatic behavior of any nation-state. I further claim that although it is revealing with regard to the United States and Japan, the cultural-psychological model is especially useful in making sense of Chinese foreign policy discourse and diplomatic behavior. However, a social constructionist (rather than merely descriptive) model of intercultural communication must be created to improve international relations in this era of unprecedented and deepening global interdependence among nation-states. Such an approach may help us avoid situations of misunderstanding, conflict, and even war.

My social constructionist model is based on the following elements: (1) the careful elaboration and reflective self-critique of the ethnocentric perceptions, premises, assumptions, and norms taken for granted by foreign policy makers, advisers, and actors about their own culture and the cultures of target nation-states; (2) a study of the pairing of local and foreign "deep" cultures, which indicates a syndrome—a recurring pattern of mutual misunderstanding— that requires constantly updated firsthand knowledge of the deep culture of the local and the target nation-states; and (3) the policy formulation of new strategies for international relations and diplomacy insofar as intercultural syndromes offer such strategies. Hence, I suggest that the China-U.S. relationship involves an intercultural syndrome of mutual misunderstanding and potential confusion, as does the China-Japan relationship. A syndrome (from the Greek *syn,* meaning "together," and *dramein,* meaning "to run") involves events that occur in concert. In this case, we are looking at a "collaboration" of mutual misunderstanding. But these intercultural syndromes also offer opportunities for discovery about oneself and one another and possibilities for mutual adjustment.

Review of the Literature

Though not widely read by mainstream scholars of international relations or advisers trained in the Cold War model of area studies, a growing body of literature argues for communication as an essential part of diplomacy and for culture as a key variable in understanding and improving international relations. For example, diplomacy is clearly communicative in nature; likewise, culture can be used as a powerful tool for institutions to shape and reshape the world order of diversity.[1] Right after World War II, in the early 1950s, there was great global dissatisfaction with the ethnocentric behavior of men and women in the American foreign service and American businesspeople. Thus, the Foreign Service Institute was created in Washington, D.C., and anthropologist Edward T. Hall, a pioneer in the field of intercultural communication, was hired to train people to overcome such ethnocentrism. Unfortunately, the Cold War intervened, followed by the Vietnam War in the 1960s. Nearly everyone is aware of Samuel Huntington's argument that the fundamental differences among the world's major civilizations function as a key variable in global politics.[2] Despite his position as one of the leading political scientists in the Western world, Huntington's understanding of cultural differences is arguably very simplistic from the perspective of the contemporary discipline of communication. However, his acknowledgment of the role of culture in world politics indicates his acknowledgment of the failure of the rationalist and universalistic paradigms of international relations, which tend to exclude culture as a central lens. Huntington's argument also signals the need for other international relations scholars and advisers to make a paradigmatic shift and consider the role of culture and communication among civilizations when managing and resolving international conflicts, in the hope of moving us toward a more peaceful world order. Obviously, Huntington's 1996 call has not been well heeded in scholarly circles. There are still not enough scholars and advisers in international relations who take culture, communication, and intercultural communication seriously; nor is there enough published scholarship that infuses culture and communication into the study of international relations to allow for the kind of pedagogical reform in international relations education that is needed.

Visionary global political leadership, such as that provided by Bill and Hillary Clinton's White House Conference on Culture and Diplomacy in 2000, confirms the significance of culture and communication in international relations. As political practitioners, the Clintons concluded, similar to Huntington, that culture is a key variable in understanding and improving relations among nation-states. Of course, their conclusion was based on their practical global experience, their direct observations of the dynamics among nation-states, and their engagement with the world's cultures. To them, culture is not an amorphous abstract construct; it is a real living force that must be well understood if the goal is improved international relations. This approach indicates a shift away from the "classic" political-economic-military models of international relations that were dominant in the Cold War era. Since the fall of the Berlin Wall in 1989, these models have become increasingly inadequate for handling conflicts among nation-states. The era of globalization calls for the formation of a cultural and intercultural communication model for handling world conflicts.

The Clintons' conference ushered in this new model, which I call the post–Cold War model. Unfortunately, this change was sidetracked by the September 11, 2001, terrorist attacks, which led to the Bush administration's unilateralist model of antiterrorism. It is hoped that eventually this model of unilateralist antiterrorism will subside and the Clintons' model, as academically affirmed by Huntington, will take over. However, there are inherent weaknesses in the views of both Huntington and the Clintons. Huntington depicts cultural differences as a key variable in the cause of international conflicts, which are inevitable, but he offers little guidance in terms of preventing, managing, and resolving such conflicts. The Clintons emphasize how the American culture could be better communicated to the rest of the world rather than how Americans could better understand other cultures. In other words, there is a lack of genuine interest in promoting intercultural communication, which is characterized by equality, openness, and third culture building to improve international relations.

Besides the generalist approach to international relations and diplomacy from the vantage point of culture and communication, there is a growing body of literature on relations between specific pairs of countries, such as the United States and China. President Richard Nixon's trip to China in 1972 paved the way and sparked academic interest in Sino-American relations from a cultural or an intercultural perspective. Some old China hands such as Richard Solomon and Lucian Pye, who participated in or observed the normalization of Sino-American relations, have written insightful accounts of the cultural differences as revealed by Sino-American political negotiations and have provided excellent tips on how Americans can adapt to and deal with their Chinese counterparts.[3] Pertinent are insightful interpretations of Chinese political culture in light of native Chinese concepts such as *guanxi* (relationship), as well as interpretations of the spirit of Chinese foreign policy from a psychocultural view.[4] These works laid the foundation for subsequent informed and intelligent engagement between the United States and China on issues beyond the political arena, such as trade, education, and mutual strategic interests.

Although such a body of literature is still of heuristic value, most of it cannot account for the political, economic, social, and cultural changes in China since 1978 and its open interaction with the rest of the world, and especially the changes in leadership since 1989. Chih-Yu Shih's account of Chinese foreign policy formulation and conduct covers the period up to 1986.[5] Shih acknowledges the importance of face (*mianzi*) in Chinese diplomacy, and Pye's account of Chinese political culture acknowledges the importance of *guanxi*.[6] However, the relational aspect of face and the emotional aspect of *guanxi* in China's international relations remain virtually unexplored by the two authors. Although some practical tips on how to deal with Chinese counterparts are provided, based on the zero-sum framework, Chinese policy makers, advisers, and actors have been given little guidance on how to improve communication with their counterparts from other countries such as the United States and Japan. Finally, none of these scholars has developed a model for such individuals to overcome their own ethnocentrism and to formulate and implement foreign policies with the target nation-state and its culture in mind.

This chapter is built on the strengths of the aforementioned literature and addresses its weaknesses by formulating a theoretical framework to help scholars and professionals in the field of foreign relations deepen their understanding of their own cultural psyche, discourse, and behavior, as well as those of their counterparts, so that communication between them can be interculturally competent.

Theoretical Framework

In this chapter, I use the iceberg concept of culture theory and social constructionism as an integrated framework to generate insights into how China and other nations can improve their relations. The iceberg concept conceptualizes culture as consisting of three layers: high culture is the most visible layer—both insiders and outsiders are fully aware of it—but it occupies only the tip of the iceberg; folk culture is the second layer, located below the tip and highly visible but occupying only a small portion of the iceberg; the third layer of the iceberg is deep culture, which, though an essential part of the iceberg and representing 90 percent of culture, is mostly hidden below the surface.[7] This deep culture governs most of the behavior of insiders but is least understood by both insiders and outsiders. Other dimensions of deep culture include fixed ways to perceive oneself and others, ways to perceive reality, ways to manage emotions, decision-making processes, and so on.

Social constructionism is a theory that conceptualizes communication as the primary force; it conceptualizes culture as open patterns that are created and re-created in and by communication.[8] Thus, communication acts as a contextual force, shaping and reshaping culture, rather than culture dictating how people should communicate. The implications of this theory for individuals who formulate and implement foreign policy are that they do not have to be constrained or trapped by their own culture, which I define as a set of taken-for-granted ways to feel, think, dwell, relate, and be. These people can learn to think, feel, act, and relate in the ways of the target culture or in a creative mix of the cultural ways of themselves and their counterparts, depending on the situation. As a result, foreign policy and diplomatic behavior can create a strong intercultural identification not only with the top decision-making elites of the target nation-state but also with the media and the public. Such policy and behavior can be much more effective in achieving intended goals, as well as creating a lasting intercultural bond that acts as a foundation for future international relations. In addition to sustaining good international relations, this bond can function as a valuable resource in transforming conflicts and crises into opportunities for mutual learning and mutual benefit. Intercultural communication from the social constructionist perspective can be defined as a complex interactive process to manage meaning and coordinate action in creating an intercultural fusion out of joint creative efforts based on mutual respect, mutual equality, and mutual openness.

The following section contains analyses and observations of several cases in light of such an integrated framework. Some aspects of these cases were handled well, but others were not. Lessons can be learned from such successes and failures.

Intercultural Syndrome in China–U.S. and China–Japan Relations

The dominant political discourse on foreign relations in the United States is primarily economic, military, and value centered (security, interests, and values). Much of the new core of the Japanese political discourse is Westernized, with a decorative Confucian coating. This is partially confirmed by Ruth Benedict's book *The Chrysanthemum and the Sword*.[9] In contrast, contemporary Chinese political discourse on foreign relations is deeply relational. This is likely to be perceived by nations of the rationalist-individualist model as a sign of weakness to be taken advantage of. In light of the intercultural model described earlier, an intercultural adaptation on both sides could minimize misunderstandings and conflicts. For example, the United States could approach China relationally by appropriating some of the Chinese relational discourse or ritual, and China could present a stronger sense of both its relational and assertive self in communicating with the United States.

Deng Xiaoping was responsible for moving China's foreign policy from the ideological track to the pragmatic track. The Jiang Zemin–Zhu Rongji era was closer to the relational model (with a stronger global awareness) than the Hu Jintao–Wen Jiabao era, which has been characterized by a stronger purposeful effort to identify with Chinese culture, a greater focus on domestic affairs, and less interest in and preparation for international affairs.

In retrospect, Chinese officials' skill in rhetorically identifying with the West has been quite evident since 1978. For example, Deng Xiaoping started a war with Vietnam (controlled by the USSR at the time) to distance China from the Soviet Union—the United States' Cold War archenemy—and to show goodwill to the United States after Deng's landmark visit during the Carter administration. This demonstrated his plan to break China's alliance with the USSR and to make the United States China's economic model. During his visit to the United States, Deng wore a cowboy hat, which became newsworthy. Likewise, during his U.S. visit, Jiang Zemin recited Lincoln's Gettysburg Address, which made a lasting impression on Americans. The strategy of "cultural translation" has been used effectively to communicate the Chinese desire for economic and political development.[10] Also, the three dialogues—political dialogue, cultural dialogue, and economic dialogue—have been used effectively by the Chinese government in engaging the West since 1989.[11] This, along with the hiring of Western public relations firms, has helped China attract the largest amount of foreign direct investment among all nations in the world, as well as realize its goal of hosting the Olympic Games and the World's Fair. Similarly, China has appropriated the human rights discourse by establishing the *China Human Rights Journal*, holding human rights dialogues with the European Union and the United States, and releasing an annual human rights white paper.

In contrast, during the Qing dynasty—a decade of intense Sinocentrism—Empress Dowager Cixi rejected railroads, and British diplomats were required to kowtow to the Qing emperor, which trigged the Opium War. The period from 1949 to the 1970s was characterized by clashes between capitalism and communism. Since the early 1990s, with the establishment of the Pudong Economic District in Shanghai to overcome economic sanctions by the West, China's efforts to culturally identify with the West have made it the country with the largest foreign direct investment, the world's largest manufacturing center, and the largest developing economy in the world. China has become more cosmopolitan with its entrance into the World Trade Organization and its hosting of the Olympics in Beijing in 2008 and the World's Fair in Shanghai in 2010. At the same time, during the Hu Jintao–Wen Jiabao era, there has been a shift toward the revitalization of native Chinese culture and the export of Chinese culture and language to the rest of the world. However, along with this shift, there should be a greater effort to internalize modern Western ideas and practices into Chinese thinking, emotions, communication, and decision making to make Chinese culture more interculturally open and competent.

It is advisable that Chinese diplomatic policy, behavior, and training be approached from an intercultural perspective instead of a solely Sinocentric perspective. First, the unspoken Sinocentric assumptions should be examined and uncovered. Then, interculturally effective diplomatic policies and skills should be consciously and creatively drawn from the deep cultures of all the nations involved. Western countries tend to adopt the rational model, which seems to be centered on self-interest, but this approach repeatedly encounters unintended roadblocks and problems. This raises the question of how rational the Western geopolitical sense really is. The Chinese model seems to be largely relational,[12] whereas the Japanese model seems to be rationalist in substance and relational in form or appearance. Thus, Japanese diplomatic behavior can be very misleading to the Chinese. Undesirable consequences of using the relational model in all cases without being sensitive to the deep culture of the other party include misunderstanding, conflict, and possibly war. China's relational model is based on the Confucian ethics of *ren,* or cohumanity, and harmony; this is out of touch with reality in today's international arena in which the prevailing attitude may be "my way or no way." The powerful yet unconscious psyche of Chinese foreign policy makers, advisers, and actors may be largely Confucian, but Marxism is the ruling ideology of the Chinese Communist Party, which helps strengthen the party but seems to have little bearing on foreign policy formulation and conduct, especially foreign policies with respect to industrialized countries. China's use of the relational model has reportedly been effective in cultivating and maintaining relationships with its smaller Asian neighbors because such countries' cultures have a long history of close affinity with China and tend to fall under the relational paradigm.[13]

Japan as a nation has developed a Western identity in terms of economics and politics, with a rationalist identity at the core and relational peripheral values, especially in dealings with other countries. However, Japan uses relational core values in promoting interpersonal, family, civic, and corporate relationships, with rational peripheral values. The Chinese do not understand this dynamic, modern Japanese identity syndrome, thanks to China's historically derived view of Japan as a country within the Confucian tradition. As a result, Chinese policy makers, advisers, and actors may use relational diplomatic discourse, behavior, and perception as the dominant approach, only to find themselves disappointed, frustrated, and humiliated by Japanese diplomatic policy and behavior toward China.

The recent twists and turns in Sino-Japanese relations richly illustrate this Chinese inadequacy. When Chinese president Hu Jintao met Japanese prime minister Junichiro Koizumi in Jakarta, Indonesia, on April 23, 2005, Hu expressed displeasure with Koizumi's visit to the Yasukuni Shrine, a temple honoring Japanese who died during World War II. When Koizumi agreed not to do so in the future, this quieted down protests in China against Japan. However, during Wu Yi's goodwill visit to Japan to improve Sino-Japanese ties, Koizumi repeatedly told the Japanese Parliament that he would pay a *personal* visit to the Yasukuni Shrine rather than an *official* visit. This reportedly outraged President Hu Jintao, who immediately recalled Wu Yi to China before she could meet with Koizumi. Hu's anger was provoked by Koizumi's purposeful violation of the Confucian ethical principle of *xin*, or mutual trust. Wu Yi's visit had been a sign of Hu's effort to repair the Sino-Japanese relationship, which had been torn apart by massive demonstrations in China against Japan's bid for a permanent seat on the UN Security Council. The visit had been meant as an honorable gesture of broad-mindedness and forgiveness, putting Hu on the Confucian moral high ground. Although Japan's acceptance of Wu Yi's visit signified a willingness to repair the torn relationship and displayed Japan's identification with the Confucian value of relationality, Koizumi chose to be true to himself and his national interest, which can only be understood under the Western rationalist model of decision making. This rational model coated with a relational flavor on the part of Japan provoked a loss of face by China and its leaders. However, Hu's public display of anger over the loss of face could easily be viewed as a sign of irrationality under the rationalist model and thus a weakness to be taken advantage of, or as a sign of image deterioration. In my opinion, Koizumi's public assertion that he would pay a personal visit to the Yasukuni Shrine during Wu Yi's visit was a provocation and manipulation of the Chinese public's emotions and the Chinese leaders' deep cultural psyche. The Chinese failure to understand Koizumi's Western-style conceptual separation of his individual persona from his organizational persona inevitably worsened the conflict. In the Chinese view, such separation is not possible; an official is always an official, regardless of time and place—a typical Confucian notion. As a result, Koizumi successfully (if on purpose) instigated the loss of face by China's leaders, as did Prime Minister Shinzo Abe, who exhibited a willingness to bring up China's human rights record in talks with Chinese officials.

However, Japan does not always take such a Western rationalist approach; it is quite capable of switching to a face-saving Confucian approach. Prime Minister Yasuo Fukuda has made it clear that he intends to follow in the footsteps of his father, who developed the so-called Fukuda Doctrine, which values "discretion over confrontation."[14] It is this split personality within Japanese diplomacy that suggests to both China and the United States quite different strategies of negotiation, especially when Japan is trying to avoid making an undesirable impression on the global audience. Therefore, China and its leaders must try to understand Japanese discourse from an intercultural perspective and learn to control their emotions over international affairs.

Rhetorical Suggestions

The United States has positioned China as neither a partner nor an enemy. This is a good illustration of the rationalist model the United States has adopted in formulating its policy and diplomatic behavior toward China. However, contemporary Chinese diplomatic policy and behavior toward the United States seem to be largely relational, driven by the hope of winning American hearts by establishing *guanxi* (relationship) with, showering *renqing* (privileges) on, and giving face to the United States. At best, the American side might express its appreciation, but because of different cultural perceptions, it might see this lavish gift-giving as something it deserves and thus feel no obligation to reciprocate, or it might perceive this as a sign of weakness to be taken advantage of. As a result, this Confucian style of diplomacy might invite further undesirable demands on China by the United States. In other words, deeply grounded in the rationalist model, the American side might treat such extravagant face-giving gestures by the Chinese as a confirmation of its own self-worth, whereas the Chinese side's intention was to make the Americans feel indebted to the Chinese and give face to the Chinese in return. The United States is unlikely to trade its own security, interests, and values for such Confucian gestures. The American culture is one of negotiation and bargaining based on individualism, not one of relational interdependence, mutual obligation, and an other-oriented perspective.[15] Assertiveness, the rational way to protect and maximize one's own interests and self-worth, is the key to success in American culture. Externally, this assertiveness in American diplomatic policy and behavior tends to be perceived as aggressiveness by collectivist cultures, including China. However, Americans may not see this themselves.[16] Because they are so goal oriented and always on the go, they tend to be inattentive to their counterparts' feelings and views and are usually focused on their own agenda. This is a pattern of the U.S. national culture that tends to spill over into the international arena.

However, Americans are willing to admit and correct their mistakes—and even apologize—when they are made aware of a problem. Therefore, one should not hesitate to be assertive and tell one's American counterparts when they are going too far. In contrast, Chinese are often unwilling to admit their mistakes, even when these are pointed out to them, for fear of losing face. Americans often fail to consider and reflect on the unintended and undesirable impact of their policies or behavior; likewise, they may be so self-confident that they do not recognize a potential mistake—even if other parties try to point it out to them—until it is too late and the mistake has already been made. Americans' perceived "aggression" may well be caused by misperception and American single-mindedness.

Chinese diplomats should not, out of a Confucian type of relational concern, simply fall into reluctant compliance with the American point of view. Americans appreciate an assertive response and do not consider it a loss of face. Therefore, failing to send an assertive message does a disservice to both parties. Deep in the American psyche, there is a strong sense of freedom, justice, and equality, and any effort to point out potential dangers to such values usually elicits a positive response from the American side. If grievances are not verbalized, Americans assume that everything is okay; they cannot be expected to read their counterparts' minds. To avoid causing the other party to lose face, Chinese tend to quietly accumulate complaints and grievances against their counterparts until the breaking point is reached. Then all these pent-up grievances are expressed in a very undesirable (both destructive and self-destructive) manner. Therefore, China would be well-advised to complain promptly whenever there is a problem, and nations such as United States, European Union, Russia, and Japan would be well-advised not to place too much pressure on China in too short a time and to inquire periodically to determine China's reaction to such pressure.

As an example, the Bush administration's recent pressure on the Chinese government to increase the exchange rate between the renminbi and the U.S. dollar has put Chinese decision makers in the position of reluctant compliance out of their Confucian-type relational concerns. China has also been forced to significantly raise export tariffs on seventy-four kinds of domestic textile products. China's decision to comply with such demands by the European Union and the United States shocked Fareed Zakaria, a well-known journalist and former editor in chief of *Foreign Affairs*.[17] A few years ago, around the time when China was accepted into the World Trade Organization, there was a popular Chinese saying that referred to transnational corporations and the countries they represent: "The wolves are coming!" I would say that the "wolves" have already settled in China. However, the Chinese need to learn how to negotiate interculturally instead of letting themselves fall prey. Quite often, when the voice is loud, the argument is weak. People in individualistic cultures are usually aware that the loudest get the most attention. Rather than reluctantly complying, China should have used a loud, assertive voice to make itself heard. China's quick compliance shocked Zakaria, because he knows the pervasive game of loud voice–weak argument played by Europe and the United States. The rule is this: If one resists long enough and is assertive enough in standing up to unreasonable demands in this world of unbridled competition, the other party will retreat. If one retreats to avoid conflict, the other party is likely to move closer. To solve this problem, China needs to educate itself and become interculturally competent; China needs to invests in the "software" of the modern mind rather than develop the hardware of modern technology. Learning from Japan's intercultural syndrome, characterized by both relationality and rationality, is a good start, thanks to the similar cultural traditions of China and Japan.

Using the iceberg concept of deep culture and the social construction-ist perspective on foreign policy making and behavior as intercultural com-munication, I argue that contemporary Chinese diplomatic behavior is still largely governed by deep Chinese culture and the dominant model for in-terpersonal communication in contemporary Chinese culture, despite the economic liberalization and social change since 1978. In other words, the Chinese model of international relations is implicitly or explicitly an exten-sion of the Chinese relational-hierarchical group (other-oriented) model of interpersonal relationships. Because international relations require dealing with other cultures, the parties involved have to understand their own deep cultures and those of their counterparts in order to be effective. That is, the Chinese international relations model has to be intercultural rather than Sinocentric. Although the Chinese relational-hierarchical model may be effective in dealing with countries bordering China, Southeast Asian countries, and Middle Eastern countries, it needs to be adjusted to deal with the rationalist-individualist (self-oriented) model represented by countries such as Russia, the European Union, and the United States, as well as the rational-relational model adopted by Japan. For such intercul-tural adjustments to be effective, Chinese foreign policy makers, advisers, and actors need to acquire a multicultural personality and mentality. The Chinese model of foreign policy must be intercultural and multicultural, in that it must be sensitive to other cultures and adapt to each accordingly. To begin with, the Chinese need to modernize their attitude without losing their own relational mind-set.

Conclusion

In some of the above scenarios, deep and nuanced mutual intercultural un-derstandings are achieved; in others, strong ethnocentrism leads to a lack of such understanding. These analyses demonstrate that the intercultural communication model, as I have formulated it, not only offers a new lens for observing, interpreting, and advising on international relations and di-plomacy but also exerts a positive impact on the formulation of diplomatic strategies, discourse, and action. Thus, improvement in the international relations and diplomacy of all nation-states is possible if both mutual interest and self-interest are maximized in a humane way in the global context of increasing interdependence.

Notes

I thank the editors of this book, the anonymous reviewers, and Dr. Richard Watson, who provided suggestions for improving the manuscript. I also thank Chapman University, Nanchang University, and the University of Macao for financial support for my presentation of this paper at two international conferences—one in Nanchang, China, in June 2005 and the other in Macao in May 2006.

1. Christer Jonsson and Martin Hall, "Communication: An Essential Aspect of Diplomacy," *International Studies Perspectives* 4, no. 2 (2003): 195–210; James Ferguson, "Lecture 4: Contested Role of Culture in International Relations" (prepared for the course Advanced International Relations and Advanced Global Politics, Department of International Relations, Bond University, Queensland, Australia, 2003).

2. Samuel P. Hungtington, *Clashes of Civilizations and the Remaking of the World Order* (New York: Touchstone, 1996).

3. Richard H. Solomon, *Chinese Negotiation Behavior* (Washington, D.C.: United States Institute for Peace, 1999); Lucian W. Pye, *Chinese Commercial Negotiation Style* (Cambridge, Mass.: Oegeschlager, Gunn and Hain, 1982); Lucian W. Pye, *Chinese Negotiation Style: Commercial Approaches and Cultural Principles* (Westport, Conn.: Quorum Books, 1992).

4. Lucian W. Pye, *The Spirit of Chinese Politics* (Cambridge, Mass.: MIT Press, 1968); Lucian W. Pye, "Factions and the Politics of *Guanxi:* Paradoxes in Chinese Administrative and Political Behavior," *China Journal,* July 1995, 35–54; Chih-Yu Shih, *The Spirit of Chinese Foreign Policy: A Psychocultural View* (New York: St. Martin's Press, 1990).

5. Chih-Yu Shih, *The Spirit of Chinese Foreign Policy.*

6. Pye, "Factions and the Politics of *Guanxi.*"

7. American Field Service, *The Cultural Iceberg: AFS Student Yearbook and Arrival Orientation* (New York: American Field Service, n.d.), 71.

8. Wenshan Jia, *The Remaking of the Chinese Character and Identity in the 21st Century: The Chinese Face Practices* (Westport, Conn.: Ablex, 2001); Wenshan Jia, "Deweyan Pragmatism and Its Implications for Intercultural Communication Studies," *Intercultural Communication Studies* 14, no.1 (2005): 100–106.

9. Ruth Benedict, *The Chrysanthemum and the Sword* (New York: Mariner Books, 1989).

10. Dong Shaopong, "Open the Historical Door to 'the Pudong Logic'—Interview with Zhao Qizheng, Director of the Press of State Council and Former Shang-

hai Vice-Mayor," 5, http//:www.people.com.cn/GB/paper66/14552/1293760.html (accessed April 22, 2005).

11. Ibid., 1.

12. Wenshan Jia, "The *Wei* (Positioning)-*Ming* (Naming)-*Lianmian* (Face)-*Guanxi* (Relationship)-*Renqing* (Humanized Feelings) Complex in Contemporary Chinese Culture," in *Confucian Cultures of Authority: China*, ed. Peter D. Hershock and Roger T. Ames (Albany, N.Y.: SUNY Press, 2006).

13. See, for example, Joshua Kurlantzick, *Charm Offensive: How China's Soft Power Is Transforming the World* (New Haven, Conn.: Yale University Press, 2007).

14. See "The Return of the Fukuda Doctrine," *Economist* 385, no. 8559 (December 15, 2007): 52.

15. See, for example, Shali Wu and Boaz Keysar, "The Effect of Culture on Perspective Taking," *Psychological Science* 18, no. 7 (2007): 600–606.

16. Ibid.

17. S. Ou, "China Must Honestly Face Her Past" by Fareed Zakaria (translated from *Newsweek*), www7.ChineseNewsnet.com/gb/MainNews/Mainland/2005_5_24_12_58_11_936.html (accessed May 24, 2005).

Conclusion

Lowell Dittmer

For the last three decades, China has been the fastest growing economy on earth. The statistics are striking: since 1978, China's gross domestic product (GDP) has grown an average of 9 percent per annum, increasing sixfold from 1984 to 2004; per capita income has risen fivefold, lifting 400 million people out of poverty. China has thus become one of the world's economic "locomotives," pulling Japan out of its long stagnation by increasing Japanese imports, and helping the United States and Europe control inflation with abundant supplies of low-cost exports. In 2004, China alone contributed one-third of the total international economic growth. If recent growth rates continue, China will rival the United States as the key driver of the world economy within two decades. Since reform and opening to the outside world were introduced in December 1978, Chinas' rise has been nonviolent (with the exception of a bloody but limited border war with Vietnam in early 1979). Thus the "China threat" seems to be nonexistent; surely, China *is* peacefully rising.

Yet the issue will not go away. Both Germany and Japan, in the early part of the twentieth century, seemed to be peacefully rising for several decades, yet they ultimately excited the apprehensions of the established powers and became involved in a world war, bringing their rise to a disastrous halt (at least temporarily). The Soviet Union, despite a rhetorical and diplomatic commitment to international revolution, rose for several decades without becoming directly involved in any foreign wars. But during that time it was deemed such a threat by the established capitalist powers that it was subjected to political and economic "containment," a forced self-reliance that contributed substantially to its eventual collapse. Even the United States could not rise without a fight—the Revolutionary War, of course, but also the War of 1812 and the Civil War (in which Britain and France were peripherally involved)—before finally emerging among the powers by the turn of the twentieth century. In each case, the status quo powers greeted the newcomer with suspicion and violent resistance.

If this turns out to be the case for China, as several distinguished analysts have already predicted,[1] the international system is likely to face considerable turmoil in the next several decades, because China is both very large and very determined to make its modernization succeed. Actually, the Chinese leadership has presumed the existence of Western resistance to Chinese modernization since liberation, although it has reacted to this presumption in slightly different ways: Mao Zedong faced it boldly, plunging into the Korean War with the Americans against the advice of the majority of the Chinese Communist Party (CCP) politburo, publicly ridiculing the repeated American threats of nuclear attack as a "paper tiger" (while at the same time focusing intensely on China's swift nuclear armament). Deng Xiaoping was pragmatically conciliatory, downgrading the "inevitable" prospect of world war and launching China's multidimensional quest for peace and development to permit an exclusive focus on domestic modernization. Jiang Zemin synthesized the approaches of his famous predecessors, sometimes confronting the United States (e.g., 1996, 1999, 2001), but otherwise focusing on summitry and the development of "strategic partnerships." Hu Jintao represented a return to the conciliatory policies of his patron, with a focus on "harmonious international society" and even "international democracy."

It is not surprising that China's apprehensions about a hostile, possibly violent reception by the outside world should revive around the turn of the millennium, given the George W. Bush administration's early commitment (and large arms sales) to Taiwan and its announced intention to reinforce U.S. military forces stationed in Asia while reducing those in Europe. Wenshan Jia contends (in chapter 17 of this volume, which is admittedly based on highly anecdotal and episodic evidence) that, to some extent, these fears are based on deeply rooted cultural preconceptions. Cumulative experience suggests, however, that this sense of foreboding, which in turn stimulated the articulation of reassuring notions such as "peaceful rise," "responsible great power," and so forth, is hardly a paranoid fantasy. In the first two decades of its existence, the People's Republic of China (PRC) was threatened with nuclear attack by one superpower or another (never simultaneously, fortunately) approximately ten times, most of them before China had acquired a nuclear deterrent. As Asia's largest country, bordering on more countries (fourteen, by land) than any other country in the world, China has been faced with border friction and even warfare from time to time with its neighbors, and many of these confrontations have threatened to escalate into major war. Since the end of the Cold War, the odds of China's most dreaded scenario—conflict with a technologically superior superpower—occurring have been reduced by half. The Soviet Union collapsed just two years after negotiating "normalization" with Beijing, and the substantially reduced successor republic, the Russian Federation, has opted to continue to nurture this relationship. Yet the collapse of the Soviet Union also divested Beijing of its triangular leverage, and Sino-American relations became more suspicious and fragile. To many Chinese strategic thinkers, the PRC is now confronted with the problem of a "nervous hegemon" dedicated to a Canute-like attempt to maintain superiority against a tide of inevitably rising contenders. This nervousness results in aggressive, unilateral foreign policy behavior that is potentially dangerous to the interests of all rising powers, particularly those not interested in emulating the American political system.

Several of the authors in this volume have traced the origins and demonstrated the substance of Chinese apprehensions. Based on the intriguing premise that it might have been otherwise, George Wei (in chapter 14) reconsiders the American decision in the context of the Korean War to terminate all aid projects and superimpose a comprehensive economic blockade on the PRC, not to be lifted until two decades later. Drawing on new research materials not previously tapped, Shen Zhihua (in chapter 15) reviews the origins of the Sino-Soviet dispute, revealing how serious flaws in U.S. intelligence estimates led American politicians to doubt the existence of a dispute between these two giants until well after it had become irreconcilable, and then to misinterpret its origins. Whereas the Americans traced it back to Khrushchev's secret speech denouncing Stalin at the Twentieth Congress of the Communist Party of the Soviet Union in 1956, we now know that Mao (and the rest of the Chinese politburo) essentially agreed with that speech. Nor was the Soviet incursion to suppress anticommunist uprisings in Poland and Hungary (which Beijing firmly supported) an occasion for controversy. The CCP also backed Khrushchev in his 1957 purge of the "antiparty clique." The first signs of disagreement do not appear until around 1958, specifically with regard to two issues. The first was Mao's bombardment of the offshore islands still occupied by Taiwan without previous consultation with Moscow (even then, the Taiwan matter was viewed as a purely domestic affair), precipitating a crisis involving U.S. nuclear threats against the PRC and the Soviets' guarantee of deterrence to its ally. The second was China's Great Leap Forward, including the introduction, with Mao's personal approval, of the People's Commune (among other daring innovations, such as collective dining and child-rearing arrangements). This was accompanied by self-confident Chinese boasts that they would be waiting at the gate of the communist utopia to greet their lagging comrades, implying that China had overtaken the Soviet Union ideologically and thereby pole-vaulted to the leadership of the international communist movement. These two bitterly contested claims—one implicitly involving a dispute over the Soviet monopoly of nuclear weapons, the other disputing Soviet ideological leadership—split the international communist movement irreparably. My own chapter 5 illustrates how that breach was healed only slowly and painstakingly in the 1980s and 1990s, resulting in a firm strategic partnership involving growing trade, international cooperation on a wide range of matters (including the North Korean problem), and even a second twenty-year peace and friendship treaty (sans a military alliance) in 2001. Thus this old and once mortal threat to China's emergence seems to have been put to rest. Russia's historical involvement with the utopian social experiment it once shared with China seems to have reconciled it to a no doubt surprising turn of events: its erstwhile student in socialism has surpassed it economically. After two decades of bitter ideological controversy, these two behemoths have reached a consensus on a form of developmental authoritarianism with minimal ideological baggage. Yet even here, a certain wariness persists about a relationship that is hot at the top but cool at the bottom, with limited popular appeal on either side of the border.

Xiaoyuan Liu, in his review of the "misty cold war in the Himalayas" (chapter 16), traces Chinese involvement in two of its more asymmetrical disputes, involving Tibet and India. The crackdown in Tibet snuffed out any prospect of an early version of "one country, two systems" that would have tolerated the survival of a Lamaist Buddhism, with which the new revolutionary leadership disagreed in principle. The brief but bruising 1962 border fight with India aggravated a dispute that is still not fully reconciled. In a review of recently disclosed materials, Liu shows the close interconnection between the two cases—that is, the Dalai Lama's flight from Tibet into India, which we now know was personally sanctioned by Mao, eventually fed into the growing Chinese conviction that the Indians were responsible for the continuing resistance to CCP authority in Tibet. This may have been partly due to the CCP's assumption that because the Tibetans protested, they must have had outside support. We learn here that there were in fact backstage string-pullers involved, but not those suspected at the time. The American CIA had quite intensive (but carefully hidden) involvement in the Tibetan situation, Liu reveals, and conceived an American strategic interest in exacerbating Sino-Indian tensions by stirring up Tibetan unrest.

At the time, American hostility to China's rise was presumably based not on sympathy for Tibetan Buddhism, in which most Americans had little understanding and less interest, but on apprehensions about the expansion of a revolutionary ideology that was perceived to have worldwide appeal and ambition. Presumably drawing on the same ideological conservatism that allowed the CIA to continue to believe in a Sino-Soviet bloc long after that alliance's disintegration had reached the point of no return, some of this suspicion has survived the end of the Cold War and China's subsequent deradicalization and opening to international capitalism. It has been reinforced by such events as the Tiananmen crackdown (which stimulated the revival of U.S. and European Union (EU) sanctions on arms sales, forcing the People's Liberation Army [PLA] to deal with Russian arms merchants) and the 1995–1996 Taiwan Strait crisis. Ideological suspicion tenaciously survived the PRC's explicit abandonment in 1979 of the "export of revolution," its belief in the inevitability of international class war, and a foreign policy orientation based on the Five Principles of Peaceful Coexistence. Intensification of propaganda efforts on behalf of Western human rights and Chinese "peaceful evolution" was particularly marked when the CCP regime was most vulnerable in the aftermath of the Tiananmen incident, as fraternal socialist regimes were toppling all over Europe. Belief in the "China threat" was now rationalized by such Western social science innovations as "democratic peace theory" and "power transition theory"—the first of which deems China dangerous because of its authoritarian political order, the latter because of its fast-growing economy. There is perhaps a self-fulfilling aspect to such thinking: if the United States expects the nature of the Chinese system to result in antagonistic contradictions, the PRC will perceive such expectations and take appropriate countermeasures, eventually leading to the coordination of Chinese foreign policies with other similarly mistrusted countries in a coalition of "illiberal regimes."[2] China's recent interest in importing oil and other natural resources to feed its rapid GDP growth has led it to tap neglected markets throughout the world, including some markets that have been avoided by the West due to human rights violations, elite corruption, or other problems, giving rise to Western suspicions that China's commercial interests have led to the strategic assemblage of a coalition of outcasts.

All these trends have been occurring at a time of unprecedented upheaval within China itself. Its population, once chained to the work unit or commune, has acquired new mobility; both wealth and inequality have grown enormously, and Western popular culture has increasingly penetrated the daydreams of the urban middle classes. One consequence of a densely modernized communication network has been heightened nationalism, as Suisheng Zhao makes clear in chapter 13. The general thrust of pragmatic nationalism (which Zhao deems the dominant trend) seems remarkably similar to the goals expressed by Yan Fu a century ago: national wealth and power. Although Zhao's analysis categorizes no fewer than six different variants of nationalism, some of them overlapping, perhaps the most important of these is the split between the nativist variant and antitraditional nationalism, with the government mediating pragmatically between the two based on current foreign policy exigencies. The former is xenophobic or at least anti-Western, while the latter carries on China's quest for the modern, for scientific enlightenment. All tend to be retrospective, obsessed with the notion that China is struggling to emerge from a "century of humiliation." Surely the public debate between these different forms of collectivism demonstrates the growing space for a serious intellectual discussion of the direction of China's unfolding modernization, although where this debate will lead, we cannot foretell. That its direction is not entirely predictable is indicated by the sudden appearance of an Internet petition in early 2005 that gathered some 20 million signatures in an effort to prevent Japan from becoming a permanent member of a reorganized United Nations Security Council. This spontaneous popular movement eventually culminated in two weekends of anti-Japanese demonstrations throughout China. This might be said to illustrate the potential of new technology to forefront opinions or attitudes that were previously only implicit in the public realm, as these demonstrations apparently originated through computer bulletin boards and chat rooms and were coordinated via cell phone text messaging.

Thus, it seems that despite the PRC's publicly expressed commitment to peaceful development, there are ample reasons to wonder whether this is in fact possible. Both geopolitical and economic conditions have been basically favorable since the end of the Cold War, but at present, Sino-American relations, described (by Colin Powell) as the "best ever" in 2001–2003, have cooled somewhat. The Bush administration has rounded up support along

China's periphery for a "hedging" strategy; the World Trade Organization seems to have stalled at the Doha round, as China's largest markets in the United States and Europe have grown saturated, raising accusations of currency manipulation and the threat of trade barriers; and despite the 2008 electoral setbacks of the Democratic Progressive Party, Taiwanese nationalism remains an irritant. Yet as the studies in this volume attest, China's commitment to peaceful development is not merely an empty slogan but a carefully considered strategy. That strategy consists of four essential pillars: (1) a diplomacy to maintain constructive Sino-American relations, (2) a revised nuclear weapons policy, (3) a new approach combining confidence-building measures with crisis prevention to deal with chronic problem areas in Asia, and (4) a new multilateral approach to regional diplomacy. The outlines of Hu Jintao's strategy have only recently become clear, and this book provides that new program's first concerted analysis and basis for critique: How comprehensive and internally consistent is it? And most important, will it succeed in overcoming the anticipated challenges?

Maintaining a stable and constructive relationship with the United States has proved to be a delicate task. The United States is acutely conscious of its position as the world's sole superpower, yet it is apprehensive that this status may be conditional and transitory. The Sino-American relationship, once sustained by collusion in a united front against the rival superpower, has ironically been complicated by the disintegration of that threat and the ensuing collapse of the "strategic triangle." Since that collapse, the U.S. electorate has become more sensitive to China's status as the world's largest and most successful remaining socialist dictatorship. Despite the deradicalization of Chinese Marxism-Leninism-Maoism, an ideological antipathy not visible during the previous decade has reasserted itself, manifest, for example, in presidential campaign rhetoric slamming Chinese human rights violations, an abortive attempt during the Clinton administration to withdraw most-favored nation status, and the Bush administration's disavowal of a "strategic partnership." Although China's market reforms and spectacular economic rise have generally made it a more attractive economic partner and helped integrate the country into world markets far more successfully than had the Soviet Union, China's current massive global account surplus has complicated the trade relationship.

More active U.S. military involvement in South and Central Asia in response to the 9/11 terrorist attacks, including the building of a number of military basing facilities (no longer called "bases" but "places") near China's western borders, has sandwiched the country strategically between West and East. This is sometimes interpreted in Beijing as a return to containment, and there is in fact evidence to support this interpretation, such as Washington's sudden volte-face on the issue of nuclear proliferation in India (promising to withdraw sanctions and cooperate in reactor construction, arms sales, and strategic coordination), the revival of the Philippine-American military alliance, the expansion of basing facilities in Singapore to monitor the Strait of Malacca, and the signing of military cooperation agreements with Vietnam in the fall of 2006.

The avoidance of negative stereotypes about China is complicated by the rhetoric's frequent fluctuation, particularly during national electoral campaigns, when the voters can be mobilized by the image of dire security threats. Jianwei Wang carefully traces the evolution of the U.S. conceptual framework over the past two decades in chapter 2. He observes that without a framework, the relationship will suffer from diplomatic drift, yet it has been difficult to settle on a new one since the rigid ideological frameworks of the Cold War were discarded. The strategic partnership, Jiang Zemin's 1997–1998 diplomatic achievement, lasted barely a year before George W. Bush decided during his presidential campaign that the relationship was not cooperative but competitive, and it was certainly not a partnership. After 9/11, it was perforce elevated to "candid, constructive, and cooperative" ("candid" still being primary) and was boosted even further to "the best yet" for the benefit of the 2004 election, only to be downgraded after the Bush victory to a complicated mixture of competition and cooperation. In September 2005, Assistant Secretary of State Robert Zoellick proffered the concept of "responsible stakeholder" to improve Sino-American relations. The term originated in the field of business management to identify the most important players in a major transaction—a somewhat flattering appellation that Beijing seems to have accepted. Yet the frequent rhetorical turnover betrays an abiding American ambivalence toward China, often turning on the issue of U.S. anxiety about falling behind. To some extent, this unease has been reciprocated in the PRC, as evinced by fierce anti-American demonstrations in the wake of the bombing of the Chinese embassy in Belgrade in May 1999 and after the Hainan incident in early 2001. The Hu Jintao administration's strategy for maintaining a positive relationship with Washington amid such shocks has been precise and nuanced: on the one hand, refusing to be distracted from a successful economic development strategy by American demands for currency adjustments on behalf of the trade imbalance; on the other hand, attempting to cooperate wherever possible with American security policy (e.g., with regard to antiterrorism efforts in Central Asia), dissenting from unilateral U.S. initiatives (e.g., the 2003 invasion of Iraq), but only discreetly, and maintaining strong security relations with Russia while attempting to build a partnership with the European Union as safe strategic alternatives to the United States. Indeed, the China-EU partnership remains robust, Xinning Song attests in chapter 6, despite U.S. debarkation from that diplomatic vehicle, and Europe often provides cover for Beijing to opt out of inopportune American bandwagoning.

Crafting a new nuclear weapons policy has clearly been a Chinese expedient in view of the mixed signals emanating from Washington—pursuing antiproliferation efforts to an almost obsessive degree (except with regard to India and Pakistan) while reviving nuclear weapons development programs and abrogating the Anti-Ballistic Missile Treaty. Beijing's response has been multidimensional. On the one hand (as Jia Qingguo's chapter 3 makes plain), China has attempted to build confidence and assuage anxiety by maintaining a policy of minimal deterrence and no first use of nuclear weapons, cooperating with efforts to prevent nuclear proliferation or missile technology transfer, promoting nuclear disarmament, and opposing ballistic missile defense efforts, which tend to aggravate arms races. On the other hand, China has engaged in the prudent strengthening of its nuclear deterrent (as documented by Baohui Zhang in chapter 4) and has accelerated spending on conventional weapons since 1989, ensuring that the PLA is not left out of the revolution in military affairs. Even minimal nuclear deterrence must be sufficient to guarantee a second strike capable of penetrating an American screen of ballistic missile defense, particularly in light of indications that the United States may have acquired nuclear primacy capable of overwhelming the defenses of any country in the world.[3] China's arsenal includes new models of solid-fueled, mobile, land-based intercontinental ballistic missiles (with multiple warheads), as well as a fleet of submarines capable of carrying submarine-launched ballistic missiles (also with multiple independently targeted warheads). Within the next fifteen years, China's deterrent capability will have improved quite dramatically, balancing the current lopsided PRC-U.S. ratio of 1:200 deliverable warheads to 1:4 or even 1:3. Given the mobility of such weapons and the technical difficulties involved in their detection, they are very difficult to destroy preemptively with a high probability of success in a first strike. As a result, China's now vulnerable second-strike capability should be much more assured. China has also demonstrated the ability to compete asymmetrically in cyberwarfare and space-based military technology, refusing to concede U.S. strategic dominance in either field.

The third pillar of Beijing's new strategy for peaceful development involves the creation of forums for the cooperative management of chronic crisis areas that have the potential to precipitate regional or international war. Asia has at least three such hot spots, and China has become constructively engaged in each. In the case of North Korea and Taiwan, Quansheng Zhao argues in chapter 7, China's participation might fit a comanagement model.

The most well-publicized conflict is the clandestine attempt by the Democratic People's Republic of Korea (DPRK) to develop nuclear weapons and the means to deliver them, beginning some two decades ago (as insightfully narrated in Yufan Hao's chapter 8) and becoming an international controversy in the 1990s. Despite the risk of invoking such severe sanctions that the DPRK economy would collapse, perhaps sending millions of refugees into China, and the possibility that the talks would simply fail, causing the Chinese to lose diplomatic face, Beijing took the initiative to host a series of six-party talks among China, the United States, the DPRK, South Korea, Japan, and Russia, winning widespread kudos for this diplomatic achievement. These talks have thus far fallen short of achieving final resolution. Pyongyang's February 13, 2007, agreement in principle to discontinue nuclear weapons construction was achieved bilaterally in another venue—an agreement that has yet to be fully implemented. Thus, the United States is not fully satisfied, and Shi Yinhong points out in chapter 9 that China is a "loser" in the deal, having forfeited the diplomatic trust of the DPRK. But perhaps the success of these talks should not be measured against the ideal outcomes of the various parties (who have different priorities); instead, their success lies in the cooling off of an issue with the potential to lead to American preemptive strikes and a North Korean invasion of the south, with consequences more lethal than the first Korean War. Although the unresolved proliferation issue leaves room for differing views among our authors, the talks have been a great procedural success, more effective than any previous functioning security forum in Northeast Asia, resulting in calls for their institutionalization in some form.

The issue of the national identity of Taiwan is one in which the PRC has long been a stakeholder, and cross-strait relations have gyrated wildly since the end of the Cold War. The Hu Jintao administration has attempted to stabilize the relationship by employing a bracketing strategy in two arenas. In the domestic arena, the PRC passed an anti-secession law in early 2005, to resounding popular approval, adding the force of law to a long-standing CCP avowal to use force to prevent any formal declaration of independence by the island state. It also implemented united-front tactics to appeal to domestic opposition to former Taiwan president Chen Shui-bian, inviting delegations from opposing parties to visit the mainland, reducing tariffs for southern Taiwan fruit and vegetable farmers, and steadfastly refusing to engage the distrusted Chen regime. In the international arena, Beijing continues to pursue a policy of diplomatic quarantine, denying Taiwan formal recognition from all but two dozen or so governments and excluding it from all international forums for which statehood is required (and many for which it is not). In the wake of Chen's relentless drive for formal independence, Beijing has appealed to Washington for help in managing the issue, tacitly relinquishing any bid to impose involuntary reunification for the time being in an effort to find common ground with the Bush administration in defense of the status quo of *bu tong bu du, bu he bu chan* (neither unification nor independence, neither peace nor war). In a December 2003 press conference, Bush (accompanied by Premier Wen Jiabao) publicly warned Chen not to pursue a national referendum. Although this interesting medley of positive and negative incentives has not resolved the issue, it offers a plausible formula for a quid pro quo that, if reciprocated positively by the new Kuomintang administration in Taipei, may offer provisional stability and facilitate further fruitful cooperation. A more stable and long-term solution may, however, need to await another generation of Chinese leaders with the courage to make the sort of concessions outlined by Zhidong Hao in his insightful chapter 11.

China has been a swing factor in the South Asian balance of power at least since the early 1960s. In 1962, a brief, victorious border war alienated India, with whom relations had been cool since the latter offered asylum to the Dalai Lama in the late 1950s. In the aftermath of this border war, this dangerous enmity was counterbalanced with China's "all-weather alliance" with Pakistan. China has remained loyal to Pakistan ever since, offering military support (but no troops) during the Indo-Pakistani wars in 1965 and 1971 and adopting Islamabad's position that the status of the disputed territory of Kashmir should be resolved by a UN-supervised plebiscite. Even when China moved toward reconciliation with India in the early 1990s, its support of Pakistani security continued, facilitating Pakistan's development of nuclear weapons and the necessary delivery vehicles, which were tested immediately after the Indian tests in early 1998. Yet in the wake of these tests, which Indian foreign minister George Fernandez claimed were justified by the Chinese nuclear threat, China has shifted to a more balanced position. For example, without abandoning the all-weather alliance, it did not support Pakistan's Kargil incursion in early 1999 and later endorsed U.S. efforts to mediate the crisis. And following the 2001 terrorist attacks on the United States, China offered full support to the American incursion in Afghanistan, where the Taliban regime had sanctioned not only al Qaeda's base but also the headquarters of the Eastern Turkistan Islamic Movement, which sponsored anti-Chinese separatist violence in Xinjiang province, as Du Youkang notes in his illuminating chapter 10. The low-level guerrilla warfare in Kashmir that had been covertly sponsored by Islamabad since the 1980s was also discredited by the terrorist attacks, and China cooperated with Washington (and admonished Islamabad) in the effort to eliminate all state sponsorship of these organizations. It has now encouraged direct Indo-Pakistani talks toward peaceful settlement of the Kashmir conflict, abandoning its historical support for a plebiscite (which Delhi adamantly refuses). U.S. intervention in South Asia in pursuit of terrorists has not only reduced the Indo-Pakistani conflict but also evened the playing field for China to improve relations with India without betraying Pakistan. Since 1998, the stubborn Sino–Indian border dispute has been relegated to two quasi-permanent negotiating teams, hoping for a replay of the successful Chinese approach to the once equally intractable Sino–Soviet border dispute.

Multilateralism is the fourth pillar of the new Chinese diplomacy. Whereas Chinese foreign policy in the Maoist era was oriented chiefly toward the superpowers, which impinged most directly on China's national security, in the aftermath of the Cold War (and post-Tiananmen sanctions), Beijing has come to appreciate the importance of the smaller surrounding countries in the region. Initially, the Chinese preference even here had been for bilateral diplomacy, under the lingering apprehension that regional blocs would be manipulated by the United States to arrange an anti-Chinese security cordon. But during the 1990s, having already made profitable use of its Security Council seat as well as the United Nations' many affiliated organizations, China discovered the accessibility and utility of regional forums. The Hu Jintao leadership has thus combined continuing support for regional diplomacy with an increasingly skilled multilateral approach, typically beginning with preferential trade agreements and progressing to include discussions of security issues as well. Already a member of the Asia Pacific Economic Cooperation (APEC) forum and the Association of Southeast Asian Nations (ASEAN) Regional Forum (ARF), China supported the ASEAN+3 (the ten ASEAN members plus China, Korea, and Japan) forum in the late 1990s and initiated the ASEAN+1 free-trade agreement in 2001, aiming for the elimination of all trade barriers for some 1.7 billion potential customers by 2010. Already engaged in semiannual meetings with the new governments in Central Asia and joint border negotiations with a Russian-led delegation since the early 1990s, China institutionalized this arrangement in 2001 in the form of the Shanghai Cooperation Organization (SCO), the first international security organization in which the United States is not directly involved. Members of the SCO are China, Russia, Kazakhstan, Kyrgyzstan, Tajikistan, and Uzbekistan; since 2006, Pakistan, India, Iran, and Mongolia have been observers. This form of multilateralism seems to have become a Chinese diplomatic preference; without downgrading bilateral relations, China has elevated talks with the European Union to a security partnership and an annual dialogue (China also has a strategic partnership with ASEAN), and in November 2006, Beijing held an unprecedentedly large conference with a continental delegation from Africa, where trade and economic engagement with China have been surging apace.

This, then, seems to be Beijing's grand strategy for rising peacefully. The obstacles, both domestic and international, remain formidable; the chances of success are perhaps no better than even. China is challenged by unsustainable trade imbalances with the developed world to reduce excessive saving and promote a consumer society, including those hitherto left behind by reform. It must do this without slackening the pace of growth that absorbs an annual influx of some 10 million rural workers—made redundant by ongoing industrialization—into the urban market economy. Economic growth remains in command, and China must somehow compete in the bidding war for natural resources (or become much more efficient in their use) to keep its economic locomotive chugging. Yet the rising tide of rural protests demands renewed attention to issues of social justice and more equitable distribution, to which the Hu-Wen administration is now turning its attention. Despite the opening of the entire eastern gold coast to trade and investment, the gateways so vital during the takeoff phase of growth should not be neglected, as Ting Wai persuasively argues in chapter 12. Although Macao has clearly been a net beneficiary of the opening policy, having surpassed Las Vegas as the gambling and gaming capital of the world, Hong Kong's status is more problematic as the city-state struggles to define "one country, two systems" in a way that is more acceptable to its wealthy and well-educated citizenry without exciting the envy of the rest of the country. Yet Hong Kong's economic future also requires that it find a functionally indispensable niche in a new, modernizing economy in which Shanghai and Dalian are keen to supplant it as a port of entry and a financial services capital. The problems are numerous and complex, but China's new leadership has thus far faced them with a well-thought-out strategy applied with impressive intelligence, patience, and shrewd judgment.

Notes

1. See, for example, Richard Bernstein and Ross H. Munro, *The Coming Conflict with China* (New York: Vintage, 1998), John J. Mearsheimer, *The Tragedy of Great Power Politics* (New York: W. W. Norton, 2001); John F. Copper, *Playing with Fire: The Looming War with China over Taiwan* (Westport, Conn.: Praeger Security International, 2006); Ted Galen Carpenter, *America's Coming War with China: A Collision Course over Taiwan* (New York: Palgrave Macmillan, 2005).

2. See Naazneen Barma and Ely Ratner, "China's Illiberal Challenge," *Democracy Journal* (fall 2006): 56–68.

3. Keir A. Lieber and Daryl G. Press, "The End of MAD? The Nuclear Dimension of U.S. Primacy," *International Security* 30, no. 4 (spring 2006).

English-Chinese Terms

Abe, Shinzo	安倍晋三
Acquisition and Cross-Servicing Agreement (ACSA)	《物品服儎务相互提供協定》
Aid India Club	援印俱樂部
American Institute in Taiwan	美國在臺協會
Annual Report to Congress: Military Power of the People's Republic of China	《中國軍力年度報告》
Anti-Secession law	反分裂國家法
APEC (see Asia Pacific Economic Cooperation)	
Article 23 of the Basic Law	基本法23條
ASEAN (see Association of Southeast Asian Nations)	
ASEAN+3	東盟+3
ASEAN-China Free-Trade Area (ACFTA)	東盟-中國自由貿易區
ASEAN Regional Forum (ARF)	東盟地區論壇
Asia Pacific Economic Cooperation (APEC)	亞太經濟合作組織
Asian cooperation dialogue	亞洲合作对話
Asian financial crisis	亞洲金融危機
Asia's world city	亞洲國際城市
Association for Relations across the Taiwan Strait (ARATS) in mainland China	海協會
Association of Southeast Asian Nations (ASEAN)	東盟

Banco Delta Asia   匯業銀行

Bandung conference   萬隆會議

Bermuda   百慕達

Bo'ao Forum   博鰲論壇

bombing of the Chinese embassy   炸舘

Boxer Rebellion   庚子拳亂

Brezhnev, Leonid   勃列日涅夫

British Virgin Islands   英屬処女島

building socialism with Chinese characteristics   建設具有中國特色的社會主義

Burghardt, Raymond   薄瑞光

Camp Hale   赫爾營

Central and South Asian Regional Security Conference   中亞與南亞地區安全會議

Chamdo   昌都

Chen Shui-bian   陳水扁

Chen Yunlin   陳雲林

Chi Mei Group   奇美集團

Chiang Bing-kun   江炳坤

Chiang Kai-shek   蔣介石

China Ocean Shipping Company   中遠輪船公司

China's reformist approach toward North Korea   中國对朝改革式方针

China's rise   中國崛起

China's strategic relationship with North Korea   中朝战略關係

Chinese character   中國性

Chinese Communist Party (CCP)   中國共產黨

Chiu Tai-san   邱太三

Christensen, Thomas J.   柯慶生

Chuo Jung-tai   卓榮泰

Cixi, Dowager   慈禧太后

Clinton, Bill   克林頓

coexistence and reconciliation   和解共生

Cold War   冷戰

collapse of the Soviet Union	蘇聯解體
Communist Party of the Russian Federation (CPRF)	俄羅斯聯邦共產黨
conceal our capacity and bide our time	韜光養晦
corporate governance	企業管治
counterrevolutionary	反動派
Cultural Revolution	文化大革命
da guo zhanlue	大國戰略
Dalai Lama	达赖喇嘛
Dalai line	达赖路綫
Democratic People's Republic of Korea (DPRK)	朝鮮民主主義人民共和國
Democratic Progressive Party (DPP)	民主進步黨
democratic reforms	民主改革
Deng Liqun	鄧立群
Deng Xiaoping	鄧小平
denuclearization of North Korea	朝鮮非核化
DF-31 intercontinental ballistic missile	東風31型洲际战略導彈
DF-31A intercontinental ballistic missile	東風31改型洲际战略導彈
double-track price system	雙軌制
dramatic transformation of Eastern Europe	東歐劇變
Duma	杜馬
East Asian Summit	东亞峰會
East Turkistan terrorist forces	東突恐怖势力
Eastern international relations culture	東方國際關係文化
Eastern Turkistan Islamic Movement (ETIM)	東突厥斯坦伊斯兰运动
ECA Mission to China	援華使團
Economic Cooperation Administration (ECA)	經濟合作總署
economic globalization	經濟全球化
economic reform and opening up	改革開放
economic system of the socialist market	社會主义市場經濟體制
EP-3 (plane collision) incident	撞機事件

fairer and more reasonable new international political and economic order	國際經濟政治新秩序
February 13, 2007, accord	六方會談2·13協議（2007年）
Financial Action Task Force	財政行動特別小組
Five Principles of Peaceful Coexistence	和平共處五項原則
Foreign Assistance Act	援外法案
Foreign direct Investment (FDI)	外國直接投資
Forum on China–Africa Cooperation	中非合作論壇
Fourteenth National Congress of the Chinese Communist Party	中共第十四次全國代表大會
Fourth Session of the Sixth National People's Congress	六屆全國人大四次會議
Fukuda, Yasuo	福田康夫
gaige kaifang	改革開放
good neighborly relationships and partnerships with neighboring countries	與鄰為善、以鄰為伴
Grand National Party	大國家黨
groping around in the pebbles to find a way to cross the river	摸着石頭过河
Group of Eight (G-8)	八國集團
Guangzhou Military Region	廣東軍區
guanxi	關係
guidelines for national unification	國統綱領
hard power	硬實力
hegemony	霸權主义
Himalayas	喜馬拉雅山
Ho, Stanley	何鴻燊
Hong Kong's Federation of Workers' Unions	香港工聯會
Hsieh Chang-ting (Frank Hsieh)	謝長廷
Hsu Wen Lung	許文龍
Hu Jintao	胡錦濤
Hu Qiaomu	胡乔木
Hu Yaobang	胡耀邦

Huang Hua	黃華
Import and Export (Strategic Commodities) Ordinance of 1995	1955年戰略物資進出口條例
Independent Foreign Policy for Peace	獨立自主的和平外交政策
Inner Mongolization	內蒙古化
international characters	國際性
international communist movement	國際共产主义运动
International Covenant for Civil and Political Rights	公民及政治權利國際公約
International Covenant for Social, Economic, and Cultural Rights	社會, 經濟及文化權利國際公約
internationalness	國際特性
Iran-Pakistan-India pipeline	伊朗-巴基斯坦-印度管道
Ivanov, Igor	伊戈爾•伊万諾伕
Jamaat ul Mujahedin Bangladesh (JMB)	孟加拉國聖戰者組織
Jiang Zemin	江澤民
jiegui (connection, convert)	接軌
JL-2 submarine-launched ballistic missile	巨浪2型潛射戰略導彈
Joint Declaration of China-ASEAN Summit Meeting	《中國—東盟首腦會議聯合聲明》
Joint Statement of September 15, 2005, on North Korean nuclear problem	朝鮮核問題六方會談9·15共同聲明 （2005年）
Kalimpong	噶倫堡
Kang Sok Ju	姜锡柱
Karzai, Hamid	哈米德•卡爾扎伊
Kashmir disputes	克什米爾爭端
Kashmir issue	克什米爾問題
Khrushchev, Nikita	赫鲁晓夫
Kim Dae Jung	金大中
Kim Jong Il	金正日
Koizumi, Junichiro	小泉纯一郎
Kuomintang (KMT)	國民黨
Langjiu incident	朗久事件
leaning to one side	一边倒

Lee Kuan Yew	李光耀
Legislative Yuan	立法院
Li Zhaoxing	李肇星
Liberation Tigers of Tamil Eelam (LTTE)	泰米爾伊拉姆猛虎解放組織
Lien Chan	連戰
Line of Control in Kashmir	克什米爾控制綫
Lord Ye's love of dragon	葉公好龍
Ma Ying-jeou	馬英九
Mahsum, Hasan	艾山・買合蘇木
Mainland Affairs Council of Taiwan	行政院大陸委員會
major non–NATO ally (MNNA)	非北約主要盟國
Mao Zedong	毛澤東
Maxwell, Neville	馬克斯韋爾
May Fourth Movement	五四運動
meet in Seattle	西雅图會晤
mianzi	面子
ming	名
missile defense	導彈防禦
Mongolian Tibetan Affairs Commission	蒙藏事务委員會
Mukden incident	九一八事變
Mukherjee, Pranab	穆吉克
Mulin, Anlin, Fulin (good neighborliness, securing the neighbors, enriching the neighbors, an amicable, secure, and prosperous neighborhood)	睦鄰，安鄰，富鄰
multilateral diplomacy	多边外交
multipolarization	多極化
Musharraf, Pervez	佩爾韋兹・穆沙拉夫
Muslim country	穆斯林國家
Mutually Assured Destruction (MAD)	相互确保摧毀戰略
Nakasone, Yasuhiro	中曽根康弘
National People's Congress (NPC)	全國人大
national reunification	祖國統一大業

National Unification Council   國統會

Naxalite   纳萨爾

negotiation of China's entry into the World Trade Organization   入世談判

Nehru (Jawaharlal)   尼赫鲁

new framework for the U.S.-India defense relationship   《美印防務關係新框架》

Next Steps in Strategic Partnership (NSSP)   《戰略伙伴後續步骤》

92 consensus   九二共識

no-first-use nuclear policy   不首先使用核武器政策

nonalignment   不結盟

nontraditional security issues   非傳統安全問題

normalization of China-U.S. diplomatic relations   中美建交

North Atlantic Treaty Organization (NATO)   北大西洋公約組織

North Korean nuclear problem   朝鮮核問題

nuclear deterrence   核威懾

nuclear facility at Yongbyon   宁邊核設施

offshore financial centers   離岸金融中心

Omar, Mohammed   穆罕默德·奧馬爾

"One Battle Line" strategy   "一条綫"戰略

one-China policy   一個中國政策

one China, two interpretations   一中各表

one country, two systems   一國兩制

open-door policy   門戶開放政策

Operation Enduring Freedom   持久自由行動

Opium War   鴉片戰爭

Organization of Islamic Conferences (OIC)   伊斯蘭會議組織

pan–Blue   泛藍

pan–Green   泛綠

pan–Pearl River Delta economic cooperation   泛珠三角經濟合作

Panchen Lama   班禅喇嘛

party's political line	黨的政治路綫
peaceful coexistence	和平共处
peaceful development	和平發展
peaceful rise	和平崛起
Peng Guangqian, General	彭光謙將軍
People First Party (PFP)	親民黨
People's Daily	人民日報
People's Liberation Army (PLA)	中國人民解放軍
Pérez de Cuéllar, Javier	佩雷斯・德奎利亚尔
period of strategic opportunities	戰略機遇期
peripheral environment	周边環境
permanent members of the UN Security Council	安理會常任理事國
permanent membership on the UN Security Council	聯合國安理會常任理事國
Persian Gulf War	海灣戰爭
plane collision incident	撞机事件
Powell, Colin	科林・鮑威爾
preventing peaceful evolution	防止和平演變
proliferation of weapons of mass destruction	大殺傷力武器擴散
psywar	心理戰
Pudong Economic District	浦東經濟特區
Putin, Vladimir	普京
Quadrennial Defense Review Report (QDR)	《四年防務評估報告》
ren	仁
renqin	人情
Republic of China (ROC)	中華民國
Republic of Korea (ROK)	韓國
resume the exercise of sovereignty over Hong Kong	香港回歸
resume the exercise of sovereignty over Macao	澳门回歸
revisionism	修正主义
revolutionary diplomacy	革命外交

Ricci Institute in Macao · 澳門利氏學社

Rice, Condoleezza · 康多莉扎‧賴斯

Rumsfeld, Donald · 唐納德‧拉姆斯菲爾德

Santong (three direct linkages: direct transport, direct mail, direct trade) · 三通

seventeen-point agreement · 十七點協議

Sha Zukang · 沙祖康

Shanghai Cooperation Organization (SCO) · 上海合作組織

Shi Chen-jung · 施振榮

Singh, Manmohan · 曼莫漢‧辛格

Sinha, Yashwant · 亞施旺特‧辛哈

Sino-Japanese Peace and Friendship Treaty · 中日和平友好條約

Sino-Russian Good-Neighborhood Treaty of Friendship and Cooperation · 《中俄睦鄰友好合作條約》

six-party talks · 六方會談

Sixteenth National Congress of the Chinese Communist Party · 中共十六次全國代表大會

Soong, James · 宋楚瑜

South Asian Association for Regional Cooperation (SAARC) · 南亞區域合作聯盟

South Asian subcontinent · 南亞次大陸

South China Sea · 南中國海

Special Administrative Region (SAR) · 特別行政區

status quo of Hong Kong · 香港既有秩序

Straits Exchange Foundation (SEF) in Taiwan · 海基會

strategic cooperative partnership · 戰略協作伙伴關係

struggle philosophy · 鬥爭哲學

Stuart, John Leighton · 司徒雷登

Summit of the Conference on Interaction and Confidence-Building Measures in Asia (CICA) · 亞洲相互協作與信任措施會議峰會

Sun Yat-sen · 孫逸仙

supervisory mechanism · 監管機制

Taiwan Relations Act · 臺灣關係法

Taiwan Strait 臺灣海峽

Takanori Kitamura 北村隆則

talk during the tour of South China 南巡講話

Tang Jiaxuan 唐家璇

tanyue 檀越

Third Plenary Session of the Eleventh Central Committee of the Chinese Communist Party 中共十一屆三中全會

"Three Worlds" "三个世界"

Tiananmen incident 天安門事件

Tibetan incident 西藏事件

Tibetan Working Committee 西藏工委

Treaty of Good-Neighborliness and Friendly Cooperation 《睦鄰友好合作條約》

Treaty of Livadia (Treaty of St. Petersburg) 中俄培城條約

Turkmenistan-Afghanistan-Pakistan pipeline 土庫曼斯坦-阿富汗-巴基斯坦管道

Twelfth National Congress of the Chinese Communist Party 中共十二次全國代表大會

two-pronged policy 兩手策略

Type 094 strategic nuclear submarine 094型戰略核潛艇

united fronts 統一戰綫

United States–Hong Kong Policy Act of 1992 1992美國香港政策法

U.S.-India civil nuclear cooperation agreement 美印民用核合作協議

Vajpayee, Atal Behari 阿塔爾‧比哈里‧瓦傑帕伊

Versailles Treaty 凡爾賽和約

Washington Post 華盛頓郵報

weapons of mass destruction (WMDs) 大規模杀傷性武器

wei 位

well-off society 小康社會

Wen Jiabao 溫家寶

Western development 西部大开發

World Trade Organization (WTO) 世界貿易組織

Wu Yi	吳儀
Xikang	西康
Xinhai revolution	辛亥革命
Xinjiang Uygur Autonomous Region	新疆維吾爾自治區
Yasukuni Shrine	靖國神社
Young, Stephen	楊甦棣
Yu Hongliang	于洪亮
Zhang Jingwu	張經武
Zhang Yintang	張蔭堂
Zhao Ziyang	趙紫陽
Zhu Chenghu, General	朱成虎將軍
Zhu Rongji	朱鎔基
Zoellick, Robert	儸伯特・佐利克

About the Contributors

Yufan Hao (introduction; chapter 8) is a professor of political science and dean of the Faculties of Social Sciences and Humanities at the University of Macao. He is also an adjunct professor at Renmin University of China and senior guest professor at Shanghai International Studies University. He is on the editorial board of several academic journals and chief editor of the series "Focusing on Sino-American Relations" published by Xinhua Press in Beijing.

Zhang Baijia (overview) is a senior research fellow and deputy director of the Party History Research Center of the Central Committee of the Chinese Communist Party.

Jianwei Wang (chapter 2) is the Eugene Katz Letter and Science Distinguished Professor in the Political Science Department at the University of Wisconsin–Stevens Point. He is also an associate fellow of the Asia Society; guest professor at the School of International and Public Affairs, Fudan University; and senior associate at the Shanghai Institute of American Studies and Shanghai Center for RimPac Strategic.

Jia Qingguo (chapter 3) is a professor and associate dean of the School of International Studies of Peking University. He is on the editorial board of several journals and is a member of the Academic Degree Program Review Committee of the State Council.

Baohui Zhang (chapter 4) is an associate professor of politics at Lingnan University, Hong Kong.

Lowell Dittmer (chapter 5; conclusion) is a professor of political science at the University of California at Berkeley and the editor of *Asian Survey*.

Xinning Song (chapter 6) is a senior research fellow of comparative regional integration studies at United Nations University in Brugge, Belgium, and the Jean Monnet Professor of European Studies at Renmin University of China, Beijing.

Quansheng Zhao (chapter 7) is a professor and division director of comparative and regional studies at the School of International Service and director of the Center for Asian Studies, both at American University in Washington, D.C. He is also a research associate at the Fairbanks Center for East Asian Research of Harvard University and a guest professor at Beijing University and Qinghua University in Beijing and at Korea University in Seoul.

Shi Yinhong (chapter 9) is a professor of international relations at Renmin University of China in Beijing.

Du Youkang (chapter 10) is the director of the Center for South Asian Studies and a senior fellow of the Institute of International Studies, Fudan University. He is also a member of the Standing Council of the China Association for South Asian Studies.

Zhidong Hao (chapter 11) is an associate professor of sociology at the University of Macao.

Ting Wai (chapter 12) is a professor in the Department of Government and International Studies, Hong Kong Baptist University. He is a member of the editorial advisory board of four academic journals and since 2007 has been president of the Hong Kong Association of European Studies.

Suisheng Zhao (chapter 13) is a professor and executive director of the Center for China–U.S. Cooperation at the Joseph Korbel School of International Studies, University of Denver. He is the founder and editor of the *Journal of Contemporary China*; a member of the Board of Governors of the U.S. Committee of the Council for Security Cooperation in the Asia Pacific; a member of the National Committee on U.S.-China Relations; a research associate at the Fairbanks Center for East Asian Research at Harvard University; and an honorary *jianzhi* professor at Beijing University, Renmin University, and Fudan University.

C. X. George Wei (chapter 14) is an associate professor and head of the Department of History at the University of Macao and a guest professor at the Institute of History Research of the Shanghai Academy of Social Sciences.

Shen Zhihua (chapter 15) is a professor at both East China Normal University and Peking University.

Xiaoyuan Liu (chapter 16) is a professor of history at Iowa State University.

Wenshan Jia (chapter 17) is an associate professor and chair of the Department of Communication Studies, Chapman University, Orange County, California. He is also a research fellow of the International Academy for Intercultural Research and president of Triwon Global Inc., an intercultural training and consulting firm.

Index

2.13 Pact, 169
3C (candid, constructive, and cooperative relationship), 6, 41–42
9/11 (9–11 incidents). *See* United States
12th National Congress, 17, 32n
14th CCP National Congress, 22
16th National Congress of CCP, 29–30
1993 five-year Military Cooperation Pact, 97

Abe, Shinzo, 136, 146, 177, 328
Acquisition and Cross Servicing Agreement (ACSA), 184
Afghanistan, 9, 32n, 41, 46, 90, 104, 183–84, 186–90, 192, 195n, 346
Afghanistan's peace and reconstruction process, 184; Al-Qaeda, 9, 105, 183, 185, 187, 346; Anti-terrorism, 31, 51, 61, 123, 128, 188, 190–91, 322, 343; Central and South Asian Regional Security Conference, 191, 196n
Akayev administration, 104
Algéria, 253
al-Qaeda. *See* Afghanistan's peace and reconstruction process
American economic policy toward China, 258, 268n
Amur/Heilungjiang River (Ussuri/Wussuli River), 87, 95, 98
an amicable, secure and prosperous neighborhood. *See* China
Angarsk, 103, 106
Angola, 253
Annual Report to Congress: Military Power of the People's Republic of China, 91, 195n
anti-American demonstration, *See* China
anti-Ballistic Missile Agreement (ABM Treaty), 103, 105
anti-China bloc, 96
anti-foreignism; *see also* nativism, 246–248
anti-Japanese demonstration. *See* China
anti-Secession Law. *See* China
anti-traditionalism, 246–48
anti-terrorism. *See* Afghanistan's peace and reconstruction process
April-May 1991 Moscow summit, 98; Arms Race. *See* Russia
Article 9 (Japanese Constitution), 136
Article 23 of the Basic Law, 229
ASEAN, *See* Asia
ASEAN-China Free Trade Area (ACFTA), 222
ASEAN+3. *See* Asia
ASEAN Regional Forum (ARF). *See* Asia
Asia: ACFTA, 222; APEC, 28, 107, 113n, 127, 193, 347; ARF, 107–8, 149, 193, 347; ASEAN, 25–26, 107–108, 116, 127, 149, 193, 222–23, 347; ASEAN+3, 108, 223, 347; Asian Cooperation Dialogue, Asian financial crisis, 22, 24–25; 193; Asia-Pacific, 363; 193; Asia's World City, 10, 225; CICA, 193, 357; "East Turkistan" terrorist forces, 189; ETIM, 189, 195; Indian-held Kashmir, 186–87; Indian-Pakistan border, 186; Indochina, 89, 263; Indonesia, 224, 263, 309, 327; Indo-Pak relations, 9, 186;

Asia (*continued*)
Indo-Pak wars, 345; Joint Declaration of China-ASEAN Summit Meeting, 25; Japan-China Consultations, 136; Japan-China 21st Century Friendship Program, 136; JMB, 9, 188; Kashmir disputes, 187; Kashmir issue, 187, 189; Line of Control in Kashmir, 186; LTTE, 9, 188; Macao, 10, 20–23, 141, 165, 169, 198, 217, 219, 221, 224, 226–27, 229–33, 332n, 348; North Korea nuclear crisis, 9, 31, 42, 62, 64, 143, 148, 162–63, 175; NSDD, 156; Pakistan-Afghanistan borders, 187, 190; SAARC, 193; SCO, 97–98, 104, 108, 193, 347; Sino-Japanese relations, 8, 106, 116, 135–36, 147, 224, 287, 327; Sino-Japanese Peace and Friendship Treaty, 15; Sino-ROK relations, 287; Six-Party Talks, 31, 52, 66, 105, 142–45, 147–49, 151n, 159, 162, 166–68, 175–76; Treaty of Shimonoseki, 137; Turkmenistan-Afghanistan-Pakistan (pipeline), 186; Vietnam War, 134, 309, 321
Asian Cooperation Dialogue. *See* Asia
Asian Development Bank (ADB), 107
Asian financial crisis. *See* Asia
Asian-Pacific Center for Conflict Prevention, 107
Asian-Pacific Institute on Security Problems, 107
Asian Pacific Region (APR), 90, 107, 109, 147, 191, 223
Asia-Pacific. *See* Asia
Asia Pacific Economic Cooperation (APEC). *See* Asia
Asia's World City. *See* Asia
Association for Relations across the Taiwan Strait (ARATS), 206
Athenian Era, 253
Australia, 48, 55n, 185
AWACS, 101
axis of evil. *See* United States

Bahrain, 253
Balkan imbroglio. *See* Russia

balance of power. *See* United States
ballistic missile submarine (SSBN), 73, 77
Banco Delta Asia. *See* China
Bazhanov, Yevgeniy, 96, 112n
Beijing, 4–5, 7–9, 12, 27, 38–41, 47–49, 51–52, 74, 87, 89–90, 92, 94, 97–98, 107–08, 119, 121, 123, 126, 133–49, 151n, 152n, 155–56, 159–60, 160, 162–65, 167–68, 171n, 174–81, 190, 198, 200, 203, 207, 217–21, 223–28, 231, 239–41, 245–47, 249–50, 251n, 262, 266, 285, 297–312, 318n, 324n, 326n, 337, 342–47
bilateral trade, 8, 89, 93, 99, 102, 125–26, 140–41, 149, 222
Blagovaschensk, 98
Bo'ao Forum, 58, 161
bombing of the Chinese Embassy. *See* China
Brazil, 185
Brezhnev, Leonid, 16
Burma, 253, 263
Bush Administration, 40–41, 47–49, 51, 53n, 77, 105, 158, 166–67, 177, 179, 184, 188, 190, 195n, 208, 322, 330, 336, 340–41, 345
Bush, George H., 39, 156, 266
Bush, George W. *See* United States
Butterworth, W. Walton, 259–60, 271n

Camp David, 184
Cam Ranh Bay, 90
cat theory, 242
Central and South Asian Regional Security Conference, 191, 196n, 350
Central Asia, 7, 98, 104–5, 186, 193, 194n, 343, 347
Chechnya. *See* Russia
Chen, Shui-bian. *See* Republican Taiwan
Chiang, Kai-shek. *See* Republican Taiwan
China: ACFTA, 222; an amicable, secure and prosperous neighborhood, 192; anti-American demonstration, 240, 250, 342; anti-Japanese demonstration, 249, 340; Anti-Secession Law, 9–10, 197–98, 201–4, 207, 211–12, 213n, 345;

April–May 1991 Moscow summit, 98; ARATS, 206; Banco Delta Asia, 165, 230; bombing of the Chinese Embassy, 27, 221, 227, 240, 249, 342; China Aid Bill, 269n; China-India relations, 190, 193; China-Pakistan relations, 9, 89, 193; China threat, 43–44, 48–49, 335, 339; China's Japan Policy, 8, 133, 138; China's Most-Favored-Nation status (MFN), 266, 273n; China's rise, 43–44, 48, 53, 111n, 130n, 214n, 227, 295, 339; China Welfare Fund, 263; Chinese characteristics, 12, 121, 129n, 242, 350; Chinese Civil War, 88, 137; Chinese foreign policy, 1–13, 16–17, 19, 21, 44, 51, 64, 112n, 122, 126, 130n, 133–34, 140, 147, 149n, 150n, 151n, 218–19, 226, 228, 239, 241, 246, 248, 250, 251n, 292n, 320, 322–23, 326, 331, 332n, 346; Chinese nationalism, 10, 12, 210–13, 239–40, 244, 247, 251n, 312; Cold War, 6–7, 11–12, 21, 25, 32, 37–38, 40, 45, 48, 53, 90–92, 96, 106, 108, 133–35, 137, 166, 183, 208, 217–18, 231, 245, 247, 253, 255–58, 261, 266–67, 268n, 269n, 272n, 273n, 275, 286, 289, 292n, 293n, 295–96, 301–3, 305–6, 308–9, 311–12, 315n, 316n, 318n, 319–22, 325, 337–40, 342, 344, 346; communism, 8, 37, 96, 102, 108, 111n, 120, 126, 129n, 221, 258, 260, 263–64, 281–82, 326; Containment, 48, 134, 158, 217, 227, 241, 245, 301, 335, 342; counterrevolutionary, 306; cross-strait dialogue, 208; cross-strait relations, 65, 141, 147, 197, 200–201, 206–7, 210, 212, 214, 224, 344; Cultural Revolution, 15, 18, 91, 108, 218, 247; Damansky/Chenbao Island, 98; Deng, Xiaoping, 15–17, 19–22, 32n, 33n, 39, 91–92, 120–21, 138, 201, 220, 241, 243, 244, 250, 325, 336; East China Sea, 136; economic reform, 15–16, 23, 48, 91–92, 126, 148, 166, 168, 176, 185, 248, 256, 266, 287; economic reform and open up, 46; EP-3 incident, 40, 221, 227, 250; EU-China relations, 115, 118–20, 124, 127–29, 129n; Five Principles of Peaceful Coexistence, 17–18, 26, 28, 192, 308, 339; Forum on China-Africa Cooperation, 27; gaige kaifang, 91; Guanxi, 83n, 94, 214n, 315n, 317n, 322–23, 328, 332n, 333n; Hua, Guofeng, 135; Huang, Hua, 262; Hu, Jintao, 44, 46, 49, 53, 58–60, 67n, 68n, 95, 120–121, 143, 161, 170n, 199, 201–202, 241, 243, 249, 325–327, 336, 341–342, 344, 346; Hu, Yaobang, 17, 91; Island of Senkaku/Diaoyu, 106, 251n; Japan-China Consultations, 136; Japan-China 21st Century Friendship Program, 136; Joint Declaration of China-ASEAN Summit Meeting, 25; Mahsum, Hasan, 189; Mianzi, 323; Mukden Incident, 88; nationalism, 10–12, 96, 98, 106, 120, 140, 201–4, 213n, 221, 239–51, 251n, 252n, 264, 288–89, 312, 340–41; negotiation of China's entry into the WTO, 24; non-alignment, 19; normalization of the China-U.S. diplomatic relations, 15–16; NSSP, 188; One-China, 61, 206, 210; Open Door policy, 253; PLA, 60, 62, 73, 75–76, 78, 80–81, 136–37, 203, 297–300, 302–6, 339, 343; plane collision incident, PRC, 2, 4, 32n, 38n, 89–90, 92, 96, 102, 133, 238, 142, 147, 150n, 151n, 197, 199–200, 202–6, 210, 217, 219, 223, 244, 293n, 294n, 295, 298–99, 301–308, 310–12, 336–40, 342–45; PRC State Council, 138; 53n; preventing peaceful evolutionary, 21; Pudong economic district, 326; Qing government, 137, 297; Ren, 326; Renqin, 328, 333n; responsible stakeholder, 45–46, 50, 191, 221, 342; resume the exercise of sovereignty over Hong Kong and Macao, 23; Sino-American economic relations, 267; Sino-Japanese Peace and Friendship Treaty, 15; Sino-Japanese relations. (see Asia); Sino-ROK relations, 287; Sino-Russian Good-Neighborhood Treaty of Friendship and

China (*continued*)
Cooperation, 27; Sino-Russo Alliance, 11; Sino-Soviet "normalization," 90, 111n; Sino-Soviet rift, 265–266; Soft power, 11, 146, 253, 333n; Special Administrative Regions, 10; sphere of influence, 88, 208; Taiwan problem, 9, 61, 66–67; talk during the tour to South China, 22; "peaceful rise," 44, 52, 122 ; Third Communiqué, 90; Third Plenary Session of the 11th Central Committee of CCP, 15; Three fundamental obstacles, 90; Three peaces, 46; Three-World, 5, 16–17, 247; Tiananmen Incident, 20, 39, 135, 339; Treaty of Good-Neighborliness and Friendly Cooperation, 190; Treaty of Shimonoseki, 137; unification, 66, 141, 146–47, 201, 205, 345; Ward, Angus, 262; *Wei*, 333n; well-off society, 29–30; Wen, Jiabao, 42, 54n, 104, 117, 136, 145–46, 190, 195n, 325–26, 345; Wu, Xiuquan, 135; Wu, Yi, 202, 240, 327–28; Xinjiang Uygur Autonomous Region, 189; Yalu River, 137; Yang, Jiawen, 265, 272n; Yu, Hongliang, 17; Zhao, Ziyang, 17; Zheng, Bijan, 44–45, 49, 54n; Zhou, Enlai, 217, 294n, 300, 303, 306, 310, 315n, 316n, 317n, 318n; Zhu, Rongji, 202, 325
China Aid Bill. *See* China
China-India relations. *See* China
China-Pakistan relations, 9, 89, 193. *See* China
China's Japan Policy. *See* China
China's Most-Favored-Nation status (MFN). *See* China
China's rise. *See* China
China threat. *See* China
China Welfare Fund. *See* China
Chinese characteristics. *See* China
Chinese Civil War. *See* China
Chinese Communist Party (CCP), 12, 15, 33n, 88, 121, 129n, 130n, 155, 197, 200, 217, 240, 256, 278, 297, 326, 336
Chinese foreign policy. *See* China

Chinese nationalism. *See* China
Church World Service, 263
Cixi, Dowager, 326
Clayton, William L., 256
Cleveland, Harlan, 258, 270n, 271n
Clinton administration, 38, 49, 184, 208, 341
Clinton, Bill, 27, 38, 158, 266
Clinton, Hillary, 321
Cohen, Warren I., 262, 272n
Cold War. *See* China
collapse of the Soviet Union, 20, 337
collectivistic and ethnic, 203
Comintern Pact, 110
Commonwealth of Independent States (CIS), 92
communism, 8, 37, 96, 102, 108, 111n, 120, 221, 258, 160, 263–64, 281–82, 326
Communist Nanjing Municipal Military Control Commission, 262
Communist Part of Russian Federation (CPRF), 96
composite dialogues, 187, 189
conceal our capacity and bide our time, 20
Confederation, 210–11
Conference on Interaction and Confidence-Building Measures in Asia (CICA), 193
confidence-building, 28, 97, 148, 157, 187, 208
constructive partnership, 94
containment. *See* China
Council of Europe, 93
counter ballistic missile (CBM), 107
counterrevolutionary. *See* China
Cross-Strait dialogue. *See* China
Cross-strait relations. *See* China
Cuba, 91, 310, 318
cultural-psychological model, 320
Cultural Revolution, 15, 18, 91, 108, 218, 247

da guo zhanlue, 94
Dam, Kenneth W., 254
Damansky/Chenbao Island. *See* China
Darfur conflict, 186
De Cuellar (Javier Pérez de Cuéllar de la Guerra), 17

deep culture, 320, 323–324, 326, 331
Delyusin, Lev, 96
democracy, 45, 47, 52, 58, 92, 161, 185,
    203–205, 207–211, 226, 233, 241,
    246–247, 255, 266, 268n, 298
Democratic People's Republic of Korea
    (DPRK, also North Korea), 26, 158, 174,
    344; denuclearization, 9, 155–56, 165,
    169, 173–77, 180, 181; IAEA, 156–58,
    165; Kim, Chong Il, 157–58, 166–69,
    178–79; Korean Peninsula, 8–9, 26, 31,
    133, 137, 140, 143–44, 155–56, 159–65,
    168–69, 170n, 173, 181, 188; Korean War,
    89, 103, 134–35, 137–38, 143–44, 150n,
    155, 217, 219, 227, 261–62, 266–67, 303–
    4, 336–37, 344; Korean Workers Party,
    155; North Korea nuclear crisis. See
    Asia; North-South Denuclearization
    Declaration (NSDD), 156; nuclear
    power plant, 169; Six-Party Talks (see
    Asia); 2.13 Pact, 169; Yalu River, 137
Democratic Progressive Party (DPP), 138,
    197, 341. See Republican Taiwan
Deng, Liqun, 92, 293n
Deng, Xiaoping. See China
denuclearization See Democratic People's
    Republic of Korea
deradicalization, 108, 339, 341
descriptive model, 320
developmental dictatorships, 109
DF-31, 73, 75–77
DF-31A, 73, 75–77
discrimination of mainlanders, 206–7, 210
double bang, 92
double-track price system, 22
dramatic transformation of Eastern Eu-
    rope, 20
Duma, 96

East Asian Summit, 193
East Asian Tigers, 141
East China Sea, 136
Eastern European satellites, 93
"East Turkistan" terrorist forces. See Asia
Eastern Turkistan Islamic Movement
    (ETIM), 189, 346

ECA Mission to China, 256, 258
Economic Cooperation Administration
    (ECA). See United States
economic globalization, 21, 23–25, 44, 46
economic reform. See China
economic reform and open up. See China
Egypt, 27, 253
EP-3 incident. See China
EU-China relations. See China
Europe, 100, 117, 127–28, 129n, 249,
    227–28, 287, 290, 339; Council of Eu-
    rope, 93; De Cuellar, 17; Dramatic
    transformation of Eastern Europe, 20;
    Eastern European satellites, 93; EU-
    China relations (see China); European
    Union, 115–17, 122, 124–25, 127, 149,
    228, 343; WWI, 253; WWII, 11, 40, 46,
    105, 122, 133, 137, 253, 261, 289, 301,
    321, 327
European Union. See Europe
extremist forces, 185

Feaver, John H., 256, 269n
Five Principles of Peaceful Coexistence.
    See China
Foreign Affairs Office, 262
Foreign Assistance Act, 258, 260
FDI (Foreign Direct Investment), 92, 97,
    100, 115, 325–26
Forum on China-Africa Cooperation, 27
Fossedal, Gregory A., 254, 268n
Fourth Session of the Sixth National
    People's Congress, 17
Fukuda, Yasuo. See Japan
Fukuda Doctrine, 328, 333n

gaige kaifang. See China
Garrison states, 109
geopolitical strategy, 191
geostrategic posture, 93
Germany, 44, 93–95, 106, 115, 185, 335
global unipolarity, 96, 109
global war on terrorism, 185
good neighborly relationships and partner-
    ships with neighboring countries, 192
Gorbachev, 90–93, 96–98, 111n

Great Leap Forward Movement. *See*
  China
great power strategy (*da guo zhanlue*), 94
groping around in the pebbles to find a way
  to cross the river, 22
Group of Seven, 93
Guanxi. See China
guidelines for the US-Japan Defense Cooperation. *See* Japan

Haass, Richard N., 254, 268n
hard power, 11, 253
heavy fuel oil (HFO), 157, 165
hedging strategy, 52, 341
hegemonism. *See* United States
hegemony, 7, 17, 19, 25, 28, 32n, 40, 80, 90,
  96, 102, 110, 134, 151n, 209, 247, 337
Heixia/Black Bear Island, 98
Hill, Christopher, 143
Hoffman, Paul, 259
Hong Kong, 10, 20–21, 23, 80, 140–41,
  204, 206, 209, 217–33, 348
Hot War, 255
Hua, Guofeng. *See* China
Huang, Hua, 262. *See* China
Hu, Jintao. *See* China
Hu, Yaobang. *See* China
Hufbauer, Gary C., 265
Huludao, 73, 82n, 83n
human rights. *See* United States

iceberg concept of culture, 323
Ilyushin transport planes, 101
imperialism, 244, 246–47, 259, 263–64,
  297, 302–3, 306–8, 310–11
Independent Foreign Policy for Peace, 17,
  19, 28
International Atomic Energy Agency
  (IAEA). *See* Democratic People's Republic of Korea
India, 26, 103, 106–07, 149, 184–90,
  192–93, 194n, 195n, 302, 306–11, 315n,
  318n, 338, 345, 347
Central and South Asian Regional Security Conference, 191; Indian-held
  Kashmir, 186–87; Indian-Pakistan bor-
der, 186; Indo-Pak relations, 190; Indo-
Pak wars, 345; Iran-Pakistan-India
(pipeline). *See* Asia; Line of Control in
Kashmir. *See* Asia; Mukherjee, Pranab,
184; New Framework for the U.S.-
India. *See* United States; Singh, Manmohan, 184; Sinha, Yashwant, 106;
SAARC, 193; U.S.-India civil nuclear
cooperation agreement, 184; U.S.-India
strategic partnership, 184
Indian-held Kashmir. *See* India
Indian-Pakistan border. *See* India
Indochina. *See* Asia
Indochina War, 89
Indonesia, 224, 263, 309
Indo-Pak relations. *See* Asia
Indo-Pak wars. *See* Asia
intercontinental ballistic missiles (ICBMs),
  73, 75, 343
intercultural communication, 319–22, 324,
  331, 332n
intercultural syndrome, 320, 324, 330
international communist movement, 18–
  19, 278, 285, 289–91, 192n, 338
international community, 6, 17, 25, 44–45,
  59, 66, 120, 122–23, 128, 147, 159, 165,
  186, 198, 217, 219, 221–23, 227, 295
Iranian nuclear issues, 186
Iran-Pakistan-India (pipeline). *See* Asia
Iraqi problem. *See* United Nations
Iron Curtain, 94, 259
Islam, 186
Islamic community, 186
Islamic extremism, 105
Islamic world, 186
Island of Senkaku/Diaoyu. *See* China
islands to the north of Hokkaido (Etorofu,
  Shikotan, Kunashiri, and the Habo-
  mais), 92, 105. *See also* Japan
Israel, 20, 101, 185
Ivanov, Igor, 106

Jamaat ul Mujahedin Bangladesh (JMB),
  9, 188
Japan: Article 9, 136; Japan-China Consultations, 136; Japan-China 21st Century

Friendship Program, 136; Fukuda, Yasuo, 328; guidelines for the US-Japan Defense Cooperation, 139, 150n; Island of Senkaku/Diaoyu, 106, 251n; islands to the north of Hokkaido, 92, 105; Japanese constitution, 136; Koizumi, Junichiro, 240, 327; Military, 139; Mukden incident, 88; Nakasone, Yasuhiro, 135; Permanent membership of the UN Security Council (*see* United Nations); Russo-Japanese territorial dispute, 92; Russo-Japanese War, 137; Six-Party Talks (*see* Asia); U.S.-Japan Security Treaty, 133, 135, 139, 146; Tanaka, Kakue, 134; Yasukuni Shrine, 13, 106, 136, 240, 327–28

Japan-China Consultations. *See* China

Japan-China 21st Century Friendship Program. *See* China

Japanese constitution. *See* Japan

Jiang, Zemin, 20–21, 24, 27, 40, 42, 94, 98, 120–21, 146, 241, 250, 325, 336, 342

Joint Declaration of China-ASEAN Summit Meeting. *See* Asia

Kakue, Tanaka. *See* Japan

Kang, Sok Ju, 158

Kanwa Defense Review, 73

Karzai, Hamid, 184

Kashmir disputes. *See* Asia

Kashmir issue. *See* Asia

Kazakhstan, 28–29, 97, 104, 347

Kelly, James, 158

Keohane, Robert, 142, 151n

Khabarovsk, 96, 98

kilo-class submarines, 101

Kim, Chong Il (Kim Jong-Il, Kim Jung Il, Kim Il Sung). *See* Democratic People's Republic of Korea

Kim, Dae Jung, 163

Kissinger, Henry, 142, 262

Koizumi, Junichiro. *See* Japan

Korean Peninsula. *See* Democratic People's Republic of Korea

Korean War. *See* Democratic People's Republic of Korea

Korean Workers Party. *See* Democratic People's Republic of Korea

Kosovo, 103, 123

Koumintang (KMT). *See* Republican Taiwan

Kozyrev, Andrei, 92, 107

Krasner, Stephen, 142

Krasnoyarsk, 90, 93

Kremlin, 92, 293n

Khrushchev. *See* Russia

Kuwait, 253

Kyrgyzstan, 28–29, 97–98, 347

Lapham, Roger, 256

Laos, 91

Lebed, 93

Liberation Tigers of Tamil Eelam (LTTE), 9, 188

Lien, Chan. *See* Republican Taiwan

light water reactors (LWR), 156

Line of Control in Kashmir. *See* Asia

Locke, Edwin A., Jr., 256

Lord Ye's love of dragon, 52

Lugar, Richard Green, 254, 267

Macao (Macau). *See* Asia

Mahsum, Hasan. *See* China

major non-NATO ally (MNNA), 185, 194n

Manas, 104

Manchuria, 88, 262

Mao, Zedong (Mao Tse-Tung), 11, 16, 88, 120, 135, 217, 243, 250, 262, 269–70, 276, 278–84, 290–91, 297, 300, 307, 336

marketization, 92

Marshall, George, 256

Marxism-Leninism, 91, 284–85, 290, 341

meet in Seattle, 27

Mianzi. *See* China

Ming, 333n

Mongol Golden Horde, 7, 87

more fair and more reasonable new international political and economic order, 25, 28, 30, 228

Moscow, 2, 7, 88–89, 92–94, 97–99, 101–2, 104, 106–7, 135, 142, 156, 259, 266, 276, 278, 280–81, 285, 287, 289–90, 310, 337

Moscow Institute of Foreign Relations, 96
Mukden incident. *See* China
Mukherjee, Pranab. *See* India
multilateral diplomacy, 28, 30
multipolarity, 30, 110
multi–polarization, 21
multipolar world, 106, 190, 247
Murawjew, N. N., 87
Musharraf, Pervez. *See* Pakistan
Muslim country, 186
Muslim militants, 186
Mutual Defense Treaty, 138
Mutually Assured Destruction (MAD), 72, 79, 81, 82n

Nahodka, 106
Nakasone, Yasuhiro, 135
name rectification, 211
National Intelligence Council (NIC), 76, 275
nationalism. *See* China
National Missile Defense (NMD), 64, 77
national reunification, 19, 138
National Security Council, 257, 260
National Security Strategy, 43, 52
nativism. *See also* anti-foreignism, 246–48
Naxalite, 9, 187
negotiation of China's entry into the WTO. *See* China
neoconservatism, 208
neo-conservatives, 158, 209, 245
Nepal, 9, 187
New Framework for the U.S.-India Defense Relationship. *See* United States
new world order, 92, 102
new thinking (*novo myshlenie*), 49, 90
New Zealand, 185
Next Steps in Strategic Partnership (NSSP), 184
Nixon, Richard. *See* United States
Noland, Marcus, 273n
nonalignment. *See* China
Nonaligned Bloc, 108
Non-Proliferation Treaty (NPT), 63, 156
non-traditional security issues, 9, 187
normalization of the China-U.S. diplomatic relations. *See* China

North Atlantic Treaty Organization (NATO). *See* United States
North Korea nuclear crisis. *See* Asia
North-South Denuclearization Declaration (NSDD), 156
nuclear power plant, 169
nuclear war. *See* United States

October 1994 Agreed Framework, 157
ODA: Official Development Assistance, 139
"One Battle Line" strategy, 16
One-China. *See* China
Open Door policy. *See* China
Operation Enduring Freedom, 183
Opium War, 87, 224, 243, 326
Organization of Islamic Conferences (OIC), 186
orthodox ("leftist") wing, 92
Outer Mongolia, 88, 90, 92

Pakistan, 107, 149, 184–90, 304, 345–46; al-Qaeda, 9, 105, 183, 185, 187, 346; Central and South Asian Regional Security Conference, 191, 196n; Indian-held Kashmir, 186–87; Indian-Pakistan border, 186; Indo-Pak relations, 9, 186; Indo-Pak wars, 345; Iran-Pakistan-India (pipeline), 186; Musharraf, Pervez, 184; Pakistan-Afghanistan borders, 187, 190; U.S.-Pakistan relations, 184, 190
Pakistan-Afghanistan borders. *See* Pakistan
Paulson, Henry, 47
peace and development, 19, 21, 193, 240, 345–46
peaceful coexistence, 187, 310
peace process, 187
peasant movement (Naxalite), 9, 187
People's Liberation Army (PLA). *See* China
People's Republic of China (PRC). *See* China
perestroika (reform and opening), 91
peripheral environment, 183
permanent membership of the UN Security Council. *See* Japan

Persian Gulf War, 20
Philippines, 185, 263
Phoenix TV, 80,
plane collision incident, 53n. *See* China
plutonium program, 168
post–Cold War period, 38, 45, 134, 267
Powell, Colin. *See* United States
pragmatism, 4, 206, 241–42, 246; pragmatic nationalism, 10–11, 240, 242, 247–48, 250, 340
PRC State Council, 138
preventing peaceful evolutionary. *See* China
Price, Harry Bayard, 264
Primakov, Evgeny, 103, 107
Primorski krai, 95–96
privatization, 92
Pro-Western bloc, 96
Pudong Economic District. *See* China
Putin, 95–96, 10, 105–106
Pyongyang, 9, 143–44, 155–60, 162–70, 177–81, 344

Qian, Qichen, 59, 164
Qing government (Manchu Dynasty), 87, 137, 244, 297
Quadrennial Defense Review Report (QDR), 52, 191, 195n

rationalist-individualist model, 325
Ren. See China
reconciliation, 46, 95, 106, 199, 206, 211–12, 291, 299, 345
Referendum. *See* Republican Taiwan
refugees, 144, 174, 218, 344
Renqin, 334
Republican Taiwan: Anti-Secession Law (*see* China); Asian financial crisis. *See* Asia; Chen, Shui-bian, 200–201, 345; Chiang, Kai-shek, 88, 138, 211, 243, 307, 314n; Cross-Strait dialogue, 208; Cross-strait relations (*see* China); DPP, 138, 197, 341; KMT, 12, 88, 98, 197–99, 205, 207, 212–13, 217, 223, 244, 296–97, 299, 302–3, 306, 313n ; Lien, Chan, 141, 197, 198, 205; nationalism (*see* China);

October 1994 Agreed Framework, 157; One-China, 61, 206, 210
Soong, James, 141, 197, 199, 205; Referendum, 201, 212, 345; Taiwan problem, 9, 61, 66–67; Taiwan Relations Act, 16, 210; Unification (*see* China)
responsible stakeholder. *See* China; United States
resume the exercise of sovereignty over Hong Kong, 23
resume the exercise of sovereignty over Macao, 23
revisionism, 284, 291
revolutionary diplomacy, 19
Rice, Condoleezza. *See* United States
robust rival, 52
Rogue States, 47, 49
Rumsfeld, Donald 184, 207
Russia, 7, 23, 26–27, 72, 78, 87, 91–95, 97–110, 127; ABM Treaty, 103, 105; anti-China bloc, 96; anti-terrorism, 31, 51, 61, 123, 128, 188, 190–91, 322, 343; April–May 1991 Moscow summit, 98; arms race, 9, 18, 64, 81, 89–90, 93, 108, 139, 143, 163, 343; Balkan imbroglio, 93; Chechnya, 97, 103, 105, 110; Cold War (*see* China); collapse of the Soviet Union, 20, 337; CIS, 92; communism (*see* China); Containment (*See* China); CPRF, 96; Damansky/Chenbao Island, 98; dramatic transformation of Eastern Europe, 20; double bang, 92; Duma, 96; Eastern European satellites, 93; Gorbachev, 90–93, 96–98, 111n; Group of Seven, 93; islands to the north of Hokkaido, 92, 105; Ivanov, Igor, 106; Kozyrev, Andrei, 92, 107; Khrushchev, 93, 276, 278–84, 286–87, 291, 309–10, 312, 337; Moscow Institute of Foreign Relations, 96; NPT, 63, 156; NATO (*see* United States); 1993 five-year Military, 97; Cooperation Pact, 97, 101; *novo myshlenie*, 90; pro-Western bloc, 96; Putin, 95–96, 10, 105–106; RFE, 88, 96, 100; Russian Federation, 92, 96, 98, 102, 106, 107–108, 337; Russo-Japanese

Russia (*continued*)
  territorial dispute, 92; Russo-Japanese
  War, 137; SCO (*see* Asia); Sino-Russian
  Good-Neighborhood Treaty of Friendship and Cooperation, 27; Sino-Russo
  Alliance, 11; Sino-Soviet "normalization," 90, 111n; Sino-Soviet rift, 265–
  66; Six-Party Talks (*see* Asia); Soviet
  Union, 2, 11, 16–17, 21, 45–46, 48–49,
  88, 90–92, 96, 99, 104, 108, 134–135,
  138, 156, 247, 253, 262, 266, 276–85,
  288–91, 309–10, 312, 325, 335, 337–338,
  341; strategic parity, 90; three fundamental obstacles, 90; Treaty of Livadia,
  87; Yeltsin, Boris, 92
Russian Far East (RFE), 88, 96, 100
Russian Federation. *See* Russia
Russo-Japanese territorial dispute, 92;
  Russo-Japanese War, 137

sanction. *See* United States
Saudi Arábia, 20, 253
security Issues, 9, 29, 120, 125, 143, 145,
  149, 187, 347
Senior Foreign Affairs Officials' Consulta-
  tion, 136
Seoul, 140, 142, 163–64, 181, 224
September 11th terrorist attack, 27, 183
Shanghai, 225, 232, 249, 260, 263, 326, 348
Shanghai Cooperation Organization
  (SCO). *See* Asia
Shanghai Federation of Emergency Relief
  (SFER), 263
Shenyang, 101, 262
Singapore, 223, 225, 232, 342
Singh, Manmohan, 184
Sinha, Yashwant, 106
Sino-American economic relations, 267
Sino-Japanese Peace and Friendship
  Treaty. *See* Asia; China
Sino-Japanese relations. *See* Asia
Sino-ROK relations. *See* Asia; China
Sino-Russian Good-Neighborhood Treaty
  of Friendship and Cooperation (Sino-
  Soviet Treaty of Friendship, Alliance
  and Mutual Assistance), 88

Sino-Russo Alliance, 11
Sino-Soviet "normalization," 90, 111n
  Sino-Soviet rift, 265–66
Six-Party Talks. *See* Asia
social constructionism, 12, 323–24
soft power. *See* China
Soong, James. *See* Republican Taiwan
South Asia, 9, 83, 185, 187–94, 345–46
South Asian affairs, 183, 186, 188
South Asian Association for Regional co-
  operation (SAARC), 193
South Asian subcontinent, 183
South China Sea, 39, 97, 250
Southeast Asia, 63, 222, 264, 309
South Korea, 26, 92–93, 140, 155–57, 163,
  166, 177, 179–81
Soviet Union. *See* Russia
Sovremenniy-class destroyers, 101
Special Administrative Regions. *See* China
Special Economic Zone (SPZ), 99, 168
sphere of influence, 88, 208
Sri Lanka, 188
Srinagar, 187
stakeholder, 43, 45–47, 49–52, 344
Stevenson, Adlai E., 254
Stillman, Charles L., 260
strategic competitor, 6, 39–43, 48
strategic cooperative partnership, 7, 27, 94
strategic opportunities, 30, 191
strategic parity. *See* Russia
strategic partner. *See* United States
strategic partnership, 7, 27, 38–39, 44, 57,
  61, 92, 94–95, 102–3, 109–10, 116–20,
  123–25, 184, 190, 336, 338, 341–42, 347
strategic raison d'etre, 109
Strategic Triangle, 8, 96, 103, 108, 134, 341
strategy of partnership, 43, 54n
Stuart, John Leighton, 262
submarine-launched ballistic missiles
  (SLBM), 72, 343
Sudan, 186
Sun, Yat-sen, 88, 217, 243

Taiping Rebellion, 87
Taiwan. *See* Republican Taiwan
Taiwan problem. *See* Republican Taiwan

Taiwan Relations Act. *See* Republican Taiwan

Tajikistan, 28–29, 97, 347

Taliban regime, 98, 183, 187, 346

talk during the tour to South China, 22

Tang, Jiaxuan, 59, 106

terrorism, 7, 25, 29, 42, 66, 98, 104–5, 158, 165–66, 184–90, 192, 230

Thailand, 231, 263

Thalweg, 98

Third Communiqué, 90

Third Plenary Session of the 11th Central Committee of CCP, 15. *See* China

three fundamental obstacles, 90

three peaces. *See* China

Three-World. *See* China

Tiananmen Incident. *See* China

Tiananmen Square, 91, 108, 209, 241, 245, 249

Tibet, 12, 296–312, 338–39

Tokyo, 106, 135–36, 143–44, 146, 148, 162, 181

Treaty of Good-Neighborliness and Friendly Cooperation, 190

Treaty of Livadia (Treaty of St. Petersburg), 87

Treaty of Shimonoseki. *See* Asia; China

Triangularity, 108

Tribal areas, 187

Truman, Harry, 137, 255

Tucker, Nancy Bernkopf, 111n

Tumen River, 98

Turkmenistan-Afghanistan-Pakistan (pipeline). *See* Asia

two-pronged policy, 250

Uighur, 97

Ukraine, 92, 100, 231

unification. *See* China

United Nations, 17–18, 28, 30–31, 59, 123–24, 147, 164–65, 180, 189, 202, 210, 239, 254, 306; Global war on terrorism, 185; IAEA (*see* Democratic People's Republic of Korea); Iraqi problem, 186; negotiation of China's entry into the WTO, 24; permanent membership of the UN Security Council, 28, 109, 185, 327; Security Council Resolution, 63, 93, 159, 178–79; sanctions, 103, 105; Stevenson, Adlai E., 254

United Nations Development Programme (UNDP), 98

United States: al-Qaeda (*see* Afghanistan's peace and reconstruction process); American economic policy toward China, 258, 268n; ABM Treaty, 103, 105; anti-terrorism (*see* China); arms race (*see* Russia); axis of evil, 105, 158; balance of power, 7–8, 39, 71–73, 77, 79–80, 107–9, 185, 291, 345; Banco Delta Asia. (*see* China); bombing of the Chinese Embassy (*see* China); Bush, George H., 39, 156, 266; Bush, George W., 27, 38–39, 53n, 54n, 105, 145, 158, 184, 336, 342; Camp David, 184; China Aid Bill, 269n; China's Most-Favored-Nation status, 266, 273n; China threat (*see* China); Cold War (*see* China); Containment (*see* China); Dam, Kenneth W., 254; denuclearization, 156; ECA, 11, 256, 258, 272n; ECA mission to China, 256, 258; Foreign Assistance Act, 258, 260; geopolitical strategy, 191; guidelines for the US-Japan Defense Cooperation, 139, 150n; hedging strategy, 52, 341; hegemonism, 16–20, 25–30, 109–10; Hill, Christopher, 143; human rights, 6, 8, 25, 37–39, 45, 103, 105, 110, 116, 119, 123, 126, 203, 208–11, 228–29, 243, 266, 325, 328, 339, 341; Iranian nuclear issues, 186; Kelly, James, 158; Kissinger, Henry, 142, 262; Lugar, Richard Green, 254, 267; Marshall, George, 256; Mutual Defense Treaty, 138; negotiation of China's entry into the WTO, 24; New Framework for the U.S.-India Defense Relationship, 184, 194n; new world order, 92, 102; NATO, 93, 103, 110, 279; NIC, 76, 275; 9/11, 6, 8–9, 49, 183–85, 188–90, 192–94, 203, 341–42; Nixon, Richard, 134, 266, 322; normalization of the China-U.S. diplomatic relations, 15–16; North

United States (*continued*)
Korea nuclear crisis (*see* Asia); NPT, 63, 156; nuclear power plant, 169; nuclear war, 72, 74, 78–79, 186; Open Door policy, 253; Paulson, Henry, 47; Persian Gulf War, 20; plane collision incident, 53n; Powell, Colin, 41, 146, 164, 185, 250, 340; responsible stakeholder, 45–46, 50, 191, 221, 342; Rice, Condoleezza, 39, 48, 166, 184; Rogue States, 47, 49; Rumsfeld, Donald, 184, 207; sanction, 20, 91, 99–100, 103, 105, 110, 135, 159, 162, 165–66, 169, 175–78, 180, 184, 190, 241, 253, 254–55, 260, 264–67, 268n, 269n, 273n, 326, 339, 342, 344, 346; Sino-American economic relations, 267; stakeholder, 43, 45–47, 49–52, 344; strategic competitor, 6, 39–43, 48; strategic cooperative partnership, 7, 27, 94; strategic partner, 6, 38–39, 41, 47–49, 95; Strategic Triangle, 8, 96, 103, 108, 134, 341; Stevenson, Adlai E., 254; Stuart, John Leighton, 262; Taiwan Relations Act, 16, 210; Third Communiqué, 90; Truman, Harry, 137, 255; U.S.-Afghanistan strategic partnership, 184; U.S. Central Command, 183; U.S.–China policy, 256–57; U.S.-China relations, 38–43, 45–46, 49, 81, 128, 201, 214, 262, 264, 266–67; U.S-China Strategic Economic Dialogue, 47, 55n; U.S.–China trade, 11, 39, 265–66; U.S.–Chinese economic policy, 255–66; U.S. Defense Department, 191; U.S. embargo, 264; U.S. foreign policy, 11, 50, 147, 152n, 214n, 230, 253, 255, 258; U.S.-India civil nuclear cooperation agreement, 184; U.S.-India relations, 184; U.S.-India strategic partnership, 184; U.S.-Japan alliance, 8, 133–35, 139, 142, 150n, 228 (a.k.a The Alliance); U.S.-Japan Security Treaty, 133, 135, 139, 146; U.S.-Pakistan relations, 184, 190; U.S. unilateralism, 109; Vietnam War, 134, 309, 321; WMDs, 66, 158, 192, 231–

32; White paper, 60, 62, 64, 138, 142, 150n; Wilson, Woodrow, 253; WWI, 253; WWII, 11, 40, 46, 105, 122, 133, 137, 253, 261, 289, 301, 321, 327; Yongbyon Nuclear Research Center, 156; Zoellick, Robert., 44, 54n, 55n, 191, 342

Ussuri, 95, 98
Ussuri/Wussuli River (Amur/Heilungjiang River), 87, 95, 98
Uzbekistan, 29, 97–98, 104, 347

Vajpayee, Atal Behari, 184
Venezuela, 253
Vietnam, 26, 90–91, 107, 289, 303, 311, 325, 335, 342
Vietnam War. *See* Asia
Vladivostok, 90

war crisis, 212
Ward, Angus, 262
Warsaw Pact Organization, 91, 111n, 279
Washington, 2, 7, 40–42, 44–46, 48, 50, 52–53, 72, 75, 101, 108, 134–38, 140, 144–48, 157–59, 164–65, 167–69, 175, 177, 181, 184–85, 217, 221, 227, 229–32, 239, 262, 301, 305, 310–11, 342–43, 345–46
weapons of mass destruction (WMDs), 66, 158, 192, 231–32
Wei, 333n
well-off society, 29–30
Wen, Jiabao. *See* China
Western Development, 189
White paper. *See* United States
Wilson, Woodrow, 253
World War I (WWI), 253
World War II (WWII). *See* United States
Wu, Xiuquan, 135
Wu, Yi. *See* China

Xinhai revolution, 88
Xinjiang Uygur Autonomous Region, 189

Yalu River, 137
Yang, Jiawen, 265, 272n
Yakub Beg Rebellion, 87
Yasukuni Shrine. *See* Japan